The History of Communication

Robert W. McChesney
and John C. Nerone,
Editors

Books in the Series

Selling Free Enterprise: The Business Assault on Labor and
Liberalism, 1945–60
Elizabeth A. Fones-Wolf

Last Rights: Revisiting *Four Theories of the Press*
Edited by John C. Nerone

"We Called Each Other Comrade": Charles H. Kerr & Company,
Radical Publishers
Allen Ruff

"We Called Each Other Comrade"

Charles H. Kerr

"We Called Each Other Comrade"

Charles H. Kerr & Company, Radical Publishers

Allen Ruff

University of Illinois Press
Urbana and Chicago

10027944 6X

Frontispiece courtesy of the Newberry Library

© 1997 by the Board of Trustees of the University of Illinois
Manufactured in the United States of America
1 2 3 4 5 C P 5 4 3 2 1

This book is printed on acid-free paper.

Library of Congress Cataloging-in-Publication Data
Ruff, Allen, 1949–
"We called each other comrade" : Charles H. Kerr & Company, radical
    publishers / Allen Ruff.
    p.   cm. — (The history of communication)
Includes bibliographical references and index.
ISBN 0-252-02277-7 (alk. paper). — ISBN 0-252-06582-4 (pbk. : alk. paper)
1. Charles H. Kerr Company—History. 2. Publishers and publishing—Political
    aspects—United States—History—19th century. 3. Publishers and
    publishing—Political aspects—United States—History—20th century. 4.
    Socialism—United States—History—19th century. 5. Socialism—United
    States—History—20th century.
I. Title. II. Series.
Z473.C455R84   1997
070.5—dc20   96-10086
                            CIP

T

In memory of Elsie and Teddy Ruff

■ Contents

■ Acknowledgments

Numerous friends and acquaintances aided this study in some way, shape, or form. My deepest gratitude is to Burton Rosen, activist, socialist mensch, and former secretary of the Kerr Company, who not only allowed me access to the records of the venture, then tucked away in storage, but also opened his Chicago home to me for a year while I completed the bulk of my research. His major contributions to the completion of this work—his critical political and intellectual insights over many a Windy City luncheonette breakfast for which he usually paid—had inestimable value. He is now warmly cherished for innumerable reasons. My sincerest thanks also extend to Katharine Kerr Moore, Charles and May Walden Kerr's daughter. She, too, welcomed me into her home and offered recollections, records, and insights that made this inquiry worthwhile. This history belongs to Katharine Moore and Burt Rosen.

I would also be remiss if I did not extol the skill and wisdom of my teachers at the University of Wisconsin. I learned about the subtleties of the historian's craft from my major professor, Stanley K. Schultz. His lessons in the nuances of the English language will stay with me for the rest of my life. I also appreciate the comments and criticisms of Thomas J. McCormick and Paul Boyer.

Special thanks must be extended to a number of radical scholars and activists who have long-term commitments to the history lessons and future of the American left. My work benefited immensely from the insights, political perspectives, and critical eyes of Paul Buhle, Sally Miller, Bob McChesney, Dexter Arnold, and Neil Basen. Many others, among them John Philips, Mary Ellen McElligott, Jeraldine Raymond, Mary Boncher,

Barbara Bordwell, Conrad Amenhauser, Michael Marcus, and Ronald Ruff also offered support and encouragement over the years.

I am also indebted to all the archivists who made this work possible. Diana Haskell, archivist at the Newberry Library, Chicago, was a special help.

Harvey Goldberg, Wisconsin's renowned activist social historian, was my friend, comrade, and zaddik. Unable to conclude his reading of my work in its present form, he nevertheless constantly informed my inquiry by extending those insights, perspectives, and wisdom that only one with his brilliance and commitment could provide. This history belongs to him as well, part of his legacy.

Finally, my loving gratitude goes to Patricia DiBiase. Her support, forbearance, patience, encouragement, and critical sensibilities enabled me to complete this project. Her companionship sustains.

■ Introduction

At some point in 1950, the human interest columnist for the local newspaper in the small community of Avon Park, Florida, approached one of the town's aging residents. Finding her an interesting character, the reporter asked May Walden Kerr, then in her early nineties, to recount some of her experiences. The article that resulted reflected on the elderly woman's years as a social and political activist in an era far removed from that of the early cold war and postwar prosperity.

May Walden informed the reporter that she considered herself a socialist, that she had been one since 1900, and that she had stumped as a soapboxer on the streets of Chicago and worked as a state officer and organizer for the Socialist Party of Illinois. Detailing some of the most significant aspects of her long life, she described her husband Charles H. Kerr and his central role as a major publisher for the socialist impetus of that bygone Debsian era. She also mentioned numerous socialist notables whom she had known and listed the radical publications, long since extinct, to which she had subscribed. May Walden completed the interview by noting that there was "nothing like a common cause—working for the betterment of humanity to bind people together." Her point was clearly important in the context of the heightening phobia, recrimination, and intolerance against "reds" during the early 1950s. Almost as an afterthought, she affirmatively and proudly, perhaps defiantly, informed her interviewer that "we called each other 'Comrade' and stood by each other with the utmost loyalty."

This book tells the story of that circle of American comrades and traces the history of the social, political, and intellectual milieux to which May Walden Kerr belonged. Its main focus is on Charles H. Kerr & Company, the most significant U.S. publishing venture of the socialist movement during the first two decades of the twentieth century. It explores the life of May Walden's husband, Charles Hope Kerr, and traces his intellectual and social background and ongoing political development, as well as those of the group of radical activists who from the 1880s through the early 1920s gathered around the Chicago publishing venture that bore his name.

The heart of this study tracks the institutional history of a unique experiment in book publishing—a cooperative business venture designed, structured, and maintained not for personal gain but for the political education, recruitment, and development of socialist activists and the advancement of the socialist cause. An authentically radical, not-for-profit concern with an ever-evolving social and political agenda, the Kerr house turned out innumerable pamphlets and books in paper and hardcover. The venture also issued four remarkable periodicals: a weekly and three monthlies that captured the mood and thinking of the several causes the publishing house served. Often used and cited by historians, the several Kerr-published magazines—the radical Unitarian weekly *Unity* (ca. 1886–93), the populist monthlies *New Occasions* (1893–96) and *The New Time* (1896–98), and the *International Socialist Review* (1900–1918)—are rich sources for tracing the institutional history of the firm and the changing political and social outlooks of their publisher and his associates.

Thematically, the work stands as an inquiry into the continuities of a specific tradition of dissent within American society. It examines an ongoing current of radical opposition to the direction and priorities of that society often denied or given short shrift by historians imbued with a consensus outlook.

Most of the activists examined in this study were indigenous, "homegrown" radicals. Most of the Kerr group came out of the American heartland, geographically and culturally. The majority came to their oppositional stance through a rational, educated assessment and conviction rather than from a sudden conversion experience or great awakening. Few, if any, made a political leap of faith. Dissidents from the main course and direction of an expansive American capitalism in the "age of laissez-faire" and the Progressive Era, their radicalism grew out of a highly educated, well-informed appraisal of the concentration of economic and political power and the mounting evidences of increased inequity and often-devastating social disparity.

Charles Kerr and his comrades also maintained an international perspective; their critique of capitalist development was global. They looked abroad for critical perspective and insights, turning to Europe for developed socialist thought and practice and establishing political and personal ties with the who's who of the Second International. Impelled by their reading of the "backwardness" of the American working-class movement, they consciously sought the best and brightest of European socialist thought. They imported, translated, published, and disseminated the most significant works of Marxian socialism, which were largely unavailable in the United States. That venture, in turn, made them the most significant English-language publisher and exporter of Marxism in the world between 1900 and 1925.

Their internationalism aside, the Kerr circle was overwhelmingly American. For the most part beneficiaries of that very system they rejected and critiqued, the Kerr group maintained a rationalist confidence in the emancipating power of education and scientific inquiry. Believers in a particular conception of progress wedded to a radical transformation of the existing social order, they held that a consummately more just society, democratic and liberatory, was not only necessary and possible but also inevitable. They could see it on the horizon through their reading of "historical development." That concept made them as American as those individuals they scorned and criticized, people whose ideal of the future and notion of mission was wedded to untrammeled corporate economic growth and imperial expansion.

The key that would unlock the door to the cooperative commonwealth, that new society based upon socialist cooperation, lay in education, in the dissemination of truth and historical fact, and in the development of political organization and social mobilization through clear, rational, scientific exposition of the socialist critique. Of that, the Kerr group remained convinced. The publisher and his associates spent decades churning out their critical message of an emancipatory, democratic socialist hope. To serve the broader socialist cause, they became a voice for the left wing within that movement. Their rationalist confidence ultimately clashed with the irrationality of war and repression, however, and with the powerful material successes of an expansive American capitalism. Their belief in the inevitability of an American socialist dawn came and went as the Debsian socialist impetus ebbed. Vulnerable from without and unstable within, that movement and its political expression, the Socialist Party of America, declined. And with the demise of American socialism's "golden age" during World War I, the fortunes of Charles H. Kerr & Company took a precipitous plunge. The firm nevertheless survived and carried on long enough to celebrate its centenary in 1986.

Something more than the mere recounting of a now-distant past, dead and gone, Kerr & Company's story is still relevant. Functioning where the distinction between the two becomes indistinct, Charles Kerr and his comrades combined their skills in an attempt to forge an independent and sustaining political culture. Pitted against a dominant corporate media in an era of ascendant mass culture, they struggled to maintain an autonomous informational and educational space unbeholding to capital, vitally critical, and actively, irrepressibly political.

Part of a larger left political culture richly laden with alternative institutions and a diversity of opinion on all questions—political, social, and cultural—Kerr and Company became the national voice of the socialist movement's left wing. Part of a diverse multilingual daily, weekly, and monthly socialist press that numbered in the hundreds by World War I and functioned independently outside the control of the Socialist Party, the Kerr venture, but one voice in a polyglot radical environment, became the most successful left publishing house of the era. Its politics ensured that it was not ignored when the United States entered the war to make the world safe for democracy. One of the first victims of the repression that accompanied U.S. involvement in the Great War, the demise of the left press tells much about the operations of the "free market place of ideas" and the liberal state's role in solidifying the ideological hegemony of America's dominant classes.

The Debsian-era socialist press provided the movement's main vehicle for propaganda and education and informed it about socialist, labor, and farmers' movements, political and economic developments, and popular expositions of Marxist theory. Offering coverage of struggles from a perspective unavailable elsewhere, it disseminated the socialist message to a broad base, reaching out to members and prospective members alike.

The way the socialist press addressed issues of class and politics was different from that of its capitalist contemporaries. Dedicated to promoting the class struggle on both the political and economic field, it allowed readers to debate issues in a manner not possible or permissible in the corporate press. It also provided a forum for mobilizing partisan support and aiding in ongoing labor struggles and political campaigns. It thereby created an ideological and political space in which workers could develop ideologies and strategies apart from the dominant media of the day. Along with other working-class institutions, that oppositional press created a vital alternative public sphere.

The left publishers of the era created a journalism very different from that of their capitalist competitors. They understood the need to counter the strong antilabor and antisocialist bias of the mainstream press. They simultaneously had to surmount several distinct sets of obstacles inherent in publishing a working-class paper within the constraints that capital imposed. Often denied significant advertising revenues, they succeeded by developing alternative sources of support through a myriad of stock, bond, and other fund-raising and investment strategies that tapped the good will, commitment, and socialist faith of the movement they served. They did so by creating an alternative press ideology that sought to erase distinctions between press and reader. The movement created and sustained its own media institutions, authentically radical and based in the working class.[1]

"We Called Each Other Comrade"

Charles H. Kerr: Early Years, Early Influences

In the prime of his life during the decade preceding World War I, Charles H. Kerr moved into the left wing of the socialist movement in the United States and aligned himself with the most radical, militant, class-conscious elements of the cause. Solidly middle class in background, highly educated and well situated, and in some ways destined for a position of comfort, a place in society regularly bestowed upon one of his background and credentials, Kerr nevertheless had long since turned toward radicalism. He had thrown in his lot with the socially disenfranchised and economically hardpressed and sacrificed virtually everything he had to a cause that promised little in immediate return—nothing, certainly, in material terms. What caused this son of the middle class to reject that birthright of relative comfort, privilege, and prestige that could have easily been his? What compelled him to take a class stand in some ways antithetical to his own immediate interest?

Although the origins of the publisher's class-conscious radicalism lay shrouded in the past, the roots of his particular radical trajectory tapped into a longer dissenting tradition anchored deeply in the social and intellectual subsoil of nineteenth-century American culture. His early environment was certainly a key factor, and Kerr's parents also played an important role. The moral and social perspectives and the dedication to service of both Alexander and Katharine Kerr had an inestimable effect on their son.

Alexander Kerr was born at Fetter Angus near Aberdeen, Scotland, in August 1828, the son of George and Helen Legge Kerr. The third of five children, he sailed with his family from Aberdeen to Quebec in April 1835.

The immigrant family first settled in Cornwell, Ontario, where George Kerr carried on his tailor's trade alongside his elder brother James, an earlier émigré. In 1838 they moved by way of the Great Lakes water route to Illinois. After landing at Chicago, they made their way to Joliet, where they remained another three years. Finally, in 1841, George Kerr purchased a farm near Rockford where he and his wife spent the rest of their lives.[1]

Alexander Kerr attended the district schools around Rockford during the winter and helped on the family farm during the summer months. In 1851 he enrolled at the Rockford Scientific and Classical Institute in preparation for Beloit College, which he entered the following year as a sophomore. Following his graduation from Beloit with highest honors in 1855, he moved to Georgia, where he taught Latin and mathematics at several small private academies.

During the Christmas holidays of 1856, Kerr returned to Rockford to marry his college sweetheart, Katharine Fuller Brown. Kate, as she was more affectionately known, was the daughter of a graduate of Amherst College, the Congregational minister Hope Brown. Born in Shirley, Massachusetts, on August 23, 1832, her formal education began at the Ipswich Academy at Ipswich, New Hampshire. The Brown family moved to Napierville (now Naperville), Illinois, in 1845. While serving as minister at the First Congregational Church at Napierville, Reverend Brown became affiliated with the Rockford Female Seminary, the "sister school" of nearby Beloit College, and Kate Brown enrolled there.[2]

Founded in 1847 to send "cultivated Christian Women [out] in the various fields of usefulness," the Rockford school developed under the disciplining guidance of Anna Peck Sill, an eastern-bred evangelical "possessed of a most passionate earnestness for Christianity in general, for the development of Christian missionaries in particular." Under Sill's tutelage, the curriculum and daily regimen combined "to inspire a missionary spirit of self-denying benevolence toward all, but toward the ignorant and the sinful." The purpose of life, as laid out by the moral and spiritual architects of the seminary, was giving oneself for the good of others.[3]

Katharine Brown came away deeply imbued with that ethic of self-sacrifice and service. After graduation in 1855, she remained at the seminary, where she worked as an instructor for the next year and a half. She had met Alexander Kerr while she was still a student at Rockford, and the two became engaged in April 1855. The bride and groom journeyed back southward to Georgia after their wedding on New Years Day 1857.[4]

Kerr resumed his teaching and became professor of mathematics at Brownwood Institute, a boys' school near LaGrange, Georgia, in 1858.

Following a stay at Brownwood, he became principal of another private school nearby. There was much more to Kate and Alexander Kerr's life than the teaching of math and Latin to the white sons of Georgia, however. Unbeknown to local authorities, the young couple was committed to the abolitionist cause. They circulated antislavery tracts and conducted a clandestine school for slaves in their spare time.[5]

Charles Hope Kerr was born in LaGrange on April 23, 1860.[6] Within a year of his arrival, animosities between the North and South flared into open conflict at Fort Sumter. Fearful that Alexander Kerr might be forced to serve in Confederate army and concerned as well for their safety and that of their young son, the Kerrs fled northward after the first battle of Bull Run in July 1861. Passing through Confederate lines by using stops along the Underground Railroad and staying with sympathetic abolitionist colleagues, the Kerr family made its way back to Rockford.[7]

Resettled in northern Illinois, Alexander Kerr became superintendent of schools for Winnebago County in 1862 to fill out the term of his brother James, who had enlisted in the Union cause. In February 1863 the family moved to Beloit, where Kerr took on the task of reorganizing that city's school system. He became president of the Wisconsin Teacher's Association in 1868. In recognition of his work as a state educator, the Board of Regents of what was then the State University of Wisconsin at Madison in 1871 elected him to fill a newly established chair in Greek. The Kerrs moved to the Wisconsin capital that year and took up residence in a large, comfortable lake-front house on Langdon Street, a thoroughfare of "quiet charm" with an "atmosphere of calm and unhasting serenity" close to campus.[8] It was there that they raised their two sons, Charles and his younger brother James.[9]

Home of the university and the state legislature, late-nineteenth-century Madison provided an exceptional intellectual environment for one as well situated as the young Kerr. The city had already become a midwestern oasis for a broad array of innovative, progressive educators. Comfortable in their new surroundings, both Alexander and Kate Kerr became active in local social, cultural, political, and religious circles not long after their arrival. They joined Madison's First Congregational Church in September 1871, where Alexander Kerr became a deacon in 1874. That same year, Katharine Kerr took up a position as secretary and treasurer of the church-related Women's Missionary Society, which supplied aid to the poor and sick at home and abroad.[10]

The active couple also joined the Madison Literary Club, where they exchanged liberal views on literature, art, and culture with such local notables as the Unitarian ministers H. M. Simmons and J. M. Crooker and the founder of the modern history department at the university, William F. Allen—all figures whose work their son would later publish.[11] Alexander Kerr also joined the Madison Board of Education while continuing to devote a good deal of energy to the State Federation of Teachers and its publication, the *Wisconsin Journal of Education*. He became a lecturer for the newly implemented university extension system and delivered talks on modern Greece and Greek poetry during visits to communities in Wisconsin and northern Illinois. While maintaining his full quota of academic duties he also found time to coauthor an edition of the Gospel of Matthew in Greek and translate the *Bacchae of Euripides* and a multivolume edition of Plato's *Republic*.[12] Kerr was a cosmopolitan man who constantly looked to Europe as a seat of classical learning and innovation, and he used his summer breaks to travel abroad and study in Athens, Berlin, London, and Paris.[13]

His method of instruction was occasionally criticized, however. Several students found him too easygoing, and he was known to have dismissed an entire class when one student took out a watch and yawned. Yet Edward Birge, the university's president, testified to the fact that "Kerr gave himself to his teaching with singular devotion," and his colleagues often spoke favorably of him as well. For several years during the 1880s Kerr conducted a class in reading the Greek version of the Gospels after Sunday morning services at the First Congregational.[14]

Young Charles Kerr was evidently much closer to his mother than his father.[15] Although Katharine Kerr's actual influence on her eldest son is difficult to assess, fragmentary evidence strongly suggests that she played a central role in imparting a degree of social consciousness, moral concern, and ethical duty. A biographical fragment published in 1880 described her as a "lady of unusual culture who found preeminent delight in the moral and scholastic training of her sons."[16] She was well known and respected throughout the Madison area, and when she died in July 1890 the city's *Wisconsin State Journal* printed a full-column obituary tribute written by one of her close associates: "From early girlhood, through college years, as a teacher and through all the cares of home and social life, she was a student, keeping up Greek, Latin, German and French with keen pleasure, and loving knowledge for its own sake but far more for the help it enabled her to give to others. She was always imparting. When we heard of some sad accident, some dying child, some wayward girl just on the verge of ruin and thought 'What can we do,' we said, 'we will go to Mrs. Kerr and we never went in vain.'"[17]

A founding member of the Madison Benevolent Society, Katharine Kerr "maintained a comprehending sympathy for the lowly and the unfortunate": "For years the dwellers on 'the worst street' in town knew her as their frequent visitor and best friend. [Their children] were in her sewing class, work for the older ones was found in good families, letters were written. All were watched over and befriended in delicate, sensible ways. All who came in contact with her felt her sincere and kindly interest."[18]

A resolution passed by the board of directors of the Benevolent Society following her death noted that the organization had "suffered an irreparable loss" and that Madison's poor had "lost an active and faithful friend, whose memory they will long cherish and revere."[19] She also clearly left an indelible impression on her son, who by 1890 was a budding activist and publisher in Chicago.

Social consciousness and commitment aside, Katharine and Alexander Kerr passed on other qualities to their son: their own training, with its emphasis on education in the classics, and also their deep interest in foreign languages and literature. Alexander Kerr also contributed certain qualities or attributes later evident in the son. As M. S. Slaughter, the elder Kerr's colleague on the faculty at Wisconsin, described him, "Gifted with a fine sense of humor, he was always good company, and a good story, especially a Scotch anecdote, brief and to the point, was sure to enliven any chance meeting with him. His most marked characteristic was a sort of Scotch persistency and he rarely gave up a scheme without accomplishing his end. He was a very kind-spirited man and preferred to be at peace with all men, but he did not mind a fight if it was necessary."[20]

The younger Kerr also maintained "a sort of Scotch persistency" and rarely gave up a scheme before attaining at least some of the goals he had set out to accomplish. Also kind-spirited, the son would also prefer peace but never shied from a struggle when it was necessary. Significantly, the younger Kerr always maintained a cordial relationship with his father. No major breach or chasm ever developed between the liberal, middle-class academic and his left-leaning socialist son, and their relationship remained amicable. Alexander Kerr contributed varied sums of money to the often beleaguered Kerr Company over the span of several decades. In return, out of devotion, gratuity, and respect, Kerr the younger published his father's translations of Greek classics. (One edition of his translation of Plato's *Republic* appeared in 1918, a year before the elder Kerr died.)

Although their direct influence remains difficult to gauge, several other Madisonians played a significant role in shaping Kerr's intellectual and social development. The young man entered the University of Wisconsin in 1877, where he excelled in romance languages and majored in French. He received consistently high grades in Greek, Latin, French, and English literature.[21] In his junior year, Kerr studied American history with his former Latin instructor, William Francis Allen, a figure typical of that liberal milieu of socially engaged intellectuals. Best remembered as the father of a modern history department at Wisconsin and as the mentor of frontier historian Frederick Jackson Turner, Allen was the leading lay figure in the Unitarian movement of Madison. A cofounder of the city's First Unitarian Society in 1878, he also was a member of the Free Religious Association, the radical offshoot of post–Civil War Unitarianism. He readily publicized the advanced positions of radical free religion while maintaining his formal Unitarian affiliation.[22] With the aid of Jenkin Lloyd Jones, then missionary secretary of the Western Unitarian Conference (WUC) at Janesville, Allen secured the ministerial services of the Rev. Henry Martin Simmons for Madison's First Unitarian in 1879. It was people like Professor Allen and Reverend Simmons who created the bridge that eventually carried Charles Kerr to the center of midwestern Unitarian activity in Chicago.[23]

Born in September 1830 and the descendant of several prominent Unitarian ministers, Allen acquired an early interest in the study of history.[24] He matriculated at Harvard University and graduated in 1851. He decided against entering the ministry, in part because of the conservative Unitarian hostility toward the radicalism of Theodore Parker.[25] Sailing for Europe in September 1854, he matriculated at the universities of Berlin and Göttingen, where he studied Roman and Greek history and romance languages and came into contact with the latest developments in German historical research and Idealist philosophy. He returned to Boston in June 1856.[26] Under the employ of the Freedmen's Aid Commission, Allen went south in November 1863 to work with former slaves on St. Helena Island, one of the sea islands of South Carolina.[27] At war's end he became chair of the Department of Ancient Languages at Antioch College before accepting the position as chair of ancient languages and history at Wisconsin in 1867. An American pioneer in the dissemination of the new European methods of historical research, Allen fostered the original research and open inquiry that gave rise to the influential Department of History at the university.[28] Socially active, Allen sat on the board of the Madison Benevolent Society alongside Katharine Brown Kerr. Always receptive to new ideas, he readily embraced the most advanced religious and secular thought of the era. He played a key role as a leading Unitarian lay figure and president of the Wisconsin Unitarian Conference and headed the

Madison chapter of the Free Religious Association, that radical offshoot of postbellum Unitarian thought. [29]

Allen assisted in the recruitment of Henry Martyn Simmons to head the First Unitarian Society. Simmons was also typical of Madison's advanced liberal milieu, and his tenure as minister in Madison spanned the period when Charles Kerr studied at the state university. Simmons helped found *Unity*, the Chicago-based Unitarian weekly that Kerr eventually came to publish, and was a close associate of Jenkin Lloyd Jones.

Born in 1841, Simmons grew up in New York state. He graduated from Hamilton College in 1864 and entered Auburn Theological Seminary to prepare for the Presbyterian ministry. Unable to ascribe to the literal terms of the Westminster Confession, he was denied ordination and shortly thereafter moved toward Unitarianism. He initially accepted a call to a Unitarian church at Kenosha, Wisconsin, but moved to Madison at the behest of Allen and Jones and assumed leadership of the newly reorganized First Unitarian in 1879.[30] Simmons was fluent in Latin, French, and German and well-versed in Greek drama, history, and philosophy. He was equally well-read in English and American literature. He maintained an avid interest in the natural sciences and has been described as an excellent botanist who also studied astronomy, geology, and biology "with great zest." He was clearly one of that generation of Unitarian clergy who readily synthesized theology with the latest disclosures of evolution.[31] In social terms, Simmons viewed evolutionary thought as a summons to "upward living" and often spoke out on political and economic matters from his Madison pulpit.[32]

The Madison Unitarians met at the Gates of Heaven Synagogue on Sunday mornings during Simmons's years as their pastor. Although not large, those Sunday gatherings contained "the choicer spirits of the city": a number of educators, members of the judiciary and local government, and "the more thoughtful youth of the University."[33] Judging from what immediately followed, in all probability among those students in attendance at Simmons's sermons in the borrowed temple sat Charles H. Kerr, taking it all in.

Kerr moved to Chicago not long after graduating from the University of Wisconsin in 1881. The figure who became his ministerial mentor during his first years there was Jenkin Lloyd Jones, a pivotal figure in midwestern Unitarianism during the decades following the Civil War. A leader of the "Unity men," the Western Unitarian faction that took its name from their organ, *Unity* magazine, Jones helped define a theological position constructed on a nondoctrinal "ethical basis" of "freedom, fellowship, and character in religion."[34] "Young for liberty," to use their historian's phrase in describing them, the Unity men explicitly disavowed any reference to either theism or Christianity. They nevertheless considered themselves Unitarian. More than any other figure among them, Jenkin Jones provided the energy, organizational drive, and religious and social outlook that drew the Unity men together.

Born in the Cardiganshire district of southern Wales in November 1843, Jones immigrated to Canada with his family in 1844. The Joneses eventually settled on the Wisconsin frontier near Spring Green. The descendant of a long line of dissenting Arminian ministers and lay folk, young Jones received his early religious training and secular education at home. He then served with a Wisconsin artillery battery that saw a great deal of action during the Civil War. Wounded in 1862 at the Battle of Corinth, Mississippi, Jones returned home to continue his education and eventually enroll in Meadeville Theological Seminary.[35]

Upon entry at the Pennsylvania college, he found that the majority of his classmates were also veterans, men inclined to associate dogmatic Christianity with army chaplains "who messed with the officers and preached asceticism and sacrifice *or* hell fire to poor devils in muddy trenches facing death."[36] This new crop of seminarians had also encountered preachers in the South who sanctified slavery and secession with biblical texts. Shaped by their collective war experience and open to new ideas, the postbellum group of Meadeville graduates energetically embraced the latest "higher criticism" and comparative study of non-Christian religions. Concerned with the here-and-now as much as the hereafter (if not more so), they also took up the questions of social reform in the early years of that "great barbecue," the Gilded Age.[37]

Away from the classroom, Meadeville's students debated the "evolution question." Jones and his fellows grappled with the problem of reconciling Darwin and Spencer with the beliefs of their professors on the ethical finality and infallibility of the Gospel. The late 1860s, after all, were a time when even the followers of Theodore Parker found their views gravely challenged by the new evolutionary thought. It was also a period when the number of articles and published sermons on the subject multiplied rapidly in the religious press. The new intellectual currents influenced Jones directly.[38]

Jones married following his graduation from Meadeville.[39] After a stint as minister at the Liberal Church at Winnetka, Illinois, he and his wife, Susan, moved to Janesville, Wisconsin, where he became head of the Independent Society of Liberal Christians. It was in Janesville that Jones began to establish himself in midwestern Unitarian circles. As minister and educator, he displayed an avid interest in the character development of children. Charles Lyttle, a Unitarian historian, has noted that the young clergyman's emphasis on the importance of a religious education for youths became "a fundamental and insistent element of his thought and activities."[40] Jones soon became known as a pedagogic innovator and active organizer of numerous education projects.

His interest in child development combined with a feeling that the Sunday school materials of the eastern-based Unitarian Sunday School Society were too formal and doctrinal. This judgment led him to found a "surprisingly modern" four-page lesson sheet, the *Sunday School* (1872), an innovative periodical dedicated "to all those who seek to work for practical Christianity, liberated from creeds and dogmas, based on Love, Service and Devotion."[41]

Concerned with the synthesis of religion and evolutionary thought, Jones used the *Sunday School* to develop a series of topical lessons on nature, outlined not according to Genesis but in scientific, evolutionary terms. Under the topic "Our Nature," the *Sunday School* imparted information on mental and physical hygiene. The lesson sheet's topical course for 1874 offered a critical study of the Bible that included a consideration of the Apocrypha of the Old Testament. The sheet also contained studies in comparative religion, responsive readings, poetry, and songs.[42] In December 1874 the *Sunday School* merged with George Cooke's the *Liberal Helper,* another educational sheet. The work of both publications continued into 1877 in the pages of the newly founded *Unity.*[43]

Jones also initiated the innovative Mutual Improvement Club while in Janesville.[44] Through these study circles he sought to improve the conventional social life of the church, specifically the role of women in it. The club met on Saturday afternoons so busy homemakers or working women might be able to participate. A combination of postgraduate Sunday school studies, adult education, and social service reform venture, the new institution encouraged inquiry and social activities around current events, recent literature, biography, classical literature, art, dramatics, current periodicals, and lectures. Social action programs included lectures and discussions on women's rights, temperance, international peace, and civil service reform. Public lectures under the club's auspices attracted young adults who belonged to many different churches or none at all. The Mutual Improvement Clubs continued an older lyceum tradition of lectures and study circles and foreshadowed numerous ventures in mass education that Kerr and his associates would initiate as socialist educators and propagandists.

Lyttle has observed that never in the history of the Unitarian movement had anyone worked so intensively on propaganda and organization as did Jones between 1875 and 1880. His energy and organizational skills were of inestimable importance in stimulating the growth and expansion of the Western Unitarian Conference. When he began his part-time work as missionary secretary, only forty-three societies with a collective debt of over $100,000 existed throughout the Midwest. By 1880 the number had increased to sixty-one, and their total debt had declined by half.[45]

The WUC nevertheless lacked a central organ or headquarters. Apparently never one to shun new duties or additional obligations, Jones helped to found *Unity* as the fortnightly Chicago-based voice of the conference in 1878, and in April 1880 he was named editor of the then-struggling periodical, which Kerr would come to publish. The following July, he resigned his Janesville ministry to become full-time secretary of the WUC. With little more than enough money for train fare and a month's room and board following nine years' hard work throughout the Upper Midwest, Jones and his family moved to Chicago in the late summer of 1880.[46]

Several fairly well-established conservative Unitarian societies existed in Chicago when the Jones family journeyed down from Wisconsin.[47] Discontented with their theological and social direction, however, Jones reorganized the defunct Fourth Unitarian Church on the city's South Side in November 1882. He hired a small hall over some shops at Thirty-fifth and Cottage Grove, and within two weeks a congregation of thirty-six had gathered. The minister told those assembled in the improvised chapel that he would start a new church, the Church of All Souls. He then proceeded to deliver a sermon on his perception of the "Ideal Church," which he eagerly awaited. The new gathering would be "a free congress of independent souls . . . the thinker's home. The student of science will handle no discoveries that it will not prize and indulge in no guesses that it will not respect. Oldest India and newest America will hold no gem of thought that will not be welcomed into its sacred scriptures. . . . Over its portals no dogmatic test is to be written to ward off an honest thinker or honest seeker."[48]

Emphatic in his plans for the future of his newly founded congregation, Jones continued, "This church must emphasize the Universal Brotherhood; it will stand upon a grand emphasis of the great word of the century. Unity. It will seek to welcome the low and the high, poor and rich, unbeliever and believer." He issued several warnings to his listeners. On guard against the elitism and ostentation of some of his potential parishioners, he cautioned that "one who enters its doors flaunting the latest achievements of dress maker or milliner in such a way as to widen the chasm between her and the family of the honest and earnest poor is guilty of impiety for she flaunts the sanctity of this church." Aware of the social distances created by earlier Unitarian practices, he notified his new congregation that there would be no pew rents, "no ownership of private boxes, where the pride of caste may enter the last hope of democracy." Jones's church would welcome blacks as well as whites, Jews as well as gentiles, members of all religious denominations "on the basis of a common Humanity, a common Moral Law, Conscience and Duty."[49]

Five years later, in 1887, a new building for the Church of All Souls Unitarian opened at the corner of Oakwood Boulevard and Langley Avenue. In conformity with Jones's ideal, the new structure had "no Gothic pretensions to frighten away the mechanic or the seamstress." Jones's son later remarked that from the time of its inception All Souls became a "seven day church," a church home, a school, a social club, and a shrine.[50] Every square inch of available space had its use. In the basement, classes were given in manual training for boys, and girls in the "domestic arts" had drawing lessons. Friday afternoon lectures in the auditorium often filled the church to capacity and adult education classes were often in session five nights a week, with Jones himself frequently leading discussions in philosophy and literature that included the works of Emerson as well as Darwin and Spencer.[51]

The seemingly indefatigable Jones launched a series of Unity Club study classes shortly after the organization of All Souls. Modeled after the Janesville Mutual Improvement Clubs, the new study groups attracted a number of young men and women, and among the participants was Charles H. Kerr.[52] Not long after his arrival in Chicago, the young man from Madison had readily found a new home for himself within the liberal spiritual community created by Jenkin Lloyd Jones at All Souls Church.

2

Kerr's Early Chicago Years

Charles Kerr completed his studies at the University of Wisconsin in the spring of 1881. In recognition of his attainments as an undergraduate, the commencement committee offered him the privilege of presenting his honors thesis at the graduation ceremony. Kerr, however, did not attend the festivities. By then, "Charly" Kerr had entered a "paper house" at Beloit, Wisconsin, "as a sort of preliminary work . . . to entering the profession of Journalism" and gave his employment as the reason for his absence.[1] After a short stint in Beloit, he went to Chicago to begin an apprenticeship in that city's flourishing book trade. He could not have realized that Chicago and its environs would become his home for the next forty-odd years.

Although the foundations of Kerr's later radicalism lay in a social consciousness first nurtured in Madison, the direct reasons for his eventual rejection of middle-class security and his later receptivity to the socialist message are unclear. After all, the young man's new hometown, vibrant and expansive as it was, projected all the promise and opportunity that one who had his background and training might hope for and expect. The city also displayed those glaring social contradictions and inequitable disparities that must have played a role in the eventual radicalization of the aspiring publisher. Life in what was soon to become the Second City must have seemed incredible, perhaps a bit overwhelming, to the young man after so many years spent in the relative tranquility of Madison.

Initially a commercial center, Chicago experienced a period of unprecedented industrialization in the two decades following the Great Fire of 1871. It had become the financial and industrial center of the Midwest within a few years of the fire and soon led the nation in farm machinery production, numbers of packing plants, lumberyards, and saw mills. Nestled at the southwestern end of Lake Michigan, it was a major Great Lakes port and the transfer hub for some twenty railroads. By 1880 only New York and Philadelphia surpassed it as manufacturing centers, and the next decade saw the city advance to second place in gross productive output. Such rapid industrial development was the result of plant expansion based on massive capitalization and combination, technological and managerial innovation, and the resultant de-skilling of established trades. Economic expansion was also fueled by massive population growth, creating an abundant, cheap labor pool. One of the fastest growing cities in the country and perhaps the world, Chicago's population doubled every ten years between 1860 and 1890. From approximately half a million people in 1880, it grew to more than a million a decade later. The city's labor force increased fivefold between 1870 and 1890.[2]

Most Chicago laborers in those years were either immigrants or the children of immigrants. The bustling industrial and shipping and rail center attracted newcomers from all over the world, and the number of foreign-born in 1890 almost equaled the city's entire population ten years earlier. Nearly 80 percent of the population by that year was of foreign parentage. As if pushed by the sheer weight of its numbers, the city's geographic boundaries rushed outward. From the time of the Great Fire until 1893, the year of the Columbian Exposition, the area within Chicago's corporate confines increased from approximately thirty-five to slightly more than 185 square miles.[3] Truly a city of immigrants, the expanding metropolis also contained a sizable middle class, mainly "old stock" or northern European in origin and composed of proprietors of small and medium-sized businesses, ascending professionals, and upper-strata white-collar employees. At the pinnacle of the city's social pyramid was a tier of white, Anglo-Saxon, Protestant industrial entrepreneurs, financial and commercial magnates, and a scattering of officeholders who had immense power and accumulated wealth.

Clearly, the Chicago of the 1880s was a study in sharp contrasts, with unprecedented squalor and poverty on one hand and unsurpassed accumulated wealth, privilege, and opulence on the other. Buffeted by cyclical economic downturns, seasonal work in many industries, and declines in purchasing power, many working-class families routinely faced destitution and unemployment, and disease and vermin-infested slum tenements abounded. Half of the children of Chicago in 1882 died before they were five. The following year, the Department of Health noted that the number of deaths in the overcrowded working-class warrens trebled those in the cleaner, more spacious residential wards of the middle and upper classes.[4] Periodic recessions and depressions, staggering inflation rates, an overabundance of cheap labor, and the de-skilling of various crafts racked the multiethnic working class that crowded into congested, inadequate living spaces close by the mills and factories.

Such inflicted hardship did not go by without response, however. Not simply a city of immigrants, Chicago had also become an émigré city where the radical milieu resembled that of Paris, London, Berlin, or Zurich. By 1880 Chicago was arguably the most radical city in America, a new home for revolutionaries and liberals fleeing repression in the aftermath of the failed revolutions of 1848 and the antisocialist laws of Bismarck's Germany. It became a temporary stopover or permanent residence for numerous socialist and anarchist members of the First International. The city also attracted former radical Republicans schooled in the abolition movement, hardened by the Civil War and the thwarted social transformation that had been Radical Reconstruction. Although some politicized émigrés, often well educated and skilled, found a modicum of good fortune and readily acquired middle-class respectability, others, class-conscious workers tempered by revolution and reaction in Europe or radicalized by the harsh realities of the American environment, soon banded together in various attempts to unite the city's diverse and often fractured working class. They soon were joined by others, the children of immigrants and native-born alike, alienated and radicalized by the struggle for existence. Such activists founded or joined existing unions, created mutual aid societies and cooperatives, an assortment of political formations, and a multilingual press that paralleled the institutions of the dominant culture.[5]

Class-conscious radical workers faced no easy task. The harsh realities of working-class life created a fertile social terrain for labor radicalism, but worker militants nevertheless had to overcome deeply antagonistic class divisions that were ethnic and linguistic as well as religious and political. They also had to transcend the fragmentation of workers' existence structured into the very nature of their labors—divisions between skilled and unskilled, between those in organized trades and the unorganized, and among the regularly employed, the underemployed, and the dispossessed. Profound tensions and heightened competition, not solely for jobs but for cramped living space and control of social, political, and educational institutions, often further strained relations among the city's foreign-born. Native-born English-speakers dominated the white-collar occupations; Germans and Scandinavians dominated the skilled trades; and Irish, Bohemians, Poles, and Hungarians provided the pool of unskilled and casual labor.

Wage differentials regularly reflected ethnic differences and discrimination as much as skill levels and competition, especially for menial, low-paying jobs, and often led to clashes away from the workplace. A deep-seated nativist streak also fueled tensions between "native" and immigrant workers. The deepest lines of division within the polyglot working class were religious, generally Protestant versus Catholic. The immigrant groups, especially the Germans, Czechs, and Scandinavians, also contained numbers of articulate and influential atheists and freethinkers. Often radical in their social outlook, they regularly attracted more concern from the city's "Yankee Puritan" elite than either Jews or Catholics.[6] The city's ethnic working classes, although deeply divided, also shared the common harsh experiences of industrialization. Regularly fragmented by differences of language and culture, occupation, skill, wage rates, and the fact of living in different neighborhoods, they occasionally joined in solidarity, especially during periods of exacerbated difficulty and agitation, when transient class solidarities overcame day-to-day divisions.

When Charles Kerr arrived in Chicago, the collective memory of all social classes in the city could readily recall the fresh images of class violence and communal wrath created by employers' responses to the severe depression of the 1870s. The city had hardly recovered from the devastation of the Great Fire when the depression of the 1870s struck. Workers who had flocked to Chicago to help rebuild the city after the fire were suddenly without jobs. Employers, eager to limit or recoup losses, cut wages and hours and dismissed thousands. Numbers of homeless men, women, and children wandered the streets in search of work or shelter and lined up at neighborhood soup kitchens. Such conditions provided a social tinderbox awaiting a spark. It came in the form of a railwaymen's strike that began in the East and spread like wildfire across the continent.

Few Chicagoans who lived through it could forget the Great Upheaval of 1877, four July days of spontaneous, unorganized class rage that resulted in the loss of dozens of lives, left hundreds injured, and necessitated the use of army regulars to quell the massive outpouring of the hard-pressed. The strikes and their accompanying violence left deep marks of bitterness and further fueled class fears and hatreds. The upheaval gave capital its first taste of mass insurrection, comparable in contemporary imaginings to the Paris Commune of 1871. Rather than turning to economic and social reform, however, Chicago's city fathers called for a strengthening of the repressive apparatus through the passage of conspiracy laws, the construction of fortresslike armories, and the reorganization of the military, state militias, and police. The city's Citizen's Association, promoted by Marshall Field "to fight communists," donated two Gatling guns to the city in 1878.[7]

Labor, in the meantime, acquired a new sense of its collective strength. The city's labor leaders, often socialist or "social revolutionaries," also drew lessons from the decade's hardships. Organization became the response as union leaders turned toward increased political and industrial action and militants formed a multilingual press, educational and social institutions, and self-defense units. Resultant class solidarities began to transcend the ethnic and linguistic divisions separating Chicago's workers. The stage was set for further contestations between capital and labor for conflict and violence as the 1880s began. Just as Charles Kerr moved to Chicago, the city's fear of class upheavals capable of rending its social fabric had become widespread. It would intensify as the decade proceeded.[8]

Tensions and conflicts nestled in the nature of the city went unresolved in the 1880s. Arthur Schlesinger, Sr., has observed that the very air the people breathed seemed to typify the sharp contrasts and contradictions of Chicago in that decade. Sometimes when the wind was from the south the city reeked with the stench of the stockyards. Then, with a sudden shift, the wind could carry fresh-blown gusts from the lake to relieve the foulness.[9] An investigation of the tenement districts by the Chicago Citizen's Association in 1883–84 revealed wretched conditions. Drainage was inadequate or nonexistent, as was plumbing, light, ventilation, and fire safety, and the working poor paid exorbitant rents for overcrowded rooms. Between 1879 and 1881, a period of relative prosperity, food prices jumped an estimated 50 to 100 percent and yet wages remained relatively stationary; the cost of living rose another 15 percent the following year. That brief period of economic advance was soon followed by another period of slowdown and deepening recession. Declines in wage rates became widespread between 1882 and 1884 while the average Illinois industrial worker remained idle one-quarter of the year.[10] By 1884, as the downturn deepened, blacksmiths, stockyard hands, steelworkers, cigar makers, and members of numerous other trades confronted further loss of wages and hours, if not loss of work.[11] The economy hit bottom during the winter of 1884–85, a period in which the city's labor force suffered more severely than in the previous decade. One-fifth of Chicago's carpenters were idle in January, and nearly 40 percent of the working class soon passed into a state of enforced idleness. An estimated twenty-five thousand people could be found walking the streets in search of employment by October 1884.

In response, the city's labor leaders called for collective action and joined agitations that culminated in strikes and demonstrations for the eight-hour day as a solution to unemployment. Calls for a general strike and the resultant work stoppages of early May 1886—pushed by increased worker desperation and militancy, improved organization, and articulate radical critiques and rhetorical attacks on the existing order—naturally heightened class tensions. So did the recalcitrance of many employers. The movement for the eight-hour day, initially successful, climaxed with the tragic events at Haymarket Square on May 4, 1886, that pivotal moment for not only Chicago's labor movement but also for a generation of social and political activists.[12]

Despite the turmoil of that decade, the 1880s also marked sheltered prosperity and comfort for some, as evidenced by the rows of stately mansions that lined the likes of Prairie Avenue on the city's South Side. Opportunities did exist. A growing middle class of professionals and white-collar workers, overwhelmingly native-born, began to leave the squalor and chaos of the industrial and business districts and immigrant working-class slums and move to quieter neighborhoods and new suburbs north and south of the city.[13] It was in the middle-class Chicago of the early 1880s that Charles Kerr, still relatively secure and confident in his class privilege, began to adjust to his new home and way of life. His move into radical politics and left-wing activism would take time. It would not be a long time, however, because the contradictory realities of Chicago's growth and development, its class cleavages, confronted the young man's understandings and future.

Shortly after he arrived in Chicago, Kerr went to work as a clerk in the sales department of the Colegrove Book Company, an independent publishing firm that produced *Unity* and other assorted religious and educational tracts for the Western Unitarian Conference. Centered in the heart of a new "Bookseller's Row" relocated on Wabash Avenue from an earlier State Street locale that the Great Fire had leveled, the Colegrove house arose in 1881 from the remains of Hadley Brothers and Keen, Cook and Company, two publishing ventures that had antebellum roots and had fallen prey to the economic hard times of the 1870s.[14] One of the oldest established "bookmen" in Chicago during the early 1880s, James Colegrove catered mainly to a large audience of professional men and women throughout the region.[15] With offices and a small shop at 135 Wabash, his company shared space with the WUC. Colegrove began to handle the conference's publishing shortly after he opened the Wabash doors, despite the early concern of some patrons that a close association with the Unitarians might prove harmful to his general trade.[16] Kerr spent a good deal, although not all, of his early Chicago days at the Wabash shop and gradually developed a keen understanding of the complex inner workings of Bookseller's Row.

He had other pursuits as well. While still a student at the University of Wisconsin, Kerr had met and fallen in love with a classmate, Helen Adams, the daughter of Chicago businessman Charles F. Adams. His affection for Nellie Adams certainly played some part in drawing him to Chicago. Wed on May 29, 1889 by Jenkin Lloyd Jones, the two carried on a lengthy courtship through Kerr's first years in the city.[17]

Kerr also became involved in the numerous cultural and educational activities inspired by the unwavering energy of Jenkin Lloyd Jones at the fledgling All Souls. His name began to appear in the church's annuals during the spring of 1883, first as a participant in the Robert Browning section of the All Souls Unity Club, the Chicago continuation of Jones's earlier Mutual Improvement groups. Clearly an admirer of Browning, he made two presentations to the study circle in March and April 1883 and a third the following November. A member of the Odyssey section as well, Kerr offered a discourse on Roman mythology the following winter. He joined the James Russell Lowell study section the next season and entertained members with a presentation on "The Yankee Dialect" and Lowell's "Autobiographical Poetry." In successive years he offered talks on "Browning's Essay on Shelley" and "Agamemnon."[18]

Kerr wrote several essays and reviews for *Unity*, which was then the conference's monthly voice. Mainly literary criticism, those pieces convey limited but suggestive insights into the young man's thinking. The varied articles reveal a fair amount about his knowledge of the classics as well as French and English poetry and drama. They also suggest a partiality for the mildly controversial and an apparent admiration for literary renegades and innovators.

In his first *Unity* piece Kerr assessed the contributions of Percy Bysshe Shelley. After noting that "Shelley was not a popular poet, he is not popular today, he never will be popular while human nature remains what it is," the young essayist launched into a highly favorable appraisal of the poet. Spanning the scope of Shelley's career from the early "Queen Mab" to "Adonais," the elegy for Keats written a year before Shelley's own death, Kerr called the poet's critics to task. In doing so, he managed to shed some light on his own predispositions and moral outlook: "Faults no doubt [Shelley] had, but they were faults that sprung from fidelity to his convictions. He never shrunk from any course of action that seemed to him right, through fear of coming into conflict with public sentiment. With his whole soul he hated tyranny and superstition in whatever form they appeared." In regard to Shelley's reputed atheism, the essay suggested that "the only God he rejected was the God of superstition, of intolerance, and of religious persecution." Kerr went on to argue that the poet's lyrics were "unsurpassed in beauty in the English language." As if to protect himself from potential criticism, he then qualified his assertion: "I say this without hesitation, for [Shelley's] poems however inferior they may be to Shakespeare's in power, to Milton's in grandeur, to Byron's in vigor, have both a depth of meaning and a grace of expression which are all their own."[19]

The editorial board of *Unity* must have been pleased with the Shelley essay, for several weeks later it extended more space to Kerr. The new piece on "Victor Hugo's Reform in the French Drama" exhibited a clear sense of historical development. In an attempt to evaluate the importance of the early-nineteenth-century French Romantic school and Hugo, Kerr discussed the evolution of Greek drama and its influence on the French tragedians of the Renaissance. While suggesting that Hugo's plays "bear marks of extreme haste, and lack the elegance which his work in other literature displays," he softened his criticism by noting that "the true excuse for the defects which appear in these works is that the dramatic art in France is still in its infancy."[20]

Kerr continued to contribute smaller essays, mainly book reviews, to *Unity* throughout the remainder of 1883 and 1884.[21] His usually favorable comments appeared irregularly in "The Study Table," the magazine's book review section. As his role in the business end of the expanding *Unity* enterprise increased, however, his contributions as essayist receded. Kerr's budding career as a literary critic soon came to a close; his energy and talents were in demand elsewhere.

While continuing his apprenticeship at Colegrove through early 1883, Charles Kerr began to volunteer more and more of his time and energy to the *Unity* bureau. Located initially at 75 Madison Street, the *Unity* office served as the general headquarters for the WUC. Sharing the limited space was the Western Unitarian Sunday School Society, distributor of Jones's Seven Year Course lesson leaflets and numerous other books and pamphlets for younger Unitarians. The society, a direct outgrowth of Jones's Janesville work, had expanded rapidly with the establishment of the Chicago office. The rooms on Madison Street also housed the Post Office Mission, which often filled the already cramped quarters with women volunteers busily at work mailing "Unity Short Tracts" and other denominational material to co-religionists throughout the country.[22]

Kerr soon became a member of the society's board of directors and took charge of a new Jones project, the Unity Church-Door Pulpit, a reprint series of sermons drawn from the pages of *Unity* and distributed to churches throughout the conference.[23]

Then, at the beginning of March 1883, Jenkin Jones informed his readers of some changes in store for *Unity.* "As one step forward," he explained, "the publishers have secured the services of Mr. C. H. Kerr, a recent graduate of the Wisconsin State University, as Business Manager and Editor Assistant." Already overburdened with his work as missionary secretary for the WUC and preoccupied with his drive to build All Souls Church, Jones maintained the editorial leadership of the fortnightly while Kerr became business manager and overseer of *Unity's* production and distribution.[24] Circulation soon expanded, and Kerr's name began to appear on the masthead as office editor, directly under Jones's listing as editor, in March 1884. There it stayed until the beginning of 1886, and Jones soon noted that Colegrove, through Kerr's effective work as business agent, had greatly improved the "practical affairs" of the struggling periodical during the previous year.[25]

Unity became a weekly and increased in size at the beginning of May 1885. With the shift to a new production schedule and format, Charles Kerr's duties at the Wabash office suddenly took on a different scope and meaning. The changeover aside, May 1885 was exceedingly hectic for the novice editor. That month Colegrove had planned to issue *Unity Songs Resung,* a volume of twenty-five poems that Kerr had compiled from the preceding six years of *Unity.* Unfortunately, fire, that arch-nemesis of the Chicago publishing trade, destroyed the Review Printing Company, Colegrove's job printer. In the *Unity* of April 18, hastily printed on borrowed presses, Kerr reassured readers that the *Unity* office itself had not been harmed, but the fire delayed the release of *Unity Songs Resung* and a run of Church Door Pulpit tracts. The compilation of *Unity* verse and the new series of missionary pamphlets were ready a few weeks later, and *Unity Songs,* Kerr's first published volume, went on to become one of the most popular publications of the *Unity* group.[26]

The *Unity* venture continued to grow. Readership for the weekly increased, and the number of published tracts and pamphlets rose as well. The enterprise went through an important restructuring at the beginning of 1886. In early January, Jones wrote "A *Unity* Prospect" to the paper's followers. After praising the unanticipated accomplishments of the previous eight years, he pointed the course of *Unity* forward. Noting that the new year heralded some important changes, he informed readers that a move to larger quarters was underway, that the editorial board had appointed a new office manager, and that the *Unity* headquarters would start carrying the publications of the American Unitarian Association and George H. Ellis, Boston's major Unitarian publisher. Jones also noted that the Colegrove Book Company, a casualty of the economic downturn of the mid-1880s, had transferred its book selling business to a nearby competitor, S. A. Maxwell and Company. He then announced that the publishing interests of the *Unity* office had been transferred to the new firm of Charles H. Kerr & Company: "Mr. Kerr, our office editor, having served over three years of apprenticeship, receives the full confidence of the Unity editorial staff. The extent of the confidence is hinted at by the mystic '& Co.' in the title of our new publishing house. He is no longer the boy we are bringing up, but the man into whose hands we place our work, and we bespeak for him the confidence of our patrons. In some slow cautious way we hope to see him become in the fullness of time the successful Liberal book-maker of the West."[27]

The *Unity* concern moved to a new office on the sixth floor of the Commercial National Bank Building at 175 Dearborn within a couple of weeks. Kerr, in turn, sublet one of the three rooms at the new location for $10 a month to house his infant publishing venture.[28] The work of editor and publisher that would occupy the young man from Wisconsin for the rest of his working life was well underway.

3

The Kerr Company's Beginnings

In his study of religious revivalism and its relationship to social reform in the antebellum era, Timothy Smith cautioned historians of American religious movements by observing that there was no typical Protestant point of view on religious or social matters. In most cases there was no commonly held perception on such issues within any of the major denominations, and "every sermon, newspaper article and essay must be studied in the light of its author's relation to the contending groups in his sect."[1] Smith's observation held true for the post–Civil War decades. They certainly remained true for the Unitarian cause. The early religious publications of Charles H. Kerr & Company acquire their full historical significance only when viewed in the specific context of various theological and social developments that reshaped the liberal faith in the three decades following the Civil War.

The Kerr Company at its inception was party to a sectarian dispute, a battle for authority and legitimacy that prefigured Kerr's later involvement in frays within the socialist camp. That particular Unitarian controversy swirled around theological concerns and also centered on the social role and direction of Unitarianism. The significance of the early Kerr list as a record of a particular tendency within that cause only becomes clear when the list is placed in context with the ongoing denominational disputes that continued to convulse post–Civil War Unitarianism.

Fundamentally a liberal conviction, Unitarian origins extended far back into the Enlightenment and Age of Reason. Unitarianism in America was also the offspring of a long series of theological and ecclesiastical disputes within New England Congregationalism during the latter part of the eighteenth century.[2] Religious liberals within the "New England faith" developed a firm stand on religious freedom based upon complete congregational independence. When conservatives within the denomination proposed tests of orthodoxy or insisted upon clear structural organization of churches, the liberals joined in opposition.[3] As the nineteenth century dawned, doctrinal and ecclesiastical disputes among orthodox and liberal Congregationalists heated to a slow boil. Various theological and organizational controversies led to successive splits within established congregations and ultimately to a final breach and the formation of the American Unitarian Association (AUA), a loose alliance of liberal coreligionists, at quarter century.

The loosely knit denomination itself soon became polarized over theological and doctrinal issues as well as social questions of the antebellum decades. A constant antagonism between those of a more rationalist and liberal inclination and those of a more evangelical bent intensified. New outlooks on theological questions, when combined with the era's socially and politically charged disputes over the role of church and individual, led to splits both within the denomination and from it. Successive controversies defined and redefined the young movement as it evolved during the nineteenth century.[4]

The First Unitarian Controversy (ca. 1810–18), which led to the founding of a formalized denomination, was led by William Ellery Channing (1778–1842), "the Luther of the Boston Reformation."[5] In his polemics against the orthodox Trinitarians and their Calvinist determinism, he insisted that the "ultimate reliance of a human being is and must be on his own mind."[6] Stressing the Arminian impulse of free will and inquiry as a modification of Calvinist predestination and revelation, he put forward a "perfectibilitarian" message that was a code of religious moral behavior for the earthbound. This liberal perfectionism helped stimulate dissatisfaction with the contemporary world and moved many of his followers toward social reform endeavor.[7] From Channing's day forward, the nature of reform and the role of Unitarians within it became issues that further fanned the flames of doctrinal and institutional dispute and dissent.

By the end of the 1830s the Second Unitarian Controversy had divided the denomination into two contending camps, a conservative majority and a small but influential number of radicals who began to question not only the necessity of belief in the miraculous but also the static authority of the Scriptures. Decrying what he termed the "pale negations" of then established Unitarianism, Ralph Waldo Emerson, in his famed "Divinity School Address" of 1838, precipitated the second schism with a scathing critique of the liberal faith. He charged that churches had lost their spirit of intuition, which they viewed as the essence of true religion. Castigating the clergy for accepting a secondhand faith in place of provocative direct inspiration, Emerson argued that religious faith had to be based on an inner light and sentiment and not on the authentication of miracles or ritualized creeds.[8]

Unlike Emerson, who withdrew from the conflict after delivering his "spiritual declaration of independence," Theodore Parker refused to relinquish his pulpit at Boston's First Unitarian, and he became the guiding intellectual force for a generation of radical Unitarians who would play key roles in shaping Charles Kerr's outlook. Parker initially entered the polemical lists in response to the attacks on Emerson. He questioned the value of miracles and asserted that the truths of Christianity were intuitive rather than dependent upon the evidence of miracles or upon any other evidence. In an essay titled "The Transient and Permanent in Christianity" he asserted that Christianity should not be based on gospels nor on the teachings of a church, but on the "great truths which spring up spontaneous in the holy heart" and suggested that "if it could be proven that Jesus never lived, still Christianity would stand firm and fear no evil." The Second Unitarian Controversy, heightened by Parker's discarding of the miraculous, intensified.[9]

Parker, significantly, was not simply some "other-worldly" theologian. A social activist and secular critic, his sermons often dealt with the present and not the past. He turned to concrete problems, "the sins of Boston, not of Babylon."[10] An irrepressible agitator, he immersed himself in the various reform initiatives of the 1840s and 1850s. He labored for numerous causes—antisabbatarianism, an end to capital punishment, reform of the justice and penal systems, temperance, and various other movements, including woman's rights and the cause of labor. An uncompromising, firebrand abolitionist who came to stand alongside William Lloyd Garrison and John Brown, Parker's antislavery activities further rankled conservatives.

The question of slavery went right to the heart of various tensions within the liberal faith. Religious liberalism could and often did blend readily with a relatively conservative perception of the social order; religious humanism and social harmony were not necessarily contradictory. During the escalating slavery debate, however, religious liberal perfectionism and social conservatism became incompatible.[11] Parker and his colleagues forced that breach. Head-on, the Parkerite radicals confronted the incompatibility of conservative Unitarian complicity with the slaveocracy. They appealed to natural law when other conservatives reacted to violations of civil law. Parker, for example, aided fugitive slaves and the militant abolitionist John Brown and premeditatedly broke secular laws of a system he deemed unjust by appealing to a higher moral order.

Parker's belief in the competence of innate, intuitive religious and moral sense enabled his successors to deal in an open, unhampered fashion with scientific and social theories that convulsed the Christian world after the Civil War. Equally as important, he and his colleagues left a legacy of moral and religious faith in progress and a commitment to a liberal perfectionism anchored in the real world. Their legacy as activists concerned for human dignity would extend far into the future, but when Parker was buried in 1860 his peers and disciples still had a long road ahead of them in the quest for a more perfect order. The path they followed led directly to the likes of Charles Kerr, born that same year in LaGrange, Georgia.

Salvation, for Unitarians, occurred through intellectual and moral growth and improvement; they believed in regeneration, not conversion. Averse to the traditional conversion experience, the movement's followers viewed individual redemption as an ongoing process. Such beliefs led to an emphasis on literacy and education as the primary vehicles to a better life. The published word in the form of pamphlets, published sermons, and periodical essays and reviews played a central role in the growth and development of the denomination. Tracts were the most important means for disseminating theology and social outlook to church members and nonmembers alike. New churches, especially those outside New England, were often established in areas where Unitarian activists had distributed tracts and books.[12] At its founding in 1886 Charles H. Kerr & Company was part of an already established institutional history; it was the direct descendant of a long line of publishing ventures wedded to Unitarianism's dissenting tradition.

In the period leading up to the Unitarian split from Congregationalism, pamphlets and periodicals provided the primary arena for the airing of differences. Public expressions of liberal views found space in the *Monthly Anthology*, begun in 1803, which the Unitarian historian George Willis Cooke has called the first distinctive literary magazine in the United States. On the orthodox side of the First Unitarian Controversy sat the quarterly *General Repository and Review*, initiated in 1812 to carry on a defense of the Trinitarian doctrine. In May of the following year, the liberals countered with the *Christian Disciple*. A family magazine that defended religious liberty, its pages also advocated temperance and condemned slavery.

The *Christian Examiner* succeeded the *Disciple* in 1824. "The organ of higher intellectual life" among Unitarians, its pages displayed continued interest in literature, general culture, and philanthropic work as well as a broad discussion of theological questions. Founded by William Ellery Channing in 1847, the *Examiner* came under the editorship of Theodore Parker's Harvard Divinity School classmate George Ellis. Ellis, in turn, went on to become the foremost Unitarian publisher in the East. His Boston-based house, after 1886, jointly issued a number of imprints in cooperation with Charles H. Kerr & Company.[13]

With unending confidence in the progressive potential of the printed word, Unitarian-related firms and institutions not only remained conspicuous in the dissemination of tracts, periodicals, and books but also devised numerous strategies and organizational mechanisms for the mass dissemination of their particular message. The American Unitarian Association was the major antebellum distributor of denominational literature and also the primary financial backer of church-related educational and missionary work on a national level. Founded in 1825, the AUA never became a formal administrative or governing body for the denomination but nevertheless came to wield considerable power as the primary clearinghouse for funds contributed for publishing projects, missionary work, and the source of support for smaller churches. The series of tracts the association published before the Civil War "was one of the most distinguished collections of denominational literature that any American church has produced."[14]

■

In 1865 most Unitarians were still relatively conservative theologically; supernaturalists, their faith relied upon an acceptance of the Gospels. By the mid-1880s the majority no longer asserted that an acceptance of the miraculous was necessary for a faith in Christ and his teachings. Instead, it placed Theodore Parker at its center. Such a change obviously did not occur overnight.

As the Civil War drew to a close, several prominent Unitarian leaders called for a meeting of all Unitarian bodies in an attempt to rejuvenate church organization at a national level. Their hope was to gather all the existing Unitarian congregations under the auspices of one national body to facilitate missionary and educational ventures. Some five hundred delegates from 195 churches met in New York in April 1865. Organizers called the meeting to deal with practical issues, not to decide doctrinal matters. They nevertheless proposed a preamble to the fledgling conference that specifically committed prospective adherents to the "Lordship of Christ."

The convention immediately erupted into a doctrinal debate as conservatives and radicals rejoined their prewar face-off.[15] The preamble met with the approval of the overwhelming majority despite Parkerite protests, and the conservatives, clearly in charge of the proceedings, successfully pressed for adoption. When the national conference reconvened the following year in Syracuse, New York, the radicals, undeterred by the previous year's events, introduced new resolutions to amend the preamble. The conservatives present suggested that the radicals go their own way. Many of them did. They left the 1866 convocation convinced that Unitarianism had repudiated its allegiance to unlimited freedom. With the idea of a "spiritual anti-slavery society" in mind, they convened several informal meetings that led to the creation of the Free Religious Association (FRA) the following spring.[16]

A new generation of ministers, followers of Parker, schooled by the Civil War, and ordained in the immediate postwar years, left the denominational fold to join the FRA. Still others, although dismayed over the credal exclusiveness of the conference's leadership, nevertheless maintained their affiliation with the national Unitarian body. The radicals who remained upheld their nondoctrinal stance while preserving close ties with colleagues in the FRA.[17] The FRA group, meanwhile, began to carry the ideas of noncredal belief and a religion unencumbered by denominational dictates to new pulpits. A seeding process of what eventually became standard Unitarianism occurred throughout the Midwest as graduates from Harvard Divinity School and Meadeville Theological Seminary scattered throughout Illinois, Iowa, and Wisconsin. Most of the western radicals, unlike their colleagues in the East, maintained the Unitarian name and affiliation. Following Parker's lead, they refused to budge from the fold.

Soon to become a central figure among this new breed, Jenkin Lloyd Jones had closely followed the ongoing denominational imbroglio as a divinity student at Meadeville.[18] He immediately rushed off to the annual meeting of the Western Unitarian Conference in Cleveland after delivering the 1870 commencement address at the seminary. He found the WUC infected with the same in-house disputes that had earlier crippled the infant national conference and the works of the AUA. Conservatives at the Cleveland meeting called for a statement of faith, an explicit doctrinal basis to bind the denomination together organizationally. Jones listened to attacks on the "spiritual vagrancy" of those concerned with such matters as comparative religion and a more active social role for the church and came away disturbed and determined to act.

The gathering, Jones's first WUC convention, became so divided that no meeting took place the following year. Jones and a number of radical allies did not remain inactive, however. They took the initiative and reconvened an annual conference in 1872 at Meadeville. Significantly, none of the more conservative, older churches had representatives present; none of the officers elected in 1870 attended. A primary issue concerned the continued funding of missionary work and the support of the more liberal churches throughout the region. The AUA, the major backer of such ventures, was firmly in the hands of eastern conservatives. The association's funding had always been contingent upon its approval of ministers and missionaries. Now, money was not forthcoming for smaller western congregations under the sway of radicals. Jones boldly suggested that the WUC leave the association and raise its own funds. Moderates among the delegates won a plea for continued affiliation, but at the annual meeting the following year, 1874, Jones again moved to have the WUC assume its own financial responsibilities. His resolution passed but went unimplemented.[19]

The breach between the WUC and the AUA widened in the meantime. In what became known as the yearbook controversy of 1874, the AUA dropped the name of William J. Potter from its annual list of Unitarian ministers on the grounds that Potter did not consider himself a Christian, but simply a Unitarian. Potter was minister of a well-known church in New Bedford, Massachusetts, and, significantly, secretary of the FRA, anathema to the conservatives. In response to his exclusion, the WUC directed its members and affiliated churches to no longer send contributions for missionary work eastward. They were instead instructed to forward funds to the conference treasurer in Chicago—Jenkin Lloyd Jones.[20]

By the early 1880s conservatives in the West had come to believe that the "Unity men" intended to transform the WUC into a branch of the FRA. They also blamed the radical's refusal to adhere to the Christian name as the primary cause for the slow rate of growth of western Unitarianism. They organized an offensive against the Unity men and their "ethical basis." In part a feud over funds, the intradenominational dispute stimulated a polemical contestation; it was a theological propaganda war, with each side vying for the hearts and minds of a highly literate and educated rank and file. Both factions regularly employed the periodical, pamphlet, and broadside to mobilize support and new adherents.

Unity, the key weekly expression of the Western Unitarian radical's position, had its origins in the desire of the younger ministers of the WUC to provide a "paper messenger" for the far-flung Unitarian societies and groups of isolated religious liberals throughout the region. Stimulated in part by the desire to supplant the publications of the conservative National

Unitarian Conference, the more radical WUC affiliates wanted a western paper to forward its own message and communications on a regular basis. After several false starts, a publishing committee of WUC ministers began the semimonthly *Pamphlet Mission* on March 1, 1878. Dedicated to "Freedom, Fellowship and Character in Religion," the first issue of the pamphlet-sized fortnightly contained a prospectus from the editorial committee; a sermon, "Not Retreat, but Victory" by Chicago's Robert Colyer; and some conference "Notes and News." Each successive number contained a reprinted sermon or essay. Among the earliest was "The Sympathy of Religions," a discourse on the universal character of religion by the noted abolitionist Thomas Wentworth Higginson.[21]

"Freedom and Fellowship in Religion," the title of a volume of essays issued by the Free Religious Association, became the group's motto. Sympathetic to much of what the FRA represented, the *Pamphlet Mission*'s founders explained in their opening issue that "each number will stand for real FREEDOM of mind, for real FELLOWSHIP between different minds, and as most important of all, for CHARACTER as the *test* and *essence* of religion." To the founders of *Unity*, "character in religion" meant opposition to an emphasis on dogmatic or literal belief based on doctrinal tests or vows; the Unity men proclaimed, "Not belief, but character is the real test of religion."[22]

The Unity men soon realized the name *Pamphlet Mission* was inadequate. Jones recalled that a new name for the publication became "the absorbing question of the first six months. Names were dropped into hats, balloted for, corresponded upon, discussed in bulk and in detail; they came singly and in squads."[23] The *Pamphlet Mission* became *Unity* on September 1, 1878. At the end of *Unity*'s first year the editorial board changed its original pamphlet design to a quarto-size format, and Henry Martyn Simmons assumed the post of editor in charge. Jenkin Jones, still missionary secretary, took charge of a "Notes from the Field" department before becoming editor the following year when Simmons departed for Madison, Wisconsin.[24]

Unity had clearly established itself as the voice of the more radical Unitarians in the West by 1880; the ministers on its editorial board became the focus of attention within national church circles. Among the other Unity men were William Channing Gannett, James Vila Blake, Charles W. Wendte, Frederick Lucien Hosmer, and Jabez T. Sunderland. Gannett played a central role in shaping *Unity*'s future. The son of William Ellery Channing's successor at Boston's Federal Street Church, he entered the Harvard Divinity School in 1861 but left shortly thereafter to join the first party of the Freedmen's Aid Society volunteers in the South Carolina Sea Islands, where he remained for four years. He was finally graduated from the Divinity School in 1868. An early member of the FRA, Gannett nevertheless retained his Unitarian ministry at St. Paul, Minnesota, from 1877 to 1883, when he became minister-at-large for the WUC. He was an ardent abolitionist and women's suffragist. Susan B. Anthony was member of Gannett's later congregation in Rochester, New York. He was also highly interested in scientific progress; one of his biographers, C. W. Wendte, has noted that "the evolution idea caught his attention immensely."[25]

Blake graduated from Harvard Divinity School in 1866. After successive ministries at Haverhill, Massachusetts, and Quincy, Illinois, he accepted a call to head the Third Unitarian Church of Chicago, where he remained for fifteen years. He published nearly twenty volumes of essays, poetry, and drama. Blake, like Jenkin Jones, was also a social radical, "in fidelity to the long Channing-Parker tradition within Unitarianism."[26] Wendte, the son of German liberal émigrés, entered Harvard Divinity School in 1866 after a brief preparation at Meadeville Theological Seminary. Ordained as minister of Chicago's Fourth Unitarian Church in 1869, he eventually accepted a call to the older and larger First Unitarian of Cincinnati.[27] Hosmer, like Blake a member of the class of 1866, was a noted Unitarian poet and hymnologist. A radical thinker in theological terms, he was less affected by the social developments of his time than were Jones and Gannett and had only limited interest in the social and political reform causes of the latter nineteenth century.[28] Sunderland had broken with the Baptist fellowship to become a prolific author for the Unitarian cause. He was also minister at Ann Arbor and the state missionary for Michigan.[29]

The Unity men were all "emphatically and enthusiastically churchmen—men of mystical and emotional dispositions, ministers of implicit and pronounced pastoral and social devotion." Their theology was fused with the evolutionary thought of Spencer, Darwin, Lyell, and Huxley as well as with the views of German New Testament scholars. They were all second- or third-generation Transcendentalists whose Emersonian convictions concerning divine immanence and intuitive notions of truth and goodness, when combined with a reverence for the cosmic order, informed their synthesis of evolution and theology. "Theirs was a rational faith, yet intensely rapturous and lyrical." Their "ethical basis" of "freedom, fellowship and character in religion" readily fused science, philosophy and an optimistic belief in progress with a true religious fervor. Such was the group that had come under attack when Charles Kerr joined the staff at the *Unity* office. They would play a significant role in the major postbellum Unitarian imbroglio, the "Controversy in the West."[30]

The controversy began in June 1883, when a minister from Brooklyn, the Rev. A. P. Putnam, addressed the London-based British and Foreign Unitarian Association. He charged that many Unitarians in the United States had turned to other faiths because the denomination had become a "medley of doubts and denials, petty criticism and secular teachings."[31] Although he had never been there, Putnam also claimed that "some Unitarian preachers in the West surpass all others in declaring that God and immortality are but fictions of the mind." Conservatives mailed Putnam's address, reproduced in London's Unitarian *Christian Life*, to every Unitarian minister in the United States.[32]

Some ministers in the West, notably Jasper Douthit, a liberal evangelist from rural southern Illinois, rejoiced over Putnam's jeremiad. Douthit had founded the monthly *Our Best Words* as a western counter to *Unity*. The *Christian Life* mailing of Putnam's address inspired Douthit to issue an extra of his monthly containing the speech and a full indictment of the ethical basis group—Jones, W. C. Gannett, and the others.[33]

Understandably, that attack led to further volleys of opposing canon. When Jones resigned as secretary of the Western Conference in 1884, Sunderland, a close friend and ally of Douthit and Putnam, succeeded him. At the WUC's St. Louis convention in 1885, Sunderland openly attacked the ethical basis adherents. Noting that Unitarianism had not grown as it should, he reasoned that too many existent churches "have been organized on so broad a basis that they included believers and non-believers. . . . if things went on as they had been going . . . , the time would come when it would be necessary to divide into two parties, the Ethical Culture one to go by themselves, those who believe in Christianity by themselves." Sunderland pledged that if reelected secretary for the coming year he would accept and recommend only liberal Christians for Unitarian ministries.[34] He did become the conference's secretary, but shortly thereafter *Unity*'s editorial board asked him to resign as a contributor. Attempting to counteract *Unity*'s influence, Sunderland then founded the monthly *Unitarian* in January 1886, "a magazine that should hold to our old freedom from dogmatic creeds and yet stand clearly for belief in God and worship the spirit of Christ."[35]

Shortly before the WUC conclave in Chicago in the spring of 1886, thousands of copies of Sunderland's pamphlet *The Issue in the West* went out to prominent Unitarian clergy and laity. This polemic against the ethical basis radicals also found its way into the hands of delegates as they arrived at the convention. It argued that the Unity men had purposefully attempted to convert Unitarianism into "Free and Ethical Religion." In resistance to the Sunderland offensive, Gannett proposed a compromise resolution: "That the Western Unitarian Conference condition its fellowship on no dogmatic tests but welcomes all who wish to join to help establish Truth, Righteousness, and Love in the World."[36] The radicals, voting in a bloc with a number of moderates who did not wish to see the WUC totally destroyed, carried the day. Gannett's motion passed.

The factional dispute did not end there, however, and Unitarian pulpits and periodicals remained "electric with the controversy" throughout 1886–87, that first year of the Charles H. Kerr & Company.[37] Implanted at the heart of the western controversy, the fledgling firm served the publishing needs of the Unity men. A torrent of publications appeared from various presses, and from its inception the Kerr venture played a central role. Commenting on the range of publications issued during the 1880s, the WUC's historian Charles Lyttle has observed that "there was never a period of Unitarian history of greater literary production in respect not only to quantity but to quality as well."[38] Kerr & Company and the two major Boston-based Unitarian publishers, George H. Ellis and James B. West, issued a broad array of sermons, poems, and hymns in book and pamphlet form. Kerr, under the auspices of the WUC radicals, issued a series of Unity Short Tracts and Unity Mission pamphlets in addition to study guides, outlines, and programs for the highly successful Unity Clubs. Every church had its literature table or lending library, and Kerr's handling of the Church Door Pulpit collection kept them all well supplied.[39]

In both quantity and quality the works of the ethical basis proponents surpassed those of their adversaries. The writings of the Unity men (and women), published initially by James Colegrove and taken up by Kerr, developed not so much to defend their position as to propagate what Sunderland derisively labeled "new religion."[40] In all of their writings, the group assayed those new insights that transformed the intellectual terrain of their age: evolution, social psychology, advanced biblical criticism, comparative religion, history, and political economy. Charles H. Kerr & Company struggled forward to help fill a growing demand for such works. Although the denominational fracas was not resolved entirely until the early 1890s, periodicals aligned with either side reviewed the literary works of their opponents. Such coverage guaranteed certain sales. In that sense the "Issue in the West" aided the infant Kerr business, but such a market alone could not ensure the company's viability. The publisher had to seek new titles and authors continually in one of the most highly competitive trades of the era. The task of running a publishing house during the 1880 and 1890s was not an easy one.

■

From the time of his firm's inception Kerr had to come to terms with a nagging dilemma. Wedded to the radical Unitarian movement with its specific religious, moral, and social outlook and limited following, the young firm nevertheless had to operate as a business in the highly competitive publishing trade. Kerr first had to succeed as a bookman in order to fulfill the goals and ambition of moral and social improvement explicit in the work of the Unity men. Constantly plagued by a lack of working capital and incessantly buffeted by shifts in the economy, mounting production costs, and changes internal to the structure of the publishing industry and challenged as well by the power of larger, better-financed houses, the young publisher had to find ways to make do, survive, and then expand. Ideals could not pay operating costs. Moral aspirations and hopes for social betterment would not assuage the ire of a petulant bill collector or hard-pressed printer when payments came due. Kerr constantly had to wage an uphill battle for survival in an environment where money talked and high ideals, no matter how lofty, regularly folded shop.

The post–Civil War publishing trade had its precedents earlier in the century. Certain Gilded Age trade practices originated in traditions established during the quieter antebellum age, when literature was identified more with gentility, scholarship, and instruction than with mass culture and entertainment. The early trade yielded small profit margins, and its leaders viewed themselves as professionals who had special dedication to literary production that overrode monetary sacrifices.[41] Leading houses were often inbred affairs, handed down from father to son and guided by certain codes of etiquette and courtesies.[42] Although successful, such older firms often eschewed what they perceived as the vulgar commercialism of other forms of business enterprise. They bemoaned the brash adventurism and violation of established norms by newcomers and upstarts who entered the field after the Civil War. As late as 1897 the editors of *Publisher's Weekly*, the major trade weekly, deplored the commercialization of the book world. "We fear it is becoming a trade," they cried futilely.[43]

The costs of entering the publishing business were relatively small in the 1880s.[44] Few publishers owned their own book manufacturing plants or print shops, in part because of the large financial outlay required for presses and typesetters and in part because of the practical difficulties inherent in gearing a publishing concern to a printing establishment. Printing and binding books had become a full-time occupation; as late as 1914, a mere 18 percent of publishing houses had their own plants, accounting for 31 percent of the books produced.[45] Publishing concerned itself with what occurred before a given manuscript reached the printer and what took place after a completed imprint returned from the bindery.

Despite, or perhaps because of, its relative ease of access, a large number of men and women who entered the field between 1871 and 1890 failed, and the business was riskier in Chicago than in the East.[46] Most titles lost money. In 1886, Kerr's first year in business, *Publisher's Weekly* lamented that "of five books . . . [published], three fail, one covers its cost, the fifth must pay a profit to cover the rest."[47] Because most published books represented a financial loss, publishers had to fund their entire operations from the success of a few titles. But even the most experienced bookmen could not predetermine a bestseller. The unpredictable and highly competitive nature of the trade forced struggling firms to find new methods in production and marketing to help ensure some modicum of profit and stability. Successive innovations in production and distribution in turn led to further instability and disruption of established practices.

One major operating expense lay in the cost of printing. Before the early 1890s, when type was still primarily set by hand, the cost of a number of small editions, each necessitating the labor of compositors and new printing plates, far exceeded that of a lesser number of larger printings. The truly profitable share of the business resulted not from the production of new books requiring the labor cost of compositors, proofreaders, pressmen, and binders, but from the continued sale of titles from existing plates. Financial stability and survival became tied to the small number of such long-term sellers on a given backlist.[48] Two methods existed for creating such a "live" list or catalog. The more difficult and time-consuming route entailed purchasing a number of quality manuscripts that could be turned into significant books, that is, works that would remain in demand over an extended period. The quicker but often more costly technique involved acquiring plates and inventories from a house that had fallen into financial difficulty. Kerr would use both methods.[49]

The marketing end of the business also had numerous drawbacks. A rapid expansion of the trade had begun in the late 1870s with the appearance of "cheap libraries," paperbound reprints of noncopyrighted titles, often by established European authors. These "pirated" editions, less expensive than original hardbound works, had a wide appeal and gave publishers a ready means of building their backlists without having to compete with the more established houses for manuscripts from notable authors. Pirating became the easiest way to get one's foot in the publishing door, and the upsurge of cheap imprint series created a flood of paperbound books in the 1880s. *Publisher's Weekly* noted an increase of 52 percent in the number of new books issued between 1880 and 1890.[50] Such growth in the number of available titles made sales by a single firm all the more difficult, and pirating continued unabated until the passage of an international copyright law in 1891. The reprinting of noncopyrighted titles, when combined with the uncontrolled discounting of retail prices and the introduction of new technologies and marketing techniques, characterized the latter part of the century as a period of unprecedented instability. The 1880s have been called the most flourishing and upsetting decade for low-priced paperbound publishing in U.S. history.[51]

Most Chicago firms distributed their works both by wholesale and retail methods. The majority of firms along Bookseller's Row were publishers as well as retail outlets, a long-time tradition of the trade. Kerr, for example, began as a clerk and agent in the retail shop of James Colegrove's operation. By the late 1880s, however, the volume of mail order and subscription sales far exceeded sales through retail outlets. At the start of that decade the Post Office Department ruled that regularly issued paperbound quartos having a price, date, and number on the cover could be sent through the mails at a periodical rate of 2 cents a pound rather than the usual 8 cent book rate.[52] The ruling substantially lowered a major expense of the trade and another barrier for enterprising newcomers such as Charles Kerr.

Subscription sales had their origin in the tradition of colporteurs, the traveling book salesmen of the antebellum era.[53] Based on a corps of independent agents, a virtual salesman army operating out of regional branch offices, distribution through subscription sales bypassed retail shops, which had additional overhead costs. By the 1890s subscription sales amounted to more than $12 million, and Chicago, with its access to the hinterlands, had become the national leader in this specific form of marketing. A number of the city's larger publishing firms maintained sizable sales staffs; by 1893 those houses specializing in the subscription market alone employed twenty thousand. Smaller firms, unable to employ large sales staffs, either enticed free-lance sales representatives with promises of commissions and discounts or explored other avenues in order to compete with the army of sales agents that the larger firms mobilized.[54]

Magazines played a crucial role in the operation of many publishing houses. A high percentage of the more notable nationally circulated week-lies and monthlies originated as subsidiaries of such firms.[55] The number of such periodicals increased 450 percent between 1865 and 1885. There were 4,400 weeklies and monthlies in circulation by 1890; two years lat-er the *Chicago Graphic*, a journal of opinion, observed that "the develop-ment of the magazine in the last quarter of a century in the U.S. . . . is paralleled by no literary movement in any country or in any time. Every field of human thought has been entered. . . . As the field has broadened new magazines have arisen to occupy the territory, and the magazine has become not only a school of literature but of science, art, and politics as well."[56]

Magazines were important outlets for advertising. Before 1885 most local retailers' advertisements were of a general nature and appeared in newspapers rather than magazines. The late 1870s and early 1880s wit-nessed a gradual increase of direct appeals to consumers by manufactur-ers and wholesalers of foodstuffs, ready-to-wear apparel, patent medicines, and such mass-market commodities as pianos, typewriters, bicycles, and popular books. Magazines, with their regional and national distribution, became a natural vehicle for such sales promotion. Publishing houses, which had given birth to new mass-market magazines, also used available page space to publicize recent releases and backlists. Editor-publishers often sold space as an additional source of income to help defray costs but reg-ularly used a considerable amount of copy to promote sales of their own inventories. As a courtesy of the trade, houses catering to a similar class of reader or audience often exchanged free advertising space to publicize available titles and new releases.

The majority of magazines circulated through the mails. The Post Office Act of 1874 set the rate of monthly and quarterly periodicals at 3 cents per pound "or a fraction thereof." In 1885, "an epochal year in magazine publishing," Congress reduced the rate to 1 cent per pound for all second-class mailings. The boom in the magazine trade that the cheaper rate helped stimulate subsided only briefly with the Panic of 1893, and publishers of all sorts scurried to enter the business.[57]

Every entry into the field did not a success story make. When a given magazine ran into financial difficulty, as so many did, it often merged with another more established venture. Such consolidations became quite com-mon toward the end of the century. Some of the resultant partnerships reflected a kinship or commonality of editorial outlook or similar social and political goals. But technical merger quite often signified the purchase of a floundering operation's subscription lists, as well as rights to any and all publications, periodical and otherwise, that the troubled firm had issued previously.

By 1883 Chicago had become the largest publishing center in the country outside of New York. Colegrove's neighbors on Publisher's Row included S. C. Griggs and Company at 87–89 Wabash Avenue, perhaps the city's leading firm in those years. Griggs had quit the general trade after the Chicago Fire to specialize in textbooks of scientific, historical, and philosophical interest. After it too moved from State Street, Jansen, McClurg and Company occupied the building at 117–119–121 Wabash on the corner of Madison Street. Described as the "central resort of the scholars and readers, the wealth and culture of the northwest," its newly constructed building was "generally admitted to be the largest best appointed, and most beautiful bookstore in America."[58] S. A. Maxwell and Company, at 134–136 Wabash, sold wallpaper as well as books and stationery. Representing the "largest wall-paper jobbing house in the world," the Maxwell firm's retail book department eventually came to rival Jansen, McClurg and absorbed the Colegrove concern. Across the street from Maxwell's, in the same block as Colegrove, were the shops and offices of a number of publishing ventures associated with various religious denominations, including the Presbyterian Publishing Board, the American Tract Society, and the Baptist Union.[59] D. Appleton and Company of New York occupied the entire second floor above the American Tract Society at 135 Wabash and used the space as the western headquarters of its national subscription business. Further down the street were the school supply houses of W. A. Olmsted and Ginn, Heath and Company. Root and Sons Music Company, a major publisher of music books and sheet music and a dealer in pianos and organs, occupied a location at the corner of Wabash and Adams Street.[60]

The rise of the city's book trade had been dynamic, in some ways astounding. Annual sales for Chicago's book business had been only a few hundred dollars in 1834; gross sales topped $9 million fifty years later.[61] The rapidly developing hinterland that the Chicago firms served was the largest book-consuming section of the country. Local book jobbers, in their attempt to meet increasing post–Civil War demands, carried inventories that often matched lists available in New York, and a number of eastern houses opened Chicago branches or contracted agents in an often desperate attempt to maintain market shares.[62]

Chicago had clearly become "the headquarters and center of western literature, book-making, and all the kindred arts" by the early 1880s.[63] By late 1887 the *Chicago Tribune* proudly proclaimed that "the growth of

Chicago as a literary center during the last seven years is unparalleled in history. In some respects the city is the greatest publishing point in the world, and in all others it rivals only second in this country to New York."[64] In 1887 the city issued more subscription books (those sold door-to-door by traveling agents) than Boston, New York, and Philadelphia combined.[65] By the end of the decade, Chicago's publishers produced some two hundred thousand atlases, between six and seven million hardbound books, and an estimated two million paperbacks annually.[66] According to the contemporary publishers' trade journal *Bookseller and Stationer,* between fifteen and twenty firms played some role in the manufacturing and publication of books "to a greater or lesser extent" in Chicago during the early 1880s. In addition to publishing houses, an unspecified number of freelance job printers and binders also produced books on special order for limited or private distribution. Chicago publishers listed more than nine hundred titles in 1881, the average sale of which was about a thousand copies. *Bookseller and Stationer* estimated that the city had sold and distributed a million volumes the preceding year.[67]

As a newcomer in the field, Charles Kerr soon learned to use all the practices that would presumably assure some semblance of solvency. *Unity* was key for the young firm. From the moment Kerr relieved James Colegrove as its publisher, the weekly's pages were the primary publicity agent for Charles H. Kerr & Company. The runs of *Unity* dating back through the late 1880s reveal a series of projects and promotional schemes that Kerr developed in a continual attempt to increase sales and reader support for both magazine and publishing house. Those first years proved difficult. Volunteer work by its editors sustained the magazine during its first eleven years, and its publishers, initially Colegrove and then Kerr, absorbed an annual deficit in the payment of printers' bills.[68] Barely solvent, *Unity* was the publishing venture's initial reason for being. In order to keep the periodical afloat, Kerr turned to other projects in an endless quest for increased receipts.

In addition to *Unity,* Kerr had also come into possession of another weekly publication, *The University,* a critical literary journal for liberal educators. At the end of February 1886, he consolidated the publications in an attempt to streamline the operation. Appearing temporarily under the title *Unity and The University,* the merged periodical used the combined mailing list of its two parents. Jenkin Jones was editor in chief, and Charles H. J. Douglas, chief editorial contributor of *The University* and the founder of its predecessor, *The Fortnightly Index,* brought his lengthy experience as a magazine editor and publisher to the venture.[69] With a hope "that our friends will be more than satisfied with the paper as it reaches them in the new and improved form," Kerr offered advertisers the benefits of combined circulation "without any increase in price."[70]

Not long after the consolidation of *Unity* and *The University*, Kerr purchased the subscription lists of *The Index*, the former organ of the Free Religious Association. He also purchased a number of plates for an extended list of pamphlet titles from the parent company, the Index Association.[71] In addition, he began to exchange advertisements with other, more established publishing houses such as Houghton, Mifflin, D. C. Heath of Boston, John B. Alden of New York, and S. A. Maxwell and S. C. Griggs of Chicago. As a fraternal courtesy (and a wise business practice), Kerr also traded advertising space with other Unitarian-related periodicals such as the *Unitarian Review* and the *Christian Register*. In addition, *Unity* carried notices for the *Political Science Quarterly*. Educational institutions such as the Chicago Athenaeum, the Chicago Female College, Knox College in Galesburg, Illinois, and the American Conservatory of Music in Chicago purchased promotional space. Despite limited advertising space, the weekly carried pitches for Columbia Bicycles, Hartley Reclining Chairs, a "cure for the Opium and Morphine Habit," and an omnipresent advertisement for Horsford's Acid Phosphate, a remedy for "dyspepsia, mental and physical exhaustion, weakened energy, nervousness, [and] indigestion."[72]

Kerr meanwhile began to explore other possibilities for increased revenues. Committed to the Unitarian cause, he took on numerous small projects for the Western Unitarian Conference. He published its annual convention proceedings and issued such items as the stationery for the Western Women's Unitarian Conference as well as various pamphlets, lesson sheets, and other materials for the Western Unitarian Sunday School Society.[73] In early July 1886, Kerr informed *Unity*'s readers that the company would furnish estimates on all kinds of printing, "from an octavo volume to a 'return envelope'." Acting as a middleman for some now-unknown job printer, he assured satisfactory work on church annuals, society proceedings, and programs for study classes. In search of new titles, he offered "special facilities to authors who are desirous of printing books or pamphlets privately or of putting them before the public" and invited distant readers to inquire about publishing rates. Promising to send proofs for the author's revision "when preferred," he guaranteed work "far superior to the best that can be obtained in country printing offices."[74]

The young firm became the Chicago agent for the London-based Robert Browning Society in October 1886.[75] The following spring, it became the midwestern distributor for a major eastern Unitarian publishing concern, Boston's George H. Ellis.[76] Kerr also began taking subscriptions for the Boston-based *Unitarian Review*.[77] The *Western Unitarian Yearbook* of 1887 notes that in addition to the Ellis concern Kerr made arrangements with Robert Brothers and the American Unitarian Association to carry their respective publications. He also began to stock the imprints of G. P. Putnam's Sons of New York.[78] The executive committee of the National Bureau of Unity Clubs, centered in New York, decided to employ Kerr's firm to handle its publishing and recommended that its local bodies throughout the country do likewise.[79]

In addition to the publications of other Unitarian-related concerns, Kerr began to issue books and pamphlets under his company's separate aegis. The first work published as a Charles H. Kerr & Company imprint was the fourteen-page poetry collection, *Beyond the Veil* by Alice William Brotherton. Published privately for the author, Kerr announced that proceeds from its sale would go to the building fund of Jenkin Lloyd Jones's All Souls Church.[80] A week or so later, Kerr released the first of several works by Chicago "Unityman" James Vila Blake. *Manual Training in Education,* Blake's initial pamphlet, discussed "the need of hand-training for all classes, the dignity of hand work, its influence on personal character, the relation of manual training to immigration and to the apprenticeship problem."[81]

Kerr spent most of that first year publishing the sermons and other writings of the Unity men. He issued two bound collections of poems and essays by Blake and a number of diverse pamphlets by W. C. Gannett and Jenkin Jones. In December 1886 the company released a collection of sermons "of practical spiritual uplift" compiled by Jones and Gannett. Published initially in two editions—the first with an "imitation parchment cover on fairly good paper" and the other in a red-cloth binding with gilt-edged pages— *The Faith That Makes Faithful* became the largest seller of Kerr & Company's early years. It had passed through seven successive printings by 1893, and by 1899 more than twenty-seven thousand copies had been sold.[82]

Kerr & Company also issued a broad range of instructional pamphlets for various Unitarian educational projects such as the Sunday School Society and Unity Club classes. Initial titles included *Robert Browning's Poetry: Outline Studies,* issued for the Chicago Browning Society (of which Kerr was an active member), *A Leaflet of Outline Studies in the Prose and Poetry of George Elliot* by Celia Parker Wooley, and a reissued collection of Theodore Parker's sermons edited by Rufus Leighton. Another early work that the company issued was Mary E. Burt's *Browning's Women.* Initially published independently by the author, the first Kerr imprint of Burt's work ("written for those who are too busy to devote sufficient time to the study of Browning's works to get at the poet's meaning") contained an introduction by Unitarian notable Edward Everett Hale.[83]

Part of a movement, able to appeal to a select audience but nevertheless hampered by a lack of capital, Kerr could turn to the movement's faithful to solicit advance sales on selected works to help cover initial printing costs. In early August 1886, for example, he announced the projected publication of *Heart's Own*, a collection of verse by Edwin R. Champlin. Although the work would not appear before the following October, Kerr asked those desiring copies to "give us notice AT ONCE, in order that the first cost of publication may be assured."[84]

Kerr that same summer took advantage of the cheaper second-class mailing rates for sets of numbered or "serialized" publications by initiating the Unity Club series, a run of approximately sixteen pamphlets of from sixteen to thirty-two pages in length. Published on a regular basis, the series included *Outline Studies in the History of Ireland* by his former teacher at Wisconsin, William F. Allen; a treatise on *The Importance of an Intellectual Life* by Jenkin Jones; and a critique of Henry George's *Progress and Poverty* by Giles B. Stebbins.[85] Kerr specifically issued the series for the Unity Club network and offered a 25 percent discount to any member group ordering five or more of a single title.

The various works of the Unity men and the countless number of pamphlets and short tracts aside, Kerr realized that he had to expand his list of titles if the company were to survive. He purchased the plates and publishing rights or remainders of potential sellers from other firms or directly from individual authors. He also issued several works of a more general interest, not directly related to the Unitarian cause. For instance, he reprinted two references works by the grammarian Samuel Fallows, *A Handbook of over Twelve Thousand Abbreviations and Contractions* and the *Complete Handbook of Nearly One Hundred Thousand Synonyms and Antonyms*, which originally appeared in 1883 under the auspices of the Standard Book Company of Chicago.[86] He acquired the rights to Stebbins's *The American Protectionist's Manual*, originally published for the author in Detroit by Thorndike Nourse in 1883. Subtitled *Protection to Home Industry Essential to National Independence to the Well-Being of the People; British Free Trade a Delusion and a Peril*, Kerr's first discernibly political title initially appeared in a "special cheap edition . . . in preparation for the use of the Republican Campaign Committee."[87] The publisher, however, soon began to promote the Stebbins tract as essential reading for advocates of free trade. One advertisement suggested that "FREE-TRADERS who are disposed to examine the tariff question from the standpoint of their opponents can find no more adequate and concise presentation of the protectionist theory." Another in the same issue, however, and on the page facing the first, hurled a pitch to the opposition: "PROTECTIONISTS who wish to diffuse a general understanding of their principles can find no better compendium."[88] A sale was a sale to the struggling young publisher, at that point apparently still lacking a political stance.

That first year in business, Kerr also reissued his original compilation *Unity Songs Resung* and two theological works published previously by other houses, Austin Bierbower's *The Morals of Christ* and *The Consolation of Science* by Jacob Straub. Toward the end of the year, he issued a short summary on the social conditions of women: *The Social Status of European and American Women* by Kate Byam Martin and Ellen Henrotin.[89]

At the beginning of January 1887 Jenkin Jones editorially noted the list of Kerr & Company publications that appeared in the weekly: "It is with a feeling of pride that we call the attention of our readers to the advertisement on our first page, which shows a year's work on the part of our publisher. It is the product of the careful industry and persistent energy of Charles H. Kerr, who a year ago assumed the responsibility, risk, and labor incident to the publication of *Unity*. He comes to his first annual reckoning in a manner that deserves our congratulations and thanks."[90] The accomplishments of that first year clearly were promising. The young publisher was off to an energetic start.

Unity Years

Charles H. Kerr & Company established itself as the major midwestern purveyor of Unitarian-related publications in the years between 1887 and 1893. The backlist expanded gradually as Kerr either released new titles or reissued works previously published by other houses. In an ongoing struggle to increase the circulation of the often-beleaguered *Unity*, he offered new subscribers discounts and other premiums on books and pamphlets.

The situation of the weekly, and the publishing house developing around it, slowly but surely improved. In the meantime, Kerr began to move in new directions, evidenced in the shifting emphasis of the company's lists. While continuing to publish the devotional theological writings of the Unity men, he also began to issue more and more materials dealing with the significance of evolutionary thought. He also distributed more of the "scientific theism" propounded by the advocates of Free Religion, that radical offshoot from Unitarianism. In addition, the views of the ethical culture movement began to nudge their way onto the company's lists. The passage of time also witnessed the increased presence of more secular writings concerned with the increasingly pressing social issues of the day.

The early Kerr Company, as the publisher of *Unity* and the various sermons, essays, and poetical works of the Unity men, catered to the reading tastes of a particular social and intellectual milieu. The continued catalog presence of a specific subject matter or genre chronicled the continuity of shared perspectives or predispositions on the part of Kerr's patrons. Occasional additions indicate alterations and shifts in the predilections, social interests, tastes, and demands of the middle-class liberal clientele that the company served. The company was not static, and beliefs, outlook, and social perspective of its founder were in transition.

A close examination of the company's lists indicates several subtle shifts in outlook on the part of the young publisher. In some ways, the gradual change in the direction of the firm's emphasis reflected a receptivity to new ideas. The change certainly mirrored the increased demand of the reading public, widespread during the latter part of the nineteenth century, for works based on the new revelations of scientific inquiry and the rise of the youthful social sciences. Like many other bookmen, Kerr had to face the constraints and demands of a highly competitive trade, but he never made decisions based solely on the vagaries and dictates of the marketplace. The works he issued reflected his own particular social and moral commitments and objectives.

Of all the religious denominations dotting the American intellectual terrain in the decades following the Civil War, Unitarianism stood out in its open receptivity to evolutionary doctrine. The liberal faith readily assimilated the views of the new science as a further affirmation of the orderly, progressive nature of a governed universe. Unitarians converted evolution into a friend and ally of "true religion."[1] Samuel Eliot noted that his "heralds of the liberal faith" were all optimistic believers in growth and progress; they maintained a confidence in a "humanity headed for brighter destinies and a more abundant life." "Tenacious nonconformists" and "essentially tomorrow-minded men," the ministers Eliot wrote about all held an open "hospitality" toward novel forms of rational thought: "Their sympathies and explorations extended beyond the boundaries of Christianity. They joined hearts and hands with all seekers after truth and right the world around."[2]

In the social and intellectual ferment that was Chicago in the 1870s and 1880s the lines of demarcation between the social attitudes and beliefs of the more radical Unitarians and those of avowedly agnostic free-thought activists or secular social reformers often became blurred and difficult to determine. A kind of "twilight zone" of belief and affiliation developed among the Unitarian radicals gathered around *Unity* and a broad array of Chicago agnostics and freethinkers.[3] In addition, individual membership in one organization or another often had more to do with shared social and intellectual outlook and personal ties than with some rigidly denominational or sectarian considerations. A great deal of associational cross-over occurred, and distinctions were often blurred. As one of their historians put it, the Chicago-based champions of the ethical basis were "spiritual democrats in the sense that they knew and respected, inside and outside of religious institutions, many thoughtful men and women of high character who were infidels and agnostics. Such folks they wanted to include in the Unitarian fellowship without the necessity of any compromise of mental and verbal honesty."[4] The list of titles Kerr published before his departure from Unitarianism in 1893 clearly illustrates that network of personal associations between the *Unity* group and a much broader milieu of advanced liberal thinkers, both within the Unitarian fold and outside it.

In 1887 Kerr released the first number of a series of short tracts under the title *Pamphlets on Living Questions.* The list of authors gathered for the effort reads like a who's who of dissent within and from liberal theology in the post–Civil War era. The majority of the *Living Questions* titles had origins as essays released by the Free Religious Association and its affiliated publishing venture, the Index Association of Toledo. The remainder of the series came directly from the pens of the Unity men and their immediate associates. Prominent in the collection of inexpensive tracts, however, were the works of a number of "schismatics," those who had left the denomination in a quest for a totally unfettered, nondoctrinal "higher truth" during those years when Charles Kerr was growing up in Madison. The series illustrates the continuity and ongoing relevancy of theological concerns central to Unitarian belief through the last half of the nineteenth century. It also represents the diversity of opinion and beliefs, acceptable by the late 1880s, that established Unitarianism held anathema a decade or so before. The collection included Theodore Parker's lecture "Transcendentalism," initially published by the FRA in 1876, and "an enlarged edition" of Thomas Wentworth Higginson's *The Sympathy of Religions* reprinted from the pages of *The Radical*, the literary vehicle for a previous generation of radical Unitarians.[5] Several works by Octavious Brooks Frothingham and Frances Ellingwood Abbot, the two most notable students of Theodore Parker and both central figures in the founding of the FRA, also appeared in the run.

A representative figure of the generation of Unitarian thinkers who spanned the antebellum years and the post–Civil War era, Frothingham's intellectual odyssey connected the generation of advanced liberals in the 1880s with their nonconforming predecessors, that earlier generation of Parkerite "transcendental Unitarians."[6] The Kerr Company initially carried Frothingham's writings as the Midwest agent for George H. Ellis, Boston's Unitarian publisher. In addition to his contribution to the *Pamphlets on Living Questions* project, the company also issued an 1887 imprint of Frothingham's *The Religion of Humanity*, originally published in 1872.[7]

Frances Abbot, a schismatic disenchanted with the doctrinal demands of the National Unitarian Conference, had played an instrumental role in the founding of the FRA.[8] He accepted a call to head an independent church at Toledo, where he founded *The Index* in January 1870 as a journal of "free religious inquiry" and "scientific theism." The initial success of *The Index* led several of Abbot's colleagues to form the Index Association as an incorporated publishing venture in April 1871. The association published *The Index*, with Abbot as its first editor, and also issued a number of tracts by a diverse group of radical Unitarians, free religionists, freethinkers, and agnostics. *The Index* moved to Boston in 1873. Burdened by financial difficulties, the weekly became the property and official organ of the FRA in July 1880. Abbot departed, and William J. Potter, then FRA secretary, became editor. He contributed the weekly editorial, but the main tasks of editing fell to his assistant editor, the well-known agnostic publicist B. F. Underwood.[9]

A future partner of Charles Kerr, Benjamin Franklin Underwood's name first appeared in association with the Charles H. Kerr & Company as a contributor to the *Pamphlets on Living Questions*.[10] Born in New York City in 1839, young Underwood had a meager formal education but nevertheless became widely read in philosophy, literature, and science. An early and zealous advocate of evolutionist theories, his thought was strongly influenced by the deism of Thomas Paine and the agnosticism of Herbert Spencer. He traveled throughout the country during the 1870s and 1880s as a lecturer on free thought and evolution. Sometimes speaking five or six times a week, he addressed audiences on such topics as "The Positive Side of Liberal Thought" and "What Free Thought Gives Us in the Place of Creeds." Described as "something of an orthodox materialist" who "possessed no little philosophic acumen," he developed the habit of challenging the clergy of the larger cities to meet him in public debate, but few dared to confront Underwood's noted forensic skills. He issued more than thirty of his lectures in pamphlet form under such titles as *The Theory of Evolution, The Genesis and Nature of a Religion,* and *Modern Scientific Materialism.*[11]

A member of the Free Religious Association after 1872, Underwood joined the staff of *The Index* in 1881. After the demise of that weekly in December 1886, he and his wife Sara, a noted agnostic propagandist in her own right, moved to Chicago, where they took up the coeditorship of the newly founded *Open Court*, a fortnightly "devoted to the works of establishing ethics and religion upon a scientific basis." Desiring to continue the work of *The Index* at their new location, the couple soon became embroiled with the *Open Court*'s owner, Paul Carus, over the new periodical's editorial direction. "Compelled by self-respect to sever all relations" with the journal, the Underwoods resigned from their editorial posts in November 1887. Remaining in the Chicago area, they worked on the *Illustrated Graphic News* through 1888. Their Chicago stay eventually brought them into direct contact with editor-publisher Charles Kerr.[12]

When *The Index* folded at the end of 1886, a number of the pamphlets and monographs previously published by the Index Association passed into the hands of Charles H. Kerr & Company.[13] Among them were those of Lewis G. Janes, founder of the Brooklyn Ethical Society. His "The Scientific and Metaphysical Methods in Philosophy" appeared as an addition to *Pamphlets on Living Questions.* Kerr also acquired the rights to Janes's historic treatise on the evolution of the Christian faith, *A Study of Primitive Christianity,* and advertised the work as one of the infant company's earliest titles.[14]

The Kerr Company at the beginning of March 1888 announced that it had become the western distributor, in conjunction with Boston's George Ellis, of the works of Minot J. Savage. Shortly thereafter, Kerr issued its imprint of Savage's autobiographical *Bluffton: A Story of Today.* He had previously included one of the Boston minister's addresses in a "sermonic symposia," *Show Us the Father.*[15] Widely recognized as the earliest American clergyman to attain notoriety through his unqualified defense of evolutionist thought, Savage had acquired a wide audience by the late 1880s, and Kerr actively promoted his arrival on the company lists.[16] Savage's most famous work, *The Religion of Evolution,* was the first systematic reconciliation of Darwinian thought and Christian theology in the United States.[17] That title and Savage's other most notable works, *The Evolution of Christianity* and *The Morals of Evolution,* made their way to the Kerr Company lists during the late 1880s. Savage became a member of the *Unity* editorial board during that same period.[18]

The writings of Solomon Schindler, a close Boston associate of Savage, also found their way to the Kerr lists with the 1888 republication of his series of sermons, *Messianic Expectations,* originally published in 1885. A noted liberal rabbi and head of Boston's Reform Temple Adath Israel, Schindler was strongly influenced by Edward Bellamy's *Looking Backward.* He joined Boston's first Nationalist Club in 1888 and subsequently became known as the "high priest of Nationalism." He translated Bellamy's utopia into German in 1890 and produced *Young West,* his sequel to *Looking Backward,* four years later. Another member of the FRA, Schindler readily substituted a confidence in scientific and technical progress for his former Judaic beliefs. He synthesized Spencer, Darwin, and views on technological progress to form a "religion of humanity." He critiqued unfettered lais-sez-faire individualism but also rejected the notion of class conflict and the use of force as a vehicle for social change. Like so many of his colleagues, Schindler considered rational education as the engine, the driving force, of positive social improvement.[19]

Such figures as Savage and Schindler exemplified the type of author who Kerr actively promoted as promising additions to his catalog at the close of the 1880s. Typical of that milieu of intellectual pacesetters who readily and actively embraced evolution and scientific revelation, such publicists spoke to and for a broad range of advanced liberals, whether "free religion-ist" or free-thinking agnostic, who considered themselves too confined by even the loose denominationalism of Unitarianism. Outside the fold, their thinking nevertheless sat comfortably well with the all-encompassing openness of Chicago's ethical basis *Unity* group. Kerr enthusiastically her-alded the arrival of Frothingham, Savage, and Janes to his fledgling com-pany's lists and actively promoted their writings in that decade of liberal conciliation between science and theology.[20]

The Unity men and their publisher also readily embraced the works of the ethical culture movement and its guiding spirit Felix Adler.[21] The Ger-man-educated son of a prominent reform rabbi, Adler had called in the spring of 1876 for the creation of a new movement "above the strife of contending sects and parties," a "common ground" open to "believer and unbeliever, . . . worshiper and infidel" based on the "practical religion" of "diversity in the creed, unanimity in the deed."[22] In addition to fostering personal righteousness or individual fulfillment, the Society for Ethical Culture also turned its energies toward active reform endeavor. Adler, pro-fessedly nontheistic or agnostic, used a commitment to social betterment as his moral or religious standard. He and his followers embarked on nu-merous reform ventures that soon won the society widespread notoriety.[23]

Following a series of Adler's lectures in Chicago in October 1882, a group of that city's liberal reformers formed a local branch of the society, which had seventy-two members by the following June. Among the list of charter members was Jenkin Lloyd Jones. Adler's New York disciple William McIntire Salter came to Chicago that same spring to head the new Society for Ethical Culture as "permanent lecturer."[24] He and Jones soon forged a close working relationship through their mutual activities at the "workingmen's school" at the Chicago Athenaeum and as participants in social issue forums at Jane Addams's Hull-House.[25] The pages of *Unity*, already open to the message of Adler and the ethical culture movement, soon found space for addresses by Salter despite his occasional outspoken critical aversion to Unitarianism.[26] He subsequently joined the weekly's editorial board, and Kerr & Company added a number of his writings to its publication lists.[27]

Modeled after the New York organization, the Society for Ethical Culture soon organized a home nursing program that sent trained nurses into working-class districts of the South and West Sides. Salter initiated a series of lectures on social ethics at the Chicago Opera House in 1885. The society also coordinated a series of monthly conferences on social issues at the Hull-House coffee shop beginning in the spring of 1886. Speakers at those gatherings included not only Salter, Jones, Adler, and other society members but also such figures as Clarence Darrow, John Dewey, and Jane Addams.[28]

Suspicious of labor radicalism, the ethical culture movement stressed education to uplift the working class and rejected change by force. The society's members were not revolutionaries in any sense. Often from wealthy backgrounds quite detached from the misery of those to whom they ministered, they were not about to sacrifice their comfort and privilege to share a slum-dweller's existence. Moral critics, they nevertheless struggled to alleviate those conditions considered unjust. Such concerns soon carried the key figures of the Chicago movement into the fight to save those convicted in the Haymarket Affair.

Salter was far more radical in his social criticisms than Adler.[29] A first-hand observer of the lives and working conditions of Chicago's laboring poor, in the spring of 1886 he readily endorsed the campaign for an eight-hour day. Then came the explosion of a bomb tossed into the police ranks at Haymarket Square. The bombing's aftermath brought anti-radical hysteria, repression, arrests, and trials, and liberal reformers who had previously joined the battle for improved conditions fell into hasty retreat from the generalized onslaught against labor. The police targeted eight outspoken anarchist labor militants and quickly hauled them to trial. Seven were found guilty of murder and sentenced to the gallows; the eighth received a fifteen-year sentence. Tainted by a frenetically vindictive atmosphere and hasty indictments, jury selection, and trial, the Haymarket case soon began to raise doubts and concerns among the city's liberal social activists.

Unconvinced of the guilt of the eight and concerned with the severity of their sentences, Salter, Jones, and Blake soon joined the battle to save the lives of the defendants. Although disclaiming any advocacy or adherence to anarchism either as a philosophy or vehicle for positive change, Jones editorialized for leniency for the condemned in the pages of *Unity* early in December 1886. Jones and Salter, along with Chicago's noted reform rabbi Emil Hirsch, were all opposed to the death penalty on moral grounds and petitioned Illinois governor James Oglesby for clemency. A meeting at the Third Unitarian to protest the death penalty and insist that the trial had been unjust and unfair "brought down violent opposition and condemnation upon the head of its pastor," James Vila Blake.[30]

Howard Radest has noted that "reasoned analysis did not impress many Chicagoans who concluded that any good word for the anarchists was treason."[31] In the forefront of the clemency fight for the Haymarket defendants, Salter and the Chicago Society soon became identified with anarchism.[32] The group lost a number of its influential moneyed supporters, and attendance at monthly meetings fell off.

The editors of *Unity*, meanwhile, conscious of the effects of guilt by association, did not set forth a position on the case until four months after the close of the trial. Jones's editorial comment began with a disclaimer compelled by still-simmering anti-radical hysteria: "With all law-loving believers in order, social progress and State authority, we abhor both the philosophy and the method of anarchy. . . . It is in direct opposition to all the lessons and methods of Evolution, and will bring confusion and disaster wherever applied." Opposed to capital punishment, Jones nevertheless stated that "those who deliberately plot for the destruction of life must themselves expect to pay the penalty of the law in the way most likely to prove a deterrent to others." Calling for "pity rather than hate" for the condemned, "poor enthusiasts of a vicious philosophy, products . . . of deep seated wrongs of Old World origins," Jones pleaded not for clemency from the hangman but for a more humane form of execution. He recognized that the state of Illinois was not about to strike down the death penalty but labeled the gallows "a ghastly reminiscence of a barbarism not yet outgrown. . . . If life must be taken by law, let the execution come according to the less revolting and more humane methods known to the physician or the electrician."[33]

Significantly, the same editorial, although equivocal, began with an open endorsement of an adjoining piece by H. Tambs Lyche, a minister from Haverhill, Massachusetts. "Socialists and Anarchists" took a bold stand on the Haymarket defendants. Written as an open letter "prompted by that brute and savage howl of revenge and hatred . . . against the condemned Anarchists and their brethren in spirit," Lyche's discussion opened with a condemnation of the "unjust, cruel, and utterly despicable" outcry for revenge and the attempts to make the anarchists "appear to the world as monsters and devils." Convinced that the eight had nothing to do with the actual bombing, Lyche argued for humane execution if they must die for their mistaken ideas: "Let them die if necessary for their mistake; but do not call them monsters, do not abuse them, do not try to blacken their characters. . . . Kill them—but do it not with savage glee or satisfaction, but with deep sorrow and pity."[34]

It was social conditions that carried men to an open advocacy of violence and "propaganda of the deed." Speaking to Chicago's liberal clergy, Lyche argued that "it is easy enough to preach patience, and peaceable means and gradual reforms when we sit in our armchairs surrounded by the comforts of civilized life . . . , but it looks very different, be sure, to him who from early morning till late at night lives in the whirl of misery, enslaving drudgery, even starvation." Amid plenty, the wealth and affluence of Chicago, people starved because they could find no work. "Perhaps most of us know little what it is to ask for work and find none, and to starve, or to see our own children grow blue and pale from hunger and cold; and under such circumstances to see silk dresses brush along the streets, and through the lighted windows catch a glimpse of tables bending under with superfluity. Let us share that kind of life for a while, and we shall better understand anarchism and bomb throwing."

Lyche also challenged other members of the clergy for their attitude toward the disinherited. "Yes, teach them patience," he cried, "but it will hardly do them much good, preached from flower-strown, [*sic*] flower scented pulpits to audiences comfortably sunk in soft cushions. . . . The Haymarket meeting marks quite a step in the progress of the world," he concluded. "We dare no longer be quite so blind as before to existing wrong and misery. The light from their bomb may be the signal of danger and need, which will call some of *our* men to the rescue out of their pulpits and churches into the saloons and streets to get acquainted with these men. . . . The death of these men will be a terrible emphasis to our duty, a terrible rebuke to our churches."

Kerr's thoughts on the Haymarket events are unknown. His company, however, plodded forward despite the illiberal frenzy that the affair stimulated. *Unity* had lost money throughout its first eleven years. Volunteer work on the part of its editors helped defray some operating expenses, but the paper's publishers, initially Colegrove and then Kerr, absorbed additional annual deficits. Plagued by *Unity's* drain of revenue from the book and pamphlet end of his struggling young firm, Kerr initiated several strategies in an ongoing quest for economic stability.

At the beginning of 1889, for example, he announced a "Clearance Sale of Books." Offering reduced prices on a large inventory, mainly material distributed for other houses, Kerr explained, "We have on hand about

$1,000 worth of books which we wish to convert into cash during January."[35] The new year's sale was "successful beyond expectations" and enabled Kerr to begin offering 30 percent discounts on the company's books and remainders from other firms. Hoping for increased sales volume, he also took to selling individual copies at a very low profit margin, which in some cases disappeared entirely with the addition of billing and bookkeeping costs.[36]

There were other avenues toward improved income as well. Numerous periodicals of the era succumbed to the lure of cheap advertising as one route. Kerr and the Unity men, however, refused to adulterate the quality and demeanor of *Unity* by opening its pages to unprincipled boosterism. "*Unity*," Kerr noted, "goes to a thinking class, and a reading class. . . . Our readers are therefore undesirable customers for those who advertise lottery schemes, quack medicines, and goods that obviously can not be furnished for the prices named, and in the interest of those misguided advertisers, we prefer to exclude such advertisements."[37]

Unity's format changed at the beginning of March 1889. The size of the page doubled, and the number of pages went from sixteen to eight, thereby lowering production costs. An accompanying reduction in the subscription price from $1.50 to $1, when combined with new book and pamphlet premiums, began to show results. The strategy secured 1,500 additional subscribers during March, April, and May, thereby doubling the periodical's circulation. The weekly was on its way to becoming self-sustaining, Kerr proclaimed, "For the first time it pays printer's bills without a deficit to be shouldered by someone."[38]

The improved situation still could not cover the costs of a salaried editorial assistant needed to relieve both Jenkin Jones, busy with the work of All Souls Church and the WUC, and Kerr, already overextended with the demands of an expanding book and pamphlet trade. Optimistic, however, Kerr called upon readers to help increase the number of subscribers in order to hire an assistant editor. In response, an additional 1,500 joined *Unity*'s mailing list early in 1890, raising circulation to approximately 4,500. The average weekly run exceeded eight thousand by mid-October, and a printing of ten thousand had become common by the following March.[39] The increase in subscribers finally engendered enough income to allow the editorial board to hire Celia Parker Wooley, a Unitarian activist, as assistant editor.[40] Kerr could turn his energies toward the improvement and expansion of his book trade.

The book-related end of the company began to expand to the extent that Kerr had to hold periodic clearance sales of materials issued by other houses previously kept in stock in order to make room for his own inventory.[41] On March 12, 1891, he announced the publication of the first of a group of new novels under the title "Unity Library." The company had released six works in the series by the following September, when Kerr explained part of the motivation behind the collection: "I found that in order to compete at all with other publishers in reaching the smaller book stores and news stands throughout the country, it would be necessary to comply with the United States postal laws governing the issue of periodicals, and issue one book a month, under some common name for the series, thereby securing the privilege of mailing at a cent a pound instead of eight cents a pound."[42] By defining a series of books as a "periodical" with a regular publication date, Kerr found it possible to lower his postal costs. Like so many of his competitors, he had realized the advantage of the cheaper periodical bulk mailing rates and greatly reduced an additional operating expense.

By mid-May 1891 the company could proudly display a catalog of thirty-six separate book titles. That spring's list also included a large number of short tracts and pamphlets, such as the run of eighteen titles called *Helps of Self Culture* published for the National Bureau of Unity Clubs and twenty Sunday school lessons for the Western Unitarian Sunday School Society.[43] As the end of his ninth year with *Unity* approached, Kerr reflected on the weekly's direction. "It has been in a certain sense uphill work all the time," he exclaimed. "There has never been a month that the paper had two hundred dollars of reserve capital to draw on. And yet it has kept growing." When he began at *Unity*, annual circulation was just over 38,000; by 1891 that number had reached 420,000. Part of the increase reflected the changeover from a semimonthly to a weekly, but the regular minimum issue had increased from 1,600 semimonthly in 1883 to 8,000 a week in 1891. "All this," he pointed out, "has been accomplished by slow, painstaking work, . . . it has all been done by slow degrees."[44]

Kerr informed readers of his regular "Publisher's Notes" column of another new development at the beginning of October 1891: "The growth of my book publishing business," he explained, "has obliged me, for lack of room, to give up carrying a stock of outside books for sale." Eager to close out the remaining inventory of those titles in order to free up office space, he once again initiated a clearance sale.[45] Kerr was about to set off in an entirely new direction. A new era in the business life of the struggling firm and the activist career of its young publisher, still in his early thirties, was about to unfold.

Unforeseen costs had continued to hound the company despite its growth and expansion. Volunteer work, so valuable to the early *Unity*, virtually ceased with the hiring of Celia Parker Wooley. In the meantime, increased circulation brought additional expenses. Unprecedented numbers of magazines appeared during the early 1890s, and the need to publicize *Unity* intensified. Kerr, for the first time, had to pay for advertising space. *Unity*'s expansion also furthered the reliance on premium offers, the key to attracting new subscribers. In response, Kerr sounded an ominous warning in mid-February 1892: "If I am to continue as publisher of *Unity* this state of things will have to be improved in some way. . . . The only way the printers of *Unity* have been paid for two years past is from the profits on my book publishing business."[46] He went on to suggest that an additional two thousand subscribers would solve the dilemma. The additional readership did not materialize, and Kerr found himself having to chide those subscribers in arrears on their payments: "*Unity*, like most papers, has three classes of readers, first those who always pay their subscriptions in advance; second, those who pay when a bill is rendered and apologize for not remitting sooner; and third, those who receive the paper for several months or years after the time has expired, and then on receipt of a bill, write indignantly to say that their name should have been removed from the list long ago."[47]

Revenues nevertheless continued to lag behind expenses, and *Unity* continued to drain capital from the book venture. Then Celia Parker Wooley resigned in late 1892. Unable and unwilling to resume his previous role as office manager for the weekly, Kerr initiated yet another fund-raising drive at the beginning of December. Significantly, the pitch marked a new course for the company. Kerr began offering "Co-operative Publishing Bonds" entitling investors to a 6 percent annual return and the privilege of purchasing publications at wholesale prices.[48] Modeled after a similar experiment in sales promotion inaugurated by the New York publisher John B. Alden, Kerr & Company's initial bonding venture had three stated goals: "We have opened a series of co-operative publishing bonds, our object being to extend our book trade to points not reached by local booksellers now handling our books, to increase our list of publications, and to avail ourselves of the liberal discounts to be obtained in the book business by payments of cash in advance."[49]

Those who purchased a $10 bond for a year were given a return either "payable in cash" at year's end or in books "at any time after the issue of the bond." Investors were entitled to wholesale prices: a 40 percent discount on Kerr's paperbound imprints, a reduction of one-third off on cloth editions, and 30 percent off on books from other houses still distributed by the company. They could also purchase books on credit, provided that "the amount charged in any one month not . . . exceed the face of the bond." Optimistic that the strategy would meet with success, Kerr anticipated that the new inducements "ought to bring us a thousand bondholders within a year, and such a number would enable us to improve *Unity* as well as to enlarge our list of publications and facilities for supplying books."[50]

Expectations for the success of this initial bonding venture soon dimmed, however. Several weeks after the beginning of 1893, Kerr notified readers of plans for an additional inventory sale. Although he did not say so, he had begun cleaning house in preparation for a move to a new office. A break with the Unity men, months in coming, had finally moved to the fore.[51]

From Unitarian to Populist and Beyond

Jenkin Lloyd Jones informed the readers of *Unity*'s editorial column at the beginning of March 1893 that Charles Kerr had decided to go it alone as an independent publisher after more than a decade of service to the cause of the Unity men. He recounted how "over ten years ago *Unity* found a willing pair of hands, a warm heart and a clear head in Charles H. Kerr," and, three years later, "*Unity*'s 'boy' had become a 'man', and . . . assumed entire business charge of *Unity*, carrying all risks, paying all bills, and running his own chances." Kerr fulfilled his obligations for seven years "in cheerful good faith." He had never made, and had often lost, money on the weekly, but in the process he had gained a practical experience and built the publishing venture "that has quietly grown until now it has reached the magnitude which is the chance, perhaps of his lifetime." On behalf of the *Unity* editorial board, Jones extended Kerr a cordial adieu and a blessing for a successful future.[1]

Kerr, in turn, notified readers of a series of important developments for his publishing house that were centered around a projected move to new offices. He had purchased the printing office of Charles H. Sergel and Company, a fifth-floor suite at 346–350 Dearborn Street, and leased half the space. The commodious new quarters, he hoped, would allow the company to merge the publishing end of the business with a printing operation previously located at 175 Monroe Street. He explained that his new office would "contain two Thorne typesetting machines, and over a ton of long primer book type which will enable us if necessary to set up a new book of 400 pages in a week or less." As planned, the new space would have the capability to handle all sorts of job printing orders, "from an octavo volume to a postal card." He invited the public to visit the new office "as soon as we have had time to make the necessary improvements in the building into which we are moving."[2]

Despite Jones's publicly espoused hopes for "continued good will," all was not well between Kerr and the Unity men. Beneath the surface of Kerr's seemingly amicable departure lay a host of tensions built up over an extended period. The separation, like a difficult divorce settlement at the end of a long-ailing marriage, engendered hard feelings and a dispute over common property. When Kerr finally decided to strike out on his own, Jones considered suspending *Unity*. The editorial board, however, decided against allowing it to die and formed a new venture, the Unity Publishing Company, to carry on Kerr's previous tasks. Kerr, in turn, agreed to continue on temporarily as printing agent for the beleaguered periodical. In the meantime, his new operation at the former Sergel office unexpectedly came to an abrupt halt after a few short weeks, and the company relocated once again to smaller quarters at 175 Monroe.[3] Unforeseen and unanticipated, the cost of the second move further exacerbated relations between Kerr and the *Unity* group as Kerr pursued a futile attempt to be compensated for contested material, including the rights and plates for various publications, from Jones and his associates. Relations soured further.[4]

Kerr reached a point during the fall of 1892 when he could no longer tolerate the losses incurred by his perpetual support of *Unity*. The weekly was impeding the growth of his publishing venture, and he had to choose between whether his company would continue to be the main source of support for the weekly or whether he would set off in a new direction. The route he selected, dictated in part by the demands of the publishing trade, came when it did because Kerr himself had changed. His outlook on the world had shifted, and a path beyond Unitarianism beckoned.

Recalling that period of transition a number of years later, Kerr recounted, "In 1891, I came into contact with the populist movement, then at the stage of its most rapid growth. I had previously read [Edward Bellamy's] 'Looking Backward' and had been charmed by it. . . . Populism seemed to me the way toward the realization of Bellamy's beautiful dream, and I went into it with ardor."[5] Jones alluded to the changes in Kerr's outlook in a letter to him during the summer of 1892, "I believe . . . [the past ten years] have differentiated your lines of conviction, aspiration, and capabilities, perhaps, from the lines upon which *Unity* was first projected, upon which we have tried to keep it and upon which it must continue to go if it goes at all."[6]

Those differing "lines of conviction" and "aspiration," although difficult to ascertain, become discernible through a close examination of Kerr & Company's list of publications during his last years with *Unity*. The catalog reflected decisions that Kerr made as a socially and morally committed publisher in the highly politicized and socially charged environment of the early 1890s. His selections did not always sit well with the Unity men. The Unity Library series, for example, contained not only the works of Jones and James Vila Blake but also several books that some *Unity* readers found objectionable. The initial title in the collection, a romantic future projection called *The Auroraphone* by Cyrus Cole, met with severe criticism from those who deemed it an intrusion in the series and not in keeping with *Unity*'s character. In response to such objections, Kerr explained that the name for the series had not been contrived to induce the purchase of material not endorsed by the *Unity* board. He apologized to those who thought otherwise.[7]

Shortly after the release of the Cole novel, Kerr issued the first of a subsequent number of populist manifestos, *The Coming Climax* by Lester C. Hubbard. An acquaintance of Kerr, Hubbard edited several populist reform periodicals in Chicago. His book described the "discouraging apathy of the mass of the middle class" and the existence of a "terrible and a growing hatred between the workers and the plutocrats" in a language filled with contempt for the upper classes.[8] Kerr publicized the Hubbard polemic as "the text-book for the Reform Campaign of 1892." Desirous of "an agent in every city and town, and in every Farmer's Alliance," he offered free sample copies to activist salesmen, promising that "the book will sell itself: it is what the people want to read." Kerr's stake in the volume's success went well beyond the pecuniary: "I have more than an ordinary financial interest in the publication of this book. It seems to me to embody ideas that are of vital importance to the welfare of the masses of the people in this country, and if what little influence I have can be used in bringing it to the speedy attention of those who are able to give powerful help to the reforms outlined, I shall be deeply gratified."[9]

Kerr wrote the book's preface. Asking, "Is not the time ripe for a word that shall open the people's eyes?" he charged that "the disloyalty of our governing class to democracy is becoming commonplace."[10] Men of peace committed to the resolution of conflict and the "unity of all," Jones and his colleagues had to disassociate themselves from such appeals. Kerr in turn proudly reprinted the favorable endorsements of *The Coming Climax* forwarded by the populist publicist Ignatius Donnelly and R. M. Humphrey, head of the Colored Farmers' National Alliance and Co-Operative Union.[11] He also carefully distanced himself from the *Unity* editorial board in his enthusiastic endorsement and promotion of Hubbard's work: "In what I say of this book, I speak for myself alone and not for the editors of this paper."[12]

Unity editorial board member Henry Martyn Simmons reviewed the Hubbard book shortly after its release.[13] Although reviews normally appeared in "The Study Table," the book review section toward the rear of the weekly, Simmons's critique ran as a front-page lead editorial. The *Unity* board apparently thought that the work necessitated an emphatic disclaimer. In lengthy editorial fashion, Simmons provided a synopsis of Hubbard's portrayal of class antagonism and the book's apocalyptic vision. He criticized Hubbard's use of harsh, unsympathetic references to the "plutocracy" and called for "wise laws" to "remove old wrongs." In place of the animosity between "producer" and "capitalist," Simmons advocated "public sentiment," which would "exalt justice and honor, and make men ashamed to live in luxury at the expense of others and ashamed to envy those who do." As a form of subtle rebuke to Hubbard, Simmons called for teachings "which shall appeal, not to the passions of any class, but to the minds and souls of all . . . [to] civilize, humanize, and soften the hearts of the capitalists and laborers alike." Significantly, *The Coming Climax*, although somewhat severe in its indictment of the "plutocrats" as the cause of the social unrest and political turmoil facing the nation, did not openly advocate further class antagonism but rather called for "an awakening" of political participation by the "Great American Middle Class" to remedy and reform existing abuses. In message if not always in tone, the book was not particularly radical. The *Unity* board's negative reception seemed to reflect its concern with Kerr's unabashed promotion and endorsement of the volume.

Other hints of a growing political and social estrangement between Kerr and his Unitarian mentors appeared in the period just before the separation. A short time before the formal split, Kerr released an anarchist tract titled *Why Government at All?* by William H. Van Ornum. In his initial announcement of the work, he informed readers that Van Ornum was an avowed anarchist but that the book warranted a careful reading as a "thought-provoking discussion." He abstained from commenting on the new release at length but promised an extensive review from the *Unity* staff.[14] Customarily, Kerr's publications received favorable notice and endorsement in *Unity*'s review section. *Why Government at All?* was a different matter, however, in an era still reverberating from the effects of the Haymarket Affair. The work received an icy reception and no recommendation in "The Study Table."[15]

Charles Kerr formally parted company with the Unitarian cause a month after that review. He came away with ten years' training and experience as a publisher, which set the foundations for the remainder of his life's endeavor. Significantly, he also came away with a score of beliefs and attitudes about progress and the potentials for constructive social change. He also believed in a perfectabilitarian possibility, the commitment to that earth-bound improvement through education and uplift that was so central to Unitarianism. He never lost the "rational faith," an informed optimism that foresaw a better world. In search of perfection on earth, he set off on a path that would ultimately carry him to Marxian socialism.

Kerr's personal life also changed markedly during the early 1890s. All Souls Church had provided him with a social mooring for more than a decade, and the dissolution of his business relationship with *Unity* also divorced him from a social circle that had been the center of his life. He also faced the pain of deep personal loss, the trauma that accompanied the deaths of people close and dear to him. Difficult to assess, such loss and the successive recuperation and reaffirmation were important in shaping the contours of his developing radicalism.

He had married his Wisconsin sweetheart, Helen Adams, in May 1889, following a lengthy courtship. The newlyweds initially moved in with the bride's parents at their Indiana Avenue residence, but soon found their own apartment on Bowen Avenue.[16] All was not well, however. A victim of a lengthy bout with bronchial consumption that left her a semi-invalid, Helen Kerr's health deteriorated seriously during the early spring of 1891, and she died of influenza that April, two years after her marriage.[17] Her death followed that of Kerr's mother, Katharine, by a year.

Ironically, the burial of the two most intimate figures in Kerr's life facilitated the transition toward his life's direction as a radical activist. With those closest to him gone and old personal, social, and institutional ties abruptly severed, he reached out for new connectedness and belonging. He found it in politics and a whole milieu of social-activist acquaintances. He also found companionship, reaffirmation, and political camaraderie in the person of May Walden, whom he would soon marry.

Of humbler social origins than her future husband, Lillie May Walden was born on September 3, 1865, in Metamora, Illinois, the daughter of Theron and Elizabeth Gribling Walden. Her father had been wounded at the Battle of Shiloh, leaving him partially paralyzed in his left arm. No longer able to farm, he became the proprietor of a small general store in Metamora. Plagued by recurrent hardship and misfortune complicated by his physical disability, he took to drink. Sixteen-year-old May Walden, driven by the desire to save her father, joined the Illinois ranks of the Woman's Christian Temperance Union, perhaps the single most significant preparatory school for a generation of women activists during that era.[18]

The Walden family moved to Highlands, North Carolina, Elizabeth Gribling's ancestral home, in 1885. Theron Walden's only source of income following the move became his meager Civil War pension. Concerned that she not remain or become a further burden for her hard-pressed parents and eager to strike out on her own, May Walden returned to Illinois. She stayed with her former music teacher until she got her bearings and then acquired a job at the public library at Peoria. She moved to Chicago shortly thereafter and went to work in the U.S. Pension Office, where she had initially ventured in search of assistance for her beleaguered father. She became close friends with Nellie Marshall, a member of All Souls Church, who in turn introduced her to Charles Kerr sometime late in 1890 or early 1891. As May Walden Kerr later recounted, the two young women had stopped by the Kerr Company office to look over some Unitarian materials. She recollected that first meeting with Kerr, "Nellie Marshall introduced me to him in his publishing office. . . . He looked tired and shabby and about forty years old. But Nellie said he was about thirty and highly educated. . . . I was searching for Unitarian literature, having contacted a group of the faith in Highland. . . . I selected a few leaflets or pamphlets and found I could get a reduction by taking several. This pleased Charles H. and he soon found out where I lived and called."[19]

Kerr, still rebounding from the loss of Helen Adams, actively pursued his new acquaintance with May Walden, and the two began to share each other's company. Both on meager budgets, they regularly strolled the grounds of the Columbian Exposition then nearing completion on the city's South Side. They went for an occasional boat outing on Lake Michigan and spent evenings at May's rooming house on Rhodes Avenue. Kerr proposed early in the fall of 1891, but May Walden, feeling that she did not know her new suitor well enough, initially rejected the offer. Undaunted, Kerr sent her a collection of poems by James Vila Blake with one page especially marked. The particular passage asked forgiveness for requesting "a love—a true heart's Love." His apology accepted, the penitent persisted. The two became engaged in October 1891 and married in a simple ceremony in Jenkin Jones's office at All Souls on April 2, 1892. May Walden Kerr by that time was already carrying their first child, Althea.[20]

The couple rented a modest flat on Walnut Street near Kedzie Avenue, not far from the Chicago Northwestern rail line so Kerr could easily commute to his downtown office. Years later May Walden Kerr recollected those early days with her new husband: "Charles was always harassed for money, but always willing I should have a little on hand, $2.50 or so, hardly as much as $5.00 at any one time. I hardly know how we got through that first year. . . . With almost no help I managed to let every possible penny go into the publishing business." An avid diarist, she noted that her husband never kept a diary himself. "His life," she suggested, "was dated pretty much by the books he published . . . his first venture with a monthly magazine began with a little thing we called *New Occasions.*"[21] Eager to assist her husband, May Walden Kerr continued on at her job at the Pension Office. She scrimped and saved enough to buy some furnishings for their home, occasionally sending small sums to her parents in North Carolina, and donated her spare moments as a Sunday school teacher at All Souls. Althea arrived in November 1892.[22]

Initiated in June 1893, just three months after his formal departure from *Unity*, *New Occasions* initially combined Kerr's skill as a publisher with the editorial expertise of B. F. Underwood. When contrasted with *Unity*, the new journal marked a clear political departure for the now-independent publisher. Designed to provide a popular platform for the discussion of political and social questions, a "magazine of social and industrial progress," *New Occasions* beckoned to a broad array of reform activists.

The first number set forward a statement of purpose, over the name of "Charles H. Kerr & Company," that would chart its course: *"New Occasions* is published in the interests of the people . . . the great majority . . . who work for a living and receive but small pay for the work that they do."[23] A "comparatively small minority" increasingly accumulated wealth, and the generalized social malaise sweeping the country had a cause: "There is no equitable distribution of the products of labor. Too large a share of industry's profit goes to capital; too little to those whose labor makes capital possible, and capital continually uses its superior advantage to encroach upon the rights and liberties of the mass of workers." Wealth, "the stored-up product of labor, . . should not be the cause of oppression or hardship to the millions whose labor capital employs." Guided by that firm belief in the power of rational argument and the value of discussion and debate that remained a constant throughout his publishing career, Kerr extended his hand: *"New Occasions* will afford what is needed at this time,—a tribunal for the discussion of questions of practical interest to the people."

The salutatory also cautioned readers that *New Occasions* was an independent journal of opinion on "questions of social and industrial reform." It would "not be for sale to any political party," nor "toady to any class or clique." Kerr tempered his declaration in a manner so typical of many late-nineteenth-century middle-class reformers: "While . . . fair and just to every honest claim of capital," *New Occasions* would "oppose class interests and aim to unite the people in defense of their rights . . . in opposition to the infamous combinations and iniquitous legislation which in this country imperil popular government."[24]

The opening issue contained a piece on penal reform by Kerr's earlier associate Lewis G. Janes and "Labor Unions and Wages" by the publisher's anarchist acquaintance W. H. Van Ornum. Underwood's editorial column, "Occasions and Duties," explored two topics. The first, an essay titled "Government" assayed the need for positive state intervention against "the evils which wealth, enormously aided by franchises and special legislation, has originated." The second essay, "Labor and Capital," chastised the advocates of violence, "wrongly called anarchism," and criticized the "unfair advantages of capital protected by legislated privilege."[25]

One of numerous reform-minded periodicals, often short-lived, which proliferated during the 1890s, *New Occasions'* pages soon attracted a host of reform theorists with various paper palliatives for the wide array of economic and political maladies convulsing the existing order. The issue of July 1893 carried "Socialism" by the Danish-born socialist writer Lawrence Gronlund, author of the highly successful *Cooperative Commonwealth* (1884). Subsequent issues that first year featured contributions by educational reformer Victor Yarros and the noted feminist Lucinda B. Chandler and a reprinted essay by Herbert Spencer. A broad spectrum of reformers in search for an all-inclusive monetarist corrective for widespread financial unrest soon filled the journal with an unending stream of banking and currency schemes. The Kerr Company's publication and active promotion of Thomas Edie Hill's *Money Found*, a proposal for the nationalization of the banking system, stimulated a series of exchanges that continued well into 1894.

A well-known Chicago publisher in his own right who had turned his entrepreneurial energies toward land speculation and suburban development, Hill developed a close working relationship with Charles Kerr during the early 1890s. He had acquired a modest fortune from the success of the Hill Standard Book Company, which he founded in 1868. He had also established a purchasing agency during the 1860s that attracted investment capital to varied real estate projects on Chicago's outskirts. The founder of Aurora, Illinois, and editor of the Aurora *Herald*, he became that town's first mayor in 1866.

Hill purchased 160 acres in the village of Prospect Park, west of the Loop, in 1885. Renaming the town Glen Ellyn in honor of his wife, Ellen, he drained the swamp on the property and dammed a small stream to form what eventually became Lake Glen Ellyn. In 1890 he organized a land syndicate that placed six hundred acres of the township up for sale to prospective homeowners. He set an additional 160 aside for a park and renamed the tiny brook running through it Apollo Springs. He soon actively promoted the town as "the recreation mecca of the midwest," where urbanites from Chicago and points east "for 11 cents . . . could take any of 30 trains to Glen Ellyn and enjoy the purest water amidst 116 acres of rolling park and lake beauty." Hill bankrolled the construction of the Hotel Glen Ellyn at water's edge as the center of this new suburban spa. He provided a pleasure boat for outings in the summer, and in winter he had ice cut and stored for summer sale and sponsored elaborate skating events.[26]

Riding the crest of his publishing and speculative successes, Hill had an elaborate mansion built surrounded by extensive outbuildings, orchards, and vineyards. There the couple, "instigators of much of the grace and glamour of earlier Glen Ellyn," entertained prospective real estate clients and local notables.[27] Misfortune soon befell Hill and Glen Ellyn, however. A fire in November 1891 leveled a portion of the town before the volunteer fire company arrived from nearby Wheaton, a number of Hill's business ventures soured during the same period, and his newly founded suburban empire fell into decline. Hurt financially, he sold off parcels of his subdivided estate.

In early 1893 Hill interested Charles and May Walden Kerr in the purchase of a small house on one of those parceled tracts. That April the couple and their daughter moved into their modest wood-frame structure at 556 Hillside Avenue, a few blocks from the Northwestern station. A second daughter, Katharine, joined the family at the beginning of August 1894. Their new home soon became a gathering place for radicals and reform-minded liberals as the couple began to host a number of informal parlor forums that brought together such notables as Clarence Darrow, Chicago's reform Rabbi Stephen Wise, socialist J. Stitt Wilson, and the reformer Robert Howe. But all was not well. Commuting daily from Glen Ellyn to tend to affairs at the publishing house, Kerr suddenly found himself struggling to survive in a business environment convulsed by the deepening depression of the 1890s.[28]

Beginning in February 1893 with the failure of a number of important railroads, the nation's severest economic crisis before the Great Depression of the 1930s reached panic proportions following the collapse of the National Cordage Company in early May. The panic led to the failure of hundreds of banks and thousands of businesses. One-tenth of the nation's railroad mileage passed into receivership, and thousands of factories cut back or curtailed production. The downturn demoralized wages and left some three million unemployed. The market for agricultural commodities was devastated. The price for a bushel of wheat, for example, fell from a peak of $1.05 in 1870 to 49 cents in 1894. The general price index fell to a level equalling that of 1860.

Chicago's regional economy, however, stimulated and bolstered by the success of the Columbian Exposition, did not initially experience the severity of the financial panic that wracked eastern banking establishments during the spring of 1893. But a deep economic and social crisis overtook the city with the closing of the exposition in the fall. Thousands of workers had flocked to Chicago in hopes of finding work at the event. With the closing of the fair grounds in October, those fortunate enough to find some employ at the numerous pavilions and concessions along the lake front joined the flood of humanity already dispossessed by foundry, mill, and retail closings. Mayor Carter Harrison's office soon estimated the number of unemployed in the city at two hundred thousand. By 1894 the city of some 1.8 million inhabitants faced a potentially explosive social crisis brought on by the desperation of the hard-pressed and the continued intransigence of its ruling elite.[29]

It was the best and the worst of times for the book firms along Publisher's Row. Technological and marketing innovations in the years just before the downturn had changed the structure of the industry and accelerated as the depression deepened. Some firms closed their doors, never to reopen, whereas others found new possibilities and potentials for growth.

As the last decade of the century dawned, Chicago was the unchallenged center of the western book trade. Printing and publishing had become the city's fourth-largest industry by 1890, and promoters, buoyant in their confidence, could boast in the *Chicago Tribune* that publishing output would soon surpass that in New York. The city would soon become "the Leipsic of the United States." Between 1885 and 1892 several factors helped lower publishing costs: the linotype and offset processes were developed, as were the half-tone and other less expensive photographic techniques, and the cost of paper dropped as more and more was made with wood products rather than cloth. Lower operating expense allowed thousands of aspiring publishers and speculators to invest in new periodicals and book ventures. The printing business, structurally separate from publishing, also received a "great impetous" from the opening of the Columbian Exposition as "an ocean of literature of all kinds relating to the Exposition was published."[30]

The depression of the 1890s spelled the failure of innumerable periodicals nationally and took a serious toll in Chicago. The dark clouds of depression contained a silver lining for some, however. The hard times led to a further lowering of magazine prices as the cost of materials and labor declined. Paper and printing costs fell to unprecedented levels with the arrival of the generalized business downswing. The drop in operating costs created new opportunity for those able to mobilize the necessary capital. The ongoing economic malaise of the mid-1890s and its related social and political crises also reshaped demands of the reading public. Reading tastes shifted. Fiction remained in high demand throughout the latter part of the nineteenth century, followed in popularity by religious works, children's stories, and legal publications in the years preceding 1893. But continued unrest greatly increased the demand for books on social questions, government, and history. With a new emphasis on economic and social problems and current events, American magazines "came to represent as never before complex currents of thought and feeling."[31] As the general crisis deepened and positions on the various pressing questions of the day came to the fore, every interest—the numerous ideological, philosophical and educational tendencies, the sciences, the professions, labor, and capital—developed a journal or journals.

The magazine business remained highly competitive despite the depression. At mid-decade *The Nation* reported that magazines "were being born in numbers that would make Malthus stare and gasp."[32] Established periodical publishers and newcomers alike had to face a serious dilemma, however. Advanced mechanical means of production often called for increased capitalization and regular short-term reinvestment, whereas price per issue had to remain competitively low. Increased circulation became key, not because of the immediate revenue from subscriptions or newsstand sales but because large circulations attracted advertisers. Advertising, the major source of magazine income, created new problems for those publishers anxious to get by or eager to expand as more and more capital went into promotion. Dependence on advertisers also created special difficulties for publishers that had political or social commitments and refused to submit to either shoddy and unethical hucksterism or to the increasing demands and economic clout of the various trusts and monopolies that had come to dominate so much of the national market.[33]

The depression posed several critical questions for the already often-beleaguered Charles H. Kerr & Company. Kerr had barely departed *Unity* and launched *New Occasions* when the forestalled impact of the deepening financial crisis hit Chicago. Unable and unwilling to turn to big capital, either at the bank or through an advertising agent, he either had to find a way to remain competitive or resign from the field. He fell back on his own resources, ingenuity, and the network of personal ties established during the previous decade. The company released several new titles between the beginning of 1893 and the following autumn, when credit tightened because of the severity of the depression and the initial financing of new books became difficult. Kerr turned for assistance to his father, Alexander Kerr, who provided a personal loan and purchased a small block of shares in the firm. That helped.[34]

Kerr next appealed to the readers of *New Occasions*. The January 1894 issue closed with a new investment scheme and an entreaty for public support. A prospectus, "Profit Sharing Realized," modestly praised the accomplishments of the Kerr venture, a firm headed "in the direction of books that help the struggle of the oppressed for fairer social conditions," and listed Hill as a reference. After surveying the assets of the company, Kerr announced the sale of 450 shares of stock. He stated his "desire to place . . . [the shares] with persons who are directly interested in the circulation of books of social reform." Such persons would find the investment "trebly profitable, first in reducing the cost of social reform and miscellaneous books required for their own reading; second, in the large margin of profit on such books as they may have the leisure to sell . . . [while] promoting the cause they have at heart; and third, in the regular dividends on stock which we confidently predict will not be less than 8 per cent after this year." To bring the $10 shares "within the reach of all," Kerr offered them for a down payment of $1 in cash and nine monthly installments. Potential investors were invited to inquire further before returning an attached application blank. Here was a method for mobilizing capital that Kerr would use in some form or another for the next thirty years.[35]

Sale of shares proceeded slowly, and the Kerr Company's situation continued to bode ill through that winter of 1893–94. In order to promote and increase the circulation of *New Occasions*, Kerr once again offered books from his catalog as premiums to new subscribers. As was the case earlier with *Unity*, he again had to subsidize a magazine by offering books from his inventory at a loss. Financially strapped and unable to pay for original articles, he began to fill the pages of *New Occasions* with reprints of lectures from Lewis G. Janes's Brooklyn Ethical Association (BEA). Although Kerr assured readers that the monthly would "continue to afford a tribunal for the independent discussion of questions of practical interest to the people, especially questions of social and industrial reform," the next several issues contained little more than reproductions of scientific papers previously presented to the BEA. Underwood resigned as editor in March 1894 to become the publisher-editor of the *Religio-Philosophical Journal*, and Kerr regretfully announced a reduction in the size and scope of future issues "until an equilibrium can be restored between income and outgo." Scaled back, *New Occasions* struggled on.[36]

In the meantime, Kerr managed to release several significant works that generated enough income to help his company weather the economic crisis. Varied debates on monetary policy and banking practices, already well underway within reform and populist circles, heightened during the downturn of 1893. With its call for the nationalization of banks, Hill's *Money Found* received a good deal of attention. Kerr sold twenty thousand copies by October 1894, revenue that helped sustain the firm.[37] Two volumes by noted radical feminists also received attention and generated sales. A major work by the noted woman's rights advocate Matilda Joslyn Gage was released in September 1893. Scathing in its critique of organized religion's teachings on the inferiority of women, Gage's *Woman, Church, and State* reached a wide audience and generated a fair amount of controversy in conservative circles. *Facts and Fictions of Life*, a collection of essays by the freethinking Helen Hamilton Gardener, was released during the summer of 1893 and also was profitable.[38]

Matilda Gage's career as an outspoken feminist militant spanned four decades. Discouraged with the slow progress made by the suffrage movement in the late 1870s, she became convinced that the teachings of churches that preached belief in female inferiority were "the greatest obstacles to woman's emancipation." In 1890 she founded the Woman's National Liberal Union to oppose moves then underway to unite church and state through the passage of a "Christian" amendment to the Constitution.[39] *Woman, Church, and State* explored the evolution of views about the "inferiority" of women. "An emphatic refutation of that assertion so often made by the clergy, that woman holds a higher position under Christianity than ever before," the book traced the history of the ancient "Matriarchate" and the "gradual encroachment" on the status of women made by canon law through its control of wills, guardianship of orphans, marriage, and divorce.

Several sections of the volume raised the hackles of conservative critics. Anthony Comstock, head of the notorious New York Society for the Suppression of Vice, vociferously condemned the work, stating, "If I found a person putting that book indiscriminately before the children, I would institute a criminal proceeding against him for doing it." Controversy naturally helped sales, and Kerr capitalized on the situation by printing advertisements for the Gage work that displayed Comstock's condemnation along with praiseworthy comments from other sources. "Condemned by Comstock!" read the bold-face heading.[40]

A close associate of the renowned agnostic Robert Ingersoll, Helen Hamilton Gardener frequently arraigned Christianity for its subordination of women. Her most famous short piece "Sex in Brain" grew out of her heightened rage with an article by a former surgeon general of the United States who had alleged the measurable inferiority of the female brain as an explanation for inequality. "Sex in Brain" persuasively critiqued the problematic correlation between brain size and intellectual capacity and received considerable attention within feminist circles. Gardener subsequently read three separate papers before the Congress of Representative Women at the Chicago's Colombian Exposition in 1893. Her appearance resulted in packed halls and repeated demands for a reappearance.[41] Kerr compiled those addresses and several earlier essays, including "Sex in Brain," and released the collection as *Facts and Fictions of Life*.

The crisis of the 1890s, meanwhile, would not allow Kerr to merely carry on as a bookman. It moved him toward increased awareness and more direct political and social engagement. The winds of depression continued to fan the Chicago's already tinderlike social terrain through the winter and into the spring of 1894. Fueled by the worsening condition of the unemployed, inadequate relief, and the paternalistic, cavalier attitude of its elites, Chicago soon became the epicenter of a pivotal conflagration of late-nineteenth-century working-class history, the Pullman Strike. Charles Kerr would not, could not, remain uninvolved.

Initiated as a struggle for redress and union recognition in response to wage cuts and evictions at George Pullman's planned industrial fiefdom south of the city, the strike simultaneously fired the ire and imagination of labor's supporters and the intransigence of monied might. Ultimately, the strike at Pullmantown became a showdown that pitted the newly founded American Railway Union lead by Eugene Debs and Chicago's dispossessed against the combined force of industrial capital and the federal government.[42]

The strike began at Pullman in early May when some four thousand workers protesting increased wage cuts and no reduction in rents or other expenses exacted in the company town walked off the job. The Pullman workers, largely unorganized until that point, turned to the newly founded American Railway Union for assistance. Counseling caution initially, the union in late June called for a boycott of all trains hauling Pullman cars. In effect, the strike disrupted two-thirds of the nation's rail system. The railway workers' solidarity opened the door for direct intervention by the federal government when U.S. Attorney General Richard Olney, a former railway lawyer, sent troops into Chicago at the request of the city's magnates and over the objections of Governor John Altgeld. The arrival of troops further fanned an already simmering situation and created a firestorm of class violence and destruction that lasted for several days. The armed power of the state, court injunctions against ARU strike activity, and arrests of the union's leaders quickly broke the sympathy strike, but not without raising a number of concerns about the implications and precedents implicit in such a use of combined federal authority and corporate might.

The strike had long-term ramifications. The class conflagration of 1894 seared numerous social consciences and led some to search for methods of conciliation between labor and capital. It forced many to question the increasing power of consolidated wealth and privilege critically. It turned others toward a search of radical alternatives. In the aftermath of the strike, Eugene Debs moved leftward, well on his way to becoming the most famous and revered voice of a homegrown socialism. Countless others, alienated further by the role of the courts, the police, the military, and the seeming usurpation of republican values and liberties, also became more receptive to radical critiques. Charles Kerr clearly was one of the latter.

In August 1894 Kerr published *The Pullman Strike*, an eyewitness exposé of the conditions at Pullman, by one of the town's pastors, the Rev. William H. Carwardine. The strikers at Pullman had continued on, alone and isolated with waning public support after the defeat of the ARU. Kerr published Carwardine's firsthand observations on the failure of Pullman's paternalism when the more established firms along Bookseller's Row, bowing to George Pullman's desire to suppress the book, refused to handle it. Committed to what he perceived as a just struggle and equally reluctant to garner any profit from the plight of the strikers, Kerr donated all proceeds from the book to the families of those still out.[43]

Kerr had incurred an additional debt in the spring of 1893, before the depression hit, through the purchase of the typesetting equipment from the defunct Sergel Company. Eager to pay off the remaining balance on the machines and also in need of additional capital to meet operating costs and begin new projects, he launched yet another campaign to attract investors during May 1894. Proclaiming in large print that "Small Sums Need Not Lie Idle," he pitched his promotional plea to those specifically interested in reform and cooperation: "Under the present conditions, those who have large sums of ready money have an enormous advantage in competition, while those with small sums are usually unable to obtain any income to help out their weekly earnings. The one remedy for this state of things is co-operation."[44] He pointed out that "the same corporation laws which often enable the rich to build up irresistible combinations for legal robbery" also allowed the "comparatively poor" to combine their resources for common profit. Smallholders interested in reform and cooperative ventures could find no better vehicle to advance the cause, he argued, than an investment in Charles H. Kerr & Company. Optimistic, he promised a cash dividend, an annual return of 8 percent on investment "after the current year." With no immediate respite in sight, however, Kerr continued on. Doubling as publisher and editor, he managed to keep the company afloat through 1896. *New Occasions*, with a meager subscription list of approximately two thousand, survived as well.

Then, with the coming of the new year, 1897, and the first glimmerings of "McKinley prosperity," the Kerr operation's course took a turn for the better. In December 1896 Kerr forged a business partnership with Frederick Upham Adams, to whom he sold approximately one-half of his interest in the company. The two agreed to devote their collective energies and resources to the improvement of *New Occasions* and the further circulation of reform books and pamphlets. Adams assumed the editorial chair of the monthly with the arrival of the new year. The Kerr-Adams partnership reinvigorated *New Occasions* and carried its publisher into new realms of reform endeavor and radical, critical thought.[45]

Frederick Adams brought a host of valuable experiences to the editorship of *New Occasions*. Born in Boston in 1859, he moved with his family to Elgin, Illinois, in 1866. His father, a mechanical engineer, trained his son to follow in his footsteps; the younger Adams spent several years as a machine designer in Chicago after completing public school in the mid-1870s. He became interested in street lighting and soon patented several related inventions, including a design for an electric street lamp post that became a standard in the United States during the 1880s. Threatened with the loss of his eyesight and forced to abandon the drafting table, he turned to journalism. Initially a writer for the *Chicago Daily News*, he became a student of the "labor question" and related social problems. He covered the labor agitations of 1886, and his reportorial skills soon won him a position as labor editor for the *Chicago Tribune*. A Democratic Party regular, he received an appointment to head the party's Literary and Press Bureau at the Democratic National Convention in 1892. His work for the party did not go unrecognized; he headed the National Press Office that publicized William Jennings Bryan's bid for the presidency in 1896.

Bryan's resounding defeat at the hands of Hanna Republicanism left Adams disillusioned with established political practice. Incensed by what he viewed as the usurpation of the democratic process by the "Monied Power," he turned to a fundamental questioning and critique of existing electoral and legislative structures and procedures. He soon became an outspoken advocate of direct legislation and majority rule.[46]

Under the guidance of the Democratic regular-cum-reformer *New Occasions* went through a rapid transformation in style, format, and content. Formerly polite, somewhat scholarly, and respectable in tone, the magazine suddenly began to mince few words with its espoused enemies: international bankers, railroad titans, and corrupt politicians. Adams's inaugural editorial of January 1897, for example, unsparingly attacked the lame duck Grover Cleveland in a language and tone that marked the monthly's future direction: "Grover Cleveland has disgraced the presidency and humiliated, disgusted and impoverished the American people. . . . He has been recreant to every trust the people have reposed in him. He has done his best to destroy and disrupt the party which thrice honored him and dishonored itself by his nominations. . . . He has made friends of the enemies of the people and of the nation." Arguing that Cleveland's presidency demonstrated "the inadequacy of the constitution . . . to protect the people against the tyranny and usurpation of an elective officer," Adams concluded with a series of political reform demands that soon became his trademark. A partisan of direct majoritarian rule, he called for an end to both presidential veto power and the authority of Congress to pass laws without the direct consent through referenda by "the people." Noting that "there is in a republic no wisdom higher than the formulated expression of a majority of the people," he also called for curtailment of the Supreme Court's power to annul any law passed by a popular plurality.[47]

Adams's premier issue also contained a lengthy disquisition by W. H. Van Ornum on "Socialism and Individualism," an article on graft and corruption in "A City without Shame, Chicago," and the first installment of a serialized *News from Nowhere*, the highly popular utopian novel by England's famed artist and socialist activist William Morris.

Clearly agitational and provocatively strident in tone and politics, *New Occasions* experienced a rapid renaissance. Beginning with a small sixty-four-page format at the start of 1897, Adams and Kerr initially hoped to enlarge the magazine by the end of the year. By April, however, "phenomenal success . . . compelled a radical departure from the original plans of its founders." Adams vowed that the monthly would double in size to become "the peer of any publication in the United States." Kerr announced that "in the future *New Occasions* will appear in the form of *Scribner's, McClure's,* and other standard magazines," primarily to provide more space and attention to the "progressive thought of the day" but also "to include departments interesting to those members of the family who will be the men and women of the coming generation."[48]

New Occasions was certainly more appealing than it had been. Liberally illustrated with reproductions of cartoons culled from the reform press and original woodcut portraits of reform notables, the monthly took on a whole new character and offered several new features. A regular column, "Socialism," presented bits and pieces about the socialist movement, broadly defined, in the United States and Europe. There was also a monthly humor page, most of it political satire, and a page of puzzles and charades. "We all like a good story or a joke now and then," Adams had noted, "the reformer who is always preaching loses his hold on those who would otherwise listen."

When Adams came to *New Occasions,* he carried in his pocket a lengthy list of the names and addresses of the national committee members of the Democratic Party, the People's Party, the National Prohibition Party, the "Silver Wing" of the Republicans, and a wide range of liberal, populist, and reform periodicals and newspapers. He used the list not only to publicize the monthly but also to promote a call for a new political organization. Distributed through the mails in March and reprinted in *New Occasions* in April 1897, Adams's "Shall We Unite" contended that the election of 1896 "was more than a defeat."[49] It would be "pure folly to expect that another battle will again be fought on similar lines. . . . Money has been crowned king and Greed made prime minister. Organized rapacity emerges victorious from the combat and regards with contemptuous disdain the scattered and disintegrated army which dared assail it." Invoking those symbols of democratic and republican virtue that recalled a seemingly more harmonious antebellum era, Adams argued that both major parties had become moribund: "No trace remains of the party of Lincoln, Sumner and the patriots who dared assail a wrong. . . . No trace remains of the party of Jefferson, Jackson, and those . . . who affirmed the right of the people to dictate what laws should govern them. Their principles are ignored, their precepts forgotten, their grand truths dispised." He called for the creation of a new mass-based, popularly elected American Party.

Such an editorial call marked a clear departure from the earlier period of *New Occasions.* Previously a mere sounding board for a broad array of reform opinion and debate, the monthly began to develop its own program and political agenda. Set in bold-faced capitals just below the masthead through the first half of 1897, "Our Platform on the Money Question" demanded "no compromise with the Gold Combine except on the basis of full restitution of all wealth Stolen, with interest at the legal rate of six per cent." Above and beyond the money question, Adams fixed his editorial sights on one central issue, the omnipresent demand for a reinvigorated popular sovereignty through direct legislation and a strict majoritarian rule based on the initiative and referenda. Emphatic in his call for a "true democracy," he contended that "there is no sovereign voter today": "We are a lot of deluded asses, who periodically march to the poles and vote for men who trade on our suffrage and deliver us as bond slaves to the men who place bribes in their hands." He maintained an unwavering commitment to parliamentary rule and republican values. "The majority," he insisted, "should have absolute dictation in formulating the platform and principles which it desires to vote for and carry into execution." As editor, he pledged that *New Occasions* would "continue to fight for public ownership of all national monopolies by means of direct legislation or the initiative and referendum."[50]

With the monthly's editorial chair in good hands, Kerr could once again devote his full energies to the more immediate task of running a publishing house. As partisan and committed to the cause of fundamental reform as his new partner, he nevertheless had to face the dilemma of subscription and circulation. Was there an alternative to the dominant business practices of the period? Could a publishing firm not merely issue reform or radical literature but also develop a structure and operational practice that differed from expected norm and dictate? Kerr thought it possible. His evolving political and social reform commitments and an evolving anticapitalist stance shaped his course. Eager to "make *New Occasions* the greatest reform magazine in the world," he nevertheless refused to use national advertisers, the major source of revenue for popular magazines of the era. This animus toward big business placed him at a disadvantage in the dynamically competitive magazine market and in a business environment dominated by the ethos of laissez-faire and survival of the fittest.

In a perpetual quest for the additional capital needed to improve the monthly and finance new publications, he turned to the popular mass movement for support. In May 1897, for example, his appeal for cooperation played not only on the pecuniary interest but also on the presumed social and political commitments of his readers.[51] Basically a promotional to attract new subscribers and independent canvassers, the appeal did not simply proffer the usual book premiums. Those willing to "take hold and help" were given several options. Along with an equivalent value of books from the company list for each annual dollar subscription to *New Occasions*, the plan also promised a 40 percent cash commission to all who sent in more than five subscriptions. A special three-month, 25 cent subscription was available for those "who want the magazine but have not a dollar." In an attempt to attract committed activist sales agents, the promotional suggested that "a reform circulating library ought to be established in every township in the United States." To this end, Kerr promised to forward $50 worth of books selected from his list to anyone sending him twenty-five subscriptions or more. In search of assistance in the form of personal loans from amenable subscribers, Kerr simultaneously issued a series of New Occasions Co-Operative Publishing Bonds.

Never content with just simply running the business, Kerr also began to contribute short pieces to the pages of *New Occasions*. In "How to Do Business without Money," which appeared in June 1897, he put forward a scheme, "a practical plan that can be tried at once," to help break the hold of the "money lender" on an already tight currency supply. A barter system of goods and services in kind based on the exchange of promissory "commodity notes" specifying the particular commodity or service in which the payment would be made, Kerr's design centered around the use of blank "New Occasions Exchange Notes" to be printed and distributed by Charles H. Kerr & Company.

The utopian scheme was based on assumptions of an idealized organic community of producers in which everyone would have barterable goods and services, a strategy that never caught hold. Nevertheless, the blueprint offered a rare glimpse into the perceptions and evolving social beliefs of the man behind the scenes at the Kerr Company. Molded by the rational liberal faith in progress and a widely held vision of evolutionary inevitability, Kerr emphatically stated that "the present commercial civilization is doomed." Voicing the widespread secular millennialism of the turn of the century, he envisioned the arrival of a new order: "A better civilization, based on brotherhood instead of robbery, is coming. Events move swiftly. I believe that most of us will live to see the new day." He articulated that confidence in the transformative power of moral suasion based on rational argument: "The friends of *New Occasions* are working for the new order by the most potent of all methods—education. We are gradually bringing people to see that the old order is wrong and the new order is right, that the old order brings want and the new order plenty, that misery is the natural outcome of the one, happiness the other. . . . Perseverance on this line will bring victory. It is only a question of time."[52]

Kerr could persevere. In business terms, what he did not have was unlimited time. What he lacked were the funds and the levels of circulation needed to enable *New Occasions* to stand on its own. Despite the various strategies put forward to help improve the monthly, increased book sales remained the major source of revenue and path to solvency. One or two bestsellers were critical to help offset the expense of works on the list that did not do well. One money-maker could mean the difference between success and ruin.

Moderate assistance did come with the release of Adams's panacea novel *President John Smith* early in 1897. Written in the autumn of 1893, the portrayal of the "peaceful revolution of 1900" pitted the archetypal populist hero John Smith against the villainies of the "fortified minority" of monied political power. Advertised as "a brilliant story based on scientific socialism," Adams's book used the by-then familiar utopian novel form to propagandize for his pet panaceas: the initiative, referendum, the nationalization of monopolies, a revision of the Constitution, and the "reign of common sense." The work sold twenty-five thousand copies within sixty days of its release and soon won the endorsements of reform notables Ignatius Donnelly, John Peter Altgeld, Tom Watson, William "Coin" Harvey, and Henry Demarest Lloyd, among others. Initial reviews proclaimed it an equal to Edward Bellamy's *Looking Backward.*[53]

With the promise of such a bona-fide bestseller in his grasp for the first time, Kerr made a seemingly curious choice. His decision must have appeared strange, even ridiculous, to his more profit-oriented peers along Publisher's Row. He opted to reproduce *President John Smith* in an inexpensive paper edition and sell it at the publisher's cost per copy, reduced even further in bulk. The decision to slash the price from $1 to 10 cents partly reflected some anticipated return on a large volume of sales. More significantly, it represented the personal commitment of a man dedicated to the popular democratic program outlined in the novel. At the beginning of June 1897 he issued the first of a number of cheap imprints at the pared retail price. The reduced price was a politically motivated "effort to place . . . [*John Smith*] in the hands of every voter in the United States."[54]

Behind the decision to forego any sizable return on the Adams book lay an optimism in the future. Such confidence arose in part from the relative success of the company and the revitalization of *New Occasions*. It also stemmed from an idealist secular millennialism, widespread in the 1890s among reformers of all stripe, which envisioned and anticipated the new century. Confident in the inevitability of an approaching progressive dawn, Kerr and Adams changed the name of their monthly to *New Time* in June 1897. The company nevertheless ran $7,000 in the red that month.

The anticipatory denotations of an approaching new epoch aside, the title change also heralded the arrival of a significant third addition to the staff. On the front cover of the June 1897 issue, under the title-in-transition, "New Occasions and *The New Time*," appeared the name of a new coeditor, B. O. Flower. His arrival, finalized by the formal change in name to *New Time* the following month, marked yet another departure for Charles H. Kerr & Company.

Already well-known within progressive circles at home and abroad as the founder and editor of *The Arena*, Boston's radically outspoken reform journal, Benjamin Orange Flower had returned to his native Illinois late in 1896 in a quest for new outlets and a new editorial home. The victim of financial difficulties owing in part to Flower's mishandling of a subsidiary book publishing venture, *The Arena* had fallen into temporary receivership in the autumn of 1896. Enticed by the possibilities already visible in the revitalized *New Occasions*, Flower met with Kerr and Adams early in 1897. He stayed at the Kerr home in Glen Ellyn while plans for a partnership took shape and finally threw in his lot with Adams and Kerr after ironing out a workable business arrangement.[55]

Described by his various biographers as a "master mechanic of dissent," "a twenty-four-hour-a-day liberal," a "full-time employee in the service of progress," and a "lay evangelist of social democracy," Flower was born near Albion, Illinois, in October 1858. Educated at home in his early years by his minister father, he completed high school at Evansville, Indiana, and entered Transylvania Bible School in Lexington, Kentucky, intent on following his father into the ministry of the Disciples of Christ. His university experience transformed his thinking, and he became a Unitarian while in Lexington. After returning to Albion, he began his lengthy journalistic career as editor of the *American Sentinel* weekly reform sheet. In 1881 Flowers moved to Boston, where he founded the *American Spectator*, a quasi-religious spiritualist monthly that explored the scientific basis of occult psychic phenomena.[56]

Flower founded *The Arena* in the fall of 1889. The "first successful muckraking magazine in America," the innovative monthly reflected the social attitudes and complex system of beliefs of its bold editor. Flower maintained the predisposition and convictions of an evangelist convinced of the possibility of heaven on earth, a mundane American millennium. Convinced in the inevitability of a "new dawn," his words and journalistic deeds elaborated a specific conception of progress based on moral idealism rather than mere material expansion. Progress, for Flower, meant change through an orderly process of reform by an enlightened, well-informed public. He was not a revolutionist. Like Kerr and Adams, he believed that positive change could only come through a public adequately educated and prepared. He contended that "changes may come from without but unless the people are made ready for them by an educational process which has touched heart and brain with holy fire of love and a passion for justice and freedom, the innovation, no matter how salutary . . . will prove dead letter."[57]

He argued that there could be no progress, freedom, or justice not based on truth, which could only be attained through free and open discussion of all things. Unwilling to place editorial restrictions on subject matter, Flower readily extended *The Arena*'s space to discussion deemed too provocative, risqué, or taboo by the more established popular journals of the 1890s. He also argued that the only cure for ailing democracy was more democracy. Opposed to monopoly and the trusts and an advocate of the referenda, recall, direct elections, and public ownership of utilities, Flower became one of the foremost early champions of a positive, interventionist liberalism. He also endorsed the populist cause, Free Silver, and designs for consumers' and producers' cooperation and maintained a firm conviction in scientific inquiry as the "source of advancement and truth." Like his new partners, Flower was typical of other end-of-the-century reformers who were optimistic about the transformative value of the new social sciences.[58]

The new coeditor's name on the masthead of *New Time* gave the monthly the immediate prestige and recognition it sorely needed. Flower's energy and skill injected the entire venture with unprecedented optimism. Kerr, as publisher, found himself unable to meet demands for the July 1897 issue. With twenty thousand copies exhausted within weeks, the editors had to apologize to those who missed out. Monthly circulation rose from ten thousand in June 1897 to more than thirty-one thousand six months later. That November, the Adams, Kerr, and Flower could proudly boast of twenty-five thousand paid subscribers—forty thousand by the end of the year. *New Time* began to cover its costs for the first time, and the trio of editors confidently began to project a monthly distribution of a hundred thousand and beyond. One editorial at the end of the year actually spoke of plans for a circulation of two million.[59]

Such optimistic projections stemmed in part from the accomplishments of the preceding half year. They also emanated from that mutually held belief—a secular faith—in the arrival of a new cooperative millennium already seemingly visible on the horizon. Convinced that a new age was inevitable and about to unfold, the *New Time* trio self-assuredly promoted their monthly as the clarion voice heralding the pending renaissance. More significantly, their periodical would be the transformative vehicle that would educate and uplift the ignorant and the uninformed.

Flower had returned to Massachusetts after consolidating the new arrangement. At times waxing evangelical, he continued to trumpet the arrival of the coming age. Considering the wondrous developments of science, industry, and technology and the advances made in all fields of intellectual endeavor, he qualified his optimistic determinism with a proviso: True progress, extending beyond material growth and technical innovation, depended on the enlightenment—the moral , spiritual, and ethical regeneration—of the people. Adams, in turn, argued that the only "the people," armed and fortified with the weapons of true democracy, could be midwives at the birth of the cooperative era. Only an informed public would be able to fend off the tyrannies of the money lender, industrial mogul, and bought politician, as well as the ominous threat of violent class strife.

A reform potpourri, what Kerr later described as a "semi-populist, semi-socialist magazine," the monthly specialized in exposés of government corruption and collusion with "the Trusts." A full list of its contributors reads like a who's who of turn-of-the-century American reform: work by Richard T. Ely, Hazen Pingree, Hamlin Garland, Ignatius Donnelly, and Frank Parsons appeared regularly. *New Time*'s pages carried occasional communications from Eugene Debs, a regular column on "Scientific Socialism" with news and views on the progress of social democracy at home and abroad, and the serialization of William Morris's *News from Nowhere* begun in *New Occasions*.[60]

May Walden Kerr contributed "The Home," a regular monthly column of advice. In her introductory piece in March 1898 she explained the rationale for such a feature. While noting that *"The New Time* declines to accept an exact line of division, cutting off woman's sphere from man's," she pointed out that the purpose of the magazine as a whole was the need for "rational action on public lines." "The Home" department had been created "to emphasize the equal need of rational action in the life of each and every home." In its faith in the inevitability of the new dawn, her column mirrored the optimism that informed every piece in *New Time.* While reminding readers that "the present social order has almost run its course, the new order must soon come, for good or for ill," May Walden Kerr suggested that it would be "in the homes of those who are already awake to the criminal injustice of present social conditions, that the leaders of the future must be nurtured and trained." Such leaders must be prepared in a "home atmosphere of liberty, helpfulness and love."[61]

The entire *New Time* team based its optimism on a secular "come outer" faith, the assumption about the willingness and the ability of all producers to take up the common collective struggle against a wrong once that wrong was exposed. Adams, Flower, and Kerr assumed that people, once enlightened, would readily volunteer and "pitch in" for the common cause through the advancement of *New Time*. Never merely out to just sell magazines, they made each subscription drive and promotional campaign an appeal for mustering reform forces and recruiting activist sales agents, investors, and secular gospel-spreading troops for the *"New Time* Army."[62]

The business end of *New Time* was restructured at the end of October 1897. Adams, Kerr, and Flower, now joined by the Chicago entrepreneur and reform advocate George E. Bowen, formed the New Time Company as a separate entity, differentiated from Charles H. Kerr & Company.[63] Incorporated under Illinois statutes and capitalized for $50,000 to publish and distribute *New Time*, the new company gave Kerr, Flower, and Adams the right to purchase 750 shares each in exchange for a mutual agreement "to contribute to the said Company all right, title and interest in the subscription list of the *New Time*, together with . . . services in behalf of the new company." In exchange for 250 shares and the option to purchase more, Bowen agreed to contribute a lengthy and "valuable" mailing list, as well as manage the business affairs of the fledgling company. Flower was listed as president of the new firm, with Adams as vice president, Kerr as treasurer, and Bowen as secretary. The agreement also stated that the Kerr Company would act as publishing agent for the succeeding four months. Kerr was now free to pursue the growth and expansion of his book firm without it being tied to the fortunes of the magazine.[64]

The son of George S. Bowen, a Chicago entrepreneur, land developer, and reform activist, George E. Bowen had established himself as a publisher's agent for a variety of reform tracts. His father, a former mayor of Elgin, Illinois, had participated in the Illinois ranks of the Greenback Labor Party in 1876 and had actively supported the bimetalist plank of the Peoples' Party platform of 1894. Father and son both worked tirelessly for Bryan in 1896. With McKinley's victory, they turned their reform energies toward the campaign against the trusts and the publication of reform literature. The Bowens were active in a number of attempts to promote the cause of free silver; when he joined the board of the New Time Company, the younger Bowen also served as secretary of the Washington-based National Bimetallic Union.[65]

Bowen became business manager of *New Time* in November 1897 and quickly transformed the marketing end of the company to be more in accord with conventional business practices of the day. Mildly contemptuous of Kerr's desire to transcend or bypass established business norms, Bowen initiated a number of costly promotional schemes to attract advertisers and subscribers as the overall reform thrust of the 1890s began to wane. Advertising and promotional costs soon began to outweigh projected returns, and subscription numbers also began to decline.

The success of *New Time* peaked in December 1897 with a sale of forty thousand. Despite announced plans to increase circulation to half a million by June of the coming year, sales had fallen by ten thousand in January. The New Time Company partially recouped in the succeeding months, and distribution again reached thirty-six thousand by April. Continually optimistic but no longer as grandiose in his projections, Kerr informed readers in April that he hoped for monthly sales of fifty thousand by the end of the year. In part the victim of a brief decline in reform impetus because McKinley prosperity and growing jingoist excitement over Cuba had diverted public concern from domestic reform, the magazine's circulation and number of paid subscribers fell.

Stating that it had become too difficult to edit the Chicago-based monthly from his vantage point in far-away Brookline, Massachusetts, Flower resigned from the editorial board in April 1898. Adams purchased his shares in the magazine and assumed full editorial responsibility once again. During the last half of 1898 expenses exceeded revenues by a little over $500 a month, in large part owing to the amount spent on advertising in the form of posters, circular letters, and other publicity Bowen had initiated.[66] The continued decline led to a dispute between the partners that took the form of a polite but somewhat contentious exchange between Kerr and Adams. Displeased with the particular course that Bowen and Adams had charted and more concerned with the future and viability of his publishing venture, Kerr resigned as treasurer of the New Time Company on July 25, 1898. New horizons and ventures beckoned once again.[67]

The First Socialist Phase, 1899–1908

As the century drew to a close, Charles Kerr once again moved politically and ideologically—this time toward Marxian socialism. The company baring his name became explicitly socialist as the twentieth century dawned. The socialist years of Charles H. Kerr & Company under Kerr's guidance have two phases: an early formative period extending from 1899 to January 1908 and a second, distinctively more radical period, that extended through the turbulent era of World War I and into the early 1920s. The first period was a time of growth and expansion for the company as well as an era of political development for its founder and the small circle of activists who gathered around him. The Kerr group, during that first phase, embarked on a number of particular projects in an ongoing attempt to introduce Marxism to American workers. They imported and translated socialist classics from Europe, published Marxian analyses by indigenous American authors, and created an ambitious monthly theoretical journal, the *International Socialist Review* (*ISR*). The years between 1899 and 1908 also marked the arrival, tenure, and exit of Algie M. Simons, next to Kerr the company's most significant figure during that first period.

Charles Kerr formally joined the socialist movement in 1899. He was no longer a young man, but rather a matured, "quiet, studious gentleman with sensitive features, small Vandyke beard, and the forehead of a philosopher."[1] He had decided to devote his energies and expertise to the creation of an ever-elusive cooperative commonwealth based on the principles, precepts, and analyses of Marxian "scientific socialism." The decision, shaped less by an impulsive and inexplicable leap of faith or conversion experience than by a rational, informed assessment of history and existing social and political conditions and a set of informed assumptions about the future direction of American society, carried him to the heart of the turn-of-the-century socialist movement. As he recalled some years later, he "had not been inside the movement" before 1899 "due to the accident of its not being presented to me" but "had not the slightest difficulty in accepting the logic of the socialist position when once perceived."[2] The small business he had initiated some thirteen years earlier would soon become the most significant publisher of Marxian socialism in the United States before World War I.

Kerr had continued on as an independent publisher after his departure from the *New Time*. During the late 1890s, "like numerous other Americans, we were looking for real socialism, but as yet knew little about it."[3] His first real connection with the international socialist movement began in the spring of 1899.[4] That March, the Chicago branch of the Socialist Labor Party (SLP) had launched a weekly, the *Worker's Call*, and Kerr immediately began to cultivate fraternal relations with the paper's editor, A. M. Simons.[5]

The SLP, one of the primary organizational expressions of scientific socialism in the United States at the time, drew from a long history. Marxian socialism had already crossed the Atlantic years before with the flight of German radicals following the defeats of 1848. Most early American socialists were European-born, and they soon divided into Lassallean and Marxian factions. The followers of Ferdinand Lassalle viewed economic activity by labor unions as futile and geared most of their activity to political action—the formation of a workers' party and the use of the ballot box. The Marxists held that political action was broader than parliamentary activity and argued for creating trade unions and organizing the unemployed. The two wings came together briefly in 1876 with the formation of the Working Men's Party. The Lassalleans won complete control of the new organization at the party convention in December 1877 and overhauled the party constitution and platform to pursue a strategy of political action at the polls. With the reorganization came a new name, the Socialist Labor Party of America.

During the 1880s socialists divided into three factions: the vote-conscious SLP, a trade union wing, and an anarchistic direct-action element. Meanwhile, a new flow of German radicals fleeing antisocialist repression at home swelled the ranks of the anarchist movement. The ineffectiveness of the SLP's electoral strategy forced numerous party sections to defect to the more militant, anarchist-led International Working People's Association. In an attempt to halt that exodus, the SLP convention of December 1883 resolved that politics was solely a means of propaganda. The privileged classes would only surrender their position when compelled by force.

In 1890 the SLP recruited a Columbia University law lecturer named Daniel DeLeon. Within a year he had become editor of the SLP's English-language paper *The People* and an acknowledged intellectual leader of the American socialist movement. In his attempt to wed the Lassallean and Marxian perspectives, DeLeon developed a series of varied strategies to raise the class consciousness of American laborers. Defeated in his attempts to "bore from within" the AFL and the anemic Knights of Labor, in 1895 DeLeon announced plans for the formation of a separate socialist labor movement around the dual union Socialist Trades and Labor Alliance (ST&LA). The separate union policy, when combined with irritations over DeLeon's dictatorial behavior, led to numerous defections from the party. In New York, approximately half of the SLP's union membership, nestled in the German-dominated crafts and the United Hebrew Trades, either departed or were expelled.

The faction fights in New York soon affected the SLP sections in Chicago, where many party members had strong ties with various AFL locals. As editor of Chicago's party organ, the *Worker's Call*, Algie Simons initially counseled neutrality and withholding recognition for either faction in the disputes between DeLeon and his opponents. But when DeLeon attacked Simons in *The People* and eventually expelled him, Simons soon joined the negotiations with Social Democrats, formed by Eugene Debs and Milwaukee socialist Victor Berger, which led to the formation of the Socialist Party of America in 1901.[6]

Kerr's junior by ten years, Algie Martin Simons still played a key role in the SLP when he and his future partner first crossed paths. An alumnus of the University of Wisconsin as Kerr was, Simons had studied history under Frederick Jackson Turner and had become acquainted with Marxian socialism as a research assistant to the professor of political economy, Richard T. Ely. Upon graduating, he worked in the University of Chicago settlement house on the city's South Side, where he collected data on living conditions in the stockyards districts for the Municipal Board of Charities. Simons's day-to-day experiences and observations in the Back of the Yards left him morally outraged and embittered at cautious gradual reform strategies based on individual uplift and personal redemption. He joined the SLP in 1897 and became editor of the *Worker's Call* with the weekly's inception during the Chicago mayoralty race of 1899.[7]

Simons's vigorous commitment to Marxian socialism had immense impact on Charles and May Walden Kerr. The articulate, analytical strength of Simons's arguments among the small circle of left-leaning activists who regularly gathered at the Kerrs' Glen Ellyn home engendered an enthusiasm "that nearly set the house afire."[8] Kerr later recounted that it was through Simons that he first came into contact with the "actual socialist movement." Recounting that period years later, May Walden Kerr recalled that she and her husband had "sopped up a lot of crazy ideas that we had to give up to make way for Marxism."[9]

Kerr and Simons began to collaborate on a number of publishing projects not long after their initial encounter. Speaking for his firm in the *Worker's Call*, Kerr announced in June 1899 that "the course of events has convinced us that half-way measures are useless, . . . our future publications will be in the line of scientific socialism."[10] He later noted that "the most important assets with which our publishing house took up the work of circulating socialist literature were Comrade Simons' thorough knowledge of the socialist movement, my own accumulated experience in the art of book publishing, and the confidence of the considerable body of widely-scattered students of social problems."[11] Simons became vice president of Charles H. Kerr & Company in January 1900.[12] Equally committed to the cause, May Walden Kerr and Simons's wife, May Wood, likewise turned their activist hopes and energies toward the seemingly inevitable promise of an approaching socialist dawn.[13]

The first joint Kerr-Simons publishing project, the Pocket Library of Socialism, began to appear that March of 1899 with the release of May Wood Simons's *Woman and the Social Problem*. Wrapped in red cellophane, the monthly series of "little red books," as they came to be called, featured socialist perspectives on a diverse range of social and political topics written by the Simonses, the Kerrs, and a number of other essayists such as Clarence Darrow and John Peter Altgeld.[14] Sold at 5 cents a copy and discounted in bulk to company shareholders, "in size convenient for the pocket, and just right for mailing in an ordinary business envelope," the series of thirty-two-page booklets soon became a popular propaganda vehicle for socialist educators, organizers, and soapboxers throughout the country. With twenty-five separate titles by April 1901, circulation of the Pocket Library reached well above 230,000. By May 1902, with thirty-five titles in print, more than five hundred thousand copies had passed into the hands of the movement.[15]

The turn-of-the-century socialist movement in the United States lagged far behind its European counterparts. Simons and Kerr attributed such "backwardness," in part, to the absence of any clear theoretical basis or scientific footing. Kerr later recounted that "when we began our work, the literature of modern scientific socialism was practically unknown to American readers. . . . The really popular and widely circulated books in 1899 were of a sentimental, semi-populistic, character and were of doubtful value to the building up of a coherent socialist movement." As Simons put it, "We were in the beginning too full of our own conceit to learn from the experience of others. Instead of accepting the time-tried doctrines which already had a literature of thousands of volumes, American socialist literature has been a byword and a laughing stock among the socialists of other nations. The most ridiculous books, based upon long exploded errors, have been hailed here as the gospel of a new redemption."[16]

With the Pocket Library off to a healthy start by mid-1900, Kerr Company activists acquired editions of socialist tracts, pamphlets, and larger works through several different channels. The company expanded its list during the summer of 1901 by obtaining the entire pamphlet inventory of the International Library Publishing Company, a New York-based concern initiated by the SLP. The purchase included the imprints, plates, and copyrights for an extensive list of European imports, including pamphlets by Ferdinand Lassalle, H. M. Hyndman, Sidney Webb, and Gabriel Deville, as well as Marx's *Civil War in France* and *Wage, Labor and Capital*. The firm also imported English editions of several socialist classics, until that time only available abroad.[17]

By 1905 the company catalog included a sizable number of works by the most influential figures of the English socialist movement. Kerr had already serialized William Morris's *News from Nowhere* and Robert Blatchford's *Merrie England* in the pages of *New Time*. He issued both works in updated form and also published Blatchford's *Imprudent Marriages* and Morris's *Useful Work versus Useless Toil* as part of the Pocket Library series. Widely read in England, Blatchford's writings received a favorable reception in the United States, and Kerr subsequently published a number of his other works such as *Britain for the British* (1902) and *God and My Neighbor* (1904).[18] The Pocket Library series also included H. M. Hyndman's essay on *Socialism and Slavery*, a critique of Herbert Spencer.[19] Perhaps the most popular English title that Kerr released during that period was Edward Carpenter's *Love's Coming of Age*, a series of candid essays on the "relation of the sexes." The company, in cooperation with the London publishing house of Swann, Sonnenschein, also imported Carpenter's *Towards Democracy* in 1905. The Kerr list of British contributors soon included the socialist philosopher E. Belfort Bax and Tom Mann, a key figure in the historic London dockers' strike of 1889.[20]

Personal ties with the European left were vital. Following the death of their eighteen-month-old son, the Simonses traveled abroad at the end of 1899. The tour of Great Britain and the Continent was undertaken primarily to recuperate from their loss and made possible through the contributions of such former colleagues in Chicago's charities and social work field as Jane Addams. While abroad, the couple established contacts with key leaders of the European socialist cause. In France, they spoke with Jules Guesde, patriarch of the *Parti Ouvrier*, and Paul Lafargue, Karl Marx's son-in-law and a central figure of the French socialist movement. They traveled about the English countryside with Independent Labourite Keir Hardie and H. M. Hyndman of the Social Democratic Federation. They were deeply impressed by the successful cooperative ventures of the Belgian movement and the accomplishments of its leader, Emile Vandervelde. Inspired, the Simonses returned to Chicago late in May 1900. They brought with them numerous publications and a list of newfound correspondents in addition to plans for a number of publishing projects and a host of new schemes that would hopefully advance the socialist cause at home.[21]

An extended list of translations began to appear in the company's catalog following the Simonses' return. May Wood had already translated an essay on Friedrich Engels by Karl Kautsky in 1899, and a Kerr edition of Marx's *Wage-Labor and Capital*, translated by J. L. Joynes, appeared as Pocket Library number 7 in September of that year. Shortly after resettling in Chicago, Algie Simons assisted in the translation of *No Compromise—No Political Trading*, a tract by Wilhelm Liebknecht, patriarch of German Social Democracy, that criticized those in the socialist movement, especially in the French party, who willingly sought to enter ministries of bourgeois governments. The company also issued an edition of Engels's *Socialism, Utopian and Scientific* previously translated by Marx's son-in-law Edward Aveling but available until then only in England. A key discussion of the differences and the theoretical break between Marxian, scientific socialism and its idealist, utopian predecessors, that work, proudly advertised as the company's "first cloth bound socialist book," soon became one of Kerr & Company's most popular offerings.[22] Kerr, in the meantime, personally translated the first of a number of works by Lafargue, who gave Kerr permission to publish an authorized version of his *Socialism and the Intellectuals* shortly after his initial meeting with the Simonses. The Simonses also translated Kautsky's *The Social Revolution*.[23]

Although Kerr Company activists continued to expend a great deal of time and energy with translations throughout the next fifteen years, their most significant work on such projects came between 1900 and 1907. Kerr, using those linguistic skills acquired as a student at Wisconsin, translated from French and Italian. The Simonses worked from German. The group succeeded in compiling an ever-increasing and impressive list of European socialist authors that included not only the shorter, standard works of Marx and Engels such as *The Communist Manifesto*, Engels's *Origin of the Family, Private Property and the State*, and Marx's *The Eighteenth Brumaire of Louis Napoleon*, but also a broad array of lesser critics, commentators, and political activists largely unknown in the United States. The company released an edition of Emile Vandervelde's *Collectivism and Industrial Development*, which Kerr had translated from the French. It also introduced several Italian theorists, such as the noted socialist criminologist Enrico Ferri and Antonio Labriola, a Marxian philosopher. Translated from Italian by Kerr and first released in 1904, Labriola's *Essays on the Materialist Conception of History* soon became another of the company's more popular offerings and passed through several imprints. Clearly influenced by it personally, Kerr continuously recommended the work as must reading for those interested in expanding their theoretical background in Marxism. He subsequently issued Labriola's *Socialism and Philosophy*, a series of letters on historical materialism and other questions of socialist theory, in 1907.[24]

In April 1900 Kerr announced the first title of the Library of Science for the Workers. He advertised the series by noting that "scientific books are a necessity for the socialist because they silently undermine the theological prejudice against the socialist principles of economic determinism, among those who can not yet be reached by direct propaganda." Imported from Germany and translated by the Kerr circle, the collection of separate volumes dealt with the natural sciences, especially geology, botany, and biology. The series included such titles as *The Evolution of Man* by Wilhelm Böelsche, *Germs of Mind of Plants* by R. H. France, and *The Making of the World* by Dr. M. Wilhelm Meyer. The series also contained *Science and Revolution*, a monograph by Ernest (Ernst) Unterman, a German-educated Kerr associate.[25]

In the spring of 1902 Kerr & Company completed an arrangement with Swann, Sonnenschein to distribute the first volume of Marx's *Das Kapital* in the United States. Sonnenschein shipped a number of unbound copies to Chicago, where Kerr had them bound in red cloth and stamped on the spine with his company colophon.[26] That first English edition had been translated by Samuel Moore and Edward Aveling under the supervision of Engels. The second and third volumes of *Capital* still did not exist in English on either side of the Atlantic. Eager to bring the additional volumes to an American readership, Kerr embarked on a search for both the necessary funds for the project and a competent translator. In need of someone fluent in both German and English and also well-versed in the complexities of Marxian economic theory, he initially sought the assistance of H. M. Hyndman in England. Hyndman expressed some interest in the project, but when that fell through Kerr procured the services of Unterman.[27]

Born at Brandenburg, Germany, in November 1864, Unterman had studied paleontology and geology at the University of Berlin before becoming a merchant marine. He first set foot in the United States in 1881 and became a citizen in 1893 after spending nearly ten years of his life aboard U.S. sailing vessels that plied the South Seas trade. A member of the SLP in the 1890s, he contributed regular columns to an assortment of socialist periodicals, including the *Worker's Call* and its successor, the *Chicago Socialist*. He subsequently wrote a number of articles for Kerr's *International Socialist Review* on a diverse range of topics and labored for the Kerr Company as the translator on a number of important works, such as Engels's *Origin of the Family* (1902) and Labriola's *Socialism and Philosophy* (1907).[28] Those earlier translations had been done on a voluntary basis with no recompense, but Unterman, with wife and daughters, required some sort of support if the monumental task of translating *Capital* was to proceed. Following an unsuccessful attempt to raise the needed funds through a company stock subscription drive, Kerr finally secured financial assistance from Eugene Dietzgen, by way of Wiesbaden, Germany, and Zurich, Switzerland.[29]

Dietzgen was a remarkable character. A philosophical radical who had a bourgeois life-style, he remained committed to the socialist cause. His father, Joseph, a close associate of Marx and Engels, had emigrated to the United States after the failure of the German revolution of 1848. A leather tanner by trade and an autodidact, well-versed in philosophy and economics, the elder Dietzgen moved back and forth across the Atlantic on several occasions. On his second stay in the United States, following the passage of the bismarckian antisocialist laws of the 1870s, he became active in socialist circles in New York and Chicago. In the aftermath of the Haymarket bombing of May 1886 he stepped forward to take up the editorial chair of the *Chicagoer Arbeiterzeitung* when its editor, August Spies, was hauled in during the police dragnet.[30]

In Germany, Eugene Dietzgen had acquired a formal education in the classics, German philosophy, and the natural sciences; his father persuaded him to move to America, where he might "become the pathfinder for the existence of our family."[31] He turned his education and entrepreneurial skills to the development of a firm that specialized in the production of engineering tools. Dietzgen amassed a comfortable sum, but around the turn of the century he contracted tuberculosis and retired from the business world. Leaving his home in the Chicago suburb of Winnetka, he removed to Germany and Switzerland and became the financial patron of various publishing ventures of the Second International, including Kautsky's *Die Neue Zeit*, the foremost theoretical journal of German Social Democracy. Charles Kerr had known Dietzgen before he left Chicago; they had been introduced by Alexander Kerr some years earlier. Algie Simons reestablished connections with him on successive trips to Europe and through a correspondence with Kautsky. Unterman also apparently had some earlier ties to Dietzgen, who agreed to subsidize Unterman's translation of Marx's opus.[32]

Unterman set to work on the massive project in the spring of 1905 while living on a chicken farm in Orlando, Florida. "I couldn't have done it on what Kerr paid me," he later recounted, "but Eugene Dietzgen paid me a total of $5.00 per page, so I built up a little chicken ranch that panned out well enough to keep my family and myself in groceries. I did the translating after I got through fighting skunks, opossums, snakes, and hawks and for a while it was doubtful whether the chicken business belonged to me or to preying animals. But I won out after a while."[33]

The transplanted Floridian not only translated volumes two and three, but he also revised and edited a new edition of volume one. Engels had edited the proofs for a fourth German edition of volume one four years after the publication of the Swann, Sonnenschein English version, and Unterman used the revised German work as the source for his translation. Kerr released the new imprint of volume one late in 1906, and the two additional volumes rolled from the press between 1907 and 1909. The Kerr edition of *Capital* immediately became the accepted English version, and Swann, Sonnenschein, in conjunction with Charles H. Kerr & Company, began to distribute it throughout the English-speaking world.[34]

The publication of books and pamphlets was not enough for the politically motivated Kerr group. Proclaiming, "The time is now here when the American socialist movement needs and is able to maintain a magazine of scientific socialism," Kerr and Simons launched the *International Socialist Review* in July 1900. Kerr as managing editor and Simons as editorial editor set three goals for the infant monthly:

In the first place we shall seek to counteract the sentimental Utopianism that has so long characterized the American movement and give it a dignity and accuracy worthy of the position it is destined to attain in the world wide advance toward the cooperative commonwealth. In the second place we shall endeavor to keep our readers in touch with the socialist movements in other countries, and through the very able corps of foreign Socialist writers and thinkers who have kindly agreed to contribute to this end, bring together each month the work and opinions of the best thought of the world on the philosophy of socialism. Finally, but perhaps most important of all, we shall aim to secure the interpretation of American social conditions in the light of socialist philosophy by the socialists of this country.[35]

They invited contributions from those committed to "co-operation" and, space permitting, from "intelligent students of social questions," not necessarily socialist. They informed readers of the first issue that their editorial policy would "be in accordance with the principles . . . of independent political action by the laborers upon the basis of a struggle of classes with divergent material interests, with the ultimate object of securing the common ownership by such laborers of the means of production and distribution."[36]

Beginning with three hundred advance subscriptions and a loan of $250 from William English Walling, a socialist notable, Kerr plotted an ambitious course for the new journal. He projected a monthly format of sixty-four pages, with forty-eight of those given to articles by European and American authors and the remaining sixteen set aside for departments dealing with events of the month "from a socialist perspective": news of the socialist movement in America, items on the "struggle in the economic field," including trade union news and "labor troubles," and a section of foreign correspondence covering the course of the socialist movement "the world over."[37] Copies sold for 10 cents, with an annual subscription costing $1. At the time of its first issue *ISR* had a secured annual list of eight hundred subscribers; it had 3,500 by April 1901. An additional 3,500 sold at news stands, and Kerr could announce that "both subscriptions and sales are increasing so rapidly that a monthly edition of 10,000 copies will soon be necessary."[38]

Kerr and Simons initially directed *ISR* toward those already somewhat acquainted with and amenable to socialist ideas. Kerr explained that the monthly did "not aim to reach the millions of laborers who know nothing of Socialism and as little of the realities of capitalism." That task belonged to the weekly socialist press and pamphlet literature. The work of the

Review was "to educate the educators." "Educators" were divided into two groups. The first consisted of workers who had already "come to a realizing sense of the truths of Socialism and who wish to make converts." They were the rank-and-filers, who "may have had no leisure for so-called higher education" but who held a "firm grasp of the fundamental fact of the class struggle." The second group consisted of "brain workers": doctors, lawyers, editors, teachers and "other well-educated but frequently ill-paid laborers." They were the "wage laborers who sell their heads instead of their hands, and who now in America, as already in Europe, are being forced by unpleasant facts . . . to realize that they are in the same slavery as the manual laborers." In addition to the educators, Kerr also hoped to reach those farmers "who ten years ago were studying the question of national finance in faulty textbooks" but who were "not afraid of hard reading."[39]

The pre-1908 volumes of *ISR* provide a sense of its political goals and agenda. The first volume, for example, contained numerous pieces about the socialist movement in Europe, either original contributions from correspondents on the Continent or articles borrowed from the European left-wing press. American contributors that first year included socialist leaders Eugene Debs and Mary "Mother" Jones, the Christian socialist George D. Herron, and Job Harriman, Debs's future running-mate from California. The first several issues carried an ongoing discussion titled "Marx on the Money Question," complete with criticisms and rejoinders, and several different positions in an exchange on the "Negro Question." Simons and Unterman edited a regular section called "Socialism Abroad," and Max S. Hayes, Cleveland's well-known socialist trade unionist, edited a monthly news update on the "World of Labor." The first volume also included what would prove to be a short-lived column called "Socialism and Religion," edited by Herron. Early volumes regularly contained poetic contributions and a monthly book review section edited by Simons. Scholarly and polite in tone and with few illustrations, the first several volumes more or less replicated the style and form of the standard academic journals of the period.[40]

The development of *ISR* and the importation of works by European socialists aside, the company turned its energies to another vitally important project—the production of an indigenous American Marxian literature, analysis of American history, industrial development, and current social and political conditions "based on the principles of the Communist Manifesto."[41] Simons articulated the sentiment of the company in May 1902 when he argued,

The time is now ready for an indigenous Socialist literature that shall combine the scientific accuracy and philosophic truth of international Socialism with the best literary style, yet which shall be expressed in the native vocabulary, whose use has done so much to popularize utopianism and muddledum. . . . The great task of the Socialist writers of this country for the next few years is to interpret American economic life in the language and style which will best appeal to the American people. . . . There is a crying need . . . for a mass of books, pamphlets and periodical articles, not so much expounding, as applying, the class struggle and economic determinism to the facts and relations of our present society.[42]

Simons, perhaps more than any other figure, played a key role in the development of the company's ever-increasing list of titles by American authors. He led the field of initial turn-of-the-century attempts to interpret U.S. history from a Marxist perspective. His *Class Struggles in America* (1903) and his discussion of the "agrarian question" in *The American Farmer* (1902) provided the foundations for the Socialist Party of America's much broader discussion and interpretation of American conditions. The company issued a fairly sizable list of his pamphlets. The works touched on a broad range of issues and had such titles as *Single Tax versus Socialism* (1899), *Anarchism and Socialism* (1901), *The Economic Foundations of Art* (1903), *Compensation* (1904), and *Labor Politics* (1904). Simons's exposé of conditions in the meatpacking industry, *Packingtown* (1899), became the basis for Upton Sinclair's exploration of that industry immortalized in the pages of *The Jungle*.[43]

Busy as he was with the day-to-day operation of the company, Kerr found time to write an occasional pamphlet or article for Chicago's socialist press. In 1899 he compiled a collection of *Socialist Songs*. Updated and revised in several editions and eventually released with accompanying sheet music, the collection included several adaptations of tunes already popular in the international movement. The first edition, for example, borrowed several tunes from the English socialist Edward Carpenter's *Chants of Labor*, originally published by Swann, Sonnenschein. Kerr wrote the lyrics for several songs and translated the words to "Internationale," the anthem of the socialist movement, from the original French lyrics by Eugene Pottier.[44]

Several pamphlets and a scattering of newspaper columns written by Kerr remain from his early socialist years and offer a rare glimpse into his developing political perspectives. He viewed himself not so much an original theorist but as a popularizer of socialist thought. He wanted "to put the accepted ideas of Socialism into such shape as to be easily understood."[45] The products of a thinker in transition, his writing varied in quality. Some of his earliest turn-of-the-century socialist essays displayed clear insights, whereas others consisted of overly simplified assertions. All contained a developed critique of the dominant institutions in American society—the schools, the church, the courts, the mass media, and marriage and the family. His critique of such institutions focused upon their role in reproducing the ideas and values that shaped social practices, the behaviors that maintained and legitimized the existing order.

Morals and Socialism (1899) put forward the instrumentalist class analysis and deterministic projection of an inevitable future society that were common elements of socialist thought during the period. Written "for the working men and working women who are outside the church," Kerr's polemic surveyed the class-based nature and historical development of notions of right and wrong from the period of "primitive communism" to the modern era. He argued that "in any state of society, the commonly accepted idea of moral or right conduct is such conduct as tends to increase the happiness and well-being of the ruling class."[46] He also noted that different kinds of proscribed or "proper" behavior existed for different classes:

> A good member of the ruling class is one who refrains from any unusually oppressive acts against his workmen that would incite them to revolt. . . . A bad capitalist is one who foolishly treats his laborers in a way that makes them rebel, or who makes a vulgar display of his wealth such as might excite discontent among those who would like to do the same thing, but cannot.
>
> A good workingman in America to-day is one who puts the most intense energy into his work for his employer's benefit, refrains from the use of beverages that might make his labor less efficient, begets and cares for enough children to keep up the supply of future laborers . . . and, last, but not least, always votes for the political party of his employer. A bad workingman is one who shows any marked interest in higher wages or shorter hours; a 'walking delegate,' who aims to unite his fellows in a better conditions, is only another name for a dangerous criminal.[47]

How did the ideas of the ruling class acquire such power and authority? How did they come to permeate society at large and gain acceptance as natural? Kerr again argued that such ideological dominance extended through the control of major institutions: "The means employed by the capitalists to impose false moral ideas on the people . . . are the same in all countries." And what were the dominant institutions of class rule? Kerr

pointed to several: "the church, the schools, the personal influence of capitalists and their hirelings, and especially books and newspapers" and "the
law, with its judges and soldiers."[48]

Morals and Socialism demonstrates the ideological distance that Kerr
had traversed since his days as a Unitarian activist. His discussion of the
origin of "false moral ideas" extended into realms of thought that he once
held dear. Long a student of evolutionist ideas, he could now note that
"within the last twenty five years the general acceptance of the evolution
theory has weakened the popular faith in heaven and hell, and the shrewder
minds of the capitalist class long ago perceived that some more efficient
means must be employed to keep the workers in subjection. With their
usual tact and promptness they redoubled their activity in moulding for
their own objects one of the strongest of all forces—PUBLIC OPINION."[49]

He further argued that "if we accept the moral standards that we find
around us, we are riveting our own fetters." Nevertheless optimistic, he
closed his analysis with a projection based on his reading of existent conditions. He seemed confident of the arrival of a new era, an inevitable new
dawn seemingly visible on the horizon. He also seemed to have a newly
invigorated sense of mission: "In the better social order that is coming, that
action will be right which is for the good of all. In the battle that is raging,
the right action for every worker and lover of justice is to do his full part,
no matter at what temporary loss, to spread the light, to marshal the army,
to shatter the last fortress of oppression and establish the reign of Liberty
over the earth."[50]

In *The Folly of Being "Good"* (1901), Kerr continued his Marxian critique
of existing institutions—church, school, and the establishment press. The
pamphlet equated the behavior of the good slave with that of the good
dog that does as his master wishes. While noting that the forms of slavery
had changed with the ascendancy of wage labor, Kerr argued that the
present masters could never rule if they relied merely on force. Never
dependent solely on the threat of force and coercion, the modern ruling
class controlled "most of the places from which most of the people get their
ideas" in order to keep nine-tenths of the population in line. Control of
such institutions meant that the new rulers and their "well paid upper
servants, . . . can and do make people think that to act in the way that is
best for their masters is 'good' and that to act in the way that is best for
themselves is 'bad.'"[51]

From 1900 on, Kerr issued yearly catalogs entitled *What to Read on
Socialism*. Each of these annuals, an annotated description of the company's offerings, also contained an introductory essay written by the publisher

on the fundamentals of Marxian thought or some similar text. Aimed primarily at the uninitiated, those essays reveal a great deal about Kerr's early Marxism.

In "The Central Thing in Socialism," for example, Kerr defined socialism as the "movement of the working class of the world toward freedom and toward better conditions of life, to be obtained by gaining control of the powers of government, which have thus far been used in the interest of the capitalist class." He also described some of the concepts key to some understanding of Marxian theory. In his attempt to simplify basics for the novice, he suggested that the definition of "historical materialism, . . . might be stated in words of one syllable by adding a word or two to an advertising catch-phrase, so as to read: Tell me HOW YOU GET what you eat and I will tell you what you are." In Kerr's understanding, "The laws and customs of a people in any stage whatever, from the earliest times to the present, grow out of the way in which the people get their food, clothing and shelter." He explained the historical origin of class struggle in the relationship of different social classes to the means of production during a particular period. He also touched on the need for a socialist party to wrest control of the state from the hands of the wealthy. The pamphlet traced the origin of the ideas that shaped social behavior and the practices that maintained the system.[52]

The company had distributed more than 125,000 copies of *What to Read on Socialism* by 1906. Regularly revised, Kerr's introductory essay in that catalog displays a growth and development in analysis and political sophistication. Some of his earlier expositions had smacked of overly simplistic economic reductionism, but by 1906 he could clearly and accurately describe the basics of Marxian analysis void of simplified arguments. Using a clear, precise language aimed at American workers he could comfortably write about the theory of surplus value (absent in his earlier writings), the tendency toward monopoly and trusts, the nature of the capitalist state, and the necessity of socialism.

Kerr wrote a lengthy statement of his socialist views in the 1907 pamphlet titled *What Socialists Think*. The thirty-two-page tract, one of the Pocket Library of Socialism series, clearly enunciated his Marxian perspectives on a number of political and social questions. Another primer written for those unacquainted with scientific socialism, the pamphlet remains the clearest statement of Kerr's views during his company's first socialist phase.

Following a brief exposition of the concepts of historical materialism, the theory of surplus value, and the origins of class struggle, *What Socialists Think* addressed a number of questions commonly raised by socialism's opponents. Primarily, Kerr argued that American society had reached a point of division between two social classes, the "hand workers" and "brain workers," the producers of all wealth, on one side arrayed against those "who live by owning" and "those who can be fooled, or bribed, into voting against the interest of the class to which they really belong," on the other. He viewed the socialist cooperative commonwealth as the logical and inevitable outcome of the class struggle between those two classes. He defined the approaching society as one "in which the good things of life shall not be produced for the profit of a part of the people, but for the use of all the people, . . . where no one who is able to work shall have the privilege of living on the labor of others."[53]

Written to dispel a number of commonly held misconceptions or apprehensions about the intent of the socialist movement, the pamphlet continually cautioned the reader. Kerr, for example, clearly defined his socialist understanding of equality:

> When I say equality, I do not mean that all the money or all the wealth of the country will be "divided up." That is something never advocated by a Socialist. It is one of the ridiculous lies told by our opponents to scare the laborer. . . .
>
> No, we don't need the money nor the houses nor the automobiles that the capitalists, or those who imagine themselves capitalists, have to-day. We want the use of the earth and of the machinery, and our labor will every year produce all the good things we need.[54]

What would the socialists do if they won state power? Although declining to venture a blueprint for future society, Kerr "thought it pretty safe" to offer some predictions about the initial actions of a socialist administration:

> It would stop paying rent, interest, and dividends to capitalists.
>
> It would take the children out of the factories and send them to school, and would at least double the force of teachers within a short time.
>
> It would give at once the least-skilled laborers enough of the comforts of life in return for their labor to let them live like human beings.
>
> It would at once reduce the hours of labor to no more than eight. . . .
>
> It would, no matter whether "money" were continued or abolished, sell the products of labor back to the laborers at actual cost, allowing for a percentage to pay for public services, furnished free, which would take the place of taxes.[55]

The "coming nation," in Kerr's vision, would be decentralized with control left "in the hands of the smallest group that can manage things efficiently." The new order "would not take away the artist's brushes, nor

the farmer's little farm." The socialists would not attempt to control people's actions; Kerr espoused the belief that "when everyone has an equal
chance to earn a living there will be little temptation to steal." With the
arrival of a socialist state, a "few policemen" would be maintained "for a
few years" to look after "those whose lives have already been wrecked
by capitalism," but the state would not be concerned with individual behavior or morality:

> When alcoholic drinks are no longer sold for profit, when cheating is no
> longer the road to social prominence, when every woman can be sure of a
> living without selling herself—then we may safely leave all questions of
> morals to the individual, while society attends to the production of the things
> people need. . . . [Socialists] do not want to do away with the freedom of
> the individual. On the contrary, they realize that to-day it is only a few here
> and there who have any freedom worth speaking of. What they mean to do
> is to make individual freedom a real thing for all.[56]

Kerr addressed the difficult question of state power and how the socialists meant to attain it: The Socialist Party stood for revolution. The
distinction between reform and revolution lay not in the use or absten-
tion of force or violence, but in the nature of class relations and social
power. The question of revolutionary means was one of practicality and
effectiveness; politics, after all, was the art of the possible. The pamphlet
defined reform as a "change in the laws or the way of enforcing the laws,
brought about by the same class that has all the time been in control."
Revolution signified the overthrow and replacement of the dominant class.
Kerr argued that socialism through piecemeal reform, "working 'for one
thing at a time,' and bidding for the votes of people who have no idea what
the class struggle means," was a "dead failure." One merely had to look at
the failures of populism and Bryanism for proof. Yet armed insurrection
was also impossible because "the capitalists to-day control the machine
guns that could in a few hours slaughter the revolutionary workers in any
of our cities."[57]

The answer lay in parliamentary political action through the ballot box,
a vote for the Socialist Party: "Elect Socialist legislators, and the laws will
be made in the interest of the laborers. Elect Socialist judges, and the injunctions will be issued to help the workers instead of the employers. Elect
Socialist Mayors, Governors and Presidents, and the policemen and soldiers will be at the disposal of the new ruling class, the working class, while
the capitalist will cease to exist as a capitalist, and will go to work so that
he can go on eating." The party, although not reformist in intent, also stood

for "every measure that may be for the immediate interest of the workers": the prohibition of child labor, shorter hours and higher wages, old-age pensions and insurance, public ownership of railways and streetcars "under working class control," the referendum, initiative and recall, and woman's suffrage.[58]

A rationalist faith in the liberatory power of education and the uplifting potential of the printed word remained key. Typical of the majority of socialists in that first decade of the century, Kerr placed his hope for a brighter future in the effectiveness of an informed, class-conscious, and politicized electorate. The route to political power lay in the study and application of scientific socialism. And there could be no educated socialists without socialist books. The key that would unlock the door to the cooperative commonwealth lay hidden in the pages published by Charles H. Kerr & Company.

As much the activist as her husband, May Walden Kerr's political development blossomed during those early years of the century. She made a series of insightful contributions to the expanding list of pamphlets issued by the company and also contributed occasional articles to the socialist periodical press. As a socialist speaker and polemicist, clearly a student of the "materialist conception of history," her primary interest centered on the role and status of women in society and the developing socialist movement.[59] She readily linked the oppression of women to an economic basis. For her, the emancipation of women could only truly take place under socialism. Speaking to America's working-class women in *Woman and Socialism* (1900), she argued that "the freedom that we crave, and which we must have, is economic freedom. We working people are all slaves, and women are in greater slavery than men, for we are slaves politically, economically and socially."[60] Her developing critique of capitalist society wedded the social subordination of women to a material basis embedded in the definition of private property defined juridically and politically by dominant males:

> Women are slaves socially because they cannot do as they choose in society. We are slaves to custom and to public opinion. We marry to get a home and we stay in it because we consider ourselves the possession of the men who furnish our food and clothes. We bring unwelcome children into the world because we are sex slaves. We dare not maintain the right to our own bodies because we have taken a vow to obey our husbands and to cleave to them until death. . . . It is only in a state of society where woman is looked upon as the private property of man, that such perversions of woman's nature can be found; the prostitute, the childless woman, and the worn-out, over-burdened mother."[61]

The most insightful passages of May Walden Kerr's *Socialism and the Home* (1901) assailed the bourgeois notion of fashion as a form of oppression imposed upon working women. Her exposition of the relationship between class exploitation and gender oppression suggested that "chasing after the fashion is one of the best evidences of the class struggle that women have. . . . As soon as a fashion is taken up by the lower classes, the upper classes change for something new. . . . Trailing skirts, pointed shoes, a pinched-up waist, and anything that keeps a woman from doing free, active, healthy work is a sign of leisure, dependence and inactivity; hence these are adopted by ladies of the upper class." She called for an emancipation from the vagaries and demands of bourgeois fashion:

> Accept the mark of your class, dear worker, and refuse to follow a fashion which is unhealthful, ungraceful, and a badge of indolence. It is not possible for any woman to be thoroughly healthy unless her body in all its parts is fully developed and so clothed that she may get about with the same freedom as a man. . . . A woman who has not freed herself from these marks of indolence and frivolity can have no idea of the independence, exhilaration and energy of mind and body that come from adopting a rational mode of dress.[62]

May Walden Kerr shared the overall socialist views of her counterparts. She believed the cooperative commonwealth was just around the corner. "Socialism," she could confidently proclaim in 1901, "is not a theory, it is the next stage in the development of society."[63] She readily pitched in to speed the arrival of the socialist epoch through work as a columnist for the socialist press in Chicago and elsewhere and as an activist stump speaker and organizer for the Socialist Party of Illinois.[64]

May Walden and Charles Kerr were divorced in 1904. The underlying tensions of their marriage and the exact reasons for their estrangement remain unclear. In part, the rift had to do with his absorption with the publishing house, a preoccupation that took the form of an obsession at times. Readily willing to sacrifice every penny for the continued operation of the company, he expected his wife and daughter to follow suit and do without on occasion. That in itself placed a strain on the relationship. In some ironic manner, meanwhile, the Kerrs' developing political and social critiques also took a toll. Both had developed analyses of marriage as a relationship based in property rights and the relegated inferiority of women. Whatever the specifics, clearly all was not well between them, and they reached a point where their marriage was untenable.

Their break coincided with the 1904 Socialist Party National Convention held at Chicago's Brand Hall. During the opening day of that conference, May Walden Kerr was introduced to another socialist woman as "Mrs. Charles Kerr." The other woman responded that "it couldn't be;" she "had just met 'Mrs. Kerr'" (apparently Kerr Company associate Mary Marcy) "in Mr. Kerr's office." The incident set off a minor scandal among the women at the convention. May Walden Kerr nevertheless maintained her composure and refused to allow her personal feelings to interfere with political principle. She went on to side with the same faction as her husband on a number of votes on key issues, to the chagrin of some of the women present.[65]

Kerr took up permanent residence in Chicago. May Walden Kerr received the house in Glen Ellyn and Kerr's agreement to assist with daughter Katharine's support. The couple, she recalled, wept upon parting.[66] She remained in the Chicago area through 1913, where she continued on as an activist for the Illinois Socialist Party. A regular stump speaker and contributor to the party press, she also worked on such projects as the Political Refugee Defense League, a group that assisted exiles fleeing political repression in Mexico. Following two lengthy speaking tours throughout central and southern Illinois in the spring and fall of 1913, she left Chicago for the last time that December and returned south to aid her ailing mother in Highlands, North Carolina. She and her mother subsequently moved to Florida, where she remained until she died in 1956.[67] Kerr, single once again, turned all his energies to the remaining constants in his life, the publishing house that bore his name and the movement it served.

Kerr's activity on behalf of the socialist cause regularly extended beyond the confines of the company offices during its early socialist years. His continuing interest in the creation of alternative socialist institutions often carried him far afield within Chicago's growing socialist circles. He had served on the National Campaign Committee of the Social Democratic Party, and with the founding of the Socialist Party of America in 1901 he became a member of Local Chicago's executive committee and served briefly as treasurer. He became secretary of the Socialist Party of Illinois in 1902.[68]

In tandem with his party work and frenetic activity at the company offices, Kerr also found time to design and implement plans for a consumers' cooperative located at the "Socialist Temple," a renovated church on Chicago's Western Avenue. Impressed by the success of similar ventures abroad, especially in Belgium, Kerr's plan for the Socialist Co-operative attempted to create the foundations for a network of alternative institutions. Groceries and coal would be sold at normal retail prices, with profits

divided quarterly. One-eighth of any profit would go toward the production of socialist propaganda, and an additional eighth would go into a reserve fund. Members would receive the remainder in the form of a rebate
based on individual purchases. Perhaps overly optimistic, Kerr viewed the
experiment as the hub of a national network of socialist-run projects.[69]

The emphasis on educational work, especially alternative education to
free the worker's mind, remained central to Kerr's thinking throughout the
period. In 1903 he and the Simonses became involved in a significant if
short-lived experiment in socialist education, the Ruskin College in Glen
Ellyn. The school evolved out of a series of previous attempts at alternative education that extended back into the nineteenth century. In 1899
two of Kerr's early socialist acquaintances, George McAnelly Miller and
Walter Thomas Mills, had founded a cooperative colony at Trenton, Missouri.[70] Miller subsequently joined the faculty of the poverty-stricken
Avalon College in Trenton, where he developed a curriculum, an "industrial plan" that allowed students to work their way through school by par-
ticipating in a series of cooperative industries and agricultural enterprises.
He procured the services of George D. Herron, the noted Christian socialist, and Frank Parsons, a progressive municipal reformer, to teach during
the summer session of 1900.[71] That same summer Miller joined forces with
the noted progressive reformer Walter Vrooman. Vrooman had just returned from London, where he had been a co-founder, along with the
American historian Charles Beard, of Ruskin Hall, a "labor college" created to train working-class leaders. When Vrooman learned of Miller's plans
for a similar project in Missouri, the two joined forces in September 1900,
and Avalon College became Ruskin College.[72]

In April 1903 the school moved lock, stock, and barrel to Glen Ellyn
after Miller had struck a deal with Thomas Edie Hill to rent several build-
ings, including Hill's once glorious Hotel Glen Ellyn, to the college. Both
May Wood and Algie Simons joined the faculty and began teaching courses
in history and economics from a socialist perspective. Kerr endorsed the
college as a school "to which Socialist parents can send their sons and
daughters from fourteen years up, with the assurance that their minds will
not be perverted by the capitalistic atmosphere such as surrounds most
colleges." He helped subsidize the operation by offering company books
and pamphlets at cost to enrolled students. The Kerrs and the Simonses
also helped launch a Glen Ellyn local of the Socialist Party to give the students some footing in the real political world.[73]

A clear experiment in socialist education, Ruskin College's stated purpose was "to bring within the reach of every young man and young wom-

an the advantages of a college education of the most practical sort; to teach the dignity of honest labor, not as a means of livelihood only, but as the glad expression of normal life . . . in order to prepare the student to aid intelligently in bringing in a more just and noble social state." In addition to standard instruction in French, Latin, German, English composition, rhetoric, and oratory, the curriculum included a course of study in "Industrial Arts and Sciences"—instruction in "mechanical arts" and the "use of tools" for men and cooking, sewing, and laundering for women. Courses in the social sciences included ancient, medieval, modern, and American history, civics, and economics. The school also offered a full list of courses in the natural sciences. Tuition cost $10 per ten-week session, with an additional $2.50 per week room and board. Students received the option to attend on a kind of work-study, self-help plan in which the value of labor done for the college or for individuals in and around Glen Ellyn was subtracted from school expenses. The school offered correspondence courses as well as on-site instruction. Regular enrollment had reached 2,500 by April 1903, and an additional eight thousand students took courses through the mail.[74]

Charles H. Kerr & Company progressed slowly through those first years of the century. Kerr continually had to face the publisher's dilemmas that had haunted him earlier and would continue to challenge his ingenuity and creativity for as long as he remained in the trade. He had to sell his publications and do so in a manner that allowed for some margin of profit in order to meet expenses and expand. But Kerr did not remain in the publishing business merely to sell books. His commitment to the socialist cause meant that political considerations took precedence over—and shaped—business concerns. Guided primarily by his desire to help bring socialism to American workers, he perpetually sought the means to produce imprints at an affordable price and make them accessible to workers. Inexpensive prices, the sale of socialist materials at or near cost, became a key political objective. As Kerr stated it, "The object of the company is to circulate the literature of CLEAR SOCIALISM IN CLEAR ENGLISH. Not merely the amount, but the quality of the Socialist literature that is circulated will determine the growth of the movement."[75]

In an ongoing quest for the mechanisms that would enable the company to flourish and still maintain proclaimed ideals and goals, Kerr continually experimented with alternative methods of book publishing and marketing. Between 1899 and 1907 he refined a system, unique to his firm, that allowed it to become the foremost socialist publisher of the era. Lack of operating capital imposed ongoing constraint on what was possible. Bank loans were available, but as Kerr developed politically he became more and more wary of the problems inherent in a dependence on large financial institutions, such as a possible loss of independence during economic hard times and the difficulties inherent in borrowing money from those who found socialism antithetical to their interests. He also viewed the percentage points paid as interest to lenders as an additional loss of investment capital. In Kerr's mind, fiscal independence and political autonomy went hand in hand.

The company had been incorporated in 1893 with an authorized capital of $10,000 divided into one thousand $10 dollar shares. In place of dividends on his stock, Kerr extended book discounts to investors. The sale of shares progressed slowly in those years, and the firm became dependent on small loans from banks and personal acquaintances and the extension of credit from printers. "Socialist" after 1899, the operation nevertheless maintained the debt incurred in the preceding period. Retirement of that debt became a top priority. As Kerr put it, "To get the company out of debt is the first concern. As long as any money is owing to non-socialists, the danger remains that in a time of industrial crisis, the creditors may act for the capitalist class as a whole in suppressing the socialist publishing house."[76]

In a quest for freedom from the demands and dictates of financial capital, Kerr turned to the socialist movement for investors. Political realities and considerations, however, created an additional set of concerns and constraints. Aware of earlier sectarian disputes and power struggles within the movement, Kerr found a debt owed to socialists even more undesirable than one owed a bank because "in the event of any acute disturbance over questions of party policy, the heavier creditors might bring pressure to bear to throw the influence of the publishing house on the side of one particular faction."[77] Retirement of the debt, dependent on the sale of company shares and inhibited by the fact that *ISR* continued to run in the red, proceeded slowly.

Until Kerr began to limit the sale of shares to one per investor, some individuals purchased small blocks of stock. Well aware of the differing factions within the socialist movement, he had become concerned that a consolidation of shares in the hands of a few investors who had an opposing political perspective might inhibit or endanger the mission of the company. When possible, he also bought back and resold stock from those who had purchased additional shares earlier. He explained that "it is best to keep the control as widely scattered among the socialists of America as possible. . . . Every share subscribed . . . will make it less and less possible for any individual in any future situation that may ever arise to use the re-sources of this publishing house in any other way than to promote the cause of international socialism."[79]

Kerr soon developed his own particular business strategy, a blueprint designed not solely to pay expenses but also to reduce the prices proffered his patrons. "Co-operation in publishing" became the key to success as Kerr met expenses with hundreds of investments in $10 shares from individuals and a growing number of Socialist Party locals.

Each publication involved three sets of fixed costs. The primary expense involved the fees paid to pressmen, binders, and paper dealers. A second fixed cost centered around the marketing of a work: advertising and correspondence, packaging, and postage. The production of electrotype plates entailed an additional major levy. Electrotyping was a costly process; it often entailed between one-quarter and one-third of the price for the first edition of an average-sized book. Normally, publishers passed the cost of plates on to the consumer. Kerr, however, used the funds procured through stock sales (and occasional assistance from friends and colleagues) to pay for electroplates. In this manner he was able to minimize the per-volume cost of company imprints and pass the savings on to patrons. The plates, once produced, could be used repeatedly to reprint new copies of a particular work. The amount of fixed cost per volume therefore declined with each successive printing.

Stock sales proceeded slowly, however. The amounts coming in through 1902 allowed the company to issue new imprints but not pay off a standing debt owed to the bank. In response, Kerr appealed to sympathetic socialists for additional loans. He took money, borrowed long-term at 6 percent, from movement activists to pay off 7 percent loans at the bank. In the meantime, he and Simons deferred any salary payments while the search for a more viable economic plan continued.

In September 1902 Kerr announced a new strategy to help promote the sale of shares. Previously, only those who had $10 to invest could purchase a share. He now began to offer shares on an "installment plan": $1 down and $1 a month. The number of shareholders increased over the next few months, and the company began paying expenses. By February 1903 Kerr announced that "the co-operative publishing house . . . has now passed the hardest stage of slow beginnings and has entered upon a period of rapid growth." That April he informed readers that the company was "now on a self-sustaining basis, every dollar of new capital goes not to make up deficits but to increase the variety of literature offered to American Socialists." Twenty-five shareholders a month began to come in by July 1903; by

December of that year Kerr could proudly announce that "our cooperative plan for supplying socialist books at cost has passed the stage of experiment. It has proved a complete success." With 750 shareholders by the
end of 1903, he noted that "we are thus able to find an immediate sale for
any new socialist book that is worth reading while we can safely let alone
such books as we believe are not worth reading." A vote of the shareholders authorized the issuance of an additional four thousand shares in January 1904.[79]

As the number of shareholders increased, Kerr found himself able to
anticipate or project the distribution and sales for a particular item. He
worked to create a secure market—a captive audience. Mass distribution
and high sales volume as well as a continued increase in the number of
shareholders became the keys to lower prices. Kerr continually experimented with a number of marketing strategies to help attract new customers.
Although they varied over time, each strategy appealed to the political
commitments of avowed socialists and socialist sympathizers. The health
and viability of the company became tied inextricably to the political
growth and vitality of the socialist movement and its organizational form,
the Socialist Party of America. Charles Kerr understood this better than
anyone. His promotionals for the company never separated the two.

Finances had genuinely improved, but all was not perfect. *ISR*, politically important as a theoretical sounding board and educational vehicle
for the movement, continued to lose money. Kerr initially planned to use
any income from the monthly and ongoing book sales to cover the daily
operating expenses of the company and use revenue from stock sales solely
to cover the cost of new imprints. But newsstand sales and subscriptions
lagged, and the journal began to drain much-needed revenue from the
firm's already taxed coffers. A marked increase in subscribed readership
became crucial, not only for the continuance of *ISR* itself but also for the
survival of the company.

Convinced that it could pay for itself as well as bring in additional revenue, Kerr poured his energies into a variety of experiments designed to
make *ISR* economically sound. He financially separated the journal from
the book and pamphlet operation. He still used discounts on his list of
publications as premiums to new subscribers, but he refused to draw on
the revenues of the firm to help defray the cost of the monthly. In February 1903 he initiated the promotional sale of "Subscription Post Cards,"
redeemable for new subscriptions to *ISR*. Offered for 25 cents to anyone
purchasing at least $1 worth of books at retail prices or to anyone purchas-
ing at least four at a time, the cards entitled the holder to a yearly *ISR*

subscription at a considerable discount. Not valid for those who had received the monthly previously or currently were doing so, the introduction of the card system stimulated sales.[80]

As a result of the new promotional, *ISR*'s financial situation improved gradually but still remained problematic. Monthly circulation was only six thousand by the end of its fourth year, and the journal still carried an annual deficit of $1,000. Some readers suggested an increase in price as a solution to the problem. Kerr dismissed the idea, however, because "we are convinced that a willingness to read and study the literature of real scientific socialism does not necessarily go along with the ability to pay high prices."[81] The *Review*'s circulation received a boost in June 1905 with the acquisition of the subscription list of *The Comrade*, a short-lived (1901–5) illustrated socialist monthly from New York edited by John Spargo.[82]

Kerr & Company continued to develop. The firm's catalog of 1904 could proudly boast of more than 180 separate titles by some 117 different authors. The list contained numerous short tracts and pamphlets that sold for as little as 2 to 5 cents apiece. It also included a sizable number of larger works of one or more volumes in length, issued in both paper and cloth editions, which sold for from $1 to $2. In addition to the ever-increasing number of socialist standards imported from Europe, the catalog also promoted a collection of poems by Walt Whitman and an edition of Plato's *Republic* translated from the classical Greek by Alexander Kerr. The 1904 list offered four titles by the noted attorney Clarence Darrow, including his *Crime and Criminals*, an address delivered to the prisoners of Cook County Jail. The catalog that election year also promoted an inventory of "socialist propaganda supplies," including "official Socialist Party design emblem buttons in celluloid or gold plate and enamel," "socialist stickers, eight kinds equally assorted," and a run of four-page leaflets written by Kerr and Algie Simons and designed specifically as propaganda for street speaking engagements.[83]

The list of U.S. authors improved both quantitatively and qualitatively throughout the decade. By the end of 1907 and the close of the company's first socialist phase it comprised a who's who of Debsian-era socialism. *ISR* published contributions by virtually every important source of social and political opinion within the movement. The Kerr press, in the meantime, poured forth an endless stream of pamphlets, tracts, and monographs by a host of theorists and propagandists, including Debs, Herron, Spargo, Jack London, and Mother Jones. The Kerr lists by 1907 also included many works by lesser known but nevertheless influential activist authors who wrote on a diverse range of social and political issues. Catalogs for those years included titles by naturalist J. Howard Moore, novelist Edwin Brenholtz, the former Unitarian minister and socialist William Thurston Brown, and such left-wing theoreticians as Austin M. Lewis, Oscar Lovell Triggs, Robert Rives LaMonte, and Charles H. Vail.[84]

Perhaps the most significant addition to the Kerr lists by an author on the U.S. side of the Atlantic during those early years of the socialist Kerr Company was Louis Boudin's *The Theoretical System of Karl Marx*. An exposition of the importance of Marx's contribution to both political economy and philosophy, Boudin's discussion eventually received recognition as the one major contribution to the canon of Marxian thought produced by an American author during the Second International. Noted for its cogent refutation of Marx's critics and its discussion of the theories of economic crisis, the book was one of the first to bring its author and publisher attention abroad.[85]

Born in 1874 the son of a Russian-Jewish shirtmaker, Boudin emigrated to New York as a teenager. A worker in New York's needle trades, he put himself through Columbia University Law School and became a labor lawyer. A socialist from his early years, he served on the national executive board of the Socialist Trades and Labor Alliance in 1898–99. He joined the Socialist Party at its founding and was a delegate to the International Socialist Congress in Stuttgart in 1907 and in Copenhagen in 1910. His *Theoretical System* first appeared as a series of monthly articles in *International Socialist Review* beginning in May 1905. Kerr requested that the series be compiled and revised but asked that the term *theoretical* be omitted from the title to enable the book to break even financially. Published in 1907 with the original title intact, the resultant monograph received its most favorable reception in Germany, where Luisa Kautsky, wife of the German socialist party leader Karl Kautsky, translated it. It soon passed into several foreign-language editions. Boudin subsequently became the American correspondent for Kautsky's *Die Neue Zeit* and an important voice in the left-wing of the American movement during the turbulent World War I period.[86]

Significantly, the general economic state of the company ebbed and flowed with the fortunes of the Socialist Party from 1901 on. Most new stock subscribers took advantage of the dollar-a-month plan, which meant that the amount of capital on hand was never great. With the opening of the presidential campaign of 1904 and its related demand for an increase in socialist propaganda, Kerr once again borrowed funds. The company at the same time owed Kerr personally an amount in excess of $8,000. Realizing perhaps that he would never see the money, he offered to deduct an equal amount from that due him for each sum donated to the company's election "propaganda fund."[87] Contributions came in, and Kerr began to promote the idea of a debt retirement fund based on appeals to socialist movement activists: "America is ripe for socialism. Whether genuine international socialism is to come at once to the front or whether we are to have a long and painful siege of opportunism, depends largely on the amount and kind of socialist literature circulated in the near future, and this again depends to a very considerable extent on the financial position of this publishing house. . . . Comrades, it rests with you to say whether the growth of our work shall be rapid or slow."[88]

With the exception of several small notes to printers and binders and an obligation to a bank in Madison, Wisconsin, by January 1905 the debt retirement fund had assisted in paying off the amount owed to those who did not hold stock. With $1,600 still owed a socialist in Wyoming, Kerr extended the fund-raising drive through March with the hope of "stopping once and for all payment of our earnings to capitalists as interest."

The financial situation of the company stabilized by mid-1905. The autumn of that year found the publishing house "in better condition than ever before." The sale of books began to cover day-to-day operating expenses for the first time, and Kerr could proclaim in July that "our co-operative publishing house is no longer a mere experiment." Although early stockholders had made initial investments with the "even chance of seeing it lost," Kerr noted that they now had "the satisfaction of being joint owners in the largest and most successful socialist book publishing house in the United States, if not in the world." The combination of stock subscriptions and donations to the debt retirement fund finally succeeded. By the end of 1905 Kerr could inform readers that the company was "no longer in distress for money to pay debts."[89]

ISR's financial state remained problematic, however. Simons had to warn readers that the monthly's deficit had reached a crucial point. "It would be criminal and disgraceful to the American socialist movement" he suggested, "to permit the *Review* to stop." He went so far as to reproduce a letter from Eugene Debs that accompanied the socialist leader's renewed subscription and called for the monthly's support. A year later the book publishing end of the business had nearly doubled, but the status of *ISR* remained "one unsolved problem, . . . about as far as ever from paying expenses." In an attempt to stabilize the monthly's fiscal difficulties, in October 1906 Eugene Dietzgen, who had helped finance the Unterman translation of Marx's *Capital*, pledged a subsidy of $1,000 a year for 1907 and 1908. Kerr, at the same time, attributed *ISR*'s problems to the ill-founded "prevailing impression" that it was only for those who were "highly educated." He announced an effort to popularize the *Review* to bring it within reach "of anyone willing to study socialism."[90]

In the meantime, Kerr continued to experiment with premium offers in an attempt to improve sales. In February 1907 he announced the purchase of the inventory from the Standard Publishing Company (formerly the Debs Publishing Company) of Terre Haute: plates, copyrights, and imprints for a number of pamphlets. The advertising campaign he began the following month offered the newly acquired pamphlets and copies of the Pocket Library of Socialism as part of a combination offer for the *Review*. The premium promised sixty socialist pamphlets and a six-month subscription for $1. Revenue increased, but Kerr nevertheless had to recognize that he had been overly optimistic as receipts fell off again the following month.[91]

The company circulated more than $22,000 worth of books and pamphlets during 1907, an increase of more than $5,000 over the preceding year. Despite the continued scarcity of operating capital, Kerr finally found himself able to announce that the company had genuinely passed from the stage of "experimentation": "We no longer have to urge socialists to send us their money in the hope that possibly it may enable us to supply the socialist books that are needed. We have the books now, and our co-operative plan offers more of the best socialist books for a given amount of money than can possibly be obtained in any other way. . . . Without the work that we have done, few of the most important writings of European and American socialists could be bought by American workingmen."[92]

ISR still remained a problem, however. Eight years old, its circulation still hovered at a little more than four thousand. A series of dramatic changes already on the drawing board would soon transform the monthly. Relatively secure and optimistic despite a downturn in the economy that occurred during 1907, Charles H. Kerr & Company turned to the future.[93]

7

The Move Leftward, 1908–11

Charles H. Kerr & Company underwent a marked shift leftward within the American socialist movement after the dismissal of Algie Simons as editor of the *International Socialist Review* at the beginning of 1908. From that time forward, Kerr also moved further to the left. In doing so, he cordially extended the pages of his monthly to the more radical "impossibilist" or "revolutionist" elements in and outside the Socialist Party. *ISR* editorially moved toward an unflinching support of the direct actionist, industrial union wing of the movement and grew in popularity and circulation as a result. The newer books and pamphlets that the company issued likewise reflected its founder's politics. Kerr's newly vested partisanship and stake in the direction of the American movement in turn incurred the wrath and resentment of the movement's conservative, "gradualist" elements.

The particularities of Kerr's developing left-wing partisanship reflected the twists and turns of socialist political development during the course of the first decade of the century. It also grew out of an assessment of changing social and economic conditions in the United States, an evaluation of both capitalist development and the contours of the "class struggle." It also mirrored the increasing tensions within the Socialist Party of America (SP), the primary organizational and institutional expression of socialist politics of the era.

The Socialist Party, founded in 1901, arose as a response to the perceived and experienced abuses of the turn-of-the-century political economy: employers' unabashed use of force in labor disputes and the favoritism they often received from state and federal authorities and the courts. It developed out of an evolved analysis and detailed critique of the tendency toward monopoly: the development of the trusts in almost every walk of American economic life and the unrestrained concentration of wealth accrued by bank, railroad, and industrial titans. The party also grew out of an assessment of the failure of major national parties as vehicles for substantive change and an evaluation of their corruption or ineffectiveness at the state or local level. In part, the Socialist Party reflected an appraisal of the failures of previous radical reform initiatives, especially the Populist Party of the 1890s. The movement envisioned an approaching cooperative dawn and promised the restoration of truly republican virtues and the reinstitution of a popular democracy based upon values and institutions usurped and denigrated by big business and corrupt government.[1]

The Socialist Party made impressive strides in the United States during the few short years after its founding.[2] The idea of working-class emancipation based firmly on the scientific socialism of Marx and his followers had extended from its initial confinement and intellectual ghettoization in the scattered communities of European, mainly German, political émigrés to become an undisputed political force throughout the country.[3] The socialist message reached a cross-section that included not only immigrant and native-born industrial workers in the shops, mills, and foundries of the Northeast and the Ohio Valley but also struggling and dispossessed farmers and agricultural laborers on the Great Plains and in the Southwest.[4] It caught the imagination of timber workers in the Pacific Northwest and the northern woods of Michigan, Wisconsin, and Minnesota. It inspired miners in the hard metal mines of Idaho, Colorado, and Montana and the coal fields of Pennsylvania, West Virginia, Kentucky, and Illinois.

The party enjoyed continuous growth and established political bailiwicks in those areas of concentrated immigrant strength such as German Milwaukee or the Jewish Lower East Side of New York, as well as in Kansas, Oklahoma, and throughout the old Southwest. The movement attracted numerous indigenous radicals who had traveled the course of post–Civil War reform. As a representative catch-all for American dissent and radicalism after the turn of the century, the party also attracted and recruited a number of middle-class professionals—lawyers, doctors, journalists, and ministers—who had experienced the demise of populist hopes and the failures of Bryanite democracy. The young party also attracted its share of bohemians—intellectuals alienated from the demands of the new industrial order and horrified, to the point of rejection, by the system of privatized aggrandizement and widespread suffering.[5]

Such growth and diversity made members confident that their organization would soon emerge as the dominant force in American political life. They were also optimistic about the inevitable arrival of the cooperative commonwealth, and that optimism colored both long-term strategies and more immediate tactics. Social and geographic diversity also gave rise to differing priorities, interests, and short-term tactical goals. Much more a loose coalition than a centralized party, the Socialist Party encompassed varying constituencies that had different needs, demands, and perceptions on the question of reform, the meaning of revolution, the nature of the approaching socialist epoch, and a host of other issues.[6]

Differences gave rise to internal tensions from the start, and the tensions developed into various factions or blocs that reflected differing goals, aspirations, and perspectives. Always fluid, defined more by specific questions and immediate, often competitive, demands than by set dogma or static, intransigent belief, the factions (commonly categorized as left, center, and right) contended for influence and political hegemony within the movement. At the same time, a shared belief in the imminence of the "socialist epoch" added a sense of urgency to the disputes that vexed and ultimately fractured the movement.

As they evolved, the several factions paralleled and reflected developments and tensions within the broader international socialist movement. The right within the American Party often took its inspiration from, and closely followed the lead of, the right within German Social Democracy (SPD). Such figures as Milwaukee's Victor Berger avidly followed the ins and outs of the revisionist controversy that shook the German party and the Second International during the first decade of the century and openly supported the evolutionary socialism of Eduard Bernstein, which disavowed the class struggle and called for social peace and class collaboration.

Many in the center and right of the Socialist Party, for example, New York's Morris Hillquit, readily embraced the increasing reformism of Karl Kautsky and other SPD theoreticians and politicians who had a cautious approach to conservative elements within the trade union movement. Many Americans openly admired the increasing numerical strength of the SPD and its growth in membership and electoral strength. They overlooked or failed to consider its increasing dependency on voters who were not of the working class and the conservatizing effect inherent in the construction of a political apparatus geared to mainstream parliamentary competition and the range of related demands, restraints, and interests of a nascent bureaucracy. Elements within the Socialist Party's right and center enviously considered the German situation and pursued a similar parliamentary strategy that disavowed direct action, that is, any strategy or tactic outside the arena of established trade union struggle and electoral campaigns that might upset or alienate those necessary for success at the ballot box. Implicit in their assessments lay acceptance of the bourgeois order, an acquiescence in the very system they sought to overthrow.[7]

Their opponents on the left simultaneously looked to Europe for inspiration and affirmation of their perspectives and tactical approach. Advocates of industrial unionism, direct action, and strategies that incorporated mass political mobilization, the movement's left-wing observers monitored the progress of the British syndicalist movement and followed the activity of their well-known popular leader Tom Mann. They also closely watched the growth and development of French syndicalism, with its call for self-emancipation of the working class. In addition, never entirely opposed to electoral strategies, American left-wingers monitored European debates on the possibilities for, and the limitations of, reform. They observed the response of the left wing within the French movement and the Second International as a whole to *l'affaire Millerand* and debated the question of coalition government and the role of elected socialists in bourgeois parliaments and ministerial cabinets.[8]

Algie Simons and Charles Kerr, both very much abreast of developments in Europe and the United States, ultimately chose different sides on a number of key questions that confronted the movement. Several issues divided them. Much more the aspirant politician than Kerr and more concerned with the creation of a viable electoral base that could attract nonsocialist voters, Simons moved to the right on the issue of municipal reform and other gradualist questions.[9] Kerr, of course, was in no way opposed to electoral strategies as long as they held to Marxian principles. But he opposed any tactic or political stratagem that diluted the class-based message of socialist goals, muted the reality of the class struggle, or opened the door to class collaboration. Simons moved precisely in that direction.[10]

The key issue that forced a wedge between the two long-time allies had to do with differing conceptions of the role of the party in relation to the trade union movement's major organizational form, the American Federation of Labor (AFL), and the future of its proclaimed rival, the Industrial Workers of the World (IWW). The AFL was an outgrowth of the failure of attempts at mass unionism during the 1870s and 1880s. Based on the bargaining power of skilled workers divided into jurisdictions defined by particular craft rather than industry, the AFL developed a strategy of "pure and simple" trade unionism—winning economic concessions and

protecting privileged skilled-craft positions. The AFL leadership generally disavowed political unionism or any form of political action based on
an appeal to solidarity of the working class. Pragmatic or opportunist (depending on one's perspective), the national organization under Samuel
Gompers' leadership steered clear of any endorsement of a socialist or labor
party. Any such backing would have diminished the ability of the AFL to
pressure the political parties already in a position to help "deliver the
goods."

The conservative nature of the AFL created two opposing schools of
opinion within socialist circles. A sizable and influential minority of socialists within the AFL from its inception in 1890 had advocated the strategy
of "boring from within," the promotion and advocacy of socialist principles and politics and the election of socialist leadership in an ongoing attempt to win existing unions to the cause. In opposition stood the dual
unionists, who denounced the AFL as an essentially backward or reactionary force and deemed its conversion a hopeless task. They advocated the
creation of industrial unions open to all workers in an industry, regardless
of skill, as the only means to protect labor and the necessary vehicle for a
unified campaign against the capitalist system.

The two opposing outlooks reflected differing assessments of ongoing
changes in the nature of industrial work wrought by the ascendancy of
large-scale mass production that demanded a cheap, "unskilled" labor pool
and eroded skilled craft positions. They also reflected a difference of opinion over Gompers' willingness to negotiate union recognition and social
peace with employers at the expense of the unorganized and his open
participation in the National Civic Federation and other groupings that
argued for a community of interest and conflict resolution between labor
and capital.[11]

Shaped by those working conditions that often led to open conflict in
the extractive industries of the American West, the IWW provided national
organizational expression to the demand for a radical opposition to the
AFL. The newer organization developed as a direct response to the severity of life in the hard-metal mines and timber forests of the West. It also
evolved out of an assessment of the ineffectiveness of the AFL and its refusal to organize unskilled migrant laborers. The IWW was a social and
political expression of workers hardened by conflicts and, on occasion, open
warfare. It mirrored the total absence of a community of interest between
employer and employee in such places as Boise, Butte, and Cripple Creek.
A child of the militant, industrially organized Western Federation of Min-

ers (WFM), the IWW evolved out of the WFM leadership's call in 1905 to gather together representatives of all those political and trade union forces opposed to the conservative, exclusivist direction of the AFL.

Algie Simons attended the preliminary gatherings and helped write the call for the "Continental Congress of the Working Class" that gathered at Chicago's Brand Hall in June 1905 to launch the IWW.[12] He energetically endorsed the new organization's firm commitment to the tenets of the class struggle and proclaimed it as "a decisive turning point in American working class history."[13] But his initial enthusiasm waned rapidly. Simons soon withdrew from the organization, in part because of his animus toward the SLP's Daniel DeLeon and in part because of other political obligations, demands, and ambitions. He also became disillusioned with the IWW's drift toward an American syndicalism and distaste for electoral activity and union contracts. He did not attend the IWW's second convention in 1906.

Simons's prestige as a party intellectual had increased, in large part because of his work with Kerr. Influential in the Illinois party, he became editor of the ambitious *Chicago Daily Socialist* in October 1906. The paper, founded as a propaganda vehicle for the local Socialist Party election campaign that fall, clearly taxed his energies, and the number of his contributions to *ISR* fell off. The daily's differing operational and political demands also helped move its editor to the right. In the meantime, Simons became a member of the National Executive Committee of the Socialist Party, which he represented at the Stuttgart Congress to the Second International in 1907. He returned more impressed than ever by the reformism of the major European parties, and their increasing electoral success based on a close working alliance with the established trade unions. Simons especially admired the inroads made by the Labour Party in Britain. He made an about-face after returning from Europe. Once one of the AFL's bitterest foes and convinced that it could not be redeemed for the socialist cause, he now moved toward it in a quest for rapprochement and votes.[14]

Kerr's political thinking also was in transition. Already in the process of developing a more radical position, he clearly differed from Simons in regard to industrial unionism and the IWW by the end of 1907. He argued that the craft-union form of organization survived solely as the inadequate vestige of an earlier stage of capitalist development based on small-scale production. Unions based on industrywide organization were the logical outcome of large-scale production and concentration. Observing Chicago's organized labor movement, however, he noted the absence of industrial unions and the fact that most local socialists also belonged to established AFL affiliates. In opposition to conservatives to his right, who opposed the industrial form, and elements on the far left, who argued that socialist unionists should leave the AFL entirely to form dual unions, he suggested that socialists already in unions should continue to work to convince the rank and file of the need for conversion to industrywide organization and membership in the Socialist Party.[15]

Simons ended his *ISR* editorial column for January 1908 with a curt single sentence informing readers that the New Year's issue was his last. He had severed "all editorial connection" with the magazine but extended no explanation for his departure. Likewise silent about the reasons for Simons's exit, Kerr assumed editorial responsibility the following month. He merely informed readers that the *Review* would "as before treat all subjects from the view-point of international socialism." He then introduced his current associates on *ISR*: John Spargo, the well-known New York socialist who would soon make his own move to the right; the German émigré, Marxist theorist, and translator Ernest Unterman; Robert Rives LaMonte, the Connecticut-based left-wing author; and Max Hayes, editor of the *Cleveland Citizen*, member of the Typographical Union, and an influential voice within the AFL.[16]

In actuality, Simons's departure completed a widening breach between the two long-time associates. Kerr had asked him to resign. Both men had changed politically since they joined forces some nine years earlier and were part of the left wing of the party. Kerr remained there in 1908. In sympathy with the IWW, he opposed the more conservative socialist elements wedded solely to electoral strategies based on alliances with the AFL. Simons, now convinced of the evolutionary nature of socialism, continued to develop his affinity for the immediatist reform elements, the strict parliamentarians, within the party. As May Walden Kerr later recalled, "Simons became better situated and turned 'right' and Charles dismissed him and assumed the duties of the editor himself with the statement that he preferred to 'please the workers rather than the college professors.'"[17]

Kerr at the end of 1907 promised to improve the *Review* by "making it no less scientific, yet easier to understand for those comrades whom capitalism has defrauded of an education."[18] At the time of Simons's departure, however, he vowed to maintain the monthly as a vehicle for airing debates and theoretical disputes internal to the socialist movement. In response to criticism suggesting that the *Review* was no good for the uninitiated, Kerr pointed to the existence of "plenty of propaganda papers" created to "bring socialism to the unconverted." *ISR* would remain a vehicle for internal debates, "full discussions of questions on which socialists differ among themselves" not normally carried in the more popular socialist press.[19]

The form, content, and emphasis of the *Review* nevertheless did begin to change. A month after Simons's resignation, Kerr introduced a new feature, a monthly letters column called "News and Views" that actively solicited and encouraged comments and contributions from rank-and-file socialist readers.[20] He also began to use simple illustrations and shortened the length of the typical article. Circulation, which had languished at somewhere around its 1901 level of three thousand, began to shoot upward. It increased by 300 percent during the course of Kerr's first year at the helm and climbed to twenty-seven thousand by June 1910. It sold forty thousand by June of the following year and continued to grow in size and circulation.[21]

Kerr advanced an explanation for the seemingly inexplicable increase in interest. With an obvious allusion to Simons, he argued that *ISR* had functioned "for too long" on the "faulty assumption . . . that the problems of social evolution must be deliberated on in advance by a select few of superior brain power, who should later on diffuse the results of their deliberations among the common man." He had come to realize that "the ordinary working people have an instinctiveness of what is good for them that is more to be trusted than the most exquisite of theories." That understanding sparked a further transformation in the magazine's direction and scope.[22]

The style and format of the monthly under Simons's tenure had remained scholarly and dry, almost somber, and certainly of little interest to those unconcerned with the finer points of Marxian theory. Having seen a "new light," Kerr revamped the magazine to make it livelier and more attractive to grass-roots socialist readers. Spiced with illustrations, cartoons, and an occasional photograph, the monthly began to reach more movement activists than ever before. With circulation up by early 1910, the *Review* began to cover expenses for the first time. The increase in revenue enabled Kerr to increase the number of pages from sixty-four to eighty. That change created more and more space for the "news and views" of the movement's rank and file. It also provided room for advertisements, which brought in additional revenue.

Although carried out in part for financial reasons, the overhaul of *ISR* also signified something deeper in Kerr's political development. The opening of the monthly to rank-and-file expression represented a deepening commitment to the popular movement. Implicit in his decision was the understanding, present in Marx and often missed by many middle-class intellectuals who subsequently filtered into the socialist movement, that the working class would ultimately have to emancipate itself.

Under Simons's tenure *ISR* had attempted to remain neutral on the numerous political debates within the socialist movement. Its pages often aired various positions on a particular question and left ultimate political decisions to readers. The revamped magazine became more and more partisan. For instance, Kerr editorialized that the election results of 1908 were "a distinct encouragement to us of the 'left wing,' who prefer to say much of the class struggle and little of the 'immediate demands,' who think it is more important to awaken the wage workers to the fact that it is to their interest to destroy the whole capitalist system, than to agitate for municipal ownership, scientific reforestation and tax reforms." He began to advise readers on how to vote in party elections. Primarily educational and theoretical in its early years, *ISR* had become more political in the overt, active sense. So had its editor and publisher.[23]

The extent of Kerr's partisanship and the leftward movement of *ISR* and its parent company became clearer during the two years following Simons's departure. In August 1908, for example, Kerr published "Constructive Socialism," a scathing critique of reformism by Joseph Cohen, a Philadelphia left-winger. Cohen, later to become a close associate of Kerr & Company, castigated the "constructivist strategy" for "introducing the idea of 'evolution,' as against the Social Revolution."[24]

That same month Kerr editorially cautioned strict parliamentarians within the party that "to think . . . a big vote is in itself an important gain for the working class is childish." Capitalism was safe, he insisted, "as long as the mass of the workers are mainly concerned about finding and keeping jobs under capitalists." Arguing that the development of trusts had already made capitalism "superfluous" and "paved the way for collectivism," he also felt that neither capitalism nor socialism was "an automatic machine independent of people's feelings and wishes. . . . The workers will not take control of industry until they desire to do so, no matter how practicable it may seem in theory. Nor will it put them in control to elect a Socialist Party president by attracting votes of people who only want cheaper railway and telephone rates. There will be no revolution without revolutionists." Revolutionaries would arise out of "changes in the mode of production," informed and guided by necessary propaganda and continued education. Kerr suggested that the needed "methods of organization" would develop as more and more workers became conscious. The "real measure of success," rather than electoral strength, would be "the number of those who begin to understand what social evolution has in reserve for them . . . and who determine to get up and go after it." That editorial position, published in conjunction with Cohen's criticisms, provided the opening shot in a protracted polemical battle against the party's right.[25]

Slowly but surely, Kerr's politics continued to evolve. Reflecting on word of socialist unity in France, he stated a somewhat more consolidated left position in December 1908: "The conquest of political power is not an end in itself, but a means to the destruction of capitalism. The test of membership in the party should therefore turn to the desire to destroy capitalism rather than on an attachment to one particular weapon." His report of developments in the French movement argued that the ballot was still "the most available weapon" and that the French "comrades" had recognized that fact but refused to proscribe those who thought differently.[26]

That same month Kerr published an article by Tom Sladden, the left-wing secretary of the Oregon Socialist Party. Annoyed with the reform tendency in the party, "a 'spirit' manifest in all sections of the country" to conceal the "foundation stone" of "class struggle," Sladden defined the "true proletarian" as having "no profession, no trade, and no property. He has no home—nor country—no religion . . . , little education, no manners, and little care for what people think of him."[27] An obvious slap at the middle-class reform elements in the movement, such arguments did not set well with the right and center and raised increased concern about the direction of *ISR*. The article led to a reproach from the Wisconsin right-winger Carl D. Thompson.[28] That, in turn, gave rise to a searing rejoinder by the Pennsylvania coal miner Louis Duchez, an articulate industrial unionist.

Duchez's "The Proletarian Attitude" argued that the official party press and platform had become dominated by middle-class intellectuals who had "cast their lot with us by adoption." They had "brought with them soured bourgeois ideals": "The Socialist press and platform do not represent the interests of the revolutionary proletariat, strictly speaking. They represent the ideals of a radical bourgeois element, out of harmony with the established order of things." Because most of the movement's writers and speakers were intellectuals from the "bourgeois class," they appealed to the "type of mind from which they sprung" and spent too much time answering the objections "which they themselves raised before coming into the movement." The solution, for Duchez, was working-class leadership: "When proletarian thinkers get the reins of the socialist movement . . . , it will not waste its energy in answering bourgeois objections to socialism, exposing capitalist grafters or fighting for social and sexual freedom for women. It will then be absorbed in but one thing: the education of the workers to class consciousness and solidarity."[29]

In the meantime, "News and Views" had become a sounding board for revolutionists throughout the country. A letter appearing in June 1909 from left-winger Charles Kohler, for instance, suggested that educated and respectable socialists, although "well-meaning comrades," should be removed from positions of leadership. Speaking as a "true proletarian," he attacked the gradualist strategy of the constructivist wing:

> We do not want benevolent feudalism; we want socialism. We want to abolish the competitive system; we want to establish the Social Republic. We are not interested in "grafters," "Votes for Women," "Right to Work" and the rest of the nonsense that is heralded as "immediate demands." We have only one "immediate demand," and that is the abolition of capitalism. We proletarians have no time to waste on "Votes for Women," "3–cent fares," "right to work," etc. We do not care about the "Spiritual Significance of Socialism." . . . We want Socialism. If we can't get Socialism, then we will abolish the present "civilization" anyhow, for no matter what the result will be, we are positive that we shall get more rest than we do now. We won't have to slave at night by the aid of electricity, making "works of art" for a lot of vampires.[30]

Such arguments couched in such language obviously did not sit well with the gradualists, but they did reflect the direction in which Kerr was moving. Speaking candidly in the spring of 1909 for those opposed to the reformist, gradualist tendencies, he could argue that the function of the party was "to prepare for the revolution, by educating and organizing" and that "the quickest way to get reforms . . . is to make the revolutionary movement more and more a menace to capitalism." He noted that reformists, "opportunists" as he now termed them, held most official leadership positions. Nevertheless, he argued that "the great mass of city wage workers" remained untouched or effected by the "propaganda of opportunism. . . . when revolutionists shape the policy of the Socialist Party, reformers will find little in it to attract them." Openly opposed to the rightward drift of the party's National Executive Committee, Kerr also opposed the gradualist attempt, emanating from Victor Berger's organization in Milwaukee in the spring of 1909, to amend the election procedure for national party office.[31]

In July 1909 Kerr responded to a suggestion from the right to place the *New York Evening Call* and the *Chicago Daily Socialist* under the ownership and control of the National Committee. Opposed to such a move while the constructivist wing controlled the NEC, Kerr argued that a "central censorship" would "stifle discussion." In favor of assisting papers that were not on a sound financial basis, he nevertheless cautioned against taking "a remedy worse than the disease." What concerned him was the threatened precedent of centralized control over the movement's propaganda vehicles. Kerr understandably took any threat, direct or indirect, to *ISR*'s independence quite seriously. Although the effort went nowhere, Kerr nevertheless correctly read it as the basis for a possible throttling of party opinion. Conservatives, vexed by the growth of support for industrial unionism and direct action and opposition to reformism, would soon turn on the major national outlet for left-wing opinion, *ISR*. The desire to control the left-wing press would eventually reappear in different form, and Kerr & Company would be the direct target as he and his comrades increased criticism of the right and support for the left.[32]

The autumn of 1909 marked a political turning point for Kerr and *ISR*. Affected by a number of specific events on the industrial front, the publisher moved still closer to the IWW. His evolving left-wing position rankled party conservatives while it endeared the company to the impossibilist rank and file. The September *ISR* opened with Louis Duchez's firsthand account of the Wobbly-led strike of unskilled immigrant steelworkers at McKees Rocks, Pennsylvania. The same issue contained another attack on reformism by Kerr regular William E. Bohn, a piece by Tom Mann on "The Way to Win," and the first installment of a lengthy report on the progress of "revolutionary unionism" (syndicalism) on the Continent.[33] The "Editor's Chair" that same month issued a clear elucidation of Kerr's political position. His enthusiasm for "revolutionary unionism" as a "new method of warfare against organized capital" was unqualified. He argued that the old form of craft unionism, essentially conservative in its attempt to limit job competition, had been outmoded and outflanked by the development of the trust. New industrial conditions had given rise to a new unionism opposed to the "aristocracy of labor." The new industrial union, not conservative "for its members possess nothing worth conserving," sought not to restrict but to enlarge membership with the ultimate aim of organizing all wage workers to "defy the capitalist, take possession of the industries, and operate them for themselves."[34]

The editorial also bemoaned the fact that many advocates of industrial unionism and numerous Socialist Party propagandists often worked at cross purposes. Many party members had to remain in the existing craft unions "in order to earn a living" and had therefore developed a prejudice against the "new unionism." It simultaneously criticized some of the "agitators" in the IWW who incorrectly denounced all electoral activity as "essentially middle class." Kerr called for a truce between the feuding factions within the movement:

A revolutionary union without the backing of a revolutionary party will be tied up by injunctions. Its officers will be kidnapped. Its members, if they defy the courts, will be corralled in bullpens or mowed down by gatling guns.

A revolutionary party, on the other hand, if it pins its hopes mainly on the passing of laws, tends always to degenerate into a reform party. Its "leaders" become hungry for office and eager for votes, even if the votes must be secured by concessions to the middle class. . . . It wastes its propaganda on "immediate demands," which either are of no importance to the working class, or else could be enforced ten times as readily by the menace of revolution.

The revolutionary party, for Charles Kerr, had two tasks: first, the dissemination of "the propaganda of revolution" to "awaken the slumbering toilers" to the value of "united action" and, second, the use of political power won at the ballot box "to obstruct the workings of the capitalist state as a weapon against the working class." He argued that both the "big capitalist" and the politician, if confronted by a "compact, revolutionary minority," would make concessions "in the hope of stopping the tide of revolution." That tide would continue unabated, regardless of reform initiatives from above.

The same issue of *ISR* that carried Kerr's "Revolutionary Unionism" also featured the first of several detailed reports from the scene of a series of heated strikes in the steel towns of Pennsylvania. The key strike in that region centered at McKees Rocks, six miles south of Pittsburgh. The fight against the Pressed Steel Car Company heralded the first victory against the steel trust since 1901. Although ephemeral, the concessions won in that Pennsylvania industrial town by a mostly immigrant work force trumpeted the first important victory for the industrial union strategy propounded by the leadership of the IWW. The advocates of direct action and industrial unionism certainly viewed it as such.

The strike began on July 10 as a walkout by the ethnically diverse, largely unskilled work force. Strikers called for an improvement in work conditions, an end to speed-ups imposed by a system of pooled wage rates, amelioration of exorbitant company housing costs, and a return to an older rate of pay that existed before the recession of 1907. By July 14 nearly five thousand workers from approximately sixteen nationalities had left the Pressed Steel Car Company yards. They effectively blocked the entry of scabs and resisted evictions from company-owned housing. The first IWW organizers did not arrive until a month later, but their willingness to "organize the unorganized," their success in bypassing the official strike leadership of the Anglo-dominated skilled trades, and their ability to transcend cultural and linguistic barriers gave the strike a cohesiveness that ultimately brought victory.[35]

ISR's lead editorial for October lauded the McKees Rock strike as a triumph. "The first great battle of the new Revolution on American soil has been WON," it proclaimed. The strike, according to the editorial, had a far greater significance than it actually came to have. But in the immediate aftermath of the Pennsylvania settlement, "The despised mass of 'ignorant foreigners,' held apart by their separate languages, half starved when at work, homeless and empty-handed, have accomplished the impossible. In a few short weeks they have welded themselves into a fighting organization that has beaten the steel trust to a stand-still. . . . Their victory is an inspiration not only to themselves but to the whole working class of the world."[36] The "steel trust" had made a critical mistake in crushing the old craft unions, which had "time-honored traditions of 'community of interest' and a 'fair day's wages for a fair day's work.'" By destroying the more conservative labor organizations, intransigent bosses had opened the door for the "in-coming of the modern revolutionary union."[37]

The McKees Rocks events led Kerr to reassess the IWW. He had watched the "checkered career" of the organization since its founding in 1905. "Firmly convinced" in the efficacy of industrial unionism as a weapon for both day-to-day labor struggles and "the final struggle for the overthrow of capitalism," he had long doubted whether the IWW "had the efficiency demanded by the tremendous task involved in organizing the working class . . . along modern lines to battle with organized capital." But McKees Rocks changed all that. The IWW now offered "the best available rallying point for socialists on the economic field." In anticipation of criticism from his right for that untrammeled endorsement of the IWW, Kerr further explained his "change of attitude." He argued that the main function of the Socialist Party was educational and propagandistic; "vote-making" was secondary but still vitally important. Prefiguring events still a decade away, he suggested that the capitalist class would seek to pass legislation to outlaw the "revolutionary unions" when industrial union tactics became generalized. Socialist legislators would be critical in combating such enactments and protecting ongoing organizing attempts, especially by government employees. Again, however, Kerr cautioned that "something more than voting is needed to overthrow capitalism." "Revolutionary unionism" was that something. In private, he suggested to Boudin in early 1910 that the most important task of the Socialist Party, once it began to win elections, would be to "block the efforts of the capitalists to crush the unions." He conjectured that "reforms will be urged by the capitalist politicians themselves as soon as the revolutionary movement becomes formidable"; it was "a waste of energy . . . to say much about them."[38]

With the November 1909 *ISR* Kerr distanced himself still further from the Socialist Party's conservative elements. His lead editorial reproduced a set of resolutions issued by a Denver branch of the Socialist Party that criticized the party for no longer being a revolutionary working-class organization. The members of Third Ward Branch, Local Denver, declared that the party had become "merely a stamping ground for faddists, careerists and notoriety seekers bent upon obtaining pelf and power at the expense of the already overburdened."[39] Their statement castigated reformist elements who had "usurped" the leadership of the party as a "conscienceless . . . crew of bourgeois buccaneers," a bunch of "muddle-headed marauders of the middle class," and a "cockroach element, composed of preachers without pulpits, lawyers without clients, doctors without patients, storekeepers without customers, disgruntled political coyotes and other riff-raff" who had "relegated the real proletarians to the rear." Affirming its allegiance to "the principles of SCIENTIFIC SOCIALISM and to the cause of OUR class," the entire local resigned from the "organization falsely called 'The Socialist Party of the United States.'"

Kerr found "some measure of truth in the indictment" but argued that it was wrong for the Denver local to leave the Socialist Party. He suggested that there were definite economic causes for the predominance of middle-class elements in the party but ongoing transformations would soon change that. Capitalist development spelled the end of conservative trade unions and signaled the rise of new revolutionary unions in which the Socialist Party would find a new strength and future. The commentary set out an independent position:

> Long enough we have cringed before the aristocracy of labor begging voters for votes that we did not get. Long enough we have experimented with "immediate demands" that might swell our apparent strength by winning the votes of people opposed to revolution. The time has come for the proletarians of the party and those who believe the party should be proletarian in its tactics to bring about a revolution inside the party. Let us not withdraw like the Denver comrades but take possession. Let us put wage workers on the National Executive Committee. Let us cut the "immediate demands" out of our platform and leave reformers to wrangle over platforms. Let us make it our chief task to spread the propaganda of revolution and of the new industrial unionism, and when we elect members of our own class to office, let us instruct them that their most important work is to hamper the ruling class in the war it will be waging on the revolutionary unions."

Although Kerr soon suggested that the charges put forward by the Denver group were all not well-founded, he nevertheless alienated the party's right. Believing that "the majority of the Socialist Party is made up of wage workers who WANT a proletarian party," he called upon party members to repudiate the conservative leadership in the upcoming NEC elections scheduled for January 1910.[40] The right maintained its hold on the NEC despite a restructuring of voting procedures that Kerr hoped would allow the "real proletarians" some entrée. His partisan stance did not go unnoticed, however. Gradualist members of the committee marked it well.

More and more opposed to the reformist direction of party conservatives on the NEC, Kerr soon became embroiled in an internal party fight, the Walling-Simons Affair. A relatively minor event in the Socialist Party history, the episode nevertheless illustrated the political distance that had developed between Kerr and Algie Simons. More significantly, it reflected increased tensions within the party and foreshadowed Kerr's allegiance in future intraparty disputes.

Confronted by the unanticipated setbacks of the election of 1908 and further declines in the socialist vote the following spring and fall, Simons and other gradualist members of the NEC had begun to explore possibilities for a more constructive working relationship with the AFL. After they had attended an AFL convention in Toronto in November 1909, Simons wrote to William English Walling, a well-known radical intellectual who was not yet a member of the Socialist Party. The letter chronicled Simons's growing dissatisfaction with the party's attitude toward the AFL and his fears over the growing strength of the IWW. "There must be a reorganization of the S.P." along the lines of the British Labour Party, he suggested; the AFL "comes much nearer representing the working class than the S.P."[41]

Simons had assumed that Walling would find his analysis and suggestions amenable. But Walling forwarded a copy of the letter to Gustavus Meyers, a New York associate of Kerr, who in turn circulated reports of the Simons "betrayal" and accusations of a right-wing plot within the NEC to convert the Socialist Party to a labor party or something worse, a political auxiliary of the AFL. Walling, in the meantime, mailed a circular letter to party notables throughout the country, notifying them of what was afoot. He charged that Simons had conspired with the gradualists on the NEC to transform the party into a political wing of the AFL. Simons responded by suggesting that Walling had distorted his letter and that he had been misquoted and quoted out of context. He denied all suggestion of an NEC conspiracy. Walling then forwarded the original letter to Kerr, who published it in entirety in *ISR*, with all of Simons's heresies set in bold-face type.

The whole matter probably would have had little significance had it not surfaced in early 1910 at the time of NEC elections. Kerr used the Simons letter and the subsequent accusations, denials, and countercharges, all re-produced in *ISR*, to wage a political fight against the party right. He went on the offensive by sending a questionnaire to all the candidates for the NEC and asked each to state their position on the idea of a labor party. He published the replies in *ISR* in January 1910. That number also con-tained an article by Walling, "Fifteen Reasons Why a 'Labor Party' Is Un-desirable," and gave prominent space to a letter from Eugene Debs to Walling. Widely respected throughout the party, Debs commended Wall- . ing for his "uncompromising spirit and attitude." He warned that "if the trimmers had their way, we [the party] would degenerate into bourgeois reform" and went on to argue that "the Socialist Party has already CATERED FAR TOO MUCH to the American Federation of Labor, and there is no doubt that A HALT WILL HAVE TO BE CALLED." Kerr also published an exchange of letters revealing that there indeed was support for a labor party at an NEC meeting in November 1909. A formal proposal put forward by Vic-tor Berger had been withdrawn when one member argued that it would create a public scandal.[42]

The partisan political function of the entire January exposé became clear in *ISR*'s lead editorial that month. Writing on "The Party Election," Kerr pointed out that party policy for the previous two years had "been largely controlled by men who think, no doubt with perfect sincerity, that the interests of the Party can best be served by catering to the 'leaders' of the American Federation of Labor."[43] Using Simons's vocabulary, again set in boldface type, the editorial argued that "some members of the present executive committee if reelected will try to make ours a SANE party stand-ing for the immediate interests of small landowners and the American Federation of Labor, and to DRIVE FROM OUR RANKS those who are SEEK-ING TO RAISE REBELLION." It recommended that "the good of the party de-mands the retirement of several members of the present executive board." Kerr listed the names of the twenty-seven candidates in three columns across the page. The left-wingers, favored by Kerr & Company, received prominent placement at the head of each column, whereas the names of those figures on the right sitting on the NEC appeared in the last column at the very end of the list. Algie Simons's name appeared last.

Simons's letter caused a fray, and when the smoke had cleared all the right-wing members, with one exception, remained in place on the NEC.

That exception was Algie Simons. Rebuked by the membership, Simons's career as an aspiring party politician had neared its finale. Charles Kerr played a key role in that event.

At the time of the Walling-Simons imbroglio, control of the major socialist press sat firmly in the hands of the right wing. The gradualists controlled all the significant dailies and weeklies with the exception of *Appeal to Reason*, which consciously remained aloof from internal party squabbles. Control of the major movement organs explained, in part, the ability of the constructivist or reformist wing to maintain control of the NEC despite the left's continued maneuverings and sizable rank-and-file support. By early 1910 *ISR* was the only major, nationally distributed voice open to the left wing.

Kerr had already announced at the beginning of 1908 that the company had finally passed the "stage of experiment." He no longer had to urge socialists to send money in the hope that his firm might possibly supply the books the movement needed. *ISR*, still too limited in circulation to cover its operating expenses, continued to drain income from book and pamphlet sales. That April, however, Kerr procured another operating stipend from the Second International benefactor Eugene Dietzgen. The gift of $1,000, supposedly earmarked to pay contributors, enabled Kerr to increase the monthly's size from sixty to eighty pages, and the fortunes of *ISR* began to change by the fall as circulation started to increase. Subscriptions doubled in two months, and the magazine finally began to reach the point of paying for itself as the end of the year approached.[44]

Kerr's political and social perspective continued to evolve in the meantime as he reassessed the condition of the working-class movement, the progress of the Socialist Party, and the position of his publishing house in relation to both. Writing on the tenth anniversary of the founding of *ISR* in July 1910, for example, Kerr evaluated the distance that the movement had traversed since 1900. He noted how capitalist productive processes had continued to revolutionize working conditions and how such transformations had wrought significant social changes over the decade: "Little capitalists have been crowded down into the ranks of the wage workers. Skilled laborers have found the market for their skill cut off. Craft unions which previously had kept their wages up have been beaten into submission, and all these have swelled the ranks of the revolutionary wage workers, with nothing to lose and everything to gain."[45] He noted a fivefold increase in the membership of the Socialist Party, caused, in his assessment, by the social changes then underway. He argued that the party rank and file had become convinced "that nothing but revolution would do." Such men and women had "learned to think for themselves" and could "no longer be swayed by reformist 'leaders.'" The rank and file, despite the "vote-catching programs" and "pet measures" of the party leadership, "wanted no compromise with reformers, no patching of the capitalist system, nothing to retard the onward sweep of the working class."

The growth and direction of *ISR* was the "outcome" and "expression" of that "rank and file awakening": "Ten years ago our aim was to 'educate the educators.' We thought the principles of socialism could be mastered by a chosen few and handed down to the many. Less than three years ago we saw a new light. We came to realize that the industrial wage-workers arrive from their daily experience at a clearer view of the class struggle than any mere theorist can possibly reach. We now see that if the *Review* is to be an important weapon in the fight against capitalism, it must be *of, by and for the working class.*"[46] Kerr announced a "new advanced step" for the monthly, a change to the format of the popular illustrated magazines of the day. The reason for doing this was not solely to further increase circulation but to transform *ISR* into "The Fighting Magazine of the Working Class." Readers were to send in concise stories and "photographs with action in them." He cautioned potential reporters to "never mind about flowery language; the *Review* reader wants the facts."[47]

The period of emergence for the "new" *ISR*, from early 1908 to 1910, was one of growth and development for a working collective that developed around the monthly. The group of regulars on the editorial board by early 1910 included trade unionist William E. Bohn as editor of a monthly section of "International Notes," as well as Robert Rives LaMonte and Max Hayes. The staff by mid-1910 also included the Wobbly poet, songwriter, and illustrator Ralph Chaplin.[48] Born in 1887, Chaplin grew up in Chicago, became a commercial artist, and joined the Socialist Party while still in his teens. As the company's chief graphic artist, he designed and illustrated books and pamphlets by such writers as Clarence Darrow, Upton Sinclair, and Edward Bellamy. He drew the cover design for *Socialism Made Easy*, the highly popular Kerr pamphlet by the noted Irish rebel James Connolly. He also created cover illustrations and interior artwork for *ISR* and designed the firm's delightfully innovative deck of socialist playing cards, for which Mary Marcy wrote the accompanying rhymes.[49]

As *ISR* entered its second decade, barely an issue went to press without a contribution of some sort from the pen of Mary E. Marcy (M.E.M.). A central figure among the left-wing militants who gravitated toward the Kerr Company, she became an associate editor of the *Review* in December 1908. A member of the company's board of directors, she served as secretary of the publishing house until her death in 1922.

Born in Belleville, Illinois, in 1877, Mary Edna Tobias lost both her parents at an early age. The eldest of three children, she purchased a book on stenography and went to work as a clerical in order to support her siblings while she attended high school. After being fired from her job as a stenographer for wearing a Bryan button during the presidential campaign of 1896, she secured a position as a secretary to the president of the University of Chicago, William Rainey Harper, through the assistance of Clarence Darrow. At Chicago, she became a student of John Dewey and studied advanced courses in philosophy and English literature. She married Leslie H. Marcy in 1901. Leaving Chicago with her new husband, she went to work as a secretary for the treasurer of a major Kansas City meatpacking firm. The resulting "Letters of a Pork Packer's Stenographer," a scathing, muckraking indictment of the Beef Trust, ran serially in *ISR* in 1904 and won Marcy instant notoriety within left circles. She soon became a regular contributor, and her husband became an associate editor in 1911. With their arrival, the "& Company" in the firm's name since 1886 took on new significance.

A member of the Socialist Party from 1902, Marcy became convinced that the teachings of Marx had to be made more accessible if the movement were to make headway among American workers. An avid polemicist devoted to socialist pedagogy and education in the fundamentals of Marxism, Marcy contributed numerous articles to *ISR*, and Kerr turned a number of her lengthier pieces into pamphlets. He first published her *Out of the Dump*, "a vivid story of working people as they really are," illustrated by Chaplin, in 1909. *Shop Talks on Economics*, "an attempt to say, in the language of working men and women, the things Marx says in his own books," initially appeared in serial installments during 1911. Published in pamphlet form that year, this now-classic primer in Marxian economics went through numerous editions and subsequently found its way into Japanese, Chinese, Finnish, Romanian, French, Italian, and Greek translations. More than two million copies of *Shop Talks* circulated by the time of Marcy's death.[50]

The Kerr group forged a distinctly independent political position between early 1908 and 1912. Unwavering in its support for industrial unionism, the collective nevertheless disavowed the "anti-political" elements to their left, the anarcho-syndicalist strategy that totally eschewed electoral campaigns. They also rebuked those socialists firmly tied to the outmoded craft unions and those party politicians who would readily dilute socialist theory and practice in order to attract middle-class votes. Kerr, the Marcys, LaMonte, Bohn, and Chaplin came to see themselves as true "revolutionists" opposed to party trimmers. The socialist dawn, looming somewhere just over the horizon, seemed inevitable. They could visualize it in the continuing concentration of wealth, the centralization of capitalist productive might, and transformations occurring in the labor process—all prerequisites, in the classical Marxian reading, for the total socialization of society. They could also see the precursors of the new era in the advances of the socialist movement internationally, no longer confined solely to Europe but also on the rise in places as far afield as Japan, Australia, and South Africa.

Such socialist inevitability nevertheless remained conditional, never totally preordained, for the Kerr group. It remained contingent on the ability of the movement to garner enough working-class political support to wrest control of the state from the hands of the capitalists. It also depended on the effectiveness of socialist organization among the proletariat, those with the most to gain and the strategic position in the productive process needed to bring the system to a standstill if necessary. That recognition of the active part to be played by the working class, that historic role of the proletarians in fulfilling the socialist mission, differentiated Kerr and his comrades (and the left as a whole) from gradualists and revisionists, who viewed socialism as an entirely inevitable outcome, the fruition of capitalist evolution extending from the logic of capitalist production.

If the working class was to rouse from its slumber, if its veil of "false consciousness" was to lift so the class could fulfill its historic mission, then socialist pedagogy was essential. Working-class political education remained central in the Kerr group's perspective. Votes for Socialist Party candidates mattered little if they were not cast by informed, class-conscious workers. Kerr company activists criticized gradualist reform schemes and short-run tactical maneuvers put forward to recruit the support of the politically transient. Enough unadulterated socialist literature—rational, readable, and scientific in its explanation of existing social conditions, class relations, and projections of the future—dispersed widely enough among American toilers would unlock the door to the cooperative commonwealth. To do so, the company turned its energy and expertise to the production of a socialist pedagogy capable of capturing the hearts and, more important, the minds of American workers. The series of influential books and pamphlets that it issued clearly influenced an entire generation of left-wing activists.

The company continued to reissue and promote those socialist works that it had brought out before 1908. New imprints, however, began to set off the catalogs of the latter period from their predecessors. New arrivals to the Kerr lists from abroad and from the pens of indigenous American radicals often reflected the shifting leftward predispositions of their publisher and the often subtle degrees of political shading and nuance that distinguished left-leaning crimson from right-wing rosé.

With *ISR* resuscitated by 1910, Kerr focused his attention on the expansion of his book list. He and his associates continued to translate those Marxian classics still not available in English. In 1908 Kerr & Company published the German socialist Paul Kampffmeyer's *Changes in the Theory and Tactics of the (German) Social Democracy*, an important polemic on revisionism and reform. They issued the third volume of the Unterman translation of Marx's *Capital* in 1909 and his *Value, Price and Profit* and *The Poverty of Philosophy* during the same period.[51] A new edition of Karl Kautsky's *Erfurt Program* appeared under the title *The Class Struggle* at a time in 1910 when elements on the Socialist Party's right had already begun to soft-peddle or abandon that central tenet of Marxian orthodoxy. A number of other European socialist notables also made their way into the Kerr catalog. The list for 1908 and 1909, for example, included yet another contribution by William Morris and E. Belfort Bax, *Socialism: Its Growth and Outcome*, along with *Anarchism and Socialism* by George Plechanoff, the father of Russian Marxism.[52]

The company issued the Connolly's *Socialism Made Easy* in 1909. A central figure in Irish left-wing circles and soon to die at the hands of a British firing squad for his role in Dublin's Easter Rising of 1916, Connolly had come to the United States in September 1903. Initially aligned with the Socialist Labor Party, he joined the Socialist Party in the spring of 1908. An advocate of industrial unionism and a supporter of the IWW, he met Kerr while attending the 1908 IWW convention in Chicago, and the latter soon agreed to publish his pamphlet. A series of essays on socialist principles and industrial unionism, *Socialism Made Easy* received a favorable reception and wide distribution, not only in the United States but also in Ireland, Australia, and Great Britain.[53]

Connolly also contributed two articles to *ISR* in 1909 and 1910. A Kerr political ally, he endorsed electoral activity and the creation of industrial unions, "the economic manifestation of Socialism," and pushed for simultaneous activity on political and economic fronts. His "Ballots, Bullets, or ——" called for the organization of industrial unions as the sole means of effective defense against usurpation of legitimate socialist electoral victories. "Industrialism and the Trades Unions" defined the craft unionism of the AFL as "the most dispersive and isolating force at work in the labor movement" and emphatically endorsed the industrial strategy of the IWW. Such statements, appearing when they did in the pages of *ISR*, further irked the more conservative elements in the party.[54]

In addition to the continued contributions of European comrades, Kerr turned more and more energy to the promotion of indigenous socialist writers. The newer works mirrored the increased sophistication and maturity of the American movement's activists and theoreticians. Most books and pamphlets that the firm issued between 1908 and 1912 also reflected the developing leftward shift of Kerr & Company and its affinity for industrial unionism, its increasing receptivity for the IWW, and its growing critique of gradualist reformism. The company, always limited as it was by economic constraints, selected its titles carefully. Each tract, pamphlet, and book was part of the political trajectory that the Kerr associates had charted and provided a specific contribution to debates or disputes that shaped the movement.

The earliest clear pamphlet indicator of the company's leftward move was William E. Trautmann's *Industrial Unionism*, released in 1908. Trautmann was an organizer for the Brewery Worker's Union and a key figure in the early years of the IWW. His exposition of the strategy for a new unionism, distinct in its goals and tactics from the craft unionism of the AFL, initially appeared in the IWW's *Industrial Worker's Bulletin*. Trautmann advocated direct action, opposed binding contracts, and discussed the use of sabotage and the general strike. Kerr felt compelled to issue a qualified disclaimer at the time of its release. Although clearly amenable to the main thrust of Trautmann's tract, he nevertheless noted the "traditional policy" of the Socialist Party to "cooperate fraternally with all trade unions, and to take no sides in disputes between unions." Kerr's preface reiterated that the concentration of capital had "made craft unions obsolete" and "the principles of industrial unionism must be adopted in the near future." It also stated that publication of the Trautmann polemic should in no way "be taken as an endorsement of any particular organization," but simply as an attempt "to put valuable information within the reach of as many workers as possible."[55]

That was 1908. By 1911 Kerr could proudly and unqualifiedly announce the publication of Austin M. Lewis's *The Militant Proletariat* as "the most important contribution to Socialist theory that has yet been produced by any American writer" and "the most important work on American economic development and the tactics of the American Socialism that has yet appeared." He endorsed and promoted the Lewis work as a logical and clear scientific exposition of the position and tactics long advocated by *ISR*.[56]

English-born and educated at the University of London, Austin Lewis had become involved in the socialist cause before emigrating to the San Francisco Bay area in 1890. Initially a lawyer in San Raphael, California, he eventually established a reputation as a noted socialist lecturer, writer, and movement attorney.[57] As a left-wing strategist and theoretician Lewis strove to produce a sound, rigorous Marxian analysis of contemporary conditions in order to bolster the left's argument for industrial unionism. Released in December 1911, *The Militant Proletariat* went further than any other book of the period to elucidate the reasons for the rise and the rational necessity for that new unionism capable of transcending the narrow confines of conservative, outmoded craft unions. Lewis's work, a clear and historically significant contribution to the Marxian discussion on the nature and composition of the American working class, helped clarify a solid and unassailable left position. It received a favorable reception within left circles, drew the expected criticism from the foes it assailed, and passed through several editions.[58]

In a quest for those revolutionary elements of the working class that could possibly function as the motor engine or driving force in the overthrow of capitalist relations, Lewis began his inquiry by assessing the various strata of the American proletariat. He dismissed the lowest strata, what he referred to as the "slum proletarians," as a force susceptible to the bribery of reaction.[59] The upper strata of the class, the organized skilled craftsmen, were just as inappropriate for leadership: "The highly skilled trades separate themselves from the mass of the proletariat and obtain for themselves a position apart and superior to the rest. . . . They have segregated themselves from the rest of the mass of their fellow workers and have independent trade contracts with their employers . . . to the detriment of members of the proletariat less fortunately placed than themselves."[60]

Lewis harshly attacked the political behavior of established craft unions. He found that the labor unions as a rule supported the established order, "the greater capitalism," in some form or another. He termed the exclusivist unions "an effective bar to progress in the industrial field" and noted that "whenever they go into politics . . . , they leave the traces of their small trader footprints." The existing trade union organizations, with their "small business ideals" and craft basis, were called the "greatest obstacle in the path of proletarian progress at present."[61]

Then, Lewis briefly assayed the potentialities of the "floating proletariat," that large mass of migrant laborers who worked the agricultural mid-section of the country during the summer and streamed into the cities during the winter. Usually dismissed as unorganizable nonvoters by the party right and the trade unions, Lewis viewed them as a "conceivably powerful force for the revolution."[62] His critique of the "intellectual proletarians," those who had entered the working-class and socialist movements from various middle-class backgrounds, was scathing. In an unsparing polemical style clearly aimed at the middle-class reform elements in the party, Lewis lambasted this "scant minority" as having "but dubious value" as a potentially revolutionary force.

> This minority which comes [into the movement] is a broken minority, generally bankrupt, not only economically but intellectually. . . . It is not the stuff out of which a strong, energetic, fighting body can be built. Its affiliations with the old system are too strong, its ideas are already fixed, and fixed wrong, before it comes into the movement. It has given and gives more trouble than any other element, and almost all the backsliding, all the hypocrisies, and all the surrenders made in the name of politics in the Socialist movement have been brought about by just this element.[63]

For Lewis, the "small trader" and "professional man" was the "curse of Socialist movement." The middle-class elements lacked those very qualities—the morals, discipline, and force—essential to a revolutionary movement and created nothing but weaknesses in the movement. The intellectual proletariat was the source of the "sham altruism, the maudlin note, the whipped dog whimper, which too frequently manifests itself in the revolutionary literature and speeches." Lewis called the clergy, lawyers, writers, and reporters "hangers on" who "lived for the favor of other people and grow into the habit of adapting manners of thought and expression accommodated to those upon whom they look for economic support." Such "material" was not "well calculated to make stalwart fighters."[64]

In his search for the truly "militant proletariat," Lewis next turned to an examination of the existent "machine process," with its specific relations between labor and capital and ongoing erosion of established skills. His lengthy exposition on the evolution and function of the modern industrial system, with its drive for standardization of product and destruction of the power long held by the skilled craftsmen, clearly defined the forces that spelled the demise of the already antiquated trade union form. The innovations that destroyed the power and autonomy of older unions simultaneously gave rise to new forms of workers' organization and new patterns of resistance and defiance. New demands and techniques in the work place created new workers who better understood the connectedness of the productive process. New labor processes also created a new psychology among workers that leveled older ways of perceiving the world. Those new perceptions laid waste to the beliefs in the inviolability of the individual and the sanctity of private property that were the ideological mainstays of the older order.[65]

From such transformations would come the most conscious militants who could understand the nature of the new industrial process and wage the struggle strategically, in a class-conscious fashion. Lewis wisely noted that the "mere fact of existence" of a proletariat did not necessarily guarantee the revolutionary nature of that class. On the contrary, the teaching of history pointed more to "failure rather than success." He nevertheless pointed to the existence of a "militant nucleus," a "revolutionary core" around which other groups, otherwise unorganized, might gather.[66]

Lewis's militant core resided at the heart of the industrial system, a product of the advanced process of production and its demands. He argued that new processes, the interplay of technological innovation and the advent and increased adaptation of scientific management to wrestle control of the workplace from producers, had created an actual "machine process state of mind," a particular psychology that transformed the antagonism of labor and capital and carried it to a new level.[67]

Lewis provided a harsh critique of the nature, composition, and direction of the Socialist Party. Ostensibly a proletarian party, the Socialist Party in reality represented only one portion of the class: the skilled laborer. At its origins a coalition of the "organized skilled laborer" and the "thoroughly whipped and correspondingly discontented small bourgeoisie," the party's platform represented the "hodge podge demands" of the discontented. Claiming to represent the proletariat as a whole, the party had also attracted those who viewed a clearly working-class platform and direction as the "only solution of the problems inherent in the present economic system." Noting the tension of interests and inherent conflict, Lewis surveyed the seemingly "unbridgeable" gulf between the advocates of the "proletarian doctrine," the proponents of "the industrial form of organization" and the "official wing" of the Socialist Party, "the representative of the non-revolutionary body." An exodus of the "proletarian element," he suggested, would leave the party "rudderless. . . , at the mercy of those leaders whom inclination or personal ambition inclines to the opportunistic role." Salvation for the "political reflex" of the workers' movement, the Socialist Party, lay in industrial unionism and direct action. The future of the movement as a whole depended upon "active, intelligent and revolutionary industrial organization and action."[68]

Lewis's work included a detailed exposition of the origins and necessity of direct action, sabotage, and that final stage of concerted worker's organization and resistance, the general strike.[69] Such discussions, already a sticking point or irritant for the party gradualists, alienated whatever remaining support for Kerr & Company that still existed on the right. The further Kerr and his associates moved to the left, however, the more the company continued to grow. The expansion of the book and pamphlet trade, when combined with the increasing popularity of *ISR* as the major national voice of the party left, marked the firm as a target for criticism and, ultimately, attack from the reformist wing.

The In-House Battle, 1911–13

The continued left-wing partisanship exhibited by Kerr & Company, the group's open support for direct action and industrial unionism, and the increasingly critical tone of the *International Socialist Review* toward the more conservative, gradualist elements within the Socialist Party ultimately marked the firm and those associated with it as targets in an ongoing intraparty imbroglio that came to a boiling point in 1911 and 1912. As the major national sounding board for the direct-actionists when most of the movement press remained under the control of the constructivists, the company came to occupy stage center in that brewing movement controversy.

The dispute eventually led to an all-out attack on the left's position by those wedded to the conservative strategy of party-building based on electoral campaigns and alliance with the skilled craft unions. By 1912 the conservatives, headed by New York's Morris Hillquit, sought nothing less than full curtailment of the left. Their offensive targeted William D. "Big Bill" Haywood, the renown IWW militant who also occupied a seat on the party's National Executive Committee, elected late in 1911 by a solid left-wing turnout. Offended by *ISR*'s editorial support for Haywood and the IWW as well as its arguments for industrial unionism and extraparliamentary action, the party's right also launched a campaign against Charles H. Kerr & Company.

The debate between left and right originated in a long series of disagreements over tactical and strategic questions dating to the earliest moments of the socialist movement. The intensified round of fractious infighting that came to a head in 1912 had its origins in the victories of the IWW at

McKees Rocks and New Castle, Pennsylvania, during the summer and fall of 1909. Viewed as the first significant triumph for the industrial union strategy, the Pennsylvania gains reinvigorated the IWW and bolstered the strength of the party's left in its ongoing debate with the "slowcialists." *ISR* hailed those triumphs as the conceivable dawn of a new era in the history of the movement.[1] As a voice for the left-wing militants, the monthly provided a rostrum for political arguments that opposed gradualist position. It also became an important organizing tool, an agitational propaganda vehicle and publicity medium, for those campaigns spearheaded by the left.

ISR played a central role in publicizing the IWW-led "free speech fights" that began late in 1909 throughout the West. It not only covered the course of various free speech battles but also editorially supported such endeavors as an important element of movement work. Party conservatives viewed the free speech campaigns differently. More concerned with marshaling employed craft union members and stationary, settled voters, conservatives showed little interest in the battles waged by nonvoting, geographically mobile vagabonds and bindle stiffs who flocked to such places as Spokane and San Diego to defend the right of soapboxers to stump for socialism on the streets. The "News and Views" section of the November 1909 *ISR*, for example, printed participants' accounts of the free speech fight in Spokane that fall. It carried a lengthy account of events in Washington submitted by a young but insightful Elizabeth Gurley Flynn, the noted Wobbly "rebel girl." More significantly, the magazine editorially endorsed the Spokane actions and called for additional rank-and-file assistance.[2] Such support for left-wing militants and their direct action also entailed the tacit endorsement of rank-and-file insurgencies by the "unorganizeable," those migrant workers, immigrants, women, non-English speaking, and blacks not actively or normally pursued by skilled craft unions or party conservatives. Such partisanship assured the further enmity of those reluctant or slow to assist such battles.[3]

That increasing antagonism soon found a focus in the character and politics of Bill Haywood. A leading spokesperson for left-wingers and an irrepressible voice for the growing numbers of "revolutionists" both within the Socialist party and outside of it, he, more than any other individual, came to personify the tensions within the movement. As such, he became the primary target for the offensive from the right that surfaced in 1912.

A hard rock miner at the age of fifteen, Haywood served his apprenticeship and toiled for years as a worker and organizer in the harsh reality of the Rocky Mountain miner's world, an environment noted for its labor militancy, solidarity, and class violence. That experience gave him a fighter's perspective and toughness and an integrity that endeared him to those for whom he spoke most fervently: the unorganized, dispossessed, unemployed, and embattled.[4] He served as an organizer for the industrially based Western Federation of Miners (WFM) for a number of years and played a central role in the founding of the IWW in 1905. In contrast to the anarcho-syndicalist elements in the movement who opposed any political (electoral) action whatsoever, Haywood argued for a dual strategy that combined militant direct action with support for electoral candidates where possible.

In 1906 Haywood won national notoriety as a defendant in the sensational trial following the murder of the former governor of Idaho, Frank Steunenburg. On the basis of a series of trumped-up charges, Haywood and two codefendants, all key WFM officers and organizers in the western mining region, became the targets of a vindictive prosecution. The case became a cause célèbre within socialist and labor circles and gave Haywood new notoriety nationally. Gaining acquittal in 1907, he criss-crossed the country between 1908 and 1910 as a socialist propagandist, IWW organizer, advocate of industrial unionism, and a critic of the AFL.

Haywood developed a close working relationship with the Kerr Company comrades between 1908 and 1910 and soon became a fairly regular contributor to *ISR*.[5] In part because of the publicity given his candidacy by *ISR*, he won election as a representative to the International Socialist Congress in Copenhagen in 1910.[6] Upon returning, Haywood embarked on a national speaking tour under the auspices of Kerr & Company as part of the *International Socialist Review* Lecture Bureau.

Kerr devised the lecture bureau scheme in part to increase circulation. The purchase of a ticket to hear Haywood also entitled the bearer to a three-month introductory subscription to *ISR*.[7] More important, however, the series of lectures helped build a political base for left-wingers who congregated around the company. *ISR* tours brought Haywood and other "revolutionists" into contact with rank-and-file activists, the so-called Jimmy and Jenny Higginses of the movement, in unprecedented fashion. Here, in essence, was a tactic that enabled the left to circumvent the gradualists' hold on the party apparatus in many locales.[8]

That "hidden agenda" underlying the creation of the national speaking tours did not go unnoticed in some quarters. Haywood did not always receive the enthusiastic greetings and cheery encouragement that most of his appearances engendered. Already a foe of those constructivists opposed to any sort of direct action that might upset the fragile work of electoral base-building, Haywood met with opposition in parts of California, for example. The State Executive Board of the California Socialist Party, dominated by the right, informed Kerr that it would not allow Haywood to address any California locals because of what the board deemed his "pronounced opposition to political action and his advocacy of direct action in lieu thereof."[9]

The action of the California conservatives presaged an eventual firestorm of reproach leveled toward Haywood and Kerr & Company as the rift between left and right widened throughout the latter part of 1911. Despite that fact, Haywood's national junket and the publicity it generated gave him enough exposure to assure his election to the party's National Executive Committee (NEC) at end of 1911.

Frank Bohn also toured regularly for Kerr & Company and the *ISR* Lecture Bureau. An Ohio native and left-wing intellectual with a Ph.D. in economics from the University of Michigan, Bohn had helped write the "Industrial Union Manifesto," which called for the founding convention of the IWW. A long-time SLP member and former organizer for Daniel DeLeon's dual union Socialist Trades and Labor Alliance, he was also a delegate to the International Socialist Congress in Stuttgart in 1907. Abandoning his position as the national secretary of the SLP in 1908 and joining Kerr & Company, Bohn contributed a number of articles to *ISR*, beginning in the spring of 1908. A regular contributor by late 1911, he dealt mostly with the IWW, industrial unionism, revolutionary socialism, and the role of a socialist party. An original member of the lecture bureau, he joined *ISR*'s editorial board as an associate editor in October 1911.[10] In August 1911 Charles Kerr announced the release of Haywood and Bohn's *Industrial Socialism*, a pamphlet exposition of the strategy of industrial unionism and direct action.[11] The most clearly defined articulation of the political line hammered out by the Socialist Party's left at that time, Haywood and Bohn's polemic raised the hackles of gradualists as few written statements had done.

A bold manifesto and declaration of purpose and intent for the left wing, *Industrial Socialism* analyzed the direction of America's dominant institutions and the shape and condition of those forces arrayed in opposition. Because Haywood and Bohn were two of the most influential voices in the movement, the pamphlet carried additional weight for those who received it favorably as well as those who found it anathema or heretical to the goals of the socialist cause. It defined and clarified the two poles, gradualist and revolutionist, that had developed within the party and the broader movement. As a call for the rank and file to choose the movement's direction, *Industrial Socialism* was the most politically provocative, significant piece that Kerr & Company issued during the period. The right would use pronouncements from it to go after Haywood in their push to oust him from the NEC, and Kerr's role in the promotion and circulation of the pamphlet was also noticed. Despite antagonism from the right, however, *Industrial Socialism* received a favorable reception.[12] Clearly delineating the differences within the movement, in an idiom that made it accessible to significant numbers of rank-and-file activists throughout the country, it soon passed through seven English and twelve foreign-language editions.

Haywood and Bohn began their exposition with a brief historical analysis. In all societies before the rise of capitalism, they argued, the ruling classes had unified their economic and political power. At the time of feudalism's overthrow, however, the ascendant bourgeoisie needed the support of the popular classes and therefore created parliaments as a mechanism of formal political power while maintaining real social power through control of the economy. The rise of the trusts, the "government of industry," was the final consolidation of actual power in the modern era. The "real government" resided in Wall Street, and the exorbitant profits made by employers were nothing more than a "tax collected without representation." The trusts controlled the dominant institutions: schools, press, church, courts, and military. In addition, the formal political state was nothing more than the tool of the industrial state. Haywood and Bohn therefore critiqued those in the Socialist Party's right "who think all we need is votes [and] expect the tool to wield the user, the shadow to change the reality, the servant to command the master."[13] The fight for ultimate control of society would have to be waged in the shop, at the point of production. Electoral strategies based on a series of immediate reform demands, devised to attract middle-class votes, were a waste of time. The only form of working-class organization capable of combating the power of the trusts was the industrial union. On the other hand, skilled craft unions faced extinction at the hands of that "great leveler" the machine process, which rendered old skills obsolete.[14]

What made *Industrial Socialism* so salient was its analysis of changes occurring at the point of production within the labor process. Haywood and Bohn's critique and disavowal of constructivist political strategies, reformism, and craft unionism flowed from their appraisal of the then visible direction of capitalist development. Their call for industrial unionism and socialism emanated from an appraisal of the rapid transformations caused by technical innovations that rendered older forms of working-class organization ineffectual and obsolete.

Workers organized not by their craft but by industry would form the bases for an industrial democracy administered by the rank and file—the true meaning of socialism. Mere government ownership brought about by elected socialists, as the gradualists advocated, was not true socialism because exploitation would still continue. "A wise tailor," argued the authors, "does not put stitches in rotten cloth." Instead of the gradual socialization of the economy preferred by the party right, industrial unions would form the framework for an industrial socialism brought to fruition through the general strike, that ultimate weapon of an organized working class.[15]

Those who later attacked Haywood would accuse him of opposing political action. He and Bohn, however, clearly spelled out a role for the Socialist Party in their scenario for social revolution. Although the state could not be used to institute socialism, it remained a deadly instrument in the hands of the capitalists. The party, therefore, had three functions in the preparatory battles for the new industrial order. First, it must win control of the state from the class enemy in order to prevent the use of the police, courts, and military as weapons in the ongoing conflict for power. Second, it must play a central educational role. Political campaigns must be used to put forward the concepts of scientific socialism—the class struggle, the theory of surplus value, and "economic determinism" or historical materialism—in order to win the majority of workers to the broader struggle. Clearly aware of the positive role of the state, Haywood and Bohn's third argument was that socialist victories at the local level would enable the party to use existing social services to aid and sustain the working class in its protracted fight. The party existed to serve the industrial union, not vice-versa. Recognition of that relationship would prevent the movement from abandoning its revolutionary role for the sake of short-term reform gains.[16]

The publication of *Industrial Socialism* helped stimulate a year-long debate over direct action that would ultimately lead to Haywood's ouster from the NEC and an attempted censure of Kerr & Company. Morris Hillquit, Haywood's major antagonist, charged that the pamphlet's strategy was not socialist at all, but rather anarchistic. He charged that specific arguments in the tract opened the door for violence, sabotage, and disrespect for the law, all inimical to his reading of the evolutionary nature of socialism. Haywood and Bohn had argued that average workers who understood Marx's notions of the class struggle and surplus value would lose all respect for the property rights of "profit takers" and use "any weapon which will win [their] fight." Aware that the laws protecting property were made "by and for the capitalists," the class-conscious worker would not hesitate to break them. Any action that advanced "the interest of the working class" was right.[17]

Constructivists such as Hillquit contended that arguments like these threatened the entire movement. The fears of the right were not necessarily ill-founded; external events over which the party had no control or say gave Haywood and Bohn's pronouncements their controversial immediacy. *Industrial Socialism* appeared at the very moment when the movement faced a crisis caused by the use of extraparliamentary tactics. The debate over direct action became urgent and evolved in a context of heightened tempers and inflamed emotions stimulated by the bombing of the Los Angeles Times Building. The event, which had far-reaching effects on the course and direction of the movement, was carried out, ironically, by two nonsocialist craft unionists.

The shock waves from the dynamite blast that demolished the offices of Harrison Gray Otis's *Los Angeles Times* during the early morning hours of October 1, 1910, reverberated through the labor and socialist movements—and took the lives of twenty-one workers. The explosion came on the heels of a protracted attempt by organized labor to open Los Angeles, a notoriously anti-union town. The *Times* immediately charged that the "anarchic scum" of the labor movement was responsible for the event. A state prosecutor, in April 1911, brought an indictment for murder against the brothers James and John McNamara, leaders of the Structural and Iron Workers' Union active in the attempt to unionize Los Angeles. The labor and socialist movements immediately responded to the charges by suggesting that the affair reeked of a frame-up similar to that Haywood and his colleagues had experienced in the Steunenberg case in 1906.

Convinced of their innocence, the entire labor and socialist press portrayed the McNamaras as victimized martyrs of a conspiracy to discredit the union cause. The collective strength of the AFL and a defense fund headed by Samuel Gompers procured the renowned counsel of Clarence Darrow. Job Harriman, who had just declared his candidacy for mayor of Los Angeles, also joined the defense team and focused his campaign on the frame-up of the supposedly innocent trade union brothers. He thereby inextricably tied his electoral effort to the defense of the McNamaras.

In a dramatic turnaround at the beginning of December 1911, Darrow convinced the McNamaras to change their plea to guilty. Their confession devastated the trade union cause on the West Coast and blackened organized labor's eye nationally. It also destroyed Job Harriman's socialist campaign for mayor. Witnesses recounted how disenchanted voters littered the streets of Los Angeles with discarded Harriman for Mayor buttons the day after the announcement. The more conservative elements of the defense coalition hastily backpedaled in repudiation of the brothers.[18]

Significantly, the Socialist Party's right used the affair as a cudgel of recrimination to assail the advocates of direct action. The case set off ripples that eventually reached Haywood, Bohn, and Kerr, leading voices in the defense of the McNamaras before and after their admission of guilt. The right soon charged that it was just the kind of thinking that had emanated from Kerr & Company that was responsible for the type of deed represented by the McNamaras' actions.[19]

Following the McNamaras' change of plea, the pages of *ISR* refused to abandon the brothers entirely and defended them as brave but misguided men forced to the wall by capital's intransigence. Writing for the *Review*, Eugene Debs castigated the "cowardly and contemptible" denunciation of the McNamaras by Gompers and the AFL. He argued that the McNamaras' crime was the "logical conclusion" of "Gompers craft unionism." He pointed out that the brothers were not members of the Socialist party, but "members of the Democratic party, . . . the Catholic church, . . . and the pure and simple labor union." He nevertheless refused to join in the "capitalist clamour and craft union clacque of denunciation" of the condemned unionists. Frank Bohn argued that the brothers had been misguided by the same sense that John Brown had been: "The hearts of the McNamaras were right. It was their heads that were in error." He, too, viewed their resort to dynamite as the logical outcome of an antiquated craft union strategy. He suggested that the outcome of the case reflected the tactical failure of party gradualists as "socialists . . . too cowardly to teach the class struggle . . . from which the McNamaras turned away in disgust and filled their suitcases with dynamite."[20] Such pronouncements, coming as they did on the heels of the Harriman defeat and the retreat of the AFL, understandably irritated the more conservative elements in the party.

The McNamara case merely exacerbated existing tensions. It appeared, by the end of 1911, that the two poles within the Socialist Party were irreconcilable. While the left increased its commitment and support for free speech fights, strikes, unemployment demonstrations, and agitations for the eight-hour day, the right had its confidence buoyed by unprecedented electoral successes in several elections through 1910 and 1911. Concern over the effects on future electoral victories of a continuing emphasis on direct action led to a number of constructivist attempts to discipline and censure the left. Both left and right, in the meantime, jockeyed for control of the party's governing bodies, the National Committee and the smaller seat of administrative power, the NEC. The McNamaras' confession merely injected a new urgency into the series of squabbles and parliamentary maneuvers, already underway, for control of the NEC and its capacity to shape the direction of the party.

The maneuvering for control of the NEC ultimately led to a coordinated attack on Charles H. Kerr & Company. Kerr had long editorialized in favor of several schemes to thwart the power of the right on the NEC. In November 1911 Robert Hunter, a New York gradualist and member of the NEC, initiated a motion requesting an investigation of Kerr & Company. Hunter charged that Charles Kerr ran the firm like a dictator, that he had attempted to create a "socialist book monopoly," and that he had built a "machine" whose express purpose was to subvert the party. The motion also charged that *ISR* "sneered at political action, advocated rival unionism, and vacillated between Anarchism and Proudhonism." Hunter suggested that "the constant emphasis THE REVIEW lays on Direct Action and its apparent faith that a revolution can be evoked by Will or Force is in direct opposition to our whole philosophy." By a vote of four to one, the NEC passed Hunter's motion and forwarded a request for action to their parent body, the National Committee. That forum approved the motion and selected a three-member panel to conduct an inquiry and report its findings before the party convention in Indianapolis in May 1912. Hunter, Hillquit, and others clearly viewed the probe of the Kerr operation as their opening salvo in an offensive against the left-wingers.[21]

With the probe of Kerr & Company underway, the gradualists shifted their sights toward that prime culprit and arch-heretic Big Bill Haywood. The IWW leader had joined the *ISR* staff as an associate editor in October 1911 and accepted a nomination to run for the NEC that November. Circulated by *ISR*, his acceptance speech criticized the activity of that body, then dominated by the right. Declaring that he did not wish to be elected under a "misapprehension," Haywood reminded readers that the party, in convention, had declared a neutral position on the labor movement, that supposed neutrality was not observed, and that numerous members had carried on a vigorous effort to ally the party with the "decadent trade unions." The mission of the party would not be achieved until it had carried the "message of industrial unionism" to the working class. He therefore called upon the NEC to carry on educational work "to the end of industrial as well as political solidarity."[22]

Frank Bohn also announced his candidacy for the NEC in that same issue of *ISR*. Not as well known as Haywood, he did not win office. His intent, spelled out just below Haywood's announcement, could not have gone unnoticed by the right, however. He, too, charted an independent position. Looking ahead to the presidential elections of 1912, Bohn warned that the Socialist Party should not compete with any middle-class reform party. The party, he argued, should concentrate on propaganda and education in preparation for the "social revolution." It should also stress industrial as well as political action. Bohn warned against any alliance with "cliques of trade union politicians."[23]

Immediately after Haywood and Bohn announced their candidacies, Morris Hillquit launched an attack. In a letter to the *New York Call* on November 20, 1911, he quoted at length from a paragraph in *Industrial Socialism*. Haywood and Bohn had stated that the worker in the fight against capital "retains absolutely no respect for the 'property rights' of the profit takers. He will use any weapon which will win this fight. He knows that the present laws of property are made by and for the capitalists. Therefore he doesn't hesitate to break them." Hillquit charged that such pronouncements were "good anarchist doctrine . . . diametrically opposed to the accepted policies of Socialism." He called upon the party press to disavow the left's position, and he argued for an orderly transition to socialism through the winning of majority opinion. Socialists, once in power, would "fight like tigers" at the barricades if the capitalists refused to obey the new regime. Any violation of the law at present, however, would label socialists as nothing more than "petty criminals and sneak thieves." Unable to resist a bout in the polemical lists, Haywood cleverly riposted by asking whether Hillquit proposed "to stand behind a barricade of law books firing a series of well-written briefs at the advancing army of capitalist minions." He insisted that the capitalist legal system could not be used to bring socialism. It, too, would collapse after the abolition of private ownership of the means of production. Haywood then challenged Hillquit to meet him in debate.[24]

The Haywood-Hillquit exchange was widely reproduced and set off an extensive discussion of the use of force, obedience to the law, and revolutionary violence. *ISR* entered the fray immediately. The Kerr group editorially stated that it hoped for a peaceful transition to socialism but noted that capitalists would not surrender political power without a struggle. The *Review* dismissed Hillquit's allusion to "barricades" by arguing that "the capitalists do not fear guns and barricades. They won't have to do the fighting." The only power that the ruling class feared was the concerted withdrawal of labor power. Electoral action not backed by industrial organization would prove "well nigh futile" when push came to shove. The

NEC refused to consider the question of industrial unionism and tended to "read out of the party" those who advocated such organization.[25]

In response to *ISR* and Haywood's candidacy, the influential New York gradualist intellectual John Spargo announced that he had decided to run for reelection to the NEC as "a duty I owed the party." Spargo stated that he could not abandon the struggle against the "pernicious influence of the *International Socialist Review* and its hired representatives," Haywood and Bohn. He charged that the two had entered the NEC contest to secure "fat and profitable contracts for the *Review*." Kerr responded immediately to both the Hunter indictment and Spargo's accusations by recounting the company's history and welcoming an investigation and the accompanying publicity. In regard to Spargo's innuendo about "fat jobs," Kerr published the salaries for Mary and Leslie Marcy, Bohn, Haywood, and himself and made note of the fact that no other socialist publication made its salary list public. In response to Hunter's charge that Haywood and Kerr had "compelled" each local on the *ISR* Lecture Bureau circuit to pay the *Review* $250 per night, Kerr again published the terms for Haywood dates.[26]

The party's voters ultimately chose seven candidates to sit on the NEC. Haywood finished third behind Victor Berger and Job Harriman and two thousand votes ahead of Hillquit. A few days after his election, Haywood appeared at a mass meeting in New York's Cooper Union. Speaking before a packed house, he launched a full-blown attack on Hillquit and his associates. The address, the final appearance in his 1911 *ISR* tour, proved to be Haywood's Rubicon as a Socialist Party leader.[27] Irrepressible as ever, he informed his audience, composed overwhelmingly of party members who had followed the ongoing in-house dispute over obedience to the law, that he would discuss the class struggle in terms so simple that "even a lawyer could understand them." In an obvious attack on the middle-class, professional elements in the party, he asserted that the class struggle was not visible "through the stained-glass windows of a cathedral" or through "the spectacles of capitalist law." One could only understand it by entering the factory or by riding above or below a boxcar.

Haywood launched into a scathing indictment of the violence and suffering inherent in the industrial order at home and abroad. Using a brief history of the Western Federation of Miners as a backdrop, he appealed for industrywide unions and a dual strategy of political and industrial action. Summing up his description of the struggles in the West, he stated, amid tremendous applause, that he "despised the law," that he was not "a law-abiding citizen," and that no true socialist could be one. He also noted in passing that he had wanted to further describe conditions he had witnessed in Europe and France in order to "justify direct action and sabotage." Haywood informed his listeners that he did not know of anything that would bring as much "satisfaction" to the worker and "as much anguish to the boss as a little sabotage in the right place at the right time." "Find out what it means," he suggested. "It won't hurt you and it will cripple the boss." Haywood finished his address by reminding his audience that a socialist's reason for being was to "overthrow the capitalist by forcible means if necessary."

The Cooper Union speech stimulated a new and heightened round of charge and countercharge. A gauntlet thrown down in a key bailiwick of gradualist strength, Haywood's address immediately drew invective from both the party's conservatives and the city's mainstream press. Initial accounts of the talk, garbled and inexact, led members of the party's right and center to suggest that he had read himself out of the organization.

In a clear attempt to force the question, and believing that the majority of the party's rank and file would uphold Haywood's position, Kerr reproduced a stenographic text of the December speech well over a month after it was made. Ironically, the *ISR* report confirmed the worst fears of the right. More significantly, it forced several key party figures to distance themselves from Haywood's pronouncements. The same issue of *ISR* also carried a piece by Debs, who stated that he had no problem with a disrespect for capitalist property laws but that he opposed sabotage and direct action as commonly interpreted by the IWW.[28] He also opposed "any tactics which involve stealth, secrecy, intrigue and necessitate acts of individual violence for their execution." He argued that the tactics of "the bomb planter" and the "midnight assassin" played directly into the hands of the "enemy." If sabotage and direct action received official sanction from the Socialist Party, "it would at once be the signal for all the agents provocateur and police spies in the country to join the party and get busy." Debs stated that he hoped to see the party "place itself squarely on record at the coming national convention against sabotage and every other form of violence and destructiveness suggested by what is known as 'direct action.'"

Coming from a long-time ally of the left highly respected in most party circles, Debs's judgment carried considerable weight. In this particular instance, however, the *ISR* team took issue with the "man from Terre Haute" and forged its own independent position. The monthly's editorial for February 1912 argued that in the struggle against capitalism, the working class and its "instrument," the Socialist Party, had access to either or both of two methods, parliamentary campaigns or direct action.[29] The

editorial noted that the European movement had long advocated and practiced both. It then criticized the confusion over the definition of direct
action as "the individual action of the bombthrower" by arguing that such
action had to be collective. By its very nature a reflection of working-class
organization, direct action should not to be confused with isolated, individual acts of desperation. Debs's argument had shared the gradualists'
confusion over the term. "Dynamite," the editorial asserted, "is the logical
weapon for the craft unionist, who is vainly trying to oppose modern capitalism with an outgrown and dying form of organization." The uproar over
the McNamaras' confession had not yet quieted down; Haywood had
voiced support for the brothers in his talk. The *ISR* editorial likewise refused to "join in the hue and cry against the McNamaras," but instead suggested that had the brothers adopted the coordinated tactics of "class direct action" and "political action" they would be helping the "Social
Revolution" rather than languishing in jail.

Commenting upon the publication of Haywood's full speech, the editors foresaw that such words might "keep some people out of the party."
They put forward the hope that "the real militant workers . . . , who wonder
whether the Socialist party members really mean what they say when they
call themselves revolutionists," would find it "a clarion call." They argued
that the question of sabotage could not be settled "in conventions or in
printed arguments," but only by the workers themselves through their day-
to-day experiences: "When they have developed the intelligence to unite
into one big union, they will be able to use this dangerous weapon when
it is needed and only when it is needed, and nothing that the *Review* may
print or that conventions may resolve will matter much."

The editors did qualify their stance over Haywood's Cooper Union
polemic by stating that they did not necessarily agree with every word of
it and that they held with the criticisms put forward by Robert Rives La-
Monte, which also appeared that month.[30] LaMonte hammered out a clearly independent position that addressed a number of questions swirling
through the dispute. He immediately took the high ground by stating that
he found Haywood "in full accord with Marx and Engels" in an understanding of the class character of the state. He also praised Haywood's understanding of the need for unified organization on both the political and
industrial fronts. Then he analyzed what he viewed as the speech's "minor defects."

The right took great issue with Haywood's comment about not being
"a law-abiding citizen." LaMonte noted that most socialists abided by the
law because "the other fellows have the law-enforcing power." He marked

the futility of individual defiance to that power and stated that he found
Haywood's support of the McNamaras "magnificent" and "refreshing" in
contrast to "the cowardly sycophancy of those trade unionists and Socialists who, in their eagerness to keep the skirts of the labor and Socialist
movement 'clean,' have joined in the bourgeois cry for blood and ven-
geance." Haywood had erred, however, in suggesting that the McNamaras
understood the class struggle. James McNamara now faced a life sentence
because he "courageously" carried the policies of "pure and simple" craft
unionism to their logical conclusion. Chief responsibility for the crime, in
LaMonte's estimation, lay with the Steel Trust and its campaign to crush
trade unionism and the "labor leaders of the Gompers type" who, in their
opposition to socialism and industrial unionism, left the McNamaras with
the choice of "supine surrender or dynamite."

Haywood had favorably recounted the dynamite destruction of a particular mill during a protracted WFM strike some years earlier, a reference
LaMonte cited as the "one fatal weakness" in a "great speech" because "the
man who believes in class organization is the last man who ought to risk
appearing to praise the suicidal tactics of the Anarchist." LaMonte then
praised the "courage" with which Haywood defended sabotage. Sabotage,
LaMonte asserted, had an advantage over the strike because it allowed a
worker to stay on the job and draw pay. Although he cautioned that "used
too freely, like whiskey, it may prove dangerous," he argued that sabotage,
if used "with brains," could be "an excellent weapon in the class war." The
election of a socialist to office was a form of sabotage on the "repressive
machinery" of the "ruling class."

LaMonte criticized the right-wing for its reliance upon the opinions of
German Social Democracy. Hillquit had solicited an opinion from the
SPD's Karl Kautsky on the question of obedience to the law. The American movement, LaMonte argued, could figure out its own difficulties.
German comrades did not necessarily comprehend the situation in the
United States. After all, the German party had a different historical position on the question of legalism. Kautsky, "like all German Socialists," had
a "touching and child-like faith in the efficacy of democratic political forms"
because they "never had a democratic government." In America, where law
was theoretically the will of the people, "We are cursed by a superstitious
and paralyzing reverence for the law. . . . Respect for law, respect for the
'sacred right of private property' are the stone walls against which every
Socialist agitation in America is continually ramming his long-suffering
head. This wall we must batter down, even though Hillquit and Spargo . . .
assisted by the convenient cowardice of the party editors, are doing their

utmost to buttress it up. It will be so much the worse for them if their heads are pushing against the other side of the wall when we topple it over."

If the socialist movement were to fulfill its "mission," LaMonte continued, it had to turn from the "painfully respectable . . . snobbish, reformist legality" of Hillquit and Spargo to the "robust, virile contempt for bourgeois property expressed by Marx and Engels in the *Communist Manifesto*'s call for the abolition of private property. The movement patriarchs' spirit of "dauntless revolutionary audacity" lay with the "indiscreet" Haywood rather than the "meticulous" Hillquit. LaMonte concluded with a list of questions that posed the historic issue of reform or revolution. The choice, he suggested, would be decided in the selection of delegates for the upcoming national convention.

The right-wingers also eagerly looked ahead to the approaching party convention in May 1912. No sooner had Haywood been elected to the NEC than his foes began to investigate ways to repudiate his politics and drive him from office. The verbatim record of his "heresies," produced for all to see by Charles H. Kerr & Company, gave them the ammunition they sought. The partisans of the right marshaled their forces and initiated a first series of proceedings against him. His supporters, in turn, rallied to his defense and arranged another appearance for him at Cooper Union. This time it would be the debate with Hillquit that Haywood had requested earlier. In the resultant January exchange, Haywood again argued that the capitalist system was too rotten to change a step at a time and that the AFL was too reactionary to reform. He charged that Hillquit had abandoned the class struggle when he helped negotiate away the right to strike during the New York Garment Worker's Strike in the autumn of 1909. He suggested that Hillquit did not understand industrial unionism as "socialism with its working clothes on."

The right was temporarily forced to ease off its campaign against Haywood. With the debate over his utterances still smoldering, Haywood had rushed off in mid-February to assist the embattled textile workers at Lawrence, Massachusetts. The resultant victory at Lawrence once again catapulted him to national notoriety and marked a high-water mark for the IWW's militant, direct-action strategies. The right bided its time.[31]

Both the right and the left prepared for a showdown at the Socialist Party's May convention. Personal attacks on Haywood reached new heights as the national gathering approached. Various constructivists went so far as to suggest that the Lawrence strike had actually been won by the Socialist Party and not the IWW. They suggested that the "revolutionists" in the party opposed majority rule and advocated the anarchists' "propaganda of the deed." The left, in response, claimed that the strikers at Lawrence had discovered the "winning tactics"; industrial unionism had withstood the test of battle and would soon sweep the entire movement. In preparation for the impending party battle, *ISR* beckoned all "clear headed revolutionists," especially individuals who had left the Socialist Party in recent years or had not yet joined, to enroll in time to help set a revolutionary course.[32]

In some ways hard-pressed to refute many of the charges leveled by the right, *ISR* published "Some Definitions" by Frank Bohn just before the opening of the convention.[33] Bohn argued that direct action was "any action taken by the workers directly at the point of production with a view of bettering their conditions." Opposition to direct action therefore entailed opposition to all trade unionism. He defined sabotage as striking while staying in the shop. It need not necessarily mean destruction of property, Bohn insisted, but included any tactic that obstructed the regular operation or output of industry; it did not necessarily involve violence. An industrial union was a union of all those who worked in a specific industry. A revolutionary unionist was someone who planned to use the industrial union and socialist political organization to overthrow capitalism and bring about "an industrial democracy." Syndicalism and revolutionary unionism were synonymous. Bohn's arguments and *ISR*'s editorial thrust anticipated the key question that drew the line between right and left.

The first skirmish of the Socialist Party's 1912 convention occurred a week before the delegates gathered in Indianapolis. At that point, the committee appointed earlier to investigate the operations of Charles H. Kerr & Company issued its report.[34] Elements on the right believed that the disclosures would decide the first round of the long-anticipated party battle in their favor. Just the opposite occurred, however. The committee surveyed the history and operation of the company and its distribution of stocks and concluded that the shareholders, mainly socialists, were "not hostile to the ideas of Comrade Kerr as far as the business of the company is concerned." The report showed that the firm's receipts for 1911 had totaled some $63,000, and profits were nearly $2,200. Kerr drew a salary of $1,500 a year, and Mary Marcy received $1,000. The ten to fifteen regular employees worked an eight-hour day, received time and a half for overtime, and enjoyed an annual week's vacation with pay. The committee found *ISR* to have seventeen thousand subscribers and an additional bulk and over-the-counter sale of some thirty-two thousand copies.

Significantly, the investigators criticized those who had encouraged the probe. They pointed out that Robert Hunter had become a shareholder in 1900 and could have checked the firm's records at any time had he wished to do so. They concluded that there was no need to call on the party to examine the company; Kerr was totally open and had cooperated fully in the inquiry. The committee members declared that "we believe no Socialist publishing house has more open methods of conducting the publishing business than this one." Quite clearly, the right's attempt to discipline the most important national platform for the left had failed.

The move to censure Kerr marked but the first of several thwarted attempts, initiated by the constructivists, to impose their will and politic on the party. Several motions introduced by the right met with opposition from the left and the center, which joined in a spirit of compromise.[35] The real issue at the convention was the future of the party's stance on industrial unionism and direct action, broadly defined. But the right found itself incapable of assailing the left directly on those questions in the aftermath of the success at Lawrence.

The Indianapolis meeting finally acquired a focus with the attempt, initiated by the right, to amend the party constitution.[36] The gradualists began their offensive by winning a place at the speaker's rostrum for Karl Legien, a representative of the German General Federation of Labor Unions and a leader of the most conservative faction of the German Social Democratic Party. On a tour of the United States arranged by Samuel Gompers, Legien had already criticized strikes as a tactic beneficial to employers and called for the dissolution of the IWW in earlier addresses. He informed the convention that the German movement had "no room for sabotage and similar syndicalist and destructive tendencies."[37] The SPD, he asserted, had always cooperated with the established trade unions in order to defeat dual unionism. His party's alliance with the trade unions, Legien argued, explained its unparalleled success at the polls.

Right-wing leaders Hillquit, Spargo, and Berger decided to put forward an amendment to the party constitution that would effectively eliminate Haywood and the left. Article 2, section 6 of the body's bylaws, as of 1908, provided for the expulsion of all members who opposed "political action as a weapon of the working class." The 1912 Committee on Constitution, chaired by Hillquit, recommended that the section be changed to call for the expulsion of anyone "who opposes political action or advocates crime against the person or other methods of violence." Amended from the floor, the motion as presented for adoption read: "Any member of the party who opposes political action or advocates crime, sabotage, or other methods of violence as a weapon of the working class to aid in its emancipation, shall be expelled from the party."[38] The amendment passed after heated debate and then went to the membership at large in the form of a national referendum.

The *Review* responded quickly. Criticizing the proposed amendment, Kerr noted that sabotage and violence were not necessarily synonymous. He suggested that the proposed clause would have no effect whatsoever on the sabotage "being practiced in a quiet way as a response to the capitalistic tactics of 'scientific management.'"[39] He called upon the membership to abide by the clause of the constitution that called upon the party to abstain from interference in controversies within the labor movement over tactics and organization in industrial struggles. Initially optimistic, he looked forward to the referendum as a "rather interesting test of the extent to which the education of the membership has proceeded." He obviously did not anticipate the result.

The amendment met with approval of the party through a vote in which only 11 percent of the membership participated. Successful in its passage of the antisabotage clause, the constructivists immediately resumed their criticisms of Haywood and Kerr & Company. Victor Berger's *Social Democratic Herald* charged that Haywood was a coward who, when on trial for his life, "hid his belief in murder; but once out of danger he not only publicly applauded the crimes of the McNamaras but has tried his best to turn Socialists into emissaries of murder and violence, backed up by the anarchistic intellectual, C. H. Kerr and his anarchistic *Review*." Referring directly to Kerr and the *ISR*, Hillquit charged that the party was endangered by "the meddling and intriguing of self-appointed leaders, who have built up powerful machines within the party . . . ; who have on their payroll a host of traveling agitators disseminating their particular vagaries throughout the movement; who . . . seek to foment discord and confusion in the Socialist Party." He described *ISR* as "an alleged socialist magazine" and "a private enterprise . . . published for the propaganda of a little Socialism, and a little anarchism and for the sale of books." He labeled the *Review*'s account of the national convention both "scurrilous" and "contemptible" and castigated Kerr for his "brazen affrontery to pose as guardian of the party." The company, he asserted, was "preying upon the Socialist movement."[40]

Not one to take such assaults lying down, Kerr responded. Hillquit had "been a dictator for so long, and loves power so well, that a general revolt against his methods naturally excites him." He countered Hillquit's invective by pointing out that *ISR* was not "the personal organ of any individual," but rather "the voice of that large and growing portion of the Socialist Party which cares more for the overthrow of capitalism than for office-seeking and office-holding." Insulted by the "slanderous" accusation of "anarchism," Kerr rhetorically asked whether it was "anarchism to advocate the abolition of capitalism, and does Socialism mean nothing but office seeking?" Meanwhile, the animosity between Hillquit and Kerr had taken other forms. The executive committee of Local New York went so far as to request that its branches halt the circulation of *ISR*. When some of its members, supporters of the left, attempted to circulate the monthly at a Madison Square Garden campaign rally for Eugene Debs, the arrangements committee responsible for the gathering called in the police to stop them.[41]

At the beginning of December 1912, Haywood attended a victory rally to celebrate the acquittal of Joe Ettor and Arturo Giovanitti, two IWW organizers charged with murder during the Lawrence strike.[42] Speaking at the gathering at New York's Harlem Casino, he once again endorsed direct action as "the shortest way home" and sabotage, "that much misunderstood word." He declared that "there is no revolutionary action that can be too strong if we will only throw the capitalistic class back." Sabotage did not necessarily mean violent action in the vocabulary of the IWW militant, but that did not matter to the constructivists. Both the *Call* and New York's German-language *Volkszeitung* editorially suggested that Haywood's language necessitated his elimination from the NEC under article 2, section 6. Both papers also erroneously charged that Haywood opposed political action. Within two weeks, the New York State Committee voted to initiate a party referendum to recall Haywood from the national body.

Kerr immediately came to Haywood's defense. He pointed out that the preamble circulated with the referendum charged Haywood with utterances he never made. His editorial correctly went to the heart of the matter when it noted Hillquit and company had devised the motion with the "deliberate intention" to drive direct-actionists and industrial unionists from the party. Kerr nevertheless urged all those upset with the direction of the party to remain in it, "no matter how the vote may result."[43]

The balloting closed on February 26, 1913. With approximately 25 percent of the membership voting, the motion to remove Haywood from the NEC passed by a vote of twenty-two thousand to eleven thousand despite the fact that article 2, section 6 said nothing whatsoever about that body. Haywood's treatment at the hands of the constructivists outraged and demoralized many party members. In the months following, membership fell precipitously. Even Haywood allowed his membership to lapse, and thousands of left-wingers followed suit. Party rolls declined by forty thousand within four months of the recall, as socialist strength in the trade union movement decreased. The Socialist Party's numerical and electoral strength also declined to an ineffectual low.

Haywood remained on the editorial board of *ISR*. Undeterred, despite what must be considered a major political setback for the left, the Kerr group continued its espousal and support for direct action and industrial unionism. The company's annual financial report, issued the same month as the Haywood recall, could proudly announce that 1912 had been its most successful year to date. The statement noted that "the summer of 1912 found the *Review* bitterly attacked by a certain faction of the Socialist Party" and that its "natural growth" suffered somewhat as a result.[44] Kerr could nevertheless announce that the subscription list had recouped by January 1913 and was "growing more rapidly than ever before," that all signs pointed to increased growth for the company "due to the constant co-operation of thousands of working men and women, whose ideas we are trying to carry out to the best of our ability." Early that year the company announced the release of the well-known French syndicalist Emile Pouget's *On Sabotage*, newly translated by the jailed IWW organizer Arturo Giovannitti.

The *Review* issued its formal response to the constructivist attack in March 1913. A strongly worded editorial written by Mary Marcy argued that the right, unable to assail the high ground of industrial unionism, had developed a straw man in the issue of individual violence. She argued that the major fear of the gradualists was the *Review*'s unequivocal stance on "revolutionary unionism" and then enunciated what the monthly stood for:

> The REVIEW is, above all Socialist party periodicals, the journal of the working class. . . .
>
> As opposed to Labor Partyism, we have advocated the Socialist Party.
>
> As opposed to Fusion with capitalist parties, we have stood for No Compromise.
>
> As opposed to middle class propaganda, we have offered proletarian literature.
>
> Instead of Craft Division, we have taught Class Unionism.
>
> We have ignored the leader in our desires to make the working class self-reliant. We have insisted that elected officials are to take their orders from the workers who elected them. . . .
>
> Instead of dynamite, we have urged industrial unionism.
>
> In place of a tiger fighting behind street barricades, we have taught organization and the general strike.
>
> Against individual violence, we have made our plea for revolutionary unionism.
>
> It profits the working class nothing to kill the scab workingman or tyrannical bosses. It would benefit them not at all if an individual smashed his machine.

But it would help them in many ways if the workers, as a class, went very slow on the job.

Class action alone counts and to have class action, we must have: Class education and class organization.[45]

Marcy conveyed the hope that the conservatives might continue their pursuit of the straw man so that they would no longer impede the real work carried out by the industrial unionist wing. She called upon the company's allies "to cease replying to the enemies of the *Review.*" Insisting that the necessary education would continue, she closed with a ringing declaration: "Our concern is the great class war. And the main things are: No compromise on the political field, and revolutionary class unionism on the economic field! Agitate! Educate! Organize!"[46]

The final comment from the *ISR* group in regard to the in-house imbroglio appeared in October 1913. Author of the lead editorial that month, Frank Bohn launched into a clear-headed analysis of the effects of the Haywood ouster and laid out a distinct plan of action for those disturbed and alienated by the behavior of the right-wingers. Noting the decline of more than 25 percent in party membership and a far greater decline in related organizational activity, Bohn pointed to what he perceived as the cause, article 2, section 6, "a living, standing insult to the whole American movement."[47] Commenting on the passage of the amendment at the Indianapolis convention, he noted that

During the thirteen years in which it has been my privilege to work in the Socialist movement, I have never heard a capitalist politician or even the most bitter Roman Catholic clerical opponent of Socialism say that we were criminals. It remained for the Indianapolis convention of the party itself to declare to the world that our ranks were so infested. When the vote was passed the hilarious leaders of the majority started to sing the "Marsalaise"—thus degrading our sacred anthem into a means of the jollification to signalize their victory in a party brawl.[48]

Following a brief discussion of criminality and sabotage, the contradictory nature of the amendment as passed, and the results on party membership and activity, Bohn called upon the thousands of comrades who had left the party or had become inactive to get involved and "stay with the fight." He suggested that the left wing simply "for the time being forget Article II., Section 6," in order to get on with more important matters. Striking a prophetic note, he suggested that "the day will come when those who passed it, realizing their shame and disgrace, will vote to repeal it." He also argued that no matter how wrong those who passed the motion were, "their error is not one-tenth as great as that of the member who deserts the standards under fire." He concluded with a call for an end to the in-fighting: "Factionalism lays hold of the ignorant member and keeps him ignorant. It seizes upon the weak man and turns his weakness into downright meanness. No man or woman can long continue engaged in internecine quarrels and come out with mind unscathed. Let us have an end to it."[49]

The party subsequently experienced a short-lived resurgence with the coming of World War I. An articulate voice in opposition to preparedness, militarism, and the nationalist bloodletting that engulfed Europe, it became a beleaguered outpost of resistance to U.S. entry into the war. Crippled and denied some of its most important militants as the result of the protracted in-house feud, the party nevertheless faced the war drive and the resultant plunge into the fray. Determined to build a political movement despite the setbacks of 1912 and 1913, the activists at Charles H. Kerr & Company stayed with it. Their persistence outlasted the decline of the intervening period and carried them to the center of agitation against preparedness and the nation's eventual entry into the Great War.

The *International Socialist Review,* 1908–18

The *International Socialist Review* (*ISR*) was a major chronicle of the socialist movement in the United States during the first two decades of the twentieth century. A richly laden source from that bygone era, it conveys more information about the particular social and political causes for which it spoke than any other contemporary record. Month by month for nearly eighteen years, the magazine's contributors, following Charles Kerr's leadership, reported and made comment on every major social, political, and economic development that had some discernible bearing on the course and direction of the movement and the society it sought to transform.

As a leading voice, at times a clarion, for the industrial-unionist, direct-action left of American socialism after 1909, the *Review* covered an immense range of topics and issues pertinent to that wing of the movement. An authentically popular monthly during that latter phase, the *Review's* style, format, and content conveyed not only the particular political culture of the movement it served but also an informed sense and critical perspective of the changes transforming society during the years leading up to and spanning World War I.[1]

During the major part of its first decade, *ISR* served mainly as a sounding board for the numerous theoretical debates facing the socialist movement at home and abroad. Its primary goal, as enunciated at its inception, was to help familiarize U.S. activists with socialist thought. It also sought to interpret developments in the United States from a Marxist perspective. Differing opinion on the strategy and tactics of the U.S. movement and comprehensive discussions and exchanges on the "correct" Marxian or scientific position on numerous questions received lengthy airings as a

result. In addition, ongoing debates on such topics as socialism's relationship to the farmer and the "land question,"[2] the "Negro problem,"[3] wom-
en and socialism,[4] and the socialist perspective on organized religion[5] often contributed to the bulk of material for any given issue in those earlier
years.

The "world of labor," the advances and retreats that trade unions made
and the role of socialists within organized labor, received limited coverage and comment, however. During the first seven years of *ISR*, most
material on the workings of the labor movement, that direct organized
expression of the working class with which Simons, Kerr, and their associates sought league, remained confined to Max Hayes's monthly columns
on "The World of Labor." Hayes, a Cleveland-based socialist trade union
leader, wrote regularly on employers' offensives and technological innovations in the work place and industrial workers' responses to them. An
advocate of socialist organizing within the AFL and a critic of dual unionism, he often reported on the tensions between the left and the more conservative "pure and simple" supporters of Gompers within the skilled crafts.
Hayes readily criticized the IWW while commenting regularly on various
strikes, lockouts, and other conflicts.

News from the labor front occasionally found its way to the *Review*'s
editorial page, too. Pieces from important movement leaders with direct
ties to the day-to-day struggles of workers appeared less regularly. The
failures and successes of socialist organizing ventures, electoral campaigns,
and educational projects garnered a large amount of space and attention
as the Socialist Party grew and developed after 1901.[6]

Thoroughly internationalist in perspective from its inception onward,
the monthly also reported on developments in the labor and socialist
movements abroad—not only from Europe but also as far afield as Australia, Asia, Central and South America, and South Africa.[7] Kerr and Algie Simons provided coverage of the advances and setbacks faced by the
various fraternal parties of the Second International Socialist Congress.
Official bulletins and communications from the International Socialist
Bureau in Brussels were given high priority. Created as a clearinghouse for
communications among the various national parties of the International,
the bureau in 1902 designated *ISR* as its "official American organ" for
publishing messages and calls for international solidarity. The monthly
supplemented such official communiqués with the services of an Austri-
an-based clipping service that forwarded items from the left-wing press
throughout Europe. It thereby kept remarkably informed of events abroad
without depending on the established transatlantic news agencies.[8]

Despite such reportage of international and domestic movements, the monthly nevertheless remained a theoretical journal until Kerr became editor at the beginning of 1908. Far more political in the active sense, both action-oriented and consciously pitched to rank-and-file worker militants, each successive issue became less and less theoretical and more and more concerned with actual struggles and the practical, tactical questions confronting the movement at home and abroad. The monthly's pages began to feature news and commentary that the direct-action industrial union wing understood and needed. Firsthand reports of labor agitations, strikes, lockouts, attempts to organize mass unions, employers' offensives, and forms of resistance created by and through workers' initiatives received top priority under the guidance of Kerr and Mary and Leslie Marcy. The new direction and commitment made *ISR* a politically active voice that soon reached thousands of left-wingers throughout the United States.[9]

Kerr enunciated the change in direction on *ISR*'s tenth anniversary in July 1910. "Ten years ago," he recounted, "our aim was 'to educate the educators.' We thought the principles of socialism could be mastered by a chosen few and handed down to the many." The magazine's staff had come to realize, however, "that the industrial wage workers arrive from their daily experience at a clearer view of the class struggle than any mere theorist can possibly reach." If *ISR* were to become an "important weapon in the fight against capitalism," the "fighting magazine of socialism," then it had to serve the needs of the movement.[10]

As part of that drive to become such a fighting magazine, the *Review* developed a detailed oppositional analysis and critique of society in general. Supported by thousands of $1 annual subscriptions and countless newsstand and left-wing "hustler" sales, it articulated hopes and aspirations and the belief in the possibility of a viable alternative to the dominant course of early-twentieth-century America. It quite clearly sat firmly in this world and was part of it. *ISR* would not have continued to exist otherwise.[11]

A perfunctory examination of any run of issues for the period between 1908 and early 1918 (the year of its suppression) reveals an immediate sense of the monthly's breadth and scope. Unyieldingly committed to the advance of scientific socialism and the rational exposition of its ideas and methods, *ISR* drew subject matter and support for its perspective from an ever-widening social terrain exposed not only by the strengths, weaknesses, abuses, and excesses of rapid capitalist development, but also by its successes. Theory, for the activists who gravitated toward Kerr & Company, became inextricably intertwined with continued engagement, a practice firmly anchored in the real world.

Liberally spiced with original illustrations, a creative layout, and photographs, the post-1908 *ISR* at first glance resembled such mass-circulation magazines as *Scribner's* and *McCall's*, which rose to unprecedented heights of popularity during the same period. The similarities stemmed from Kerr's conscious decision to make the monthly popular and accessible to as large a readership as possible.[12] Format aside, *ISR's* ideological intent and political objective demarcated it from most of its mainstream journalistic contemporaries. Here was a magazine, popular in form, with an unflinchingly radical outlook and agenda. It had few, if any, rivals.[13]

As oppositional voice in the Progressive Era, *ISR* stood out as a critic of the multileveled reform impetus emanating from the major political parties and the advanced liberal sectors of the corporate world. Unswervingly Marxist, the Kerr group closely monitored the "tendency toward monopoly," an increased concentration of wealth and social power in fewer and fewer hands, which proceeded in seemingly unabated fashion throughout the period. Firmly convinced of the conflictual nature of a class society based upon the privatized accumulation of wealth and the ideology of free enterprise, they turned a critical eye toward attempts to mediate or resolve the nature of the class struggle within the confines of existing institutions. That radical perspective provided them with a vantage point, lacking in the mainstream press, on the dynamics of reform and the ideology of "progress." They viewed the underpinnings of capitalist development and called for markedly different solutions than those which liberal and conservative reform advocates put forward.

Significantly, the Kerr group's particular perspective and support for the movement's left wing did not stem from some subjective infatuation with militant direct action or a romanticized notion of "the revolution." It emanated instead from experience and an informed, ongoing assessment of numerous changes taking place within society. The *ISR* group filtered that experience, of course, through a particular prism—a specific reading of Marx that projected both the necessity and inevitability of a radical transformation in the course and direction of society. The group observed and chronicled the unabated concentration and organized strength of capitalist economic and political power and continually analyzed the strengths and weaknesses of the forces in opposition. Their commitment, promotion, and support for industrial unionism, and the dual strategy of direct action and electoral challenges, emerged from an evaluation of that particular correlation of forces. Their call for a social revolution and their related critique of reformist assumptions and gradualist strategies flowed logically from that same assessment.[14]

Kerr and his associates maintained the orthodox Marxian view that the "laws of motion of capital" made monopoly inevitable. Increased consolidation, the classical argument asserted, would ultimately polarize society into two classes: the exploiters (the bourgeoisie) and the exploited (the proletariat). Transformations in the productive process seemingly confirmed that perspective. The lead editorial marking *ISR*'s tenth anniversary clearly articulated the Kerr group's argument: "Capitalist production has gone on revolutionizing its processes day by day." Those new techniques, in turn, had created new working conditions with far-reaching effects. "Little capitalists have been crowded down into the ranks of the wageworkers. Skilled laborers have found the market for their skill cut off. Craft unions which previously kept their wages up have been beaten into submission, and all these have swelled the ranks of the revolutionary wageworkers, with nothing to lose and everything to gain."[15] Social reality had verified the scientific observations that formed the basis of the Marxian critique and call for social revolution.

One constant theme that emerged concerned changes in the nature of work. The monthly chronicled transformations not simply in the forms of technological innovation but in the reformulation of the social aspects of labor, those effects of innovation broadly defined as "scientific management" and engendered by the application of new techniques and corporate strategies for control of the workplace. *ISR* continually monitored the degradation and erosion of skills and the displacement of workers caused by the introduction of new machinery and the advancement of new managerial offensives forwarded by corporate leadership. Those fairly regular informative articles substantiated and bolstered support for the particular social critique and political position that the Kerr group held. Analysis of changes in the labor process provided the foundation for the group's radical critique and call for action. It remained a key element in the development of the group's broader social outlook and political trajectory.[16]

A double-edged sword, the *Review*'s line of argument on the labor process often cut in several different directions. New productive techniques often simultaneously displayed a progressive and a retrograde face. Changes in the productive process, in the "social relations of production," bore the promise of relieving humankind from the toil and drudgery of earlier epochs. Such technological advances, in the orthodox Marxian view, created the necessary preconditions for socialism by furthering the "socialization of production." The introduction of new productive processes, usually accompanied by speed-up, increased managerial control, and the erosion of workers' skill and say over the conditions of work, simultaneously created new horrors for the displaced, the degraded, and the disorganized. Technical and managerial innovations were accelerating the proletarian- ization and the further "immiseration" of labor.

Writing on technological changes in numerous industries, a long list of *ISR* contributors after 1908 asserted that such changes successfully under- mined the power of the "outmoded" skilled craft unions, which had inher- ent animus toward the "unskilled." Industrial unionism, the organization of all workers in a particular industry regardless of skill, the contributors argued, had become the necessary and logical response to new conditions.[17] A number of such pieces contained an argument that linked innovation to the need for revolutionary industrial unionism, what *ISR* associate ed- itor Robert Rives LaMonte referred to as the "new socialism."[18]

The series of articles on the changes in production also chronicled workers' resistance to numerous employers' offensives on the shop floor. Quite often spontaneous and carried out by hard-pressed, rank-and-file laborers against the wishes of skilled craft union leadership, or by suppos- edly unorganizable immigrants and women in "unskilled" or "semiskilled" positions, the new unionism further substantiated the strategic and tacti- cal line of argument that *ISR* championed. Such resistance in turn paved the way for *ISR*'s examination of tactics and strategy that the AFL com- monly disavowed. Debates and exchanges on the meaning and efficacy of sabotage, the continuing value of the sympathy strike and the boycott, and the strategic hope for a general strike appeared more and more frequent- ly despite criticism and opposition from the movement's right wing.[19]

The *Review*'s critique functioned on several different levels. The regu- lar contributors developed a detailed analysis of reform tendencies with- in the labor movement, especially the propensity on the part of the na- tional AFL leadership to sit down and talk "harmony of interest" or "conflict resolution" with the representatives of capital. Criticism of the route cho- sen by the right within organized labor followed logically from the ongo- ing assessment of changes at the base of American society and also stemmed from the practice of the AFL leadership on the industrial front. The conservatism of the AFL under Samuel Gompers' leadership—the disavowal of politics, the pursuit of economistic "pure and simpleism," and the presence of AFL notables in the National Civic Federation—furthered *ISR*'s analysis of the antiquated nature of the skilled craft union. AFL ac- tions, especially the behavior of its national leadership, bolstered the monthly's support for the industrial union alternative.[20]

The ongoing concern with the often subtle shifts in the nature and condition of work, changes at the point of production, also fueled broader analysis of the inadequacies of liberal reform. Political and social reform, from the perspective of *ISR*'s regular contributors, could not and would not resolve the basic sources of conflict and antagonism within society. Kerr and his associates continually argued that such tensions were inherent in the very nature of capitalist growth. Their origins lay in the dynamics of class exploitation, in the privatized expropriation of wealth from those who produced it. They argued that although reform promised some redress from the most flagrant abuses of the system, it would neither address nor alleviate the structural foundations of poverty and suffering inherent in the "anarchy of capitalist production." Socialism alone promised a solution to that antagonism. Reform only promised to buy time for the existing order and derail the movement. It was therefore a major impediment to the cause.[21]

Such analysis clearly set *ISR*'s major contributors apart from the advocates of liberal reform in the Progressive Era. It also delineated them from the more conservative reformist elements within the socialist camp. The critique of reformism, with its often-implicit renunciation of social revolution, became another foundation stone upon which the Kerr group's politics rested. If the majority of the working class necessary for the political victory of socialism were to be won over, then it must not be diverted by the lure and promise of reform. *ISR* did not stand against the existence of reform demands within the Socialist Party platform, but recognized the incidental value of such demands for the working class. Its contributors argued, however, that most reforms would "prove even more beneficial to the capitalist class." One of the "old parties" or some new reform party would eventually enact existing socialist reform demands. The election of socialist candidates could clearly assist the general movement, but the "principle battlefields of the Social Revolution must be in the shops, mines, factories and fields."[22] The Kerr group, by 1912, argued that the "ultimate aim" of the Socialist Party should be the education and organization of the working class for the "complete overthrow of capitalism." They held that the party should nominate candidates for office wherever possible but should never conceal or obscure its "revolutionary principles" to win votes from people "not in sympathy with our ultimate aim."[23]

An activist periodical as well as an oppositional voice that had a clear political agenda, *ISR* also maintained an ongoing belief and commitment to workers' education as a key to the cooperative commonwealth. Charles Kerr remained convinced that enough rationally presented factual information would unlock doors for others. The group that gathered around him was also confident in the emancipatory power of a broad education.

The emphasis on the dispersal of scientific socialism and the recruitment of working people to the socialist perspective and cause remained central. *ISR*'s editorial board also sought to deepen the understandings of those already involved in the movement. Rarely did an issue appear after 1908 that did not contain some discussion of a topic from the broad range of Marxian inquiry. What made such articles distinct from those appearing earlier was their style, form, and perspective. The earlier *ISR*, aimed clearly at movement intellectuals, was academic in tone and somewhat exclusivist. Kerr and his associates after 1908 consciously geared discussions of such topics as the theory of surplus value and the scientific basis for the class struggle to industrial workers and migrant laborers, who were directly involved in the conflicts of the period. In effect, *ISR* developed a "pedagogy of the oppressed," a distinct method of instruction that attempted to accommodate its analytical arsenal to worker militants and their ongoing battles.[24] The Kerr group simultaneously developed a detailed critique of the inadequacies and class nature of mainstream, or bourgeois, educational institutions.[25]

The commitment to workers' education extended far beyond the political economy of Marx, Engels, and the theorists of the Second International. The movement needed well-educated working men and women. To that end, Kerr and his associates promoted a number of works from the natural and social sciences. Popular discussions on evolution, botany, zoology, and anthropology found their way to the pages of the *Review*, as did essays by Mary Marcy on prehistoric society and serializations of essays by naturalists J. Howard Moore and Wilhelm Böelsche.[26] *ISR* promoted several collections of Kerr titles that were of a general educational nature, such as the Library of Science for the Workers and the Library of Sociology.[27] The monthly also regularly offered such works as George Earle Buckle's *History of Civilization*, the writings of Charles Darwin, Herbert Spencer, and John Tyndall, John Ridpath's *History of the World*, and Noah Webster's *Universal Dictionary* as premiums during subscription drives.[28]

Education took many forms. Incorporating numerous stylistic and formating techniques common to popular mass-circulation magazines, *ISR*, by 1911, used cartoons, lively and often moving original illustrations, and photographs on nearly every page—a far cry from those earlier years when lengthy, dry paragraphs of black type filled its pages. Each worth a thousand words, the illustrations often supported the political position and social perspective of Kerr & Company. Every issue carried discussions of current events and items of topical importance to the cause, as well as political commentary and analysis of importance to the left wing. In addition, every number featured book reviews, an editorial page, several pages of reader's "News and Views," a section of "International Notes," and a page or two of promotional "Publisher's Notes" and announcements that Kerr had written. The monthly regularly allowed room for satire and bits of humor in prose and illustrated form. Its pages also became a vehicle for a number of radical poets and short story writers, such as Jack London and Carl Sandburg and the Wobbly lyricists Ralph Chaplin and Joe Hill, and occasionally ran articles on the fine arts and their depictions of the working class.[29]

The editorial board also published a wide range of instructional pieces to assist rank-and-file socialists involved in day-to-day organizational and agitational work. A long list of contributors, including Mary Marcy, the artist and poet Ralph Chaplin, Philadelphia militant Joseph Cohen, and *ISR* editorial board members Robert Rives LaMonte, Bill Haywood, and Frank Bohn, not only presented their views on the broad range of tactical and strategic questions but also developed numerous how-to articles on such topics as local organizing, the techniques of effective street speaking and soapbox agitation, and the best methods for promoting socialist literature at public gatherings. Militants from across the country in turn forwarded practical suggestions and organizing tips, which Kerr reproduced in the "News and Views" correspondence section. *ISR* in such fashion became an invaluable and inexpensive reference guide and instructional manual for the daily nuts-and-bolts mechanics of the cause.[30]

Few groupings on the left understood the notion of solidarity better than Kerr & Company; the broad range of services it provided the movement helped explain the company's relative success and the popularity of its monthly.[31] Activist and agitational, *ISR* became a nationwide hot line for movement events and calls for action. It developed into a communications hub and organizing center for the geographically dispersed left, and its pages continually contained messages of support and calls for assistance. The monthly not only carried accounts of every major labor struggle and socialist political campaign of the era but also communicated descriptions of tactics developed in specific areas to other locales, widely dispersed and often isolated, across the country. By doing so, it forwarded information that helped provide the industrial union, direct-action wing with a coherence of theory and practice that it might have lacked otherwise.

With each successive month *ISR* became more and more political. In the process, it came to play a key role in the national recruitment of movement activists through numerous calls for physical assistance and funds to assist strikes, free speech fights, and political campaigns. As the major national monthly organ for the geographically dispersed left wing, it served a vitally important function for direct-action militants, especially after Haywood's ouster from the NEC in 1912 and 1913.[32]

The *Review* remained unconditionally and incessantly internationalist during its second phase. Sections of any given issue often resembled a left-wing, politicized *National Geographic* as the group's sense of working-class solidarity continuously caused them to look far beyond the geographic confines of the United States for news of class struggle and left-wing tendencies within the world's labor movement. *ISR* also went far afield in search of stories that would deepen an understanding of changes wrought by the intrusion of capitalist relations—that is, the disruption of traditional societies by the market economy with its demand for wage labor and cheap commodities. In a constant quest for material that would verify and support its particular social and political reading the *ISR* staff turned not only toward Europe but also to Japan, China, South Africa, and Latin America as articles from as far off as Puerto Rico, the Philippines, India, Argentina, and Australia found their way to the monthly's pages. Written either by an activist from the particular region or by a Kerr associate, each piece carried a social analysis that further confirmed and advanced the monthly's ongoing critique.[33]

The *ISR* group played a central role in the Atlantic community of left-wing socialism. Paralleling the American movement, each major European socialist party had developed a revolutionary and a reformist wing. Where Kerr and his associates had earlier looked to Europe for guidance and inspiration, they now sought political support and affirmation. The Kerr circle, as a result of established personal ties and shared political experience, soon acquired a list of regular contributors active in the direct-action, syndicalist, and revolutionary wings of European socialism. Issues in the years preceding U.S. entry into World War I often contained correspondence from such figures as the British syndicalist Tom Mann, the Irish rebels James Connolly and Jim Larkin, the Dutch left-wingers Anton Pannekoek and S. J. Rutgers, and the French revolutionary socialist Emile Pouget. The Kerr & Company office became a common meeting place and stopover point for a lengthy list of radicals on temporary sojourn in the United States.[34]

The *Review* continued to be the primary promotional vehicle for Charles H. Kerr & Company throughout the teens. As such, each issue chronicled the history of the firm, its difficulties and successes, and the often subtle shifts and changes in its founder's ceaseless effort to maintain the magazine and the book and pamphlet ends of the operation as parts of a viable socialist cooperative business venture. But one of innumerable book and magazine concerns in the highly competitive publishing industry of the 1910s, the company had to face the vagaries of a market buffeted by swings in the economy. In addition, the firm also remained susceptible to shifts in the political climate and mood. As inextricably intertwined with socialist movement as it was, the fortunes of the company ebbed and flowed with the progress and setbacks of the broader cause. It nevertheless had to meet expenses and expand, despite numerous obstacles, in order to supply the movement with the propaganda and educational material it required.

Whenever possible or desirable, Kerr continued to use the marketing techniques and strategies common to the publishing trade, for example, the purchase of backlist inventories, copyrights, plates, and mailing lists from other firms.[35] He promoted the circulation of *ISR* by discounting his list of books and pamphlets and occasionally "clubbing" the monthly with allied periodicals such as *The Masses* in order to offer savings to subscribers.[36] He continually worked and reworked various types of combination offers, discounting package deals on *ISR* subscriptions, company stock, books, and pamphlets.[37] He used endorsements by movement notables such as Eugene Debs.[38] He also continued the sale of $10 shares in the company and occasionally, in time of need, solicited loans and contributions from friends in the movement. When money was really tight, he went so far as to offer returns of 4 to 6 percent on loans from movement activists.[39]

Kerr also offered numerous premiums, everything from copies of the works of Karl Marx and reproduced charcoal portraits of Debs, Bill Haywood, Mother Jones, and Marx to slide projectors, phonographs, and sets of encyclopedias.[40] He usually promoted such enticements for their value to the movement. For example, advertisements at the end of 1911 offering a "Lyric Columbia Graphophone" as a premium for twenty-five yearly *ISR* subscriptions or a bundle order of 250 copies hyped the phonograph as "exactly the thing for use at a Socialist meeting, either in a hall or in the open air" and "just the thing for the young soap-boxer."[41]

Subscription drive contests increased circulation and stimulated revenue as well. Again, Kerr pitched such offers from a socialist perspective and offered prizes that included an all-expense-paid trip to the Second International Congress at Vienna in 1914, and free train fare to the San Francisco World's Fair of 1916.[42]

Kerr initiated the *Review*'s seventeenth year at the beginning of July 1916 with a remarkable subscription drive. In exchange for seven hundred subscriptions, he offered readers "a free Ford touring car for you or your

Socialist local." Socialists of the period were clearly not immune to America's infectious love affair with the automobile, and Kerr & Company understood that. At the same time, the drive promoted the Ford in a unique manner. Noting that "nothing attracts the crowd like a GOOD SPEECH from an automobile," *ISR*'s promoters argued the automobile's virtues as a socialist organizing tool. Suggesting that the "old Socialist soap-box had served its time" and "must be relegated to the scrap-heap in favor of the Automobile Way," advertisements for the contest lauded the economy, mobility, and efficiency of the Ford as the vehicle of choice for socialist speakers and organizers.[43]

In an ongoing attempt to help finance the enlargement of the monthly from sixty-four to eighty and, briefly, to a hundred pages, Kerr opened its pages to more and more advertisements as a major source of revenue. The increase in *ISR*'s circulation during the decade made it more attractive to advertisers, and many small firms took advantage of its space. Each number contained numerous promotionals for medications and treatments promising cures for ailments ranging from backache and hernia to acne. There were plans for weight loss and schemes to put on weight. The magazine also displayed occasional advertisements promising a secure income through land speculation and other ways for workers to improve their lots. Advertisements for correspondence courses offering law degrees, for various people's or socialist colleges, and for workers' schools also filled a fair amount of advertising space, along with a regular list of offerings from kindred publishers. Conspicuously absent were the "name brands" of the day that were offered by the major national firms, or trusts.[44]

Some of the advertising seems glaringly out of place or contradictory. What, after all, are promotionals for land and mining investment schemes and other possibilities for self-aggrandizement doing in a socialist magazine? They brought in revenue, but there was more to it. Such advertisements fit Kerr and his associates' worldview. A common theme of improvement and uplift tied the broad range of advertisements together. Individual betterment of one's material condition was not necessarily contradictory to the broader collective uplift of the socialist promise. Conscious individuals (i.e., "good socialists") had to take care of themselves and improve their minds, bodies, and general circumstances in preparation for the important struggles that lay ahead.[45]

Quite clearly, Kerr used nearly any practice of the trade to help advance the company. His social and political commitments placed one important voluntary constraint on the operation, however. Kerr refused to use banks. Concerned with the possible loss of control and conceivable political costs inherent in an overextended dependence on private financial institutions, he and his associates constantly experimented with and searched for the best way to expand their inventory and yet remain independent. That reluctance to establish long-term banking credit required him to turn to the mass movement for the support needed to keep the company going. That continually increasing dependence on movement demand also meant that the firm often teetered on the edge of insolvency.

Devised by Kerr earlier as an alternative to dependence on outside capital, the sale of $10 shares in the company, although helpful, was inadequate for financing new projects and expansion. Some 2,200 supporters had purchased approximately 3,600 of the available 5,000 shares by late spring of 1910. But stock sales, promising nothing more than sizable discounts on the company's offerings and a vote at the annual shareholders' meeting, proceeded slowly throughout the decade.[46] Increased circulation of *ISR*, as a source of revenue and the firm's own best advertising medium, became critical.

Kerr continually searched for the most viable distribution method for *ISR*. In January 1909, for example, he contracted with the American News Company, the foremost national magazine distributor, to distribute the *Review* to newsstands throughout the country. The experiment proved too costly, and he halted newsstand sales after a year-long trial.[47] He next turned to the movement and began offering marked discounts on bulk or bundle sales to individual sales agent hustlers and Socialist Party locals. He also again promoted *Review* subscription cards that allowed individual sellers to recoup initial investments immediately and simultaneously receive discounts on offerings from the company's lists.[48] A reflection of both the popularity of the monthly and the effectiveness of the mass-based sales strategy, circulation shot from twenty-six thousand in July 1910 to more than fifty thousand by May 1912. Annual receipts increased proportionately, going from a mere $2,500 in 1907 to almost $24,000 in 1911.[49] In 1910 the company experienced a nearly 50 percent increase in sales and receipts over the previous year, and sales of the magazine and books reached new heights with each successive month into 1912.[50]

Movement support, ultimately based on the development of a widely dispersed corps of grass-roots socialist sales agents who hustled the *Review* and the full list of Kerr titles, managed to provide the margin of revenue that kept the venture viable.[51] That dependence on rank-and-file movement hustlers or "live-wire" agents also meant, however, that the firm's marketing apparatus and distribution network remained fragile and vulnerable.

First, the company drew more and more of its political and financial support from the most economically hard-pressed and least stable sectors of the work force. During any part of a given "prosperous" year, the very workers who Kerr and his political allies sought for the movement's ranks—the countless thousands of "unskilled" and unorganized in the Great Lakes industrial belt or the garment and textile workers' ghettoes of the Northeast, for example—regularly faced sectoral layoffs and seasonal unemployment. With no permanent home or mailing address, thousands joined the great floating pool of migrant transient or casual laborers who followed the rails and harvests across the Great Plains and the West Coast agricultural belt or "hoboed" the vast stretch of the interior in search of work. Such workers had to think twice about investing in books or magazines, even during "good times." Second, a marked shift in the direction and fortunes of the left wing, shaped either by economic factors or by a dramatic swing in the political climate, could carry with it the fate of the company's inner circle and the lifetime investment of its founder.

Kerr remained fully aware of such factors and continually attempted to steer a course that would manage to keep the firm afloat. The first major obstacle that he and his associates had to face was the in-house Socialist Party imbroglio that heated to a slow boil through 1911 and 1912. Clearly aligned with the left wing, Kerr moved to insulate the firm from any attack engineered by the right. He notified readers of a new limit on the sale of company shares to no more than ten per individual or local in July 1911. Concerned with maintaining control of the house at a time that party conservatives had initiated talk of centralizing the dissemination of movement literature under the aegis of the Socialist Party National Office, Kerr took the step as a "necessary precaution to make it as difficult as possible for a majority of stock to be bought up by those who would like to change the general policy of the publishing house."[52] He also made occasional offers to buy back or trade literature for stock during that period.[53] Speaking for the company at the end of 1911, he restated the goal "in the future as in the past, to use our entire income in the work of socialist education and propaganda rather than to divide any money as dividends" and reinitiated sale of stock on a monthly installment basis in order to make it more accessible to rank-and-file supporters. He reaffirmed his confidence in the system of socialist sales agents by calling upon rank-and-file activists to take advantage of his offers: "We want the publishing house owned for the most part by the activist socialist hustlers, the ones who are pushing the sale of our literature."[54]

In the thick of the intra-party fight in the fall of 1912 Kerr actively solicited support for more "socialist partners" in the company. In his estimation, the main reason for an individual to buy stock was not the discounts they allowed but that the $10 investments would help assure the survival of the publishing house as the "rallying point of the loyal revolutionists" and the "most important educational factor in recruiting more revolutionists." He argued that the "greatest danger to the Socialist movement" came from within. Some members of the Socialist Party might "forget the ultimate aim, the abolition of wage-slavery, and become mere office seekers, ready to desert the field of the class struggle in the pursuit of votes, no matter how obtained." Noting that the company had become "warmly loved" and "bitterly hated," he assumed that at some point it would "be attacked with every possible weapon."[55]

From May through December 1912 the operation experienced a serious slump in receipts. In anticipation of an increased demand for socialist literature during that election year, Kerr ordered additional printings of a number of books and pamphlets and had even repaid several outstanding personal loans to company supporters. He had also enlarged *ISR* to one hundred pages, but monthly receipts from increased circulation could not keep pace with additional production costs. The downturn in the company's fortunes proved temporary, however, and by January 1913 Kerr could announce that the year had turned into "the most successful in the history of the publishing house."

The next year brought another wave of unforeseen difficulties "for all Socialist publishers." Kerr attributed the difficulties to several political factors: "bitter controversies within the Socialist party"; a "natural reaction" following a "strenuous year of . . . presidential elections"; and "the near-Socialist policies of President Wilson, which distract the interest of many sympathizers not well grounded in Socialist policies." The January 1914 annual report showed that the company had once again weathered a downturn, however, and improved its financial position. Indebtedness had decreased, and *ISR* had "survived the attacks made upon it by those who regard offices as more important than Socialist education." Kerr closed the 1914 report on a optimistic note: "We look forward to the new year with confidence in the rank and file of the revolutionary movement, and with the hope that during 1914 we can make the publishing house more useful to the movement than ever before." Those present extended Kerr a vote of confidence. None could foresee that the approaching year would initiate the most difficult period for Charles H. Kerr & Company.[56]

From its earliest days *ISR* had been concerned with the question of war and peace. Always a key issue of the socialist movement, that ongoing discussion of the causes and implications of violent international conflict became a constant topic from 1905 forward. Rarely an issue of the monthly passed from the press without some comment on the evils of war and great power confrontations. Convinced that military conflict among the reigning superpowers spelled no good end for workers and that wars of national rivalry meant nothing but increased casualty figures and mortality rates for the working class, *ISR* consistently spoke out against militarism, intervention, and imperialistic forays. The magazine editorially opposed U.S. interventionist policies in Latin America and elsewhere throughout the early part of the century. Opposed to World War I from the start of hostilities in August 1914, the *Review* also protested U.S. entry into the war almost three years later. That opposition and espoused resistance to involvement in the mass slaughter of the Great War, when combined with support for popular upheavals against the war in Russia and elsewhere, assured the monthly's demise once the United States joined in.

The War Years and After

The world came out of the Great War transformed. Very much a part of that prewar world, the socialist movement, both in the United States and internationally, came away from the war years changed, something quite different. The war ultimately, perhaps inexorably, drew the United States in, and with its entry the American socialist cause, avowedly antiwar, immediately found itself caught in the whirlwind of ultra-nationalism and heightened intolerance that accompanied mobilization. The socialist impetus endured an onslaught of legal and extra-legal repression but came away a mere ghostlike shadow of its former self, lacking neither the unity of vision, purpose and politic, nor the organizational and institutional cohesion that might usually define a movement.[1]

A vital oppositional voice and institutional center for the prewar American movement's left wing, Charles H. Kerr & Company could not avoid the storm. It, too, became a target for war-bred harassment and state repression not long after U.S. entry into the fray. The firm survived as well but came away severely injured. The majority of movement publishing ventures did not weather the first year of American involvement.[2] Kerr & Company, however, resuscitated itself enough to move toward the future, but only as a ghostlike fragment of what it had been before the war.

The company belonged to a diverse social and political movement. Extending ideologically and politically from the authentically anarcho-syndicalist elements within the IWW that disavowed politics, that movement spanned a range from those who favored dual strategies of parliamentary campaigns and militant direct action to those who concentrated on gaining stable, respectable electoral strength and office through legal means. Diverse as it was, the movement functioned in the name of the working class. That stance posed serious concerns for numerous vested interests within U.S. society well before the opening of hostilities in Europe. The war, after all, followed on the heels of one of the most hotly contested and violent eras in U.S. labor history. Class politics had discomfited innumerable influential and powerful people well before 1914. As the country drew closer to the fray, the movement further raised the ire and eyebrows of its enemies through its persistent wail of warning against preparedness and involvement. That continuing oppositional cry ultimately called for concerted working-class action against U.S. entry.

The call for class struggle against war, quite distinct from the dissenting voices of various pacifist opponents, clearly marked all factions of the movement as immediate targets as soon as the country became a belligerent. Those deeply opposed to socialism readily took advantage of and used the era's heightened jingoist and xenophobic sentiment to isolate and hobble the left as treasonous "slackers," "war resisters," "pro-Kaiser" or "Bolsheviki" agents, "anti-Americans," or simply "troublemakers." The political stances of the various movement groupings up to and well into the war made such attacks inevitable. Outspokenly oppositional on the issue of war and peace, Charles H. Kerr & Company would not pass unnoticed.

The Kerr circle had articulated its animus toward militarism and war long before the outbreak of hostilities in August 1914.[3] Well informed by the often-contradictory debates within the Second International, they readily condemned the Russo-Japanese conflict of 1904 and 1905.[4] *ISR* applauded the key resolutions against war at the various Second International Congresses—in Amsterdam in 1904, in Stuttgart in 1907, and in Copenhagen in 1910. The firm circulated not only the International's official declarations but also distributed such notable statements as the famous antiwar polemic *My Country, Right or Wrong!* by French socialist Gustave Hervé, which called for an open insurrection against war and the repudiation of all forms of "bourgeois and governmental patriotism, which lyingly asserts the existence of a community of interests among all the inhabitants of a country."[5]

Kerr and his associates used the language of imperialism and "rich man's war" to analyze the economic causes of war. They argued that international conflict was the result of the financial and industrial rivalries inherent in capitalism—a critique they unwaveringly supported and deepened. Part of their argument led to an examination of the role of the state apparatus and mainstream institutions—the press, churches, and schools—in marshaling support for interventionist ventures. It contrasted the wealth of banks and trusts, especially the armaments and other war-related industries, with the poverty and suffering of the lower ranks of the working class. The message was clear: Workers had no interest whatsoever in such wars.[6]

The ongoing discussion of socialist response to the use of military might as an extension of foreign policy became focused and more immediate as U.S. intervention in Mexico became more and more probable after 1910. The Kerr group's position in regard to "dollar diplomacy" and the counter-revolutionary "big stick" laid the groundwork for the lines of argument it would use later.

A revolution against the thirty-five-year dictatorship of Porfirio Diaz broke out in November 1910. Diaz's brutal reign had granted numerous concessions to U.S firms, but the revolution compelled many Americans to abandon their holdings. Francisco Madero, a democratic reformer, replaced Diaz, but in February 1913 the new leader fell victim to a counter-revolutionary coup d'état headed by Victoriano Huerta. The new dictator promised to protect foreign investment and sought to reinstall a Diaz-type despotism. Although the Taft administration had recognized Madero, Woodrow Wilson withheld recognition of Huerta's regime and eventually attempted to pressure him through the promise of loans and assistance to his opponents. Wilson lifted an arms embargo early in 1914, facilitating the arming of Huerta's opposition. He also set up a blockade of Vera Cruz to impede the flow of supplies to the regime. Following a provocation, the Tampico Incident of April 1914, Congress granted the president permission to use force to uphold U.S. interests. Indeed, U.S. troops had already intervened by bombarding and occupying the port of Vera Cruz. Events ultimately led to Huerta's ouster and the recognition of Venustiano Carranza as Mexico's de facto president. With the collapse of Huerta, however, various other leaders openly contested for power. Pancho Villa's actions on both sides of the border provoked yet another direct military intervention that began in March 1916. The U.S. expeditionary force under the command of Gen. John J. Pershing remained in Mexico until January 1917, despite opposition from all Mexican political elements.

The Kerr group closely watched developments in Mexico and U.S. responses. Several of the company's associates, including *Review* illustrator Ralph Chaplin, traveled to Mexico to witness and assist the revolution, and Kerr warmly received a number of Mexican revolutionists on their brief sojourn to Chicago.[7] During the spring of 1909 *ISR* carried a series of exclusive firsthand accounts of conditions under the Diaz dictatorship and the growth of *insurrecto* forces. The reports, by John K. Murray, told of the potentially explosive revolt in the making.[8]

Articles by Murray and others tied problems in Mexico to the intrusion of U.S. capital. A piece in December 1909 by Cy O. Brown, for example, suggested that "nothing must be permitted to interfere with the plans of American Capital to secure further control of the bases of industrial and economic supplies in Mexico." Diaz, he argued, had "sold out one economic vantage point after another to the American capitalists." A later piece pointed out that Diaz always was "a warm friend of American capitalists" and asserted that it was "chiefly because the United States Government stands back of the American plutocracy and the Diaz regime of blood, that Mexico has become known over the whole world as the home of the murder and brutality to workingmen and women."[9]

In December 1910 *ISR* carried the first of a series of articles by John K. Turner, the famed Mexico correspondent. An extract from the advance sheets of Turner's *Barbarous Mexico* titled "The American Partners of Diaz" concluded by pointing out U.S. complicity in the counter-revolution: "Three times during the past two years the United States government has rushed an army to the Mexican border in order to crush a movement of Liberals which had risen against the autocrat of Mexico. Constantly during the past three years the American government through its Secret Service, its Department of Justice, its Immigration officials, its border rangers, has maintained in the border states a reign of terror for Mexicans, in which it has lent itself unreservedly to the extermination of political refugees."[10]

ISR's editorial page that same month pointed out that "the real slaveholders" in Mexico, "for whose profit men, women and children are being bought and sold, starved and tortured are not Mexicans, but American capitalists." American capital used the U.S. government to keep Diaz in power; if such backing did not exist, "slaves would free themselves" and Diaz would topple without the "active help" of the United States. [11]

Turner concluded an exclusive article in *ISR*'s next issue by citing the probability that U.S. troops would cross the border if the revolution threatened Diaz's rule. The following March, Taft ordered twenty thousand troops to the border and dispatched warships into Mexican waters. That April, *ISR* opened with an anti-interventionist proclamation from the National Executive Committee of the Socialist Party. That protest and the several articles that followed tied U.S. involvement to the interests of the trusts and Wall Street in maintaining Diaz. The April lead editorial contended that "what the capitalists are doing to Mexican toilers they would do to Americans also." Only "organized resistance" would maintain "what little freedom and comfort" U.S. workers had. The *ISR* group argued that in the absence of a "fighting organization," the United States "would sink into the terrible slavery of the Mexican peons." In June, an article argued that "workers of the United States have nothing but their lives to lose in Mexico" and pointed to the "general strike mass movement" as "the most effective and practical attack" against the "brutal wars the capitalists make the workers fight."[12] The Kerr circle continued to examine and assess events in Mexico through 1913.[13]

When Wilson scrapped his proclaimed policy of "watchful waiting" in April 1914 and sent troops and shells into Vera Cruz, the socialist movement rallied in protest. Mary Marcy, destined to become the most articulate and militant antiwar voice of the Kerr group, took the lead in denouncing Wilson's actions. She scathingly assailed the intervention as a war for the benefit of the Rockefellers, Guggenheims, and Hearsts and argued that neither the Mexican people nor the young American men involved had anything to gain. She lambasted the patriotic rationales for the military move and discussed the international nature of the working class as a "class without a country," with no interest in such nationalist entanglements. She reminded readers that the same interests lay behind the conflict in Mexico and the open class warfare then underway in places such as Ludlow, Colorado: "The wars in Mexico and in Colorado are BOTH Standard Oil wars, to a very large extent," she contended. "American working men have no quarrel with Mexican working men. . . . We are both robbed by the capitalist class and the only way we can stop this robbery is by uniting under the banner of SOCIALISM." Her polemic concluded with a line of argument that must have raised concerns among any antisocialist readers: "The CLASS WAR—the war of the propertyless and exploited working class against those who live off their labor—this is the ONLY WAR worthwhile. This is the ONLY war that can benefit OUR class because it will give every working man and woman the right to work and to have the FULL VALUE OF HIS PRODUCT! . . . The only war in which we should engage is the working class war, which will abolish Poverty from the face of the earth!"[14] With the eruption of war in Europe, that particular argument—the call for class war against the makers of war—would acquire new salience.

The Kerr group's antiwar critique became less abstract and more direct as events abroad further stirred the winds of war and the jingoist appetite for intervention throughout the teens. Their class analysis of the causes of war led to direct criticism of the military itself. In an attempt to counter much of the patriotic emotionalism and martial spirit that accompanied the preparations for intervention in Mexico, *ISR* turned its reportorial sights toward exposés of life in the military that focused on the working conditions and rights of men in the service. Such criticisms appeared well before any discussion of a conscription bill.

Contributors also examined notions of nationalism and patriotism and made connections and comparisons between the use of the police, state constabularies, and militias during domestic labor disputes and the use of sailors and marines abroad. Clearly aimed at discouraging enlistment, such articles appeared as international tensions increased. The United States had already completed the naval buildup for which global strategists and expansionists such as Alfred T. Mahan and Theodore Roosevelt had long called. Such arguments in and of themselves, especially those aimed at discouraging military recruitment, set Kerr and his associates on a collision course with established power when the country's gloves did come off in 1917.[15]

Still concerned with U.S. involvements in this hemisphere, *ISR* writers turned their sights toward Europe as the temperature rose on long-simmering tensions throughout the summer of 1914.[16] The outbreak of open hostilities on the Continent had almost immediate political and economic repercussions in the United States. As a result, the American socialist cause soon found itself in an intensely volatile and precarious situation that only worsened as the country moved toward direct involvement. The new situation forced a reappraisal of socialist strategy and tactics within the movement. Charles H. Kerr & Company, as a national voice of the left wing, played a critical role in that discussion.

The war's opening salvos immediately eviscerated the Second International. Socialist parties in almost every country rapidly abandoned their internationalist principles and readily succumbed to nationalist calls to defend their respective homelands. That development left the U.S movement shocked, confused, and demoralized. Numerous members of the American cause, after all, had long turned to the European parties, especially Germany's SPD, for theoretical guidance and inspiration. They now looked on in dismay and disbelief as their comrades joined the rush to the abyss.

Some American socialists initially excused or rationalized the behavior of the European parties by parroting the specific justifications put forward by either the German, French, or British leadership. The overwhelming majority of the movement, safely cushioned temporarily by the Atlantic, maintained its clear antiwar stance, however. The movement, both within and outside of the Socialist Party, gradually regained its political footing and slowly but surely developed a deeper analysis of the causes of the conflagration and the underlying political and structural weaknesses of the Second International. Such new analyses, in turn, forced further debate and reappraisal. Although certain elements of the party's right and center in the United States continued to excuse the European comrades, the movement as a whole began to find a new grounding in the position of various antiwar voices on the Continent. Elements of the American left wing also soon developed a critique of the failure of the fraternal parties and moved rapidly to an adamant and vigorously active opposition to U.S. involvement.

The *Review*'s coverage and commentary at the beginning of the war mirrored some of the broader movement's disarray, as well as its naive optimism and hope in the ability of the International to maintain a common oppositional front. Editorially, however, it maintained the class-based critique of war and patriotism developed earlier, and it soon began to examine the failures of the various socialist parties of the belligerent nations. In keeping with its political trajectory of the preceding years, it quickly developed and put forward a left-pole position on the causes of the war.[17]

The issue for September 1914 contained firsthand reports by Kerr associate Phillips Russell, who had traveled to Europe to attend the Second International Congress at Vienna, which had been scheduled for August but was now canceled.[18] October's number carried a significant lead article by the Dutch-born voice of Germany's "Left Radicals," Anton Pannekoek, who analyzed the causes of the war and the collapse of the Socialist International from a revolutionary left position. An early opponent of revisionism, the astronomer-turned-revolutionary examined the "imperialistic" nature of the conflict and argued that it had its origins in the "general antagonisms" of states "rooted in the competition to win world power," in "nothing else but the struggle of every country to win for its capital colonies, contracts, spheres of influence and favorable opportunities for investment." Pannekoek lambasted the reformist tendencies within the various parties and dissected the structural and political weaknesses of German Social Democracy. He viewed mass action, the political strike by an organized proletariat, as the only possible defense against the rush to war that capital had fostered.[19] Mary Marcy had already castigated the leadership of the German party for its opposition to the general strike against war, that tactic long called for by the left wing within the Second International. She called upon the U.S. movement to go on record for a general strike and endorse "a tactic that shall make a repetition of the European tragedy impossible in America."[20]

Discussion of the causes of the war and the failure of European Social Democracy continued in *ISR* for a number of months.[21] Long-time editorial board member William Bohn used his monthly "International Notes" column to carry on lengthy discussions of the questions posed by the collapse of the Second International. He regularly kept up on developments within the European left and was one of the first Americans to report on the surfacing of a new socialist opposition within Germany headed by Karl Liebknecht, Rosa Luxembourg, and Franz Mehring.[22] Associate editor Robert Rives LaMonte had traveled to Europe to attend the Vienna Congress and remained for a number of months. He took the occasion of his time on the Continent to visit a number of key leaders of the Second International and spent time with Karl Liebknecht and Mehring in late spring 1915, but German authorities refused him a visit with Rosa Luxembourg, then in jail.

Mary Marcy, in the meantime, continued to develop an editorial line that eventually carried the group into alignment with emerging antiwar and anti-imperialist elements abroad.[23] The *ISR* board in October 1915 enunciated the firm stance that it would maintain from then on. Writing for the group, Marcy declared an unflinching opposition to "ALL capitalist wars." Although noting that it might be impossible to preempt such wars, she nevertheless argued that "we must do all in our united power to prevent them" and called for a no vote on any war funds and appropriations. If the prevention of war proved impossible, she suggested that the war be used as an "eye-opener," as "the greatest educational force the world has ever known" for workers' understanding of "the old double-cross system by which the worker loses, no matter which nationalist capitalist group may win."[24]

The discussion of possible socialist responses to U.S. entry became more immediate as war preparations accelerated. Marcy took up the question as early as June 1915. Noting that there was no legal machinery, no method open to oppose war if the country decided to enter, she saw the "need to paralyze the industrial machinery that makes war possible." She called upon workers to organize on the job, in factory and shop, "to demoralize the whole plant if it seems that war is about to be declared." She then criticized those in the movement opposed to the violence of direct action, sabotage, and the general strike by noting that "the violence that may attend the putting of a steam engine out of business, a shop or mill temporarily out of commission in ORDER TO PREVENT WAR, would be like burning a match in order to prevent a forest fire." Calling for "rebellion rather than war," she remained unequivocal in what it would take to stop the war: "We do not need pink tea society ladies and sissies to talk against war. We want MEN AND WOMEN who will demoralize the wheels of industry so that there CAN BE NO WAR. And a general strike can accomplish this purpose better than any other weapon. Votes can't help us tomorrow—because we will have no opportunity to vote on any war issue."[25]

In December 1915 President Wilson called for America to embark on a preparedness campaign and asked Congress for legislation to deal with the "disloyal activity" of war opponents. His declaration led to a shift in the political thrust of *ISR*. From that month forward, each issue contained material that voiced opposition to preparedness at all levels, especially on the industrial front. Each number linked the drive toward war and related patriotic posturings to the push for profit by the trusts and America's ruling families and opposed "capitalistic slaughter" at every opportunity.[26] That opposition took many forms.

In addition to numerous antimilitarist articles, editorials, and informational pieces on the corporate profitability of the war drive, the editors regularly used photographs, illustrations, political cartoons, and poetry to convey their antiwar message. For example, the opening pages for the June 1916 number contained Carl Sandburg's poem "Ready to Kill" opposite three photographs of partially decomposed, mutilated peasants and soldiers taken after a battle in Mexico.[27] Some of the cartoons and illustrations likely raised the hackles of the wartime censors more than the text did. The front cover of the June 1917 issue, for example, featured a drawing entitled "Empty Shells"—a towering mound of human skulls and empty artillery casings. Atop the mound was a chair and a tattered flag, and on the thronelike chair was a bulging money bag labeled "capitalist interests." The July 1917 cover portrayed a man dressed in a military uniform and staring into a shop window that displayed various prosthetic devices— artificial arms and legs. Issues through the spring 1917 also contained often hard-hitting or satirical caricatures of pot-bellied war profiteers and military figures pitted against heroically stylized antiwar workers. Stark, realistic original cover designs by "Machia" and numerous cartoon reproductions from such allied periodicals as *The Masses* carried *ISR*'s message in a manner that made reading its text almost unnecessary. Various issues also carried photographs of disemboweled, charred bodies or juxtaposed photographs of domestic conditions that contrasted the disparities between wealth and poverty and hammered home a class-based antiwar message.

The total opposition to preparedness voiced by various socialists launched an extended debate within the American movement over correct tactics. Distinguishing between the historical opposition to standing armies and "huge military establishments" and the "nonresistance" now advocated by some, Henry L. Slobodin began a lengthy exchange in the

January 1916 *Review* by arguing that socialists had never entertained "the idea of leaving a country exposed defenseless against foreign aggression." He also expressed distress over the "sudden and indignant abhorrence of arms and force" in the movement. Underlying his discussion lurked the question that upended the European movement: the issue of "wars of national defense." The varied responses and rejoinders to Slobodin's piece from William Bohn and others proceeded for a number of months.[28]

Kerr and his associates, in the meantime, continued to monitor developments within the European left. They cheered Karl Liebknecht's refusal to vote for a second war credit in the Reichstag and reported as best they could on the meetings of the antiwar socialists in Lugano, Zimmerwald, and Kienthal.[29] The monthly readily carried longer analytical pieces by representative voices of the Continent's antiwar and anti-imperialist left. It played a central role in acquainting the American movement with such voices of the revolutionary left as the Dutch-born militants Herman Gorter and S. J. Rutgers.

Soon to become an important figure during the formative stages of the communist movement in the United States, Rutgers had spent a number of years in Asia and arrived in the United States in 1915. Well-versed on the debates of the European left, he soon became an influential voice within the left wing as a regular *ISR* contributor. The monthly provided a forum for his opinions on the need for new direction, and Kerr regularly ran Rutgers's lengthy articles on imperialism, the consolidation of a revolutionary pole in Europe, and other developments leading to the formation of the Third, or Communist, International as lead articles or editorials. The editorial board endorsed his series of June and July 1916 on "The Left Wing" as "the most valuable series . . . ever published in the *Review.*"[30] Rutgers's *ISR* contributions played a significant political role in helping frame the debates and political currents that eventually launched American communism. No one within the Kerr group could foresee such developments in 1916, of course. Nor could they know or assess the important role that their monthly played in molding such thought.

Mary Marcy, again writing editorially at the end of 1916, set forth a position on the necessary direction for the American movement. Endorsing Rutgers's argument, she agreed that "mass action is today the only remaining form of democracy left open to the workers." It had become obvious to any "revolutionist" that "socialist parties which restrict themselves to legislative contests alone are in no position to rally to the support of the working class in any sudden emergency." "Old party tactics" represented nothing more than "suicidal folly" in the presence of a declaration of war.

Besides, mass action offered something more than a possible antiwar tactic. It represented "the best school for revolutionary activity," and therein lay its significance. Prefiguring events in the not too distant future, Marcy noted that belligerent governments everywhere had discovered that they had merely to arrest socialist leaders or suppress a dissident press in order to "check any incipient revolt." She hoped that mass action would develop initiative in the rank and file and thereby neutralize such moves. Addressing herself to the "Left Wing comrades" in Europe, she clearly defined the position of the *Review:*

> We, too, in this class-war-torn Land of "Liberty," will do our small part in the great work you are doing to build up a true working class International that shall have for its aim the joining of the hands and hearts and heads and aims of the revolutionary workers of all lands for the overthrow of the Capitalist System.
>
> We hereby wish to repudiate all so-called socialists, those traitors to the working class, whether they be at home or abroad, who march at the heads of military preparedness parades, who vote war appropriations, who advocate aggression on weaker nations, and sing the siren song of Nationalism as opposed to Internationalism.[31]

The European left wing urged that industrial struggles be broadened into political strikes, a goal, Marcy pointed out, that had long been part of *ISR*'s propaganda work. The monthly stood for "Political Action in the broadest sense, Mass Action, Industrial Unionism, Class Unionism and for International Socialism" and opposed "Imperialism in all its forms." She drew a clear line in the polemical sand between the Kerr group and elements of the movement's center and right: "We are for such reforms as shorter hours and higher wages only for the reasons that the struggles of the workers for these things are one of the best means of education in the class struggle. No reforms can materially benefit the working class as long as the present system of product-taking continues."[32]

With such statements, Mary Marcy and her fellow Kerr associates had set a clear course some five months before the United States became a belligerent. With their position mapped in November 1916, they crossed a political point of no return well in advance of U.S. entry into the war and the Russian revolution.

The war, in the meantime, affected the day-to-day operations of the Kerr publishing venture. Always vulnerable to marked downturns in the economy, the company felt the pinch of the recession that began in mid-1913 and deepened throughout the winter of 1914. The opening of hostilities in Europe had initially upset the regular functioning of the transatlantic economy, and it further exacerbated an already difficult situation for the publishing house.[33] Confronted with the severest downturn of the period and with potential opportunities constrained by economic realities, the company nonetheless managed to move forward. The *Review*'s circulation increased toward the end of 1914. Most demand came in the form of increased bulk bundle orders from left-wing locals or individual socialist salespeople. That was not sufficient, however; the book end of the business had fallen off by half. Kerr attributed the decline in pamphlet and book sales to the deepening recession and the war excitement. It also reflected a general disillusionment with socialist politics related to the utter failure of the international movement on the war issue.[34]

The company's operating expenses continued to increase, in the meantime, as a direct result of a war-bred price inflation. The cost of paper, always a vital factor in the publishing business, nearly doubled between the fall of 1914 and the spring of 1916 and continued to rise as war demand pushed the price of commodities upward. Electrotyping and other costs of printing increased dramatically as well. Confronted with declining revenues and mounting costs, Kerr once again called for short-term loans from movement supporters and an increase in stock subscriptions. In addition, he contributed $1,000 from his personal savings and took a reduction in his already meager salary to help forestall a projected deficit for 1915. He asked others to give what they could. Significantly, he refused to raise company prices and maintained a long-held commitment to "circulate the greatest possible amount of the best socialist literature at the lowest possible prices." He looked forward to an upsurge in the demand for socialist material once the war ended.[35]

As the war continued, European demand for U.S. goods stimulated a general economic upswing. The economic recovery, although uneven, improved labor's general bargaining power. It also aided Kerr & Company. Both a victim and a beneficiary of the war economy, the company sustained a loss for 1915 but then experienced a period of relative growth through 1916. Still hard-hit by the steep rise in the cost of paper, the firm, rather than raise prices, reduced its pamphlet inventory, curtailed certain types of discounts and premium combination offers, and limited publication of new works. Financial statements for 1916 were positive based on assumptions of increased demands for socialist literature at the close of the war. The firm managed to accumulate a small reserve during the first few months of 1917, and Kerr urged readers to take advantage of the war-

induced demand for labor in order to form "fighting working class industrial unions." Still optimistic, he and his associates had no way of knowing
what the next few months would bring.[36]

Woodrow Wilson convened a special session of Congress on April 2,
1917, and asked for a declaration of war against Germany. Congress readily
complied, and the United States became a formal belligerent on April 6.
Gathering that same week at an emergency convention in St. Louis, almost
two hundred representatives of the Socialist Party of America approved a
wartime program. The "majority resolution on war and militarism" passed
overwhelmingly and branded the declaration of war a "crime against the
people of the United States." Defining the conflict as the result of preda-
tory capitalist competition for markets, the St. Louis Manifesto proclaimed
loyalty to the principle of international working-class solidarity and called
for "continuous, active and public opposition" through "demonstrations,
mass petitions, and all other means." It called for "unyielding opposition
to . . . military or industrial conscription" and promised "vigorous resistance" to press censorship, restrictions on free speech and assembly, compulsory arbitration, and limitations on the right to strike. The report, co-
authored by representatives of the right, center, and left, also called for
"consistent propaganda against military training and militaristic teaching"
and "widespread educational propaganda to enlighten the masses as to the
true relation between capitalism and war." It demanded that all socialist
officeholders vote against any military appropriations and loans. Such language and espoused goals did not go unnoticed.[37]

The government soon passed a number of war measures, including the
Liberty Loan Act (April 24) and the Selective Service Act (May 10), which
immediately provided a focus for the socialist oppositional campaign. The
already widespread general sentiment and agitation against war intensified
with the passage of the conscription law demanding compulsory registra-
tion.[38] Long-standing foes of military recruitment, the *ISR* staff readily
joined in that broad-based campaign against conscription. Its vociferous,
class-based stance against the draft, present in each issue throughout the
spring of 1917, clearly marked *ISR* as a target.[39]

The entire U.S. left faced widespread repression during the war. That
often-concerted assault on the formal and informal institutions and leadership of the movement, unprecedented in scope, fashion, and sophistication, turned into a generalized offensive against all those who spoke out
against the war from an anticapitalist vantage point. Socialists who opposed
the war became suspect and were the subjects of official surveillance, harassment, arrests, detention, lengthy and costly trials, imprisonment or

deportation, and extra-legal violence.[40] In order to pursue its proclaimed democratic war aims to the fullest and simultaneously deal with dissent at home, the Wilson administration used the Espionage Act of June 15, 1917, to restrict and curtail any and all opposition to the war.

The act made it illegal to "willfully cause or attempt to cause insubordination, disloyalty, mutiny, or refusal of duty in the military or naval forces . . . or [to] obstruct the recruiting or enlistment service of the United States." Congress approved the measure after defeating a section giving the president the right to censor the press. But section 12 of the legislation prohibited the mailing of any materials "advocating or urging treason, insurrection, or any forcible resistance to the laws of the United States."[41] That clause, in effect, gave the postmaster general the extraordinary power to determine who might use the mail at a time when the survival of hundreds of left-wing periodicals depended on easy access and the savings afforded by second-class mailing privileges. Encouraged by a sensationalist mainstream press, heightened jingoist and antiradical sentiment, and zealous employers and ambitious politicians eager to rid the land of agitators and Reds, police and military authorities rapidly formed a vast network of informants, spies, and provocateurs to seek out and prosecute violators of the war enactments. The several governmental agencies, often assisted by thousands of patriotic volunteers, watched, listened, took notes, and compiled dossiers in a frenetic quest for that incriminating bit of evidence of some proscribed utterance or action banned under the war strictures.[42]

At various moments, such as in early September 1917, nationally coordinated local, state, and federal agents descended on the pivotal institutional centers of Socialist Party and IWW dissent—local and national offices, meeting halls, book shops, printing establishments, social clubs, and the homes of movement members. They rounded up activists and boxed and carted off any materials that might incriminate and help indict those apprehended. Once in tow, dragnet victims defined as citizens regularly faced jail before and after their day in court, and those defined as non-citizens or aliens found themselves detained incommunicado and deported with little or no legal recourse.[43] Meanwhile, postal authorities, under the leadership of Albert Burleson, immediately used section 12 of the Espionage Act to open an out-and-out assault on the socialist and IWW press.

Postal officials surely must have seen red, regardless of the actual color of the printer's ink, upon opening any *ISR* of the period. The monthly immediately became a ready target of Post Office Department surveillance, probably because of the fact that it was still a national voice for the socialist movement's left wing. Speaking in unabashed oppositional class terms on the range of war-related issues that section 12 intended to silence, *ISR* continued to report on labor's fight for better conditions after the country entered the hostilities. Such coverage, in and of itself, placed the monthly in a precarious position.

Left-wing worker militants had stepped up their drive for union recognition and improved working conditions as labor's bargaining power increased throughout 1916 and early 1917. The IWW-led strikes aimed not so much at disrupting the war effort as at improving working conditions throughout Pacific Northwest's lumber camps and the copper mining regions of Montana and Arizona. Most of those labor agitations, although commonly infused with class-based, antiwar rhetoric, had accelerated well before the country entered the war. Employers and politicians from the affected areas, especially in the West, had long clamored for Washington's assistance against radicals. Federal authorities, concerned with vital war-related production, finally came to their aid after June 1917, when the declaration of war and related legislation provided the authority and power to do so. Following U.S. entry, employers immediately took advantage of patriotic sentiment by labeling any strike activity as pro-kaiser and un-American. Not about to yield to either the jingoist demagoguery of some bosses or the no-strike pledges of pro-war labor leaders in the AFL, IWW organizers and rank-and-file activists accelerated agitation. The anticapitalist politics and antiwar rhetoric of their labor campaigns made them more vulnerable to legal and extralegal attacks.

Rhetorical in its own right, *ISR* gave such struggles full partisan coverage and publicity. The monthly readily relayed IWW calls for solidarity (general) strikes and actively protested state and employer-inspired assaults on labor and the left. It carried messages of support and encouragement, for example, for labor organizers Tom Mooney and Warren Billings, already incarcerated in California for their alleged roles in the bombing of a San Francisco preparedness parade in 1916.[44]

ISR also vigorously protested the brutal deportation of striking miners from Bisbee, Arizona, during the summer of 1917. Arizona produced 28 percent of the nation's copper, which was essential to the war effort. The mining region centered around Bisbee became a zone of contention between IWW-led strikers and intransigent mine operators during the summer of 1917. Demanding improved working conditions, the right to organize, and better pay in response to the war-induced price inflation, miners throughout Arizona had walked out in June. Joined by workers organized by the International Union of Mine, Mill and Smelter Workers (IUMMSW), the strikes spread, and more than twenty-five thousand workers had left the mines by early July. When federal mediation failed, mine owners took the law into their own hands. On July 12 some two thousand specially deputized and heavily armed vigilantes rounded up more than twelve hundred strikers in Bisbee, placed them in box cars, and had them hauled out into the desert across the New Mexico state line. In response, *ISR* provided full coverage, accompanied by graphic photos and illustrations, of the Bisbee affair. The front cover for the September 1917 number, for example, carried a group portrait of the deportees. The thrust of the reportage likened the strikers' deportation to the exile of Belgian citizens under the direction of the kaiser.[45]

The *Review* also decried and mourned the lynching of IWW field organizer Frank Little in Butte, Montana. A well-known Wobbly militant, Little had arrived in open-shop Butte in late July 1917. Copper and zinc production in the city had already been crippled by a hard-fought strike by some ten to twelve thousand miners. Irrepressible, Little infused his strike agitation with outspoken antiwar and anticapitalist rhetoric. Such activity made him a choice target. On the night of July 31, six masked men abducted him as he slept in his boardinghouse. They dragged him through town tied to the back of an automobile before taking him to the city's outskirts, where they hung his castrated body from a railroad trestle. The lynching outraged the Kerr associates, and they gave the Butte tragedy full coverage. The frontispiece for the September issue of *ISR* contained a full-page portrait of the "Wobbly martyr" and a poetic eulogy by Phillips Russell on the facing page. The lead article that month gave a full account of the affair, complete with a photo of Little taken in the Butte morgue.[46] Such journalism did not pass unobserved by federal postal censors who already had the *Review* under surveillance.

Meantime, on the political front and in tandem with the upswing of labor activism at the beginning of the war, membership in the Socialist Party and the IWW increased markedly despite mounting legal assaults and illegal pressure on both organizations to desist in agitations. Socialist candidates campaigning on a straight antiwar message in local elections during the fall of 1917 (the only barometer of socialist electoral strength in that off-election year) tallied unprecedented percentages across the country.[47] The *Review* simultaneously heralded national Socialist Party gains and monitored the increasing frequency of mob assaults and prosecutions against left-wing political activity. It featured news of unabated and ongoing antiwar and antimilitarist agitation and cried out against continuing attacks on socialist antiwar demonstrations and the harassment of Socialist Party officers and speakers. The monthly denounced a rising tide of vigilantism, mob attacks, and the participation of uniformed servicemen in assaults on socialist and IWW halls in Seattle, Boston, New York, Cleveland, and elsewhere. It also defiantly spoke out against the dragnet raids and mass arrests of Socialist Party and IWW members carried out by federal, state, and local authorities during the first week of September 1917.[48]

Perhaps most significant for those who monitored the monthly was its optimistic belief in future revolutionary potentials. It was an optimism no longer based on secular faith in some future socialist inevitability, but rather on an informed projection of a possible future seemingly prefigured by the Russian revolution.

The major news during the early spring of 1917, as viewed by *ISR*, was not so much U.S. entry into the war but the events in Russia. It carried an initial report of the first stages of the revolution in April 1917, featured lead-article coverage of developments under the newly proclaimed provisional government throughout the summer, and heralded the Bolsheviks' seizure of power and the developments that ensued through February 1918. Encouraged by the sudden collapse of the Romanoff dynasty and the rise of a popular government, *ISR*'s position during the months following struck a variant chord quite different from the tune of socialist inevitability that it had aired in the past. The war had clearly forced an important although initially subtle shift in the group's analysis and politics.[49] Mary Marcy, as adamant as ever in her opposition to "capitalist war," now speculated that the opportunity for revolution might only come during such cataclysms, "when social institutions are crumbling and men and women are torn from their old habits of thought and action, and Misery, Hunger and Death stalk abroad among the working class." Heartened by the first stage of the revolution, she observed that "people only *act* . . . at a time when they are torn away from their old moorings and thrust into a new set of conditions, a new environment; when they are jolted from their old habits and customs, when they *suffer*, in short." She articulated continual optimism in the possibilities the war might create for revolutionary action.[50]

The question of war and peace for the Kerr group had become inextricably tied to the question of revolution. Analyzing the causes of World War I, Marcy argued in July 1917 that the only way to avert such tragedies in the future lay in abolishing the "Profit System." That same month, in an article clearly aimed at an American readership, Phillips Russell, upon receiving news of municipal elections in Petrograd, chided Russian comrades for "making use of the old-fashioned, futile political machinery which is in bad enough odor even in the political democracies like the United States,

England and France." He argued instead that it was "not the business of revolutionists to elect governors or mayors or sheriffs or pound-keepers to fill the seats left open in the machinery of a republican form of government . . . but to organize a new world." He called for the construction of a new society that would be an "industrial democracy," with political representation based on industrial organization rather than states, counties, and districts. The "great issue" for the *ISR* circle, as enunciated editorially in August 1917, was not when the war would end but "whether . . . it would end with the working class . . . strong enough to stop future wars, and to demand and take control of the processes of production." Noting that the "impossible had come to pass" in Russia, the editorial suggested that all the belligerent nations, including the United States, should follow the Russian example.[51]

The *Review* energetically hailed the Bolshevik ouster of Aleksandr Kerensky's provisional government. It carried eyewitness reports of the event and procured permission to run the introduction of Leon Trotsky's *The Bolsheviki and World Peace* as a lead article in February 1918.[52] The October Revolution, of course, sent an entirely different message to U.S. leaders. *ISR*'s support for those events, along with its antiwar line and emphatic support for the continuation of politicized labor struggles on the home front, placed it outside the already narrowing boundaries of acceptable and allowable public discourse.

Within days after the passage of the Espionage Act the Post Office notified Kerr that it had found the June 1917 *International Socialist Review* unmailable. Although most of the June issue had already been mailed, Post Office attorney W. H. Lamar ordered Kerr to submit a copy of the July issue for consideration before mailing it. In compliance, Kerr sent several copies to Washington and requested that Lamar identify any offending material so the rest of the issue, prohibited passages omitted, could pass through the mail. The Chicago postmaster, acting on instructions from Washington, informed the company that the entire issue was unmailable. In response to further queries about specifics, Lamar sent Kerr a copy of the Espionage Act. Undeterred, Kerr again attempted to find out the precise bases for Post Office determinations. Lamar, responding on July 2, stated that it was "utterly impossible" for his office to point out specific passages. Officials in his department stopped reading and ruled the entire issue unmailable whenever they came across an offending passage.

Kerr sent out the July issue by railroad express and submitted the August number for inspection. Postal authorities allowed that issue to pass after he deleted three paragraphs from an article that had previously appeared in the *Chicago Daily News*. Awaiting word on the status of the September issue, Kerr declared, "We have published and intend to publish nothing contrary to any constitutional law passed by Congress." All attempts to comply with the letter of the law made no difference to Burleson and his aides, however. They temporarily halted the September *ISR* and all subsequent issues through February 1918. The months-long harassment forced a marked decline in advertising revenue, which deeply hurt the monthly. Loss of revenue and concern for censorship led to a decline in quality as well. Kerr decreased the number of pages and had to combine the November and December issues.[53] Undeterred, he continued by using express delivery and informal distribution networks— "the cooperation of . . . friends in many cities who ordered bundles"— and went so far as to send subscribers free pamphlets as replacements for suppressed issues.[54]

In February 1918 Kerr assured readers that the company would continue to circulate books if the monthly succumbed. Meanwhile, federal agents had intercepted bundles of the *Review* shipped by express. Holding them until a ruling could be made in Washington, authorities in Chicago and other locales induced Wells Fargo and other private express companies not to forward bundles of the monthly pending such ruling. That same month, Kerr received word from Burleson's office that *ISR* could no longer pass through the mail or express. Postal authorities had finally blocked the one remaining vehicle of *ISR* distribution by invoking a section of the Trading with the Enemy Act of October 1917 that prohibited express companies from disseminating seditious material, broadly defined. Banned and without recourse, *ISR* became a casualty of war-bred intolerance and antiradical animus after serving nearly eighteen years as a voice for socialism in America.[55]

Kerr & Company carried on as best it could, severely hampered by the suppression of the *Review* and a resultant decline in revenues. Post Office harassment continued unabated as well. Department censors barred from the mails such works as Paul LaFargue's *The Right to Be Lazy*, Marx's *Wage Labor and Capital*, and the 1917 edition of Kerr's *What Socialism Is*. The publisher gave up entirely on the postal service and began sending all books by express.[56] The additional cost of private delivery, in turn, further exacerbated the financial state of the already beleaguered firm.

Down but not out—and not about to disavow its politics—the Kerr group nevertheless slowly turned its energies and meager resources toward issuing reprints and new releases. The company, despite increasing hardships in 1918, issued an updated seventh edition of *Industrial Socialism*, the militant left-wing manifesto by William D. Haywood and Frank Bohn. It also released several analytical studies of contemporary capitalist development, for example, Herman Cahn's *The Collapse of Capitalism* and Frederick Haller's *Why the Capitalist?* and *The Economic Causes of the War* by the Italian socialist Achille Loria. It briefly distributed copies of the famous antimilitarist tract *On Militarism* by Karl Liebknecht until it, too, was banned. Kerr & Company also found the time and resources to issue *The Labor Movement in Japan*, a landmark work by that major figure of the early Japanese socialist and communist movements, and Kerr's longtime acquaintance, Sen Katayama.[57]

Undaunted in their determination to provide the movement with news and analysis, in March 1918 the Kerr group issued the first number of *The Labor Scrapbook*, a projected sixty-four-page replacement for *ISR*. Containing an essay entitled "To Fight All Capitalism" by one Nicholas Lenine and reproduced from the *Chicago Examiner*, an abridgment of Herman Kahn's recently released *The Collapse of Capitalism*, and a number short articles on socialism and the effects of the war culled from mainstream press sources, the first *Scrapbook* immediately came under the scrutiny of federal censors. Released in late May, the second issue contained a primer on Marxian theory, "The New Era" by Mary Marcy, a number of reports on the first IWW trial then underway in Chicago, and an additional series of articles from the mainstream press predicting radical changes in the postwar capitalist order. The ever-vigilant Post Office Department soon ruled that the *Scrapbook* should be barred from the mails and express services under the wartime restrictions.[58]

Kerr also brought out a remarkable pamphlet on the status of women, *Women as Sex Vendors* by Mary Marcy and her brother, Roscoe Tobias, in 1918. Seemingly as irrepressible as ever despite the accompanying stress and difficulties of the war period, Marcy continued her left-wing educational work. In addition to numerous columns and editorials in *ISR* and *The Labor Scrapbook*, she also churned out a diverse number of longer pamphlets and several book-length works between 1917 and 1921.[59] Marcy joined the IWW in 1918 and became active in political defense work following the arrest of several tiers of the organization's leadership in 1917 and after. Those activities brought her and Leslie Marcy under closer scrutiny from the authorities.[60]

Government surveillance of the Kerr group increased rather than ceased with suppression of *ISR*. Not surprisingly, the firm's activities and the political conduct of its close associates had come under the watchful eye of several intelligence-gathering agencies, including the Justice Department's Bureau of Investigation and the War Department's Military Intelligence Division (MID). In an attempt to acquire some hard, incriminating evidence that would place the business in further violation of the Espionage and Sedition Acts, MID agents attempted to entrap Kerr on several occasions. Apparently, only his extreme caution, careful attention to security, and close observation of the letter of the law as interpreted by the authorities kept the company alive throughout the period.[61]

At some point in mid-July 1918, for example, a Chicago operative for the MID named Lloyd Canby visited Kerr's offices at 341 East Ohio Street. On instructions from his superiors, Canby purchased a stock of books after casually questioning a shipping clerk who had apparently grown suspicious about his queries. The catalog Canby acquired listed *The Crimson Fist*, described as "a book of propaganda against war," and he immediately attempted to purchase the volume. Hoping to set a snare, he had book dealer A. C. McClurg & Company place an order for three copies, but Kerr returned the McClurg request, stating that the company was "not allowed to circulate copies of the book." Undeterred, Canby then asked a local acquaintance, E. C. Carlson, to write to Kerr and request a copy of *The Crimson Fist*. Again Kerr returned the order with a note explaining that the book was not for sale.[62]

Canby, in the meantime, forwarded the fruits of his investigation to Washington. He sent his superiors a number of recent Kerr imprints of Marx, Engels, Kautsky, Wilhelm Liebknecht, and Lafargue. The package also included a translation of *The Republic of Plato* by Kerr's father, Alexander, at the time an emeritus professor of classics at the University of Wisconsin. An evaluation of his report at military intelligence headquarters stated that Canby was obviously "very badly informed about Socialism," and that the books he had purchased were "mostly 19th Century Classics of Socialism . . . absolutely without point in the present war." In his follow-up instructions to Chicago, Colonel M. Churchill of the MID General Staff suggested that "further investigation of C. H. Kerr & Co. be called off or that an investigator be selected who possesses some discerning knowledge of Socialism."[63] Surveillance continued, however, and the Kerr associates learned to work around it and accept it as a fact of life for those upholding revolutionary views as the decade drew to a close.

The war's repression had already taken a toll on Kerr activists even before the suppression of *ISR*. Chaplin and Haywood were key targets of the nationally coordinated arrest of IWW leaders that began with a raid on the organization's Chicago headquarters in September 1917. That first of several Wobbly roundups, undisputedly aimed at crippling the radical union, detained some 160 activists. Indicted and arraigned within weeks on more than ten thousand separate charges, 113 "Wobs," among them the two Kerr associates, sat in Cook County Jail awaiting a mass trial that finally got underway on April 1, 1918. Found guilty on all counts by a highly prejudicial court that acted in an inflamed political environment, the group was sent to Leavenworth Penitentiary by Judge Kenesaw Mountain Landis. Chaplin and Haywood each received twenty-year sentences.[64]

A number of the prisoners' friends and comrades, including the other members of the Kerr circle, immediately joined a broad defense effort organized to aid those facing trial and assist the incarcerated with appeals and clemency campaigns. The work of the Marcys in defense campaigns for the IWW and other radicals brought them under further scrutiny from authorities.[65] The Marcys managed to procure enough security by putting up their personal properties and cash to obtain Haywood's release on a $30,000 bond, pending appeal, in August 1919. Those contributing to the bail fund included Mary and Leslie Marcy, Roscoe Tobias, and Charles Kerr. Haywood resumed an activist role while awaiting the outcome of his appeal and again faced arrest during the Red Scare raids of early 1920. When the U.S. Supreme Court, on April 21, refused to hear his appeal, Haywood, aging, in poor health, and facing twenty years behind bars, dropped from sight and made his way to the Soviet Union.

Failure to appear meant that he had forfeited his bond. The loss of that bail fund left the IWW, already hard-pressed, in financial shambles. More directly, it created additional havoc in the lives of Haywood's longtime associates at Charles H. Kerr & Company. Posting company property as security, Kerr had furnished $2,000 to the bail fund. Wanting to contribute more, he attempted to put up the mortgage of the family home in Glen Ellyn, then occupied by his daughter Katharine Kerr Moore, as security. After consulting with her mother, she rejected the idea. Not so fortunate, the Marcys placed their Bowmanville bungalow on the line and lost it when Haywood failed to appear.[66]

Haywood's flight took an exceptionally heavy personal toll on Mary Marcy. Their relationship had been a close one, and his departure came as the movement she so selflessly had served, attacked from outside and fractured within, reached an extreme state of disarray. Although she was never in good health, she continued writing and poured out pamphlets and essays, including *The Right to Strike* (1920) and *Open the Factories* (1920). She also composed the text for a beautifully illustrated hardbound collection of children's stories and poems titled *Rhymes of the Jungle Folk* (1922). Marcy became physically and emotionally drained, however, by the results of the war period and its aftermath. Her marriage to Leslie Marcy had become strained as well. Neither could she draw strength; by 1921 or 1922, from those glimmerings of revolutionary potential that had fueled her confidence but a few years earlier when the beacon of the international revolution seemed to burn so brightly. The central figure in the Kerr circle, whom Eugene Debs once described as "the brainiest woman in the American movement," committed suicide in December 1922.[67]

Sixty years old in 1920, Charles Kerr continued on amid the turmoil of the postwar period. He made plans for another periodical entitled *Every Little While a Shop Book*, projected to appear in June 1921.[68] While the firm bearing his name, now in its fourth decade, survived mainly by reprinting its long list of Marxian classics, it also managed to issue several significant new imprints as well. Always one to publish books that other publishers showed a reluctance to handle, in 1923 Kerr released an important work on the Red Scare, *The Deportations Delirium of Nineteen-Twenty*, by one of its influential liberal critics, former Assistant Secretary of Labor Louis F. Post. The publisher also brought out R. F. Pettigrew's *Imperial Washington*, an insider's historical view of political life in the nation's capitol; the now-classic story of one of America's great labor militants, *The Autobiography of Mother Jones* (1923); and a collection of essays by Lenin, S. J. Rutgers, and Nicholai Bukharin on *The New Policies of Soviet Russia*.[69] With an American audience for his socialist inventory drastically decreased for numerous reasons—the war repression, the Red Scare of 1919 and 1920, the splintering of the broader socialist movement, the annihilation of industrial unionism, the return to "normalcy," and the "new prosperity" among them—Kerr looked for new markets overseas.[70] The movement that Charles H. Kerr & Company served never recovered the vitality of its prewar years, however, and with the fortunes of that cause rode the future of its most important publishing house.

Cast adrift ideologically and organizationally by the tumult of the immediate postwar years, the company's guiding spirit meanwhile sought a new political home. He found it for a short period in the Proletarian Party, a small communist grouping that arose as one of several splinters from the disrupted and fragmented Socialist Party of 1919.[71] But more than forty years had passed since young Charlie Kerr had first journeyed to Chicago to take up a career in the book trade. The promise of a cooperative commonwealth that he held so dear for so many years had come and gone. So had many of his friends, associates, and comrades. He traveled to Mena, Arkansas, in mid-1927 to stay for awhile with Kate Richards O'Hare, the famous radical voice of the antiwar crusade.[72] Returning to Chicago shortly thereafter, he handed the reins of the company over to John Keracher, one of the founders of the Proletarian Party. Charles Kerr retired in 1928 at the age of sixty-eight. He left Chicago and settled in Los Angeles, where he lived out the remainder of his life with Mary Marcy's sister, Inez. He died on June 1, 1944.[73]

■ Conclusion

The fortunes of Charles H. Kerr & Company during the decades follow-ing the retirement of its founder became tied to the trajectory of the Pro-letarian Party, a small communist group with origins in the war-bred disruption and postwar fracturing of the Debsian-era socialist movement. Under the management of party cofounder John Keracher and a handful of his committed comrades, the publishing house continued to promote works on socialism into the 1960s, when Al Wysocki, the last of the Pro-letarians capable of running the enterprise, almost eighty at the time, closed the firm's office and placed the remaining inventory of books and pam-phlets in warehouse storage. How did the company survive across that span of years from the 1920s to the 1960s? The answer lays hidden, in part, in some understanding of the politics and personalities that were the Prole-tarian Party.

The party cannot be understood without some knowledge of its cen-tral figures, most prominent among them John Keracher, who would come to maintain Kerr & Company for the good part of three decades. The self-taught son of a shoemaker, Scottish-born Keracher had arrived in Detroit in 1909, not long after his arrival in the United States. He was in his early twenties and a committed socialist when he joined the Michigan Socialist Party in 1910, and he soon began holding regular evening classes on Marx's *Capital* in the rear of his small shoe store. Keracher quickly forged a close working alliance with two key figures within Detroit's socialist circles, the militant trade unionist and tool-and-die maker Dennis Batt and Al Ren-ner, a left-wing organizer. Staunch partisans of a militant industrial social-ism firmly based on a systematic understanding of Marxism that would

combat the Michigan Socialist Party's reformist leadership, the trio organized the "Proletarian University," an alternative network of study classes
and lectures for workers that was centered at Renner's "House of the
Masses" and various locations throughout the city.[1]

With their university as an institutional and organizational base, Keracher, Batt, and Renner successfully forged the left-wing poll that effectively challenged conservative control of the Michigan party. Keracher,
described as a "scholarly and reasoning man" and a "good lecturer" with
"personal charm," won election as secretary of the state organization in
1916.[2] He also became editor of the monthly *Michigan Socialist*, which was
soon halted by the Espionage Act's restrictions, and its successor, the *Proletarian*, which was launched in late 1918.

With a monthly press, alternative institutions, and control of the state
apparatus, Detroit left-wingers proceeded to revise the Michigan party's
constitution and bylaws. They made any state socialist who advocated the
"immediate demands" of the national platform liable to expulsion. The left-
dominated 1917 state convention also passed a resolution urging members to take a firm stance against religion "on the basis of the material
conception of history." That motion placed the Michigan party in direct
opposition to the long-standing national policy of neutrality on the "religious question." The National Executive Committee, determined in its
attempt to discipline an increasingly intransigent left, seized upon the
opportunity created by the stand against religion and revoked the state
party's charter in June 1919.

The first of several state party organizations expelled by the national body,
and de facto leader of the left wing for a short time, the Michigan group cast
about for allies. Meeting in emergency session that month, they called for a
national convention to organize a socialist party to be aligned with the Mos-
cow-based Third, or Communist, International. A delegation of "Reds" from
Detroit, including Keracher, Batt, Renner, the printer John MacGregor, and
Oakley C. Johnson, a teacher, attended a conference of left-wing elements in
New York.[3] From that meeting emanated a July call signed by Keracher and
Batt for a National Convention for the Purpose of Organizing the Commu-
nist Party of America to be held in Chicago on September 1.[4]

The Michigan group was well represented at what became that founding meeting of the Communist Party. Batt, already known in left-wing circles as a fiery orator and to some the "American Trotsky," gave the opening address, called the Michigan Manifesto, but he and his Detroit comrades
already differed politically with the mood and reading that prevailed at
that gathering.[5]

The majority of left-wingers gathered in Chicago were either immigrant members of the recently expelled Socialist Party's foreign language federations or recent movement arrivals propelled by a belief in the proximity of a revolutionary situation. After all, the pace and scope of events at home and abroad, accelerating that spring, suggested to many on the left that the long-anticipated "final contest" was inexorably near. It would be only a short matter of time before the world revolution would successfully expand outward from its base in the Soviet Union.[6]

[margin, handwritten: not all the language federations were expelled at this time.]

The Michigan representatives did not share that reading of conditions, more a hope than a reality. They differed with those gathered in Chicago, primarily over the issue of minority action, the notion influenced by the example of the Russian Bolsheviks, that a small, disciplined organization could successfully seize power. The Detroit communists instead insisted that conditions in the United States were far from revolutionary; that America at war's end, although tumultuous, was not akin to Russia; and that the Bolshevik experience and opportunity were unique. They contended that the American working class was ill-prepared and nowhere near as class conscious as its European counterparts. More significantly, they argued that capitalism in the United States was nowhere near the brink of collapse, but had actually emerged from the war far stronger than before and the system was likely to survive indefinitely. They also held that the working class as a class in itself would have to be prepared over a long period for that moment when it could enter the world stage of history as a class for itself. The strategic response, for the comrades from Michigan, lay not in a vanguardist minority incapable of leading a reluctant mass but in a long-term commitment to working-class education.[7] Keracher, dismayed by the tenor of the convention, left before it ended, and the rest of the Michigan group soon followed.[8]

The October 1919 issue of the *Proletarian* carried the "Manifesto and Program of the Communist Party of America."[9] The Detroit minority group that same month, however, circulated a confidential critique of the infant Communist Party's analysis and strategy and a "program of action submitted as a basis for discussion" to kindred left dissidents around the country. In response, the newly formed Central Executive Committee of the Communist Party directed members to disassociate themselves from the Proletarian University, the Proletarian press, and the affiliated Proletarian clubs.[10] The future caretakers of Charles H. Kerr & Company thus became the first group purged from the party.

The opening rounds in the sectarian contests for the leadership of American communism had hardly been settled when national round-ups of left-wing militants, the infamous Palmer Raids, named for Attorney General A. Mitchell Palmer, began. The arrest of some six thousand radicals in January 1920 forced the contentious Communist and Communist Labor Parties underground. A number of the people who would form the Proletarian Party the following June were, in Keracher's words, "given a taste of American democracy in action." Keracher himself was arrested, briefly held for deportation, and released. Renner, native-born, was arrested and held under Michigan state antisyndicalist laws. Looking back, Keracher would recall that the period "was not the best time, nor presented the most favorable circumstances, for forming a new party." The repression, however, "had eliminated the timid ones who had been frightened away from the movement."[11]

Founded by Batt and Keracher in June 1920 and for a brief period the only public communist party, the Proletarians turned all their energies toward recruitment and political education—street agitations, study classes, expanding their Proletarian clubs in numerous cities, and circulating their newspaper and other party literature. Concerned with building a viable organization of informed cadre well versed in scientific socialism, Keracher and his comrades, centered in Chicago after the early 1920s, soon became involved in the ongoing business of Charles H. Kerr & Company.[12] As Keracher later recalled, "From the outset, the proletarians realized that it would take time to build a substantial Marxian party, and that it would have to recruit its ranks mainly from new people."[13] Their activities melded nicely with the party's role as caretaker for Kerr & Company.

Keracher's work in Detroit's Proletarian University had brought him into close contact with Charles H. Kerr & Company, and he became a member of the Kerr board in 1924. Upon his retirement in 1928 Charles Kerr sold the bulk of his controlling shares in the firm to Keracher, who, over the next several decades, worked with his Proletarian comrades to issue a number of remarkably nonsectarian pamphlet popularizations of Marxism, including Keracher's *How the Gods Were Made* (1929), *Producers and Parasites* (1935), *The Head-Fixing Industry* (1935), *Crime: Its Causes and Consequences* (1937), *Frederick Engels* (1946), Christ Jelset's *Money and Money Reforms* (1931), and several others. Kerr & Company, under the auspices of Keracher and the Proletarians, never became a narrow party press, but it continued to serve the broader left-wing movement. Primarily a publisher of Marxian classics, in 1935 the company issued the first English translation of Engels's *Anti-Dühring*.

The party grew, as did other organizations of the left, during the 1930s, and it eventually opened offices in an estimated thirty-eight cities from coast to coast. Although the group never had more than several thousand members, party organizers played a significant although unheralded role in the sit-downs and early struggles of what became the CIO in Detroit and other cities. Considering its relative size, it provided the United Auto Workers with a disproportionately large number of its ablest organizers—figures such as Emil Mazey and Frank Marquart. A number of its onetime cadre also went on to occupy significant leadership roles in other major unions: Al Renner of the Restaurant Workers, Carl Berreiter of the International Typographical Union, and Samuel Meyers of the Retail Clerks.

The party carried out occasional expulsions, and now and then someone defected to the Communist Party. The largest opposition group to the Communist Party for some fifteen years, it also carried out its own occasional expulsions. Dennis Batt, for instance, after moving rightward in the mid-1920s, met that fate, as did the one-time member and Marxist theorist Paul Mattick. Keracher remained at the helm of the organization until his retirement in 1953. He died in 1958.[14]

The office of the Proletarian Party and the Kerr Company came under the care of long-time party activist Al Wysocki, who succeeded Keracher as national secretary.[15] By the late 1960s the company had been reduced to a small mail-order firm. Stricken with cancer in 1970, Wysocki looked for some way to save Kerr & Company from extinction, and in 1971 he contacted Fred Thompson, a long-time socialist and IWW activist historian. Thompson organized a meeting at Wysocki's apartment that included the Chicago socialists Burt Rosen and Virgil Vogel and a life-long anarchist, Irving Abrams, who had been a law partner of Clarence Darrow. Wysocki transferred control of the firm to those present. The new caretakers formed a board of directors, eventually expanded to ten members, which elected Vogel as president, Thompson as vice president, and Rosen as secretary. The newly constituted board adopted a statement of policy that committed the company to the nonsectarian publication and dissemination of socialist literature. During the summer of 1971 Rosen and Vogel rented office space in the old Manhattan Building on Dearborn Street, just south of the Loop. They placed a few small advertisements, orders began to trickle in, and Charles H. Kerr & Company was back in business.

While circulating imprints of socialist classics from the dwindling inventory, the new board established a warm working relationship with the Illinois Labor History Society and one of its founders, Les Orear of the Amalgamated Meat Cutters' education department. With his assistance and the help of the amalgamated's secretary-treasurer Pat Gorman, the ILHS aided Charles H. Kerr Publishing Company, now reorganized as a nonprofit corporation, in reissuing several historically significant reprints, including the Rev. William H. Carwardine's *Pullman Strike* (originally published in 1893), *The Autobiography of Mother Jones* (1923), and a collection of Eugene Debs's writings, *Walls and Bars* (1926). The company also reprinted Clarence Darrow's *Address to the Prisoners of Cook County Jail* and *The Right to Be Lazy* by Paul Lafargue.

Virgil Vogel resigned as president of the Kerr board in March 1973, and Joe Giganti, another long-time Chicago labor activist, replaced him. Often assisted by the aging Fred Thompson, Burt Rosen selflessly maintained the firm's business through the next decade by spending part of his normally long workday at the Kerr office before taking a bus uptown, where he earned his living as a television repairman. In 1983 Rosen handed over the management of Kerr to Franklin and Penelope Rosemont, two members of a younger generation who joined the Kerr board of directors during the late 1970s.[16]

Charles H. Kerr & Company survived. It survived long enough to experience a revival—a renaissance of sorts—during the mid-1980s under the guidance of a fourth generation of Chicago-based activists. The publishing house, in the process of a revitalization, celebrated its hundredth anniversary in 1986: the oldest socialist publishing house in the world.

■ Epilogue

The exact impact of Charles H. Kerr & Company, still alive and well in 1996, is difficult to assess. Lasting as long as it has and distributing as many works as it has among the left, its influence has been considerable. In terms of sheer output, the numbers of books, pamphlets, and periodicals distributed, the company touched thousands, if not hundreds of thousands, of lives over a century. Its historical import, however, remains at various levels intangible and certainly unquantifiable. Certain assertions, admittedly speculative and conjectural, can be drawn, however. Those, in turn, will hopefully lead to a closer examination of the significance of the left press in shaping the contours of twentieth-century America.

The Kerr history, a history of independent socialist activism, has taken on new significance in the post–cold war era. A left no longer encumbered by all the political baggage of the bipolar cold war system—the obstacles of deeply rooted anticommunism, an identification with the Soviet system, and the crippling sectarianism on the left—still has much to learn from the era of Second International socialism in America. Kerr & Company evolved, both institutionally and ideologically, within a distinctly left-wing political culture that appears ever more distant and remote as the twentieth century draws to a close.

Barred ideologically and politically from the mainstream media of the Debsian era and often hindered economically, many of the socialist left's editors, publishers, writers, and publicists sought alternative means to disseminate their messages and create an alternative community and an alternative political space. Conscious actors, they collectively created an oppositional political and cultural space despite innumerable obstacles.

Their primary medium of expression, the periodical press, played a key role in that process by providing a counterhegemonic political forum as well as a sense of community and camaraderie that those far afield from urban concentrations of left-wing labor and political activity yearned for and needed. In that sense, Kerr & Company and its socialist allies played a significant role in the history of American public expression by providing a marginal but nevertheless influential alternative political discourse.

Diverse rather than monolithic in its perspectives on a broad range of political and social questions, the left-wing press of the Debsian era gravitated toward two poles reflecting tendencies within the broader socialist movement. Wedded to a reformist strategy of winning support within the exclusivist trade unions and at the polls, the movement's conservatives, often in charge of the Socialist Party organs, faced off against a left wing committed to industrial unions, direct action, and a secondary role for electoral work. Siding with the latter while maintaining a commitment to agitational work on the political front, Kerr & Company developed a political line that still holds lessons for contemporary activists.

The company was always something more than the major disseminator of socialist theory in the United States. Never under the direct control of the national leadership of the Socialist Party and critical—at times defiant—of that leadership, the Kerr group plotted an independent political course with its own strategic and tactical perspective. After 1908 the Kerr venture played a unique role in publishing a national political forum, *The International Socialist Review,* for the movement's left wing and also a broad range of pamphlets and book-length works that provided an ideological counter to the more conservative movement right. The *Review,* although never attaining the circulation of its socialist cousin, the weekly *Appeal to Reason,* maintained its authentically radical—indeed, revolutionary—edge and paid the price for doing that during World War I. The *Appeal* weathered the war-born repression by taking up a pro-war position while Kerr and Company called for further resistance.

Significantly, Kerr and his associates and those who succeeded them provided continuity in the history of radical dissent and opposition to the mainstream trajectory of U.S. development. Kerr's parents were abolitionist activists in the mid-nineteenth-century crusade against slavery. Nurtured in a midwestern rationalist culture and initially an activist at the heart of the most radical tendency within Unitarianism, Kerr moved through populism to Marxian socialism and then aligned with the revolutionary wing of the movement. Continuing Kerr's legacy of dissent, his successors at the company's helm from the late 1920s through the early 1970s remained unaligned communists, an independent dissenting voice unbeholding to the Comintern and Moscow. The company's reins were eventually passed to a small but dedicated collection of independent left-wingers, who ultimately passed the legacy of the Kerr house to its present stewards. The details of that history, now spanning more than a century, remain unique in the annals of American publishing.

Surviving as long as it has, the company has provided a legacy for successive generations of socialist activists, especially the propagandists and publishers. In that sense, the firm's structure could be viewed as the forerunner of latter-day independent left-wing publishing ventures such as *Monthly Review Press* and the more recent *South End Press*. The Kerr venture participated in a much broader seeding process that disseminated socialist ideas across the political landscape. It also helped shape political discourse and thereby influenced debates throughout society on political and social reform.

Much of the social and political history of the United States during the last half of the century was shaped by the catastrophe of the Great Depression of the 1930s and liberalism's response to that crisis, the New Deal. Most New Deal historians readily acknowledge the precedents and antecedents of that earlier "age of reform," the so-called Progressive Era that arose in response to the preceding capitalist crisis of the 1890s. Historians of both periods, the depression decade of the 1930s and the period of crisis and response in the Progressive Era, have rarely considered the significant role of the socialist left in shaping and influencing mainstream response to reform and the general impetus for it. In much the same way that the New Deal had origins in the Progressive Era, the history of radicalism of the 1930s, that heyday of the American left, originated in the political and social experience, the lessons, successes, and failures, nestled in the political culture and politicized popular memory of the Debsian era.

The popular mass media of the left, primarily its periodicals, transmitted a complex message of socialist hope and progress while demanding the extension of true democracy, improved working and living conditions, and social protections. Unwilling to take up the notions of class struggle, and certainly unamenable to the slightest suggestion of revolution, American liberalism at times readily and at times begrudgingly took up the reform demands that the socialist left had proposed well back in the nineteenth century. The most advanced liberal elements did so in many instances primarily to offset and placate demands for radical change and to deflate insurgency from below and the threat of a burgeoning left during the 1910s and the 1930s. In some sense, many of the reform ideas of American social democracy, especially the notion of a positive interventionist state, became mainstream during the course of several decades because of the small but influential socialist press. The fact that part of that press's message ultimately reached America at large may have been one of its most important legacies.

More to the point, the Kerr project transmitted a popular left culture "of, by and for the working class" that has rarely been surpassed. A truly independent socialist voice, it set an example in left journalism and publishing that continues to provide lessons. Kerr and his associates constantly struggled to maintain their freedom along with their ability to remain critical. Clearly aware of the constraining strings of self-imposed political caution and censorship that came attached to loans and credit line obligations, they refused financial ties to banks and well-heeled movement patrons. In a constant quest for unencumbered capital, they turned to the movement they served and ultimately succeeded in developing an alternative strategy of support. Incessantly innovative in their search for a political alternative based on an authentically egalitarian and democratic impulse, their experience still provides vital examples. Political autonomy and economic independence remained central for Kerr and his associates and their heirs. So did their principled adherence to socialist fundamentals and their unswerving class perspective on the origins and causes of society's core antagonisms. As they saw it, those class antagonisms, embedded at the very heart of capital, could only be eliminated through a profound social transformation. They never lost sight of that fact, and for that very reason their story still remains salient.

■ Notes

Introduction

1. For a provocative discussion of the significance of the left-wing press in the Debsian era, see Jon Bekken, "The Working-Class Press at the Turn of the Century," in *Ruthless Criticism: New Perspectives in U.S. Communications History*, ed. William S. Solomon and Robert McChesney (Minneapolis: University of Minnesota Press, 1993).

Chapter 1: Charles H. Kerr

1. Unsigned handwritten memoir, Alexander Kerr Papers, University of Oregon Archives, Eugene (hereafter Alexander Kerr Papers, Eugene); M. S. Slaughter, "Minute on the Life of Alexander Kerr," read at the University of Wisconsin faculty meeting, Oct. 19, 1919, Alexander Kerr Papers, Eugene; "Alexander Kerr," in *History of Dane County, Wisconsin* (Chicago: Western Historical Company, 1880), 1006; Ruben Gold Thwaites, ed., *The University of Wisconsin* (Madison: J. N. Purcell, 1900), 327–28; "Professor Alexander Kerr, A.M.," *Dane County Biographical Review* (Chicago: Biographical Review Publishing, 1893); Consul W. Butterfield, *History of the University of Wisconsin* (Madison: University Press, 1879), 152–53.

2. Material on Katharine Fuller Brown Kerr from "Death of Mrs. Kerr," *Wisconsin State Journal* [Madison], July 24, 1890, 4; *Fiftieth Anniversary of the First Congregational Church, Madison, Wisconsin, 1840–1890* (Madison: Tracy, Gibbs, 1890), 79–80.

3. Sally Lou Coburn, "Anna Peck Sill, 1852–1884," in *Profiles of the Principals of Rockford Seminary and the Presidents of Rockford College, 1847–1947* (Rockford: n.p., 1947), 5–8; James Weber Linn, *Jane Addams* (New York: D. Appleton-Century, 1935), 42.

4. "Death of Mrs. Kerr"; May Walden Kerr to Katharine Kerr Moore, June 18, 1944, box 2, May Walden Kerr Papers, Newberry Library, Chicago (hereafter May Walden Kerr Papers).

5. Interview with Katharine Kerr Moore, Glen Ellyn, Illinois, Nov. 18, 1981. The only other remaining hints of clandestine abolitionist activity appear in correspondence between Kate and Alexander when he was in Georgia and she was still in Rockford before their marriage. In one instance, Alex cautions his betrothed to wrap some abolitionist material carefully before sending it to him so that it might go undetected by the authorities. Alexander Kerr Papers, Eugene.

6. Family members have long since taken delight in noting the coincidence of Charles's birthday with that of William Shakespeare. Interview with Katharine Kerr Moore.

7. Ibid.

8. Frederic Pike, *A Student at Wisconsin Fifty Years Ago* (Madison: Democratic Printing, 1935).

9. James Bremer Kerr was born at Beloit, Wisconsin in September 28, 1867. He graduated from the University of Wisconsin in 1889 and from the law school there in 1892, becoming "one of the most scholarly members" of the Dane County bar before moving first to St. Paul, Minnesota, and then Portland, Oregon, where he worked as a corporate attorney for the Northern Pacific Railway. *Dane County Biographical Review* (1893), 405; Thwaites, ed., *The University of Wisconsin*, 725–26.

10. First Congregational Church of Madison, Wisconsin, Collection, State Historical Society of Wisconsin (hereafter SHSW); *Our Paper* 15 (Jan. 1878): 1, 4; First Congregational Church of Madison, *Annual Reports, 1897–1949* (Madison: n.p.), vols. *1896, 1898–1902*; First Congregational Church Record Books, *1891–1914*; *The Seventy-fifth Anniversary of the First Congregational Church of Madison, Wisconsin, 1840–1915* (Madison: n.p., 1915[?]).

11. *The Record of the Madison Literary Club of Madison, Wisconsin, 1878–1887* (Madison: David Atwood, 1887); *The Madison Literary Club, Twenty-fifth Anniversary, 1877–1902* (Madison: Parsons Printing, 1904).

12. Merle Curti and Vernon Carstensen, *The University of Wisconsin: A History, 1848–1925* (Madison: University of Wisconsin Press, 1949), 1:337; Thwaites, ed., *The University of Wisconsin*; Pike, *A Student at Wisconsin*, 51.

13. Thwaites, ed., *The University of Wisconsin*.

14. Curti and Carstensen, *Wisconsin: A History*, 1:337.

15. Interview with Kathryn Kerr Moore.

16. C. W. Butterfield, *History of Dane County* (Chicago: Western Historical Company, 1880).

17. "Death of Mrs. Kerr."

18. Ibid.

19. "In Memory of Mrs. Kerr," *Wisconsin State Journal*, July 26, 1890, 4.

20. Slaughter, "Minute on the Life of Alexander Kerr."

21. Transcript of Charles Kerr's grades at the University courtesy of the registrar, the University of Wisconsin. Little trace exists of Charles Kerr in the university's archives. Writing to her daughter at the time of his death in 1944, May Walden

Kerr made note of the fact that he was "always a brilliant student, especially in literature and languages, Greek, Latin, and especially French," and that "he was not at all given to athletics." May Walden Kerr to Katharine Kerr Moore, box 5, folder 4, May Walden Kerr Papers.

22. William F. Allen, *Nature and Aims of Free Religion: An Address Delivered Before the Free Religious Association of the University of Wisconsin, November 17, 1881* (Madison: Democrat Publishing, 1881).

23. For background on the early Unitarian movement in Madison, see First Unitarian Society of Madison MSS, SHSW.

24. Allen's family extended back seven generations and were among the original inhabitants of colonial Dedham, Massachusetts. His father was the noted Unitarian minister Joseph Allen; his mother, Lucy Clarke Ware, was daughter of Henry Ware, Jr., another well-known Unitarian minister whose father was a key figure in the Unitarian schism from New England Congregationalism. David B. Frankenberger, "Memoir of William Francis Allen," in William F. Allen, *Essays and Monographs, Memorial Volume* (Boston: George H. Ellis, 1890), 3–20.

25. Frankenberger, "Memoir of William Francis Allen."

26. Ibid.

27. The William F. Allen Papers, SHSW, contain accounts of his Sea Islands experience. A number of radical Unitarians played an active role in the educational experiments at St. Helena. Most notable among them was Thomas Wentworth Higginson, the militant abolitionist colleague of Theodore Parker and a founding member of the Free Religious Association. W. C. Gannett, a central figure among the group of Unitarians with whom Charles Kerr later became involved, also spent time in the Sea Islands. See Willie Lee Rose, *Rehearsal for Reconstruction: The Port Royal Experiment* (New York: Vintage, 1964).

28. Frankenberger, "Memoir of William Francis Allen, 13–17."

29. Allen, *Nature and Aims of Free Religion.*

30. Samuel Atkins Eliot, ed., *Heralds of a Liberal Faith*, vol. 4: *The Pilots* (Boston: Beacon Press, 1952), 214–16; Raymond Bennett Bragg, *Henry Martyn Simmons* (Minneapolis: n.p., 1944), 17; "Henry Martyn Simmons Memorial Number" *Unity*, Dec. 12, 1905. While at Kenosha, Simmons also served as the superintendent of schools for that city. Presumably, he must have been acquainted with Alexander Kerr, who occupied the same position in Rockford and Beloit during the same period.

31. In regard to Simmons's outlook toward the rise of new scientific ideas, his biographer had the following to say: "Coming to the ministry when the names of Darwin, Fiske, and Spencer were disturbing the world of thought, when their teachings were considered a menace to religion, Simmons forcefully, persistently talked about the Unending Genesis. For him the world was forever unfolding. He interpreted not only Darwin and Spencer but Huxley and Tyndall and their associates in terms if moral and religious truth. . . . He made many a man and woman familiar with the flower and insect, with leaf and crystal. His book was that of Nature,

not enclosed within covers but open for unceasing investigation." Bragg, *Henry Martyn Simmons*, 17. For a sense of Simmons's views on Social Darwinism see "Mr. Spencer's Social Anatomy," *Wisconsin Academy of Sciences, Arts, and Letters Transactions, 1876–77* 4 (Madison: 1879): 56–61. H. M. Simmons, "Strikes," *Unity*, April 10, 1886, 73.

32. Eliot, ed., *Heralds of a Liberal Faith*, 4:214–16.

33. Ibid.; Joseph Henry Crooker, *The New Unitarian Church at Madison* (Madison[?]: n.p., 1883). Simmons served as minister of the Unitarian society in Madison between 1878 and 1881—the very period when Charles Kerr studied at the university. Simmons's direct connection with or influence on Kerr remains difficult to document, but enough evidence exists to ascertain some clear, although speculative, links between the two. While in Madison, Simmons maintained a close friendship with Jenkin Lloyd Jones, Kerr's future Chicago mentor. He also maintained an active relationship with *Unity*, the Chicago-based Unitarian periodical that Kerr came to publish. Simmons likely provided a Madison connection to the center of Unitarian activity in Chicago—and Kerr took full advantage of that connection.

34. Conrad Wright, "'Salute the Arriving Moment': Denominational Growth and the Quest for Consensus, 1865–1895," in *A Stream of Light: A Sesquicentennial History of American Unitarianism*, ed. Wright (Boston: Unitarian Universalist Association, 1975), 84–85.

35. While a student at Meadeville Theological Seminary, Jones wrote Unitarian notable Edward Everett Hale a letter that claimed nine uncles settled over Unitarian parishes in Wales. Recounted in Charles W. Wendte, *The Wider Fellowship* (Boston: Beacon Press, 1927), 1:163. Biographical material on Jones compiled from Richard D. Jones, "Jenkin Lloyd Jones," in *Heralds of a Liberal Faith*, ed. Eliot, 4:164–73; Richard W. Seebode, "Jenkin Lloyd Jones: A Free Catholic," master's thesis, Meadeville/Lombard Theological Seminary, 1927; Charles H. Lyttle, *Freedom Moves West: A History of the Western Unitarian Conference* (Boston: Beacon Press, 1952), passim; Richard Harlan Thomas, "Jenkin Lloyd Jones: Lincoln's Soldier of Civic Righteousness," Ph.D. diss., Graduate School of Rutgers, New Brunswick, 1967; and A. T. Andreas, *History of Chicago from the Earliest Period to the Present Time* (Chicago: A. T. Andreas, 1886). Jones published an account of his Civil War experiences; see Jenkin Lloyd Jones, *An Artillery Man's Diary* (Madison: Wisconsin History Commission, 1914).

36. Lyttle, *Freedom Moves West*, 125.

37. Ibid., 125, 118.

38. Ibid., 119. Upon completion of his studies with the class of 1870, the young man from Spring Green delivered a commencement address on "The Theological Bearings of the Developmental Theory," a discourse on evolution and theology.

39. Jones married Susan C. Barber the day after his graduation from Meadeville. She was the amanuensis for Frederic Huidekoper, head of the divinity school and an active participant in Unitarian Sunday school work. "A lady of superior lit-

erary attainments and social qualifications," she became "an invaluable helpmate to her husband." Andreas, *History of Chicago*, 825–26.

40. Lyttle, *Freedom Moves West*, 127.

41. Ibid.; George Willis Cooke, *Unitarianism in America: A History of Its Origins and Development* (Boston: American Unitarian Association, 1902), 276.

42. Lyttle, *Freedom Moves West*, 128.

43. Ibid.

44. Ibid., 130.

45. Ibid., 136–37. During his first nine months as missionary secretary of the WUC in 1876 Jones traveled ten thousand miles by rail and carriage, preached and made addresses on more than a hundred occasions, attended twelve conferences, visited sixty-five different towns in eight states, and helped establish twelve new Unitarian societies. Wendte, *The Wider Fellowship*, 1:363.

46. Lyttle, *Freedom Moves West*, 136–37.

47. The First Unitarian Church of Chicago organized in 1836. *Western Messenger* 2 (Sept. 1836): 140–41. *The Unitarian Yearbook* (Boston: American Unitarian Society, 1885), 3:26 notes the founding of the Third Unitarian Church in 1868. See Lyttle, *Freedom Moves West*, 51–53.

48. Jenkin Lloyd Jones, *The Ideal Church: A Discourse* (Chicago: Colegrove Book, 1882), 4, in "Chicago All Souls Church Scrapbook (Activities), Nov. 1882–May 1890," Jenkin Lloyd Jones Collection, Meadeville/Lombard Theological Seminary, Chicago (hereafter Jones Collection).

49. Jones, *The Ideal Church*, 4–5.

50. Jones, "Jenkin Lloyd Jones," 169.

51. Ibid., 170.

52. Kerr's name began to appear in the list of Unity Club participants in 1883 as leader of the Robert Browning section. All Souls Church, Chicago, *All Souls Church Annual, 1884*, Jones Collection.

Chapter 2: Kerr's Early Chicago Years

1. Kerr was "excused from speaking at the commencement" of the state university on June 22, 1881. He had been scheduled to present his honors thesis on "Victor Hugo's Reform in the French Drama." See *University Press*, July 20, 1881, University Archive Collection, University of Wisconsin-Madison.

2. Bessie Louise Pierce, *A History of Chicago*, vol. 3: *The Rise of a Modern City, 1871–1893* (New York: Knopf, 1957), 146; Paul Avrich *The Haymarket Tragedy* (Princeton: Princeton University Press, 1984), 15.

3. Arthur M. Schlesinger, Sr., *The Rise of the City, 1878–1898* (New York: Macmillan, 1936), 64; Pierce, *A History of Chicago*, 3:20, 22, 50.

4. Pierce, *A History of Chicago*, 3:55.

5. Bruce C. Nelson, *Beyond the Martyrs: A Social History of Chicago's Anarchists, 1870–1900* (New Brunswick: Rutgers University Press, 1988), 25–26.

6. Nelson, *Beyond the Martyrs*, 22.

7. For the events of the Great Upheaval, see Robert V. Bruce, *1877: Year of Violence* (Indianapolis: Bobbs-Merrill, 1959); Jeremy Brecher, *Strike!* (San Francisco: Straight Arrow, 1972).

8. Avrich, *The Haymarket Tragedy*, 35; Almont Lindsay, *The Pullman Strike* (Chicago: University of Chicago Press, 1966), 8; Stanley Buder, *Pullman: An Experiment in Industrial Order and Community Planning, 1880–1930* (New York: Oxford University Press, 1970), 35.

9. Schlesinger, Sr., *The Rise of the City*, 86.

10. Pierce, *A History of Chicago*, 3:237–38, 240; Henry David, *The History of the Haymarket Affair* (New York: Collier Books, 1963), 34.

11. David, *The History of the Haymarket Affair*, 34; Pierce, *A History of Chicago*, 3:241.

12. David, *The History of the Haymarket Affair*, 31; Avrich, *The Haymarket Tragedy*, 17.

13. Schlesinger, Sr., *The Rise of the City*, 86.

14. Madeleine Stern, "Keene and Cooke: Prairie Publishers," *Journal of the Illinois State Historical Society* 42 (Dec. 1949): 442.

15. "Bookselling in Chicago," *Unity*, Aug. 15, 1883, 230–32.

16. "Bookselling in Chicago."

17. All Souls Church, Chicago, "Marriage Record," Jones Collection.

18. All Souls Church, Chicago, *All Souls Church Annual, 1884–1888*, Jones Collection.

19. Charles H. Kerr, "Percy Bysshe Shelley," *Unity*, Jan. 16, 1883, 451–52.

20. Charles H. Kerr, "Victor Hugo's Reform in the French Drama," *Unity*, March 1, 1883, 6–9.

21. See, for example, "The Patriot: A Story from Browning," *Unity*, Dec. 16, 1883, 424. Other essays by Kerr that appeared in *Unity* included a review of A. P. Russell's *Characteristics* (Jan. 16, 1884, 463–64); a discussion of *Verses* by William S. Lord (April 1, 1884, 55); a review of Sarah Orne Jewett's *A Country Doctor* (July 1, 1884, 190); a book review of *Round about Rio* by D. Y. Carpenter (Dec. 1, 1883, 401); and reviews of Thomas R. Landsbury and James Fenimore Cooper (Feb. 1, 1883, 481), L. Clarkson's *The Shadow of John Wallace*, and Rev. T. T. Munger's *Lamps and Paths* (March 7, 1885, 14).

22. Lyttle, *Freedom Moves West*, 143.

23. Western Unitarian Sunday School Society, *Unity Festivals with Words and Music* (Chicago: Colegrove Book, 1884). For a list of Unity Church-Door Pulpit tracts, see advertisement signed by Charles Kerr in back of J. W. Chadwick, *The Poetry of Rational Religion* (Chicago: Unity Office, 1885).

24. *Unity*, March 1, 1883, 1; Susan Quackenbusch, "History of *Unity*," *Unity*, March 5, 1928, 9. Kerr's name first appeared as "office editor" of *Unity* in advertisements for the paper's coming year, 1884; see Feb. 16, 1884, 508. Susan Curtis Mernitz, "The Religious Foundations of America's Oldest Socialist Press: A Cen-

tennial Note on Charles H. Kerr Publishing Company," *Labour/Le Travail* (Spring 1987).

25. *Unity*, March 1, 1884, 20.

26. *Unity*, April 18, 1885, 5, May 2, 1885, 69. Charles H. Kerr, comp., *Unity Songs Resung* (Chicago: Colegrove Book, 1885). For a favorable review of *Unity Songs Resung*, see "The Study Table," *Unity*, May 16, 1885, 107. The collection, a small volume of seventy-five poems, had initially been scheduled for release about May 1. Announcement, *Unity*, March 7, 1885, 1.

27. "A Unity Prospect" *Unity*, Jan. 9, 1886, 234–35. Jenkin Jones and W. C. Gannet, as representatives of the Unity Committee, signed a formal contractual agreement with Kerr that defined the young publisher's management of *Unity* and the periodical's relationship to the new firm. See "Articles of agreement," handwritten contract, March 19, 1886, Charles H. Kerr & Company Papers, Newberry Library, Chicago (hereafter Kerr Company Papers).

28. "A Unity Prespect"; "Report of the Rev. J. T. Sunderland, Secretary of the Western Unitarian Conference," *Unity*, June 5, 1886, 198; Ellen T. Leonard, "Thirteenth Annual Report of the Western Unitarian Sunday School Society," *Unity*, June 5, 1886, 199. The infant Kerr Company paid $10 a month for rental space at the new Unity office at 175 Dearborn. See "Treasurer's Report of the Western Unitarian Conference for Financial Year 1885–1886," *Unity*, June 5, 1886, 198.

Chapter 3: The Kerr Company's Beginnings

1. Timothy Smith, *Revivalism and Social Reform* (New York: Abingdon Press, 1957), 32.

2. A number of the standard works on the history of Unitarianism in the United States include Cooke, *Unitarianism in America;* Conrad Wright, *The Beginnings of Unitarianism in America* (Boston: Beacon Press, 1955); Conrad Wright, *The Liberal Christians; Essays on American Unitarian History* (Boston: Beacon Press, 1970); Wright, ed., *A Stream of Light;* Daniel Walker Howe, *The Unitarian Conscience, Harvard Moral Philosophy, 1805–1861* (Cambridge: Harvard University Press, 1970); Stow Persons, *Free Religion: An American Faith* (New Haven: Yale University Press, 1947); Sydney Ahlstrom, *A Religious History of the American People*, 2 vols. (Garden City: Doubleday, 1975).

3. Cooke, *Unitarianism in America*, 26.

4. Ibid., 122; Persons, *Free Religion*, chs. 1, 2.

5. Ahlstrom, *A Regligious History*, 1:483.

6. William Ellery Channing, *The Works of William Ellery Channing*, 6 vols. (Boston, 1841–43), 1:226.

7. Ahlstrom, *A Religious History*, 1:483–84, 486–87.

8. For the Divinity School Address, see *Theology in America*, ed. Ahlstrom. On the influence of Emerson, see Persons, *Free Religion*, ch. 2; Ahlstrom, *A Religious History*, 2:36–42.

9. Henry Steele Commager, *Theodore Parker: Yankee Crusader* (Boston: Beacon Press, 1936), 65–66; Theodore Parker, "The Transient and Permanent in Christianity," in *Theodore Parker: An Anthology*, ed. Henry Steele Commanger (Boston: Beacon Press, 1960). Aside from Commager's biography, the standard work on Parker is John White Chadwick, *Theodore Parker* (Boston: Houghton Mifflin, 1901); see also Perry Miller, "Theodore Parker: Apostasy within Liberalism," *Harvard Theological Review* 54, no. 3 (1961): 275–95.

10. Commager, *Theodore Parker*, 65–66.

11. Howe, *The Unitarian Conscience*, 271.

12. Cooke, *Unitarianism in America*, 149, 169.

13. Another notable periodical in the antebellum period was the *Massachusetts Quarterly Review*. Begun in 1847 and halted in 1850, the short-lived publication grappled with the numerous social problems of its day. Concerned more with political and economic issues than with the literature of formal criticism, the *Review* carried a large number of articles on the slavery question. Its major influence was Theodore Parker. Although never officially a Unitarian publication and not religious in character, the *North American Review* (1815–) had Unitarian editors for more than sixty years. Cooke, *Unitarianism in America*, 95–101; J. Wade Caruthers, *Octavius Brooks Frothingham: Genteel Reformer* (University: University of Alabama Press, 1977), 53. For the *Massachusetts Quarterly Review*, see Commager, *Theodore Parker*, 130–34; see Cooke, *Unitarianism in America*, 116, on the *North American Review*; also see Clarence Gohdes, *The Periodicals of American Transcendentalism* (Durham: Duke University Press, 1931).

14. Ahlstrom, *A Religious History*, 1:482.

15. This sketch of the postwar denominational dispute draws from Conrad Wright, "Henry Ward Bellows and the Organization of the National Conference," in *The Liberal Christians; Essays in American Unitarian History*, ed. Wright (Boston: Beacon, 1970); Wright, "'Salute the Arriving Moment'"; Lyttle, *Freedom Moves West*; and Persons, *Free Religion*.

16. Lyttle, *Freedom Moves West*, 122–23; Persons, *Free Religion*, 14–17; Cooke, *Unitarianism in America*, 201–2. The Free Religious Association (FRA) formed in May 1867 "to promote the interests of pure religion, to encourage the scientific study of theology, and to increase fellowship in the spirit" following a dispute over doctrinal issues within the National Unitarian Conference. Promoted initially as "a spiritual Anti-Slavery Society," the new association's first formal gathering opened with an endorsement by Ralph Waldo Emerson. Also present at the initial meeting were Lucretia Mott, Robert Dale Owen, and Thomas Wentworth Higginson.

Never a formal denomination as such, membership in the FRA was open to all those who held that the improvement of spiritual and moral existance was the substance of "pure" religion. The organization served as a magnet for liberals "theologically too naturalistic to be Christians and too religious to be militant atheists." Henry W. Schneider, "The Influence of Darwin and Spencer on American Philosophical Theology," *Journal of the History of Ideas* 6 (Jan. 1945): 15; Persons, *Free*

Religion. Unitarian chronicler C. W. Wendte asserted in *The Wider Fellowship* (Boston: Beacon Press, 1927) that the FRA was "perhaps the first religious body of thinkers in America to acclaim and espouse evolution." The group's founders were "all impassioned converts to the scientific method" (1:221). Their affinity for evolutionary development reaffirmed a belief, universal among them, in the essential rationality of humankind. The neccesity of absolute individual freedom, the idea that humanity not be bound by any creed, was fundamental for the association. Members shared a reverence for progress, evolution, and scientific inquiry, but they held no consensus or unanimity in regard to social philosophy.

The FRA's diverse following maintained earth-bound individual perfection as a goal but attained no agreement over the role of the body in social reform activity. The dominant outlook on reform within the FRA centered around the need for individual ethical transformation. The organization emphasized education, the full development of rational and spiritual powers, as the true vehicle to social betterment. It devoted its energies to the dissemination of liberal thought through tracts, books, periodicals, and the lecture platform.

The FRA's critique of established Christianity never gained wide currency, however. Overly intellectual, the body lacked the popularizers it needed to articulate its ideas in a form that appealed to broad numbers of people. For the history of the FRA, see Persons, *Free Religion;* Cooke, *Unitarianism in America;* Sydney Warren, *American Freethought* (New York: Columbia University Press, 1943); and Wright, "'Salute the Arriving Moment.'"

17. Persons, *Free Religion*, 22; Lyttle, *Freedom Moves West*, 65–66.

18. Lyttle, *Freedom Moves West*, 119–25.

19. Ibid.

20. Ibid., 131–36.

21. Charles W. Wendte, "The Founding of *Unity*," *Unity*, March 5, 1928, 6–7.

22. Jenkin Lloyd Jones, "Ten Years Old Today," *Unity*, March 3, 1888, 3, 4, emphasis in the original.

23. Jones, "Ten Years Old Today," 3.

24. Ibid.; *Unitarian Church Directory and Mission Handbook, 1884–1885* (Chicago: Colegrove Book, 1885), 56; Cooke, *Unitarianism in America*, 451.

25. Alfred Walters Hobart, "William Channing Gannett," B.D. thesis, Meadeville/Lombard Theological Seminary, 1928; Wendte, *The Wider Fellowship*, 1:187–88, 189, 190. For further information on this central figure in the Western Unitarian Conference, see William H. Pease, "Doctrine and Fellowship: William Channing Gannett and the Unitarian Creedal Issue," *Church History* 25 (Sept. 1956): 210–38; Eliot, ed., *Heralds of a Liberal Faith*, 4:142–46.

26. Lyttle, *Freedom Moves West*, 198–99: Eliot, ed., *Heralds of a Liberal Faith*, 4:182.

27. For Wendte, see his two-volume autobiography *The Wider Fellowship;* Eliot, ed., *Heralds of a Liberal Faith*, 4:244–48.

28. Wendte, *The Wider Fellowship*, 1:193, 194, 197–98. Hosmer succeeded the

elder Joseph Allen, father of Charles Kerr's Wisconsin teacher William Francis Allen, at Boston's Northborough Church.

29. Eliot, ed., *Heralds of a Liberal Faith*, 4:219.

30. Lyttle, *Freedom Moves West*, 194.

31. Ibid., as quoted, 165.

32. Ibid.

33. Ibid., 165–67

34. Ibid., 178.

35. Ibid., 180.

36. Ibid., 185, as quoted. For the full text of Gannett's compromise resolution, see Celia Parker Wooley, *The Ideal Unitarian Church* (Chicago: Charles H. Kerr & Company, 1887). For a more detailed discussion of the role of W. C. Gannett in the Western Controversy, see Pease, "Doctrine and Fellowship," 210–38.

37. Lyttle, *Freedom Moves West*, 187.

38. Ibid., 192.

39. Ibid., 193.

40. Long noted for its liberal stance toward the emancipation of women, Unitarianism as a denomination led the way in accepting women as full and equal members. Women often shared pulpits and received ordination as ministers. Although men continued to dominate positions of power in the denomination, women activists carried on the countless endless organizational tasks—the office work and staffing of numerous missionary and educational ventures—that formed the structures and institutions of established Unitarianism, especially in the West.

41. Donald Henry Sheehan, *This Was Publishing: A Chronicle of the Book Trade in the Gilded Age* (Bloomington: Indiana University Press, 1952), 3–6.

42. Sheehan, *This Was Publishing*, 8–9.

43. *Publisher's Weekly*, Nov. 13, 1897, 794.

44. Georg Eugene Sereiko, "Chicago and Its Book Trade, 1871–1893," Ph.D. diss., School of Library Science, Case Western Reserve University, 1973, 6.

45. Sheehan, *This Was Publishing*, 21.

46. Sereiko, "Chicago and Its Book Trade," 332.

47. *Publisher's Weekly*, April 24, 1886, 542.

48. Sheehan, *This Was Publishing*, 30–31.

49. Sereiko, "Chicago and Its Book Trade," 10–11.

50. Ibid., 2.

51. Freeman Lewis, *Paper-Bound Books in America* (New York: New York Public Library, 1952), 3.

52. Sereiko, "Chicago and Its Book Trade," 26–27.

53. Gerald H. Carson, "Get the Prospect Seated and Keep Talking," *American Heritage* 9 (Aug. 1958): 38–41.

54. Sereiko, "Chicago and Its Book Trade," 284–85; Sheehan, *This Was Publishing*, 190–91; Pierce, *A History of Chicago*, 3:169; John Tebbel, *A History of Book*

Publishing in the United States, vol. 2: *The Expansion of an Industry, 1865–1919* (New York: R. R. Bowker, 1975), 16.

55. Numerous well-known national magazines had their beginnings as subsidiaries to publishing houses. The book firms used their related periodicals to serialize new novels—a form of advance publicity. The New York house of Harper & Bros. led the field at midcentury with *Harper's Monthly* (1850) and *Harper's Weekly* (1857). From 1865 to 1885 few leading firms could get along without a magazine, but toward the turn of the century major independent magazine enterprises won the field from their book-firm-related predecessors. Tebbel, *Book Publishing in the United States,* 14; Helmut Lehman-Haupt, *The Book in America: A History of the Making and Selling of Books in the United States* (New York: Bowker, 1952), 211. In *A History of American Magazines,* vol. 4: *1885–1905* (Cambridge: Harvard University Press, 1957) Frank Luther Mott chronicles the large number of notable magazines that had their origins as the subsidiaries of publishing ventures.

56. As quoted in John Tebbel, *The American Magazine: A Compact History* (New York: Hawthorn, 1969), 119–20.

57. Mott, *Magazines,* 20.

58. "American Paternaster Row," *Chicago Evening Journal,* May 1, 1883; [Sherman W. Booth], "Chicago's Book Trade," *Publisher's Weekly,* July 5, 1884, 11.

59. "Bookselling in Chicago," *Unity,* Aug. 12, 1883, 230–32.

60. Ibid.

61. [Booth], "Chicago's Book Trade," 9.

62. Sereiko, "Chicago and Its Book Trade," 139–40.

63. *Bookseller and Stationer* 4 (July 1882): 45.

64. *Chicago Tribune,* Nov. 6, 1887, 28.

65. Sereiko, "Chicago and Its Book Trade," 284–85.

66. Ibid., 333.

67. The actual number of published works was far greater. Such estimates, gleaned from existing trade sources, did not count books produced privately for individuals and not customarily listed in publisher's catalogs.

68. Susan Quackenbusch, "*Unity:* 1878–1918," *Unity,* March 7, 1918, 10.

69. A one-time instructor of grammar and rhetoric at the State University of Wisconsin, Douglas published the *Fortnightly Index* at Madison in 1884. The educational journal featured the contributions of Wisconsin faculty members John Bascom, John Birge, Willian F. Allen, and Kerr's father, Alexander. *The University* began as a monthly at Ann Arbor in 1882. It became a biweekly upon absorption of the *Fortnightly Index* and two other short-lived educational periodicals: *Weekly Magazine* and *Educational News. Unity,* before 1886, absorbed or merged with a number of ephemeral midwestern Unitarian papers with such titles as *The Liberal Helper, The Spectroscope, The Church of the Unity, The Unitarian Advocate,* and *The Liberal.* Pike, *A Student at Wisconsin,* 125, 127; Herbert E. Fleming, *Magazines of a Market Metropolis* (Chicago, 1906), 507, 531; Mott, *Magazines,* 55n; Quack-

enbusch, *"Unity,"* 10. Kerr distributed Douglas's *Syllabus of Rhetorical Training* and his *Douglas Genealogy: A Collection of Family Records with Bibliography* during 1886.

70. "Announcement of Consolidation," *The University,* Feb. 27, 1886. Kerr & Company, before the merger, had handled the "business management" of *The University* as noted by Douglas the preceeding January. Douglas's paper moved to Chicago in late 1884 or early 1885, and James Colegrove handled its publication before the birth of the Kerr firm. *The University,* Jan. 9, 1886, 13, Jan. 16, 1886, 36.

71. Gohdes, *The Periodicals of American Tanscendentalism;* Persons, *Free Religion,* 90.

72. *Unity,* Aug. 21, 1886, 350.

73. "Western Unitarian Conference Annual Report," *Unity,* June 4, 11, 1887, 198–99.

74. *Unity,* July 10, 1886, 269.

75. *Unity,* Oct. 2, 1886, 64.

76. *Unity,* May 21, 1887, 161.

77. *Unity,* May 28, 1887, 174.

78. *Unity,* June 4, 1887, 198–99.

79. *Unity,* Sept. 17, 1887, 31.

80. Letter (dated April 1886), "All Souls Church Scrapbook, Apr. '85–Mar. '89," Jones Collection; *Publisher's Weekly,* May 8, 1886.

81. *Publisher's Weekly,* May 29, 1886, 670.

82. *Publisher's Weekly,* Jan. 22, 1887, 85; Lyttle, *Freedom Moves West,* 196.

83. *Publisher's Weekly,* Dec. 18, 1886, 953.

84. *Unity,* July 10, 1886, 56.

85. The National Bureau of Unity Clubs was founded in 1887 in Boston "to render assistance in the social, literary, philanthropic, and religious work of churches and communities." A list of the Unity Club series pamphlets is available in "National Bureau of Unity Clubs" and "Unity Club Scrapbook, 1883–1886," Jones Collection.

86. A religious leader, soldier, and educator, the grammarian Samuel B. Fallows was born in December 1835 in Pendleton, England. He emigrated to Wisconsin with his parents in 1848. He was graduated from the University of Wiscosin in 1859 and entered the Methodist Episcopal ministry in 1862. Highly decorated in the Civil War, he became state superintendant of public instruction after serving as the pastor to a number of Wisconsin's M.E. churches. He became the president of Illinois Wesleyan Uuniversity in 1875, entered the Reformed Episcopal church that same year, and went on to become a well-known Episcopal bishop in Chicago. Thwaites, ed., *The University of Wisconsin,* 436; *Dictionary of Wisconsin Biography,* 127.

87. Advertisement, *Unity,* July 10, 1886, 56.

88. *Unity,* Sept. 4, 1886, 121.

89. The book was called "an interesting little summary of social conditions of

French, German, English, and American women." *Publisher's Weekly,* Jan. 22, 1887, 87.

90. *Unity,* Jan. 8, 1887, 239.

Chapter 4: *Unity* Years

1. For a full discussion of Unitarian receptivity to evolutionist ideas, see Persons, *Free Religion;* and Cooke, *Unitarianism in America.*

2. Eliot, ed., *Heralds of a Liberal Faith,* 4:xxiii–xxv. Unitarianism was never monolithic in its theological and social perspectives. Certain adherents of the "liberal faith" often shared the conservative social complacency so prevalent among the more orthodox denominations in the decades following the Civil War. No direct relationship existed between liberal theology and progressive social thought or activism. In Boston, the seat of established Unitarianism, the wealthy and respectable members of the denomination in most instances "always agreed with the orthodox in everything but theology." Although congregants maintained a leadership in numerous charitable and philanthropic endeavors, such activity rarely if ever elicited a serious critique of the social order. Henry F. May, *Protestant Churches and Industrial America* (New York: Harper, 1967), 80–81.

3. Francis P. Weisenberger, *Ordeal of Faith: The Crisis of Church-Going America, 1865–1900* (New York: Philosophical Library, 1959), 274–75. Weisenberger argues that during the period following the Civil War, "The Unitarian emphasis on reason, the Transcendental emphasis on intuition, and the scientific emphasis on the accumulation of facts, had tended to separate theology from its earlier intimate connection with philosophical studies." Philosophy in America became more and more secularized and less dependent on scriptural or other religious sanctions and therefore came to constitute at least a potential threat to the intellectual bulwarks of church-going America.

4. Lyttle, *Freedom Moves West,* 198.

5. For a discussion of *The Radical,* an antebellum predecessor of *The Index,* see Gohdes, *The Periodicals of American Transcendentalism,* 229–56.

6. The descendant of Mayflower stock and the son of the prominent Unitarian minister Nathaniel Frothingham, Octavius Brooks Frothingham was born in 1822. He graduated from Harvard University twenty years later and then continued on at the Divinity School as all good sons of Unitarian ministers did in that era. German higher criticism and Idealist philosophy permeated Harvard Yard in the 1840s. By the time young Frothingham enrolled at the theological school, Theodore Parker's "natural religion" and abolitionism, although not part of the regular curriculum, had become the diet of informal exchange among the student body. Under the personal discipleship of Parker, Frothingham studied the works of the new German scholarship and gradually moved beyond the confines of a Christian confession to a radical transcendentalism strictured by no creed whatsoever. Affected by the evolutionary doctrines of Darwin and Spencer in the post–

Civil War years, his thinking shifted once again from the transcendentalist position to a more rationalist scientific theism propounded by his colleague Francis
Ellingwood Abbot. Caruthers, *Octavius Brooks Frothingham*.

7. Octavius Brooks Frothingham, *Fear of the Living God* and *The Present Heav-
en* (Chicago: Charles H. Kerr & Company, 1887).

8. Kerr published a number of works by Abbot as contributions to the Pamphlets on Living Questions series. See *Christian Propagandism* (ca. 1887), *Compulsory Education* (ca. 1887), *The Proposed Christian Amendment to the Constitution of the United States* (ca. 1887–88), *A Study of Religion* (ca. 1887–88), *Truth for
the Times* (1888), and *The God of Science* (1889). Born in November 1836, Frances
Ellingwood Abbot was graduated from Harvard University in 1859. He then proceeded on to Meadeville Theological Seminary, that western outpost of Parkerite
radicalism. He joined the Unitarian ministry in 1863 but left it five years later in
the aftermath of a dispute with his Dover, New Hampshire, parishioners. The
nonconformist minister accepted a call to an Independent church in Toledo, Ohio,
in September 1869, after that body agreed to drop the name *Unitarian* from its
title. Abbot was a key figure in the founding of the FRA. Persons, *Free Religion*, 31–
37; Joseph McCabe, *A Biographical Dictionary of Modern Rationalists* (London:
Watts, 1920); *Dictionary of American Biography* (New York: Charles Scribner's Sons,
1928), 1:11–12 (hereafter *DAB*).

9. For the history of *The Index*, see Gohdes, *The Periodicals of American Transcendentalism*; Persons, *Free Religion*, 38.

10. B. F. Underwood, *Evolution in Its Relation to Evangelical Religion* (Chicago:
Charles H. Kerr & Company, 1887).

11. Marshall Brown and Gordon Stein, *Freethought in the United States* (Westport: Greenwood Press, 1978), 47–48; Weisenberger, *Ordeal of Faith*, 278; McCabe,
A Biographical Dictionary, 826; *DAB*, 19:11–112.

12. McCabe, *A Biographical Dictionary*.

13. Charles H. Kerr, "Publisher's Notes," *Unity*, March 17, 1892, 24.

14. *Unity*, Aug. 7, 1886, 328; Lewis Janes, *The Scientific and Metaphysical Methods in Philosophy* (Chicago: Charles H. Kerr & Company, 1887). The son of Al-
phonse Janes, a Providence, Rhode Island, merchant and "pioneer in the antislavery movement," Lewis Janes moved to New York in 1866. While teaching Sunday
school at Brooklyn's Second Unitarian Church, he became deeply engaged in the
study of science and religion. By the late 1880s he had become widely known as a
proponent and defender of Spencerian philosophy. Janes founded and assumed the
presidency of the Brooklyn Ethical Association and lectured on sociology and civics at the Brooklyn Institute of Arts and Sciences. He subsequently joined the
department of history at Long Island's Adelphi College in the mid-1890s. *DAB*
(1936), 9:606; *Who Was Who in America, Historical Volume* (Chicago: A. N. Marquis, 1963), 276; *National Cyclopedia of American Biography* (New York: J. T. White,
1904), 12:114.

15. "Minot J. Savage's Works," *Unity*, March 3, 1888, 19. A sheaf of six sermons,

Show Us the Father (Chicago: Charles H. Kerr & Company, 1887), contained writings by Jenkin Jones, Henry Simmons, W. C. Gannett, Samuel R. Calthrop, and John White Chadwick as well as Savage.

16. Born in rural Maine in 1841, Minot Judson Savage became a Congregational minister following his service in the Civil War. While pastor at the Congregational church at Framingham, Massachusetts, he began a reading of Darwin and Spencer that lead him to the conclusion that "a Ptolemaic theology cannot live in a Copernican universe." In 1872, after three years as head of the liberal Congregational church in Hannibal, Missouri, Savage joined the Unitarian fold. He became pastor of Chicago's Third Unitarian Church before accepting the call in 1874 to head Boston's Church of the Unity, where he remained for twenty-two years. During the early years of his Boston tenure, Savage became a leading disciple of Herbert Spencer. He contended that unfettered individualism and competition would perfect the human species and ultimately lead to a form of socialism. He posited his view of the natural progress of evolution as a counterweight to the "short-cuts" of communism, the single tax, state socialism, or Bellamyite nationalism—any schemes that attempted to build perfect societies with "imperfect bricks." Schneider, "The Influence of Darwin and Spencer," 9–10. After the hard times induced by the Depression of 1893, however, Savage acknowledged weaknesses in his conservative Spencerian outlook. He turned to support of the poor and actively endorsed tenement reform legislation and ordinances opposed to child labor, the sweated trades, and the saloon. Savage was a prodigious author. His regular Boston sermons, delivered extemporaneously and transcribed by stenographers, reached a large readership. His published sermons between 1879 and 1896 numbered seventeen volumes. His words served "as a godsend to thousands of people troubled and confused in their religious thinking by the discoveries of science" in the last two decades of the nineteenth century. Arthur Mann, *Yankee Reformers in the Urban Age: Social Reform in Boston, 1880–1900* (New York: Harper and Row, 1966), 82; Eliot, *Heralds of a Liberal Faith*, 4:206–10; Weisenberger, *Ordeal of Faith*, 66.

17. In its pages Savage argued that the central tenet of Christianity, the fall of man, had been devastated by evolutionary disclosures and that evolution had invalidated the orthodox notions of God, man, revelation, heaven, and hell. He further argued that God's will was not revealed in scripture but in natural law; that the Divinity did not stand outside the universe but was immanent and therefore humanity was perfectible; and that the true Christian must therefore be a reformer. Mann, *Yankee Reformers in the Urban Age*, 82–83.

18. For Savage, see Robert T. Handy, ed., *Religion in the American Experience: The Pluralistic Style* (Columbia: University of South Carolina Press, 1972); Minot Judson Savage, *The Change of Front of the Universe* (Chicago: Charles H. Kerr & Company, 1889).

19. Mann, *Yankee Reformers in the Urban Age*, 53–67, 69.

20. Rarely did an issue of *Unity* pass from the press in the years between 1886 and 1890 without some promotional for Frothingham, Savage, or Janes. Charles

H. Kerr & Company also regularly advertised their works in his catalogs. See "Catalogue of Books for Sale by Charles H. Kerr & Co., Publishers and Booksellers," supplement to *Unity*, March 24, 1888.

21. Young Adler had gone to Germany to prepare for the rabbinate after receiving a bachelor's degree at Columbia University. His studies at Heidelburg and Berlin altered his future course, however. Influenced by neo-Kantian idealism, with its critique of religion and emphasis on the autonomy and centrality of ethics or practical reason independent of any theological system, Adler spurned his formal religious training and beliefs. His stay in Germany also brought him into contact with that country's growing labor movement and a broad spectrum of social thought on the nature of industrial society and the labor question. Returning home, he refused to succeed his father as rabbi of New York's Temple Emanu-El and took a position teaching Hebrew and Oriental literature at Cornell University in 1874, biding his time until the founding of the ethical culture movement two years later. Howard Radest, *Toward Common Ground: The Story of the Ethical Societies in the United States* (New York: Frederick Ungar, 1969), ch. 1; *The Fiftieth Anniversary of the Ethical Movement, 1876–1926* (New York, London: D. Appleton, 1926), passim; McCabe, *A Biographical Dictionary*; Aaron I. Abell, *The Urban Impact on American Protestantism 1865–1900* (Cambridge: Harvard University Press, 1943), 19–20, 102; M. W. Meyerhardt, "The Movement for Ethical Culture at Home and Abroad," *American Journal of Religious Psychology and Education* 3 (1908): 71–153.

22. Felix Adler, "Address of May 15, 1876, Standard Hall, New York City," cited in Radest, *Toward Common Ground*, 27–28.

23. The society founded a District Nursing Department, forerunner of the Visiting Nurse Service, to administer care to the poor of the city's slums. Under Adler's guidance, the New York Society founded a free kindergarten in 1877. That same year they began a workingman's school, where laborers received combined instructions in the manual arts and a nonsectarian morality. Adler's investigations of the "housing question" prompted the New York tenement house inquiries of the early 1880s and that state's first legislation against sweatshops. Adler received appointment to the state Tenement House Commission in 1882. Radest, *Toward Common Ground*, 37, 40; Moses Rischin, *The Promised City: New York's Jews, 1870–1914* (Cambridge: Harvard University Press, 1962), 202.

24. Radest, *Toward Common Ground*, 40.

25. Both Salter and Jones appear in the lists of charter members of the Athenaeum. See the Chicago Athenaeum, *Annual Reports*, Chicago Historical Society. For a brief discussion of the history and activities of the Atheneum, see Lyttle, *Freedom Moves West*, 203.

26. William McIntire Salter, *Why Unitarianism Does Not Satisfy Us* (Chicago: Max Stern, 1883); William McIntire Salter, "Unitarian Churches and Ethical Societies," *Unity*, July 6, 1889, 146. The heir of a family with deep Congregational moorings, William McIntire Salter was born in Burlington, Iowa, in 1853. He entered Knox College in Illinois at fourteen and proceeded on to Yale Divinity

School, still a bastion of Congregational orthodoxy, in 1871. Disenchanted with the theological demands at New Haven, Salter transferred to Harvard two years later, "thinking I might hold on to enough to be a Unitarian minister if I could not be an Orthodox one." Still dissatisfied, he refused a call to a Unitarian pulpit following his ordination in 1876. Interested in the ancient Greeks, particularly Plato and Aristotle, he accepted a Theodore Parker Fellowship from Harvard University to pursue studies abroad at Göttingen, but illness foreshortened his stay in Germany and he returned to the United States. While en route to Boston in late 1879 after a recuperative stay in Colorado, Salter met Felix Adler in New York. Impressed by Adler's aversion to dogma and creed and the man's commitment to social betterment, Salter joined the ethical culture cause. After a year and a half under his new mentor's tutelage in New York, Salter took up his position as head of Chicago's newly founded Society for Ethical Culture. Radest, *Toward Common Ground*, 63; *Fiftieth Anniversary of the Ethical Movement, 1876–1926* (New York: D. Appleton, 1926), 234–35; McCabe, *A Biographical Dictionary*, 704.

27. William McIntire Salter, *What Can Ethics Do for Us?* (Chicago: Charles H. Kerr & Company, 1891); William McIntire Salter, *First Steps in Philosophy, Physical and Ethical* (Chicago: Charles H. Kerr & Company, 1892).

28. Radest, *Toward Common Ground*, 65.

29. Ibid., 66.

30. Quackenbusch, "History of *Unity*," 10.

31. Radest, *Toward Common Ground*, 65. The society's work slowly began to recoup, however. In 1888 Salter and associates sponsored a series of talks on "Justice for the Friendless and the Poor" that called attention to the inadequate services for those unable to afford attornies' fees. That forum, in turn, led to the founding of Chicago's Bureau of Justice, forerunner of the Legal Aid Society. Also beginning in 1888, the group organized a series of economic conferences on the relationship between workers and employers, with the aim of bringing the leading representatives of capital and labor together. Held at the Madison Street Theater, the initial set of seven meetings included an address by Thomas J. Morgan, the socialist leader of the construction trades, on "The Labor Question from the Standpoint of a Socialist" and "An American Trade Unionist's View of the Social Question" by A. C. Cameron, an executive officer of the Illinois Federation of Labor.

32. The Haymarket Affair affected Salter markedly. In the words of one historian of that tragic episode, Henry David, "Salter experienced a disturbing inner struggle from the clash of his Ethical Culture ideas, his desire to see justice done, his predisposition to side with the underdog, and his conviction that the men as anarchists threatened the existence of the State and society." "What Shall Be Done with the Anarchists?" was the title of Salter's address before the Ethical Society at the Grand Opera House two weeks before the scheduled execution of the condemned, a talk that displayed a "deep emotional concern and inner turmoil." While concluding that the identity of the actual bomb-thrower was unknown, Salter

nevertheless felt that three of the defendants were guilty as accessories. He argued that the case against the other four "is not such as to convince any fair-minded, unprejudiced man beyond the reasonable doubt" but then qualified his statement: "I do not say because the four I have mentioned are not guilty, they are therefore guiltless of any connection with the Haymarket crime. They are not guilty simply of the crime with which they were charged." While arguing that the four were not accessories in the murder of the police officer killed at the scene, he nevertheless found them "guilty of sedition, of stirring up insurrection. They were all members of a conspiracy against the State." He called for leniency for Michael Schwab, Albert Parsons, Samuel Fielden, and August Spies, recommending imprisonment of several years for each. He termed it a "public crime" to hang them and called for life imprisonment for the other defendants. David, *History of the Haymarket Affair*, 335; William McIntire Salter, *What Shall Be Done with the Anarchists?* (Chicago: Open Court Publishing, 1887).

33. Jenkin Lloyd Jones [editorial], *Unity*, Dec. 4, 1887, 176.

34. H. Tambs Lyche, "Socialists and Anarchists," *Unity*, Dec. 4, 1887, 177–78.

35. *Unity*, Jan. 5, 1889, 549.

36. "Special Prices on Books to *Unity* Subscribers," *Unity*, Feb. 9, 1889; "Special Clearance on Standard Books," *Unity*, May 25, 1889, 103.

37. [Charles H. Kerr], *"Unity's* Advertising," *Unity*, March 5, 1891, 1.

38. "To The Friends of *Unity,*" *Unity*, Feb. 1, 1890, 169.

39. *Unity*, Jan. 25, 1890, 161; Jenkin Lloyd Jones, "Ten Times One Is Ten," *Unity*, March 5, 1891, 1.

40. Born in Toledo, Ohio, in 1848, Celia Parker Wooley passed her girlhood years in Coldwater, Michigan. Following a short stint in the Unitarian pastorate at Geneva, Illinois, in 1876, she moved to Chicago, where she became active in civic and literary life. A notable figure in educational reform endeavors, woman's rights activities, and the movement for racial equality, she also found time to write three novels, all published by Kerr: *Love and Theology* (1887), *A Girl Graduate* (1889), and *Roger Hunt*. Eliot, *Heralds of a Liberal Faith*, 58; "Reverend Celia Parker Wooley Memorial Number," *Unity*, April 18, 1918.

41. "Clearance List of Books," *Unity*, March 5, 1891, 1.

42. "Unity Library," *Unity*, March 12, 1891; "Publisher's Notes," *Unity*, Sept. 17, 1891, 2.

43. "Catalogue of Religious and Miscellaneous Books Published and Sold by Charles H. Kerr and Company," *Unity*, May 12, 1891, 110–11.

44. C.H.K. [Charles H. Kerr], "Publisher's Notes," *Unity*, Sept. 24, 1891, 32.

45. *Unity*, Dec. 1, 1891, 40.

46. *Unity*, Feb. 18, 1892, 282.

47. *Unity*, March 15, 1892, 24.

48. C.H.K. [Charles H. Kerr], "Publisher's Notes," *Unity*, Dec. 8, 1892, 120; Quackenbusch, "History of *Unity*."

49. *Unity*, Dec. 15, 1892, 132.

50. Ibid.

51. *Unity*, Jan. 26, 1893, 184.

Chapter 5: From Unitarian to Populist and Beyond

1. Jenkin Lloyd Jones, "Fifteen Years of Struggle," *Unity*, March 2, 1893, 1–2.

2. Charles H. Kerr, "Publisher's Notes," *Unity*, Feb. 23, 1893, 216, Feb. 16, 1893, 208.

3. Jones, "Fifteen Years"; Kerr, "Publisher's Notes," *Unity*, March 2, 1893, 8, April 6, 1893, 48. The name "Unity Publishing Company" first appeared on the front page of *Unity* on March 2, 1893.

4. For a sense of the growing distance between Kerr and the *Unity* group and the continuation of contention between the parties involved, see the series of letters between Jones, Kerr, and W. C. Gannett: Jones to Gannett, and Jones to Kerr, June 21, 1892; Kerr to Jones, Feb. 16, 1893; Jones to Kerr, May 8, 1893; Kerr to Jones, May 11, 1893; Jones to Kerr, May 16, July 26, Aug. 9, and Aug. 27, 1893, April 23, 1894, Nov. 8, 13, 1895. Jones Letter Books and Correspondence Files, Jones Collection.

5. Charles H. Kerr, *A Socialist Publishing House* (Chicago: Charles H. Kerr & Company, 1904), 10.

6. Jenkin Lloyd Jones to Charles H. Kerr, Aug. 25, 1892, Jones Collection.

7. C.H.K. [Charles H. Kerr], "Publisher's Notes," *Unity*, Sept. 17, 1891, 24.

8. "Publisher's Notes," *Unity*, Sept. 17, 1891, 24.

9. *Unity*, Dec. 3, 1891, 114.

10. Ibid.

11. Charles H. Kerr, "Publisher's Preface," *The Coming Climax* (Chicago: Charles H. Kerr & Company, 1891).

12. "Publisher's Notes," *Unity*, Jan. 14, 1892, 163. See advertisements for *The Coming Climax* in the issues of *Unity*, Jan.-Feb. 1892.

13. Henry Martyn Simmons, "*The Coming Climax*" [editorial], *Unity*, Jan. 7, 1892, 139.

14. *Unity*, Jan. 5, 1893, 165.

15. *Unity*, Feb. 2, 1893, 197.

16. Little has been learned about Helen Adams aside from the fact, discernible from May Walden Kerr's memoirs, that Kerr loved her deeply, held her in high esteem, and mourned her loss greatly, always referring to her as "my darling Nellie" even after he and May Walden were married. Charles Kerr and Helen Adams were married on May 29, 1889. "Marriage Record—All Souls Church," Jones Collection. The *All Souls Church Annual, 1890* listed "Mr. & Mrs. C. H. Kerr" living at the same address as the bride's parents; the newlyweds moved to Bowen Avenue sometime in 1890. *All Souls Church Annual, 1890, 1891*, Jones Collection; *Chicago City Directory*, 1889–91. For traces of Helen Adams's past, see transcript of her academic record, Office of the Registrar, University of Wisconsin-Madison; "Unity Club Scrapbook, 1883–1886," Jones Collection.

17. For a note on Helen Adams Kerr's death, see *Unity*, April 16, 1891, 57; Funeral Record, All Souls Church, Jones Collection.

18. Interview with Katharine Kerr Moore; family record, Kerr family Bible, courtesy of Katharine Kerr Moore. Walden's experience with the WCTU as the first experience with reform endeavor was not unusual. By the 1880s temperance had become the issue that drew tens of thousands of women into more general reform causes. It was through the WCTU, the first mass movement that involved women, that numerous liberal and radical feminists received their initial political education and experience. Ruth Bordin, *Woman and Temperance: The Quest for Power and Liberty, 1873–1900* (Philadelphia: Temple University Press, 1981).

19. May Walden Kerr, "How I First Met My Husband, C.H.K.," handwritten memoir, box 1, folder 2, May Walden Kerr Papers.

20. Ibid.; certificate of marriage, Marriage Record, All Souls Church, Jones Collection.

21. Kerr, "How I First Met My Husband."

22. Ibid.

23. *New Occasions* 1 (June 1893): inside front cover.

24. Kerr's statement of purpose would occupy the inside front cover of the first several issues of *New Occasions*.

25. B. F. Underwood, "Occasions and Duties" [editorial], *New Occasions* 1 (June 1893): 1–2.

26. Thomas Edie Hill, *Money Found: Recovered from Its Hiding-Places, and Put into Circulation through Confidence in Government Banks* (Chicago: Charles H. Kerr & Company, 1893). Hill became well known in publishing circles as the author of *Hill's Manual of Social and Business Forms*. A secretarial guide for the preparation of business forms and letters and the only standard text of its kind then in existence, the manual went through forty editions and sold nearly three hundred thousand copies. Hill built his publishing business, the Hill Standard Book Company, around the manual and several other reference books. By 1885 he had 1,200 agents throughout Canada and the United States circulating his textbooks, but the firm nevertheless passed into bankruptcy in 1889. Hill wrote a sizable list of reference books and pamphlets, including *Hill's Album of Biography and Art* (1881), *Hill's Souvenir Guide to the World's Fair* (1892), *Hill's Political Facts of the United States* (1894), and *Hill's Practical Encyclopedia* (1901). Tebbel, *Book Publishing in the United States*, 2:429; Sereiko, "Chicago and Its Book Trade," 288, 291–92.

27. An ostentatious eccentric with a keen sense for a quick financial turnover, Hill often strolled about the town in a plum-colored overcoat, cape, and black slouch hat. Always concerned to make a favorable impression, he regularly sent his private carriage with its black coachman and "spic and span" horses to retrieve guests from the local train depot. Frederick S. Weiser, *Village in a Glen: A History of Glen Ellyn, Illinois* (Glen Ellyn: Anna Harmon Chapter, Daughters of the American Revolution, 1957), 65–72; Ada Douglas Harmon, *The Story of an Old Town— Glen Ellyn* (Glen Ellyn: Glen New Printing, 1928), 74–75; Blythe Kaiser and Dor-

othy Vandercook, *Glen Ellyn's Story* (Itasca, Ill.: Graphic Arts Production, 1976), 110–13; "Thomas Edie Hill," *Who Was Who in America* (Chicago: A. N. Marquis, 1968), 1:565.

28. May Walden Kerr, handwritten memoir, May Walden Kerr Papers.

29. For background on the depression of the 1890s see Edward C. Kirkland, *Industry Comes of Age* (Chicago: Quadrangle, 1967), 5, 9; Thomas C. Cochran and William Miller, *The Age of Enterprise* (New York: Harper and Row, 1961), 219; Lindsay, *The Pullman Strike;* and Sidney Lens, *Radicalism in America* (New York: Thomas Crowell, 1969), 191–92. For the effects on Chicago, see Ray Ginger, *Altgeld's America* (Chicago: University of Chicago Press, 1965), 92.

30. *Chicago Tribune*, Dec. 12, 1892, 1, Jan. 1, 1894, 19; Sereiko, "Chicago and Its Book Trade," 239.

31. Schlesinger, Sr., *The Rise of the City*, 250–51; Mott, *Magazines*, 5, 10, 15. For general information on the structure and workings of the publishing industry during this period, see Sheehan, *This Was Publishing;* and Tebbel, *Book Publishing in the United States*, passim. For the particularities of the publishing industry and book trade in Chicago, see Sereiko, "Chicago and Its Book Trade," passim.

32. *The Nation*, Nov. 14, 1895, 342.

33. Harold S. Wilson, *McClure's Magazine* (Princeton: Princeton University Press, 1970), 31.

34. Alexander Kerr regularly assisted his son during the various phases of the company's development. He offered to mediate the dispute between his son and the *Unity* group in 1893, he loaned Charles money on several occasions, and the company later issued several works by Alexander Kerr, in part out of appreciation for his assistance. See the correspondence between Charles Kerr and Jenkin Jones, 1893, Jones Collection; "New Time Company Applications for Dividends—Stock," box 53, George S. Bowen Papers, Archival Collection, Chicago Historical Society (hereafter Bowen Papers).

35. [Charles H. Kerr], "Profit Sharing Realized," *New Occasions* 2 (Jan. 1894): 121–23. Charles Kerr & Company formally incorporated under laws of the state of Illinois on February 4, 1893. See "Certificate of Incorporation from the Secretary of State, the State of Illinois," Kerr Company Papers.

36. "Announcement," *New Occasions* 1 (Dec. 1893); *New Occasions* 2 (March 1894): 193.

37. Advertisement for *Money Found* in *New Occasions* 2 (Oct. 1894): 306.

38. Matilda Joslyn Gage, *Woman, Church, and State: A Historical Account of the Status of Woman through the Ages; with Reminiscence of the Matriarchate* (Chicago: Charles H. Kerr & Company, 1893); Helen Hamilton Gardener, *Facts and Fictions of Life* (Chicago: Charles H. Kerr & Company, 1893).

39. Edward James, Janet James, and Paul S. Boyer, eds., *Notable American Women, 1607–1950* (Cambridge: Harvard University Press, 1971), 2:4–6.

40. "Condemned by Comstock!" *New Occasions* 2 (Oct. 1894): inside front cover. Anthony Comstock became well known during the 1870s as the self-appoint-

ed guardian of public morals. His campaign on behalf of "public decency" led to the passage of the postal laws of 1873 and 1876 that banned obscenity in the mails. Comstock's definition of obscenity made no distinction between pornography and "un-Christian" free thought and atheism. The term *Comstockery* became synonymous in liberal parlance with intolerance and fanatical incursions into individual freedoms. J. Wade Caruthers, *Octavius Brooks Frothingham, Gentle Radical* (University: University of Alabama Press, 1976), 132. For a further discussion of Comstockery and the liberal response to it, see Hal D. Sears, *The Sex Radicals: Free Love in High Victorian America* (Lawrence: Regents Press of Kansas, 1977); Warren, *American Freethought;* and Heywood Broun and Margaret Leach, *Anthony Comstock* (New York: A. C. Boni, 1927).

41. James, James, and Boyer, eds., *Notable American Women*, 2:11–13.

42. Lindsay, *The Pullman Strike*, passim; Buder, *Pullman*, passim; Philip S. Foner, *The History of the Labor Movement in the United States*, vol. 2: *From the Founding of the American Federation of Labor to the Emergence of American Imperialism* (New York: International Publishers, 1988), 261–63.

43. Charles H. Kerr, "Publisher's Preface," in William H. Carwardine, *The Pullman Strike* (Chicago: Charles H. Kerr & Company, 1894).

44. [Charles H. Kerr], "Small Sums Need Not Lie Idle," *New Occasions* 2 (May 1894): 301–2.

45. Frederick Upham Adams, "To the Board of Directors of the New Time Company," typescript memo, dated July 12, 1898, Bowen Papers. Kerr and Adams formalized their partnership in April 1897 with an agreement, by Adams, to purchase 336 shares in the company, paid for either through a series of six promissory notes or from the royalties resultant from the sale of any of Adams's writings published by the firm. Signed typescript agreement between Charles H. Kerr and Frederick Upham Adams, dated April 3, 1897, Kerr Company Papers.

46. Adams played a central role in the formation of the short-lived Majority Rule League. See Frederick Upham Adams, *The Majority Rule League of the United States, a plan for the organization of the people . . . with a view of substituting direct legislation by majority vote for the existing system of corporation legislation by purchased votes* (Chicago: Charles H. Kerr & Company, 1898). For material on Adams, see *The National Cyclopedia of American Biography*, supp. 1 (New York: James T. White, 1910), 14:455; *DAB* (1928), 1:58–59; *Who Was Who in America*, vol. 1.

47. [Frederick Upham Adams], "Grover Cleveland," *New Occasions* 4 (Jan. 1897): 1–2.

48. "Important Announcement," *New Occasions* 4 (April 1897): 257–58. See volume 4, numbers 1–4 for a sense of change and improvement in the format and style of the monthly.

49. "Shall We Unite?" *New Occasions* 4 (April 1897): 267.

50. "The One Issue," *New Occasions* 5 (May 1897): 12.

51. "Workers Wanted," promotional inside front cover, *New Occasions* 5 (May 189); "Financial Prospectus of *New Occasions*" (printed circular), Bowen Papers.

52. Charles H. Kerr, "How to Do Business without Money," *New Occasions and the New Time* 5 (June 1897): 96–99. See also "A Plan for Extending the Labor Exchange" *New Time* 1 (Aug. 1897): 116–17. See Kerr's short article on the currency question, "Break the Evil Chain," *New Occasions* 4 (April 1897): 325–27.

53. "An Epoch-Making Book," *New Occasions* 4 (April 1897): 122; also see the advertisement, rear cover, *New Occasions* 4 (March 1897).

54. "Announcement: A Novel Plan to Place 'President John Smith' in the Hands of Every Voter," *New Occasions* 4 (March 1897): 123–25.

55. May Walden Kerr, handwritten memoir, box 2, 1935, May Walden Kerr Papers; Roger E. Stoddard, "Vanity and Reform: B. O. Flower's Arena Publishing Company, Boston, 1890–1896," *Papers of the Bibliographical Society of America* 76, no, 3 (1982): 273–337.

56. Roy P. Fairfield, "Benjamin O. Flower, Father of the Muckrakers," *American Literature* 22 (Nov. 1950): 27–82; David H. Dickason, "Benjamin Orange Flower, Patron of the Realists," *American Literature* 14 (May 1942): 148–56; H. F. Cline, "Benjamin Orange Flower and *The Arena*, 1889–1909," *Journalism Quarterly* 17 (June 1940): 139–50; H. F. Cline, "Flower and *The Arena*: Purpose and Content," *Journalism Quarterly* 15 (Sept. 1940): 247–57; Mann, *Yankee Reformers in the Urban Age*, 163, 145–46; McCabe, *A Biographical Dictionary*, 258; *DAB* (1931), 1:478; *Who Was Who in America*, 1:408; *National Cyclopedia of American Biography* (1899), 9:228.

57. *Coming Age* 1 (March 1899): 322, as cited in Cline, "Benjamin Orange Flower," 142.

58. Cline, "Benjamin Orange Flower," 145–46; Mann, *Yankee Reformers in the Urban Age*, 102.

59. "Editorial," *New Time* 1 (Aug. 1897): 68; "If You Read This Advertisement Others Will Read Yours," *New Time* 1 (Nov. 1897): xii; "Editorial: To Our Readers," *New Time* 1 (Dec. 1897): 385; "On to Victory," *New Time* 1 (Dec. 1897): 387; "'The New Time' Is Growing," *New Time* 2 (March 1898): x.

60. Kerr, *A Socialist Publishing House*, 8; Eugene V. Debs, "From Eugene V. Debs," *New Time* 1 (July 1897): 42; "The Social Democracy," *New Time* 1 (Aug. 1897): 78–79; "The Martyred Apostles of Labor," *New Time* 2 (Feb. 1898): 79–82.

61. May Walden Kerr, "The Home," *New Time* 4 (March 1898): 201–5.

62. "Soldiers of *The New Time*," *New Time* 1 (July 1897): 15; "An Earnest Word to the Friends of *The New Time*," *New Time* 1 (Sept. 1897): xi; "This Is Your Magazine," *New Time* 1 (Oct. 1897): xi; "Our Financial Plan," *New Time* 1 (Dec. 1897): xi; "You Must Do Your Share," *New Time* 2 (Jan. 1897): xi; "Personal," *New Time* 2 (May 1898): 342. *New Time* was not alone in viewing itself as the journalistic harbinger and vehicle for the arrival of the cooperative commonwealth. Most notable was its natural ally, Julius Wayland's *Appeal to Reason*, published in Gerard, Kansas. Successor to the *Coming Nation*, a heartland populist periodical that promoted homespun Great Plains socialism, the *Appeal* would become the largest left-wing weekly in the country. Its initial success rested on founder Julius

Wayland's entrepreneurial and promotional skill and the strategy he devised—the recruitment of a large number of committed sales agents, the "Appeal Army" who hawked the magazine far and wide across the Mississippi basin and the Southwest. For the best history of the *Appeal to Reason* to date, see Elliot Shore, *Talkin' Socialism: J. A. Wayland and the Role of the Press in American Radicalism, 1890–1912* (Lawrence: Univesity Press of Kansas, 1988).

63. "Business Manager George E. Bowen," *New Time* 1 (Nov. 1897): xi.

64. "Memorandum of an agreement between B. O. Flower . . . Frederick U. Adams . . . Charles H. Kerr . . . and George E. Bowen," typescript, dated Oct. 19, 1897, Bowen Papers. A similar document spelling out the same terms of the partnership among Kerr, Adams, Flower, and Bowen, dated Oct. 26, 1897, exists in the Kerr Company Papers.

65. Hugh S. Desantis, "George S. Bowen and the American Dream," *Chicago History* 6 (Fall 1977): 143–54; "George S. Bowen (1829–1905)," typescript, Bowen Papers.

66. "To Whom It May Concern," typescript financial statement for *The New Time,* dated Dec. 1898, Bowen Papers; "Valedictory," *New Time* 2 (April 1898): 254. For an example of the type of promotion Bowen undertook, see "Do You Quarrel with a Customer's Politics Before Soliciting His Trade?" (brochure), box 53, folder 4, Bowen Papers.

67. Kerr resigned as treasurer of the New Time Company on July 25, 1898. Kerr and Adams filed formal papers dissolving Kerr's partnership in the New Time Company that same day. Charles H. Kerr to George S. Bowen, July 25, 1898, box 52, folder 6, Bowen Papers; "Agreement . . . between Charles H. Kerr & Company . . . and the New Time Company," typescript signed by Kerr and Adams, Kerr Company Papers. For a discussion of the difficulties and problems that had developed between the New Time Company and Charles H. Kerr & Company, see Frederick Upham Adams, "To the Board of Directors of The New Time Company," typescript, dated July 12, 1898, Bowen Papers.

Chapter 6: The First Socialist Phase, 1899–1908

1. One of the few fragmentary bits of personal description that remains of Charles Kerr exists in Ralph Chaplin, *Wobbly: The Rough and Tumble Story of an American Radical* (Chicago: University of Chicago Press, 1948), 71.

2. Kerr, *A Socialist Publishing House,* 10–11.

3. Charles H. Kerr, "Our Co-operative Publishing Business: How Socialist Literature Is Being Circulated by Socialists," *International Socialist Review* (hereafter *ISR*) 1 (April 1901): 669–72.

4. Kerr, "Our Co-operative Publishing Business."

5. Kerr, *A Socialist Publishing House,* 10.

6. For detailed discussions of the SLP, see Howard Quint, *The Forging of American Socialism* (Columbia: University of South Carolina Press, 1953), 3–71, 142–

74; Ira Kipnis, *The American Socialist Movement 1897–1912* (New York: Monthly Review, 1952), 6–42; Daniel Bell, "Marxian Socialism in the United States," in *Socialism and American Life*, ed. Donald Drew Egbert and Stow Persons (Princeton: Princeton University Press, 1952), 1:236–49; Kent Kreuter and Gretchen Kreuter, *An American Dissenter: The Life of Algie Martin Simons, 1870–1950* (Lexington: University Press of Kentucky, 1969), 42–45.

7. Biographical material on Algie Simons from Kreuter and Kreuter, *An American Dissenter*, passim; Robert S. Huston, "A. M. Simons and the American Socialist Movement," Ph.D. diss., University of Wisconsin-Madison, 1965. Initially a four-page weekly that appeared every Saturday, the *Workers' Call* served as an educational propaganda vehicle for the Chicago movement. Advertisements for the Kerr Company soon began to appear regularly in its pages. See "Wanted— Socialist Agents for Socialist Books," *Worker's Call*, April 15, 1899; the full-column advertisement "Socialist Books," June 17, 1899; and an advertisement for the company's Pocket Library of Socialism, May 15, 1899. In an attempt to increase the circulation of the weekly during the autumn of 1899, Kerr, in cooperation with Simons, offered a list of his publications as a premium bonus to new subscribers. "Socialist Books Free," *Worker's Call*, Nov. 25, 1899.

8. May Walden Kerr, "Notes on C.H.K.'s Ancestry," handwritten memoir, box 1, folder 2, May Walden Kerr Papers.

9. Kerr, *A Socialist Publishing House*, 10–11; May Walden, "How Come?" handwritten memoir, ca. 1950, box 7, folder 1, May Walden Kerr Papers.

10. "Socialist Books," *Worker's Call*, June 24, 1899.

11. Kerr, *A Socialist Publishing House*, 12.

12. Kerr, "Our Co-operative Publishing Business," 669.

13. May Wood Simons played a vital role as translator of some of the early European socialist tracts that Kerr & Company imported. A native of Baraboo, Wisconsin, May Wood entered Northwestern University in 1893, planning to become a Christian missionary. She left Northwestern, however, after two years and returned to Wisconsin. She married her high school classmate Algie Simons in June 1897 and joined him in his activities with the Chicago Bureau of Charities and the University of Chicago Settlement in the "Back of the Yards." Disenchanted with liberal reform and outraged by the conditions that she witnessed among Chicago's working poor, she readily joined the Socialist Labor Party with her husband. She worked alongside him on the *Worker's Call* and its successors, the weekly *Chicago Socialist* and *Daily Socialist*. She made the move into the Socialist Party in 1901, soon became one of the best-known women in the organization, and simultaneously contributed to a number of nationally circulated socialist periodicals. In the years after her husband's break with Charles Kerr, she served as a delegate to a number of national party conventions. She attended the International Socialist Congress in 1910 and narrowly lost election to the National Executive Committee of the Socialist Party in 1912. She served on the party's National Woman's Committee and was a major advocate of woman suffrage. A party intel-

lectual, she emerged as a leading expert on the various components of the "woman question." She eventually earned a Ph.D. from the University of Chicago and turned a great deal of her energy toward socialist education. Strongly influenced by John Dewey and Maria Montessori, she lectured for the Intercollegiate Socialist Society and the National Lyceum Bureau of the party. She taught classes at the experimental Ruskin College in Glen Ellyn, Illinois, and for a short while in the Milwaukee schools. May Wood Simons, "How I Became a Socialist," *Comrade* 2 (Nov. 1902): 32; Huston, "A. M. Simons," 29–31; Kreuter and Kreuter, *An American Dissenter,* 36–37; Kent Kreuter and Gretchen Kreuter, "May Wood Simons: Party Theorist," in *Flawed Liberation: Socialism and Feminism,* ed. Sally M. Miller (Westport: Greenwood Press, 1981), 37–60; Mari Jo Buhle, *Women and American Socialism: 1870–1920* (Urbana: University of Illinois Press, 1981), 166–68; Sally M. Miller, "Other Socialists: Native-Born and Immigrant Women in the Socialist Party of America, 1901–1917," *Labor History* 24 (Winter 1983): 84–102.

14. Kerr, *A Socialist Publishing House,* 11.

15. [Charles H. Kerr], "Publisher's Department," *ISR* 2 (May 1902): 529; [Charles H. Kerr], *Catalogue of Books* (Chicago: Charles H. Kerr & Company, 1901), 21–22, 30; Charles H. Kerr, *What to Read on Socialism* (Chicago: Charles H. Kerr & Company, 1902), 19. The Pocket Library series contained forty-five separate titles by November 1906. For a complete list of authors and titles, see Charles Kerr, *What to Read on Socialism,* rev. ed. (Chicago: Charles H. Kerr & Company, 1906), 51–54.

16. Kerr, *A Socialist Publishing House,* 14; Algie Simons, "Salutatory," *ISR* 1 (July 1901): 54.

17. "Announcement," *ISR* 2 (Aug. 1901): 160.

18. *Merrie England* had a larger circulation than Edward Bellamy's *Looking Backward* according to the observations of B. O. Flower. B. O. Flower, *Progressive Men, Women and Movements of the Past Twenty-Five Years* (Boston: New Arena, 1914). For a discussion and appraisal of Blatchford's importance, see Stanley Pierson, *Marxism and the Origins of British Socialism* (Ithaca: Cornell University Press, 1973; Stanley Pierson, *British Socialists: The Journey from Fantasy to Politics* (Cambridge: Harvard University Press, 1979).

19. H. M. Hyndman, *Socialism and Slavery* (Chicago: Charles H. Kerr & Company, 1905).

20. The company developed a close working relationship with Swann, Sonnenschein over a period of years. It initially imported a number of works issued by that firm and eventually exported several of their own imprints to England, where Sonnenschein handled distribution. *ISR* 2 (Dec. 1901): 479. On Carpenter, see Sheila Rowbotham and Jeffrey Weeks, *Socialism and the New Life* (London: Pluto Press, 1977); and Sheila Rowbotham, "In Search of Edward Carpenter," *Radical America* 14 (July-Aug. 1980): 49–60. For Bax and Mann, see Pierson, *Marxism;* Pierson, *British Socialists.*

21. Kreuter and Kreuter, *An American Dissenter,* 46–54; Huston, "A. M. Simons,"

73, 75–78. Simons, upon returning from Europe, reported to his former Wisconsin mentor Richard T. Ely that he had brought back "a very large amount" of original documents on European socialism and that he was "doing considerable corresponding with foreign socialists." Algie Simons to Richard T. Ely, May 2, 1900, box 16, folder 1, Richard T. Ely Papers, SHSW (hereafter Ely Papers). For Simons's list of European socialist correspondents see box 3, folder 2, Algie M. Simons Papers, SHSW (hereafter Simons Papers).

22.   Karl Kautsky, *Friederich Engels: His Life, His Work and His Writing,* tr. May Wood Simons (Chicago: Charles H. Kerr & Company, 1899); Karl Marx, *Wage-Labor and Capital,* tr. J. L. Joynes (Chicago: Charles H. Kerr & Company, 1899); Wilhelm Liebknecht, *No Compromise, No Political Trading!* tr. Marcus Hitch and Algie Simons (Chicago: Charles H. Kerr & Company, 1900). Kerr's *Socialism, Utopian and Scientific,* translated by Edward Aveling, passed through numerous printings in cloth and paper. Issued initially as part of the company's Library of Progress in February 1900 and included in the Standard Socialist series after 1901, cloth editions of the work sold for 50 cents. Kerr sold more than twenty thousand copies by early 1906; it still appeared on the company's lists in the early 1980s. [Charles H. Kerr], "Publisher's Department," *ISR* 6 (Feb. 1906): 508.

23.   Paul Lafargue helped to found the French Socialist Party with Jules Guesde. An important polemicist and propagandist for the socialist cause in France, Lafargue wrote on numerous subjects, including philosophy, history, religion, and literary criticism. For a brief critical sketch of Lafargue and his writings, see Leszek Kolakowski, "Paul Lafargue: A Hedonist Marxism," in *Main Currents of Marxism,* ed. Leszek Kolakowski (New York: Oxford University Press, 1981), 2:141–48. Karl Kautsky, *The Social Revolution* (Chicago: Charles H. Kerr & Company, 1903).

24.   Emile Vandervelde, *Collectivism and Industrial Development* (Chicago: Charles H. Kerr & Company, 1904); Enrico Ferri, *The Positive School of Criminology,* tr. Ernest Unterman (Chicago: Charles H. Kerr & Company, 1906). Labriola's *Materialist Conception* received a favorable reception on the American side of the Atlantic. See the lengthy review by John Spargo in *The Comrade* [New York] 3 (March 1904): 141–42. For an insightful and informative philosophical and historical appraisal of Antonio Labriola, see Paul Piccone's Introduction to the reprint of Labriola's *Socialism and Philosophy* (St. Louis: Telos Press, 1980); and Leszek Kolakowski, "Antonio Labriola: An Attempt at an Open Orthodoxy," in *Main Currents of Marxism,* ed. Kolakowski (New York: Oxford University Press, 1981), 2:175–92.

25.   "Library of Science for the Workers," advertisement on back cover of Robert Rives LaMonte, *Science and Socialism* (Chicago: Charles H. Kerr & Company, 1905); [Charles H. Kerr], "Library of Science for the Workers," *ISR* 5 (April 1905): 638–39; [Charles H. Kerr], "Publisher's Department," *ISR* 23 (May 1905): 701–2.

26.   Kerr publicly discussed the desire to publish and translate an edition of *Capital* as early as November 1902. The company, in cooperation with the *Worker's Call,* had imported a number of the Sonnenschein English edition in October

1901. Kerr & Company sent a cash order for 250 copies to London in May 1902. [Charles H. Kerr], "Publisher's Department," *ISR* 2 (May 1902): 830, 3 (Nov. 1902): 317–18, 6 (Dec. 1902): 379–83. An original copy of the Sonnenschein edition of *Capital* with the Kerr colophon stamped on the spine exists in the collection of the former secretary of Kerr & Company.

27. H. M. Hyndmann to Algie Simons, April 3, 1902, Simons Papers.

28. For Unterman's biography, see Solon DeLeon, *American Labor Who's Who* (New York: Hanford, 1925); Ernest Unterman Collection, SHSW. For a sampling of writings by Unterman, see his lengthy series of articles on "The Second, Third and Fourth Volumes of Marx's *Capital*," *Chicago Socialist*, Feb. 22, March 4, 11, 18, 25, April 1, 8, 15, 1905; and "Anarchism and Socialism," *The Comrade* 3 (Oct. 1903): 18; "The Decline of Capitalist Democracy," *Chicago Socialist*, Jan. 23, 1901, 4; "The Tactics of the German Socialist Movement," *Chicago Socialist*, Sept. 26, 1903; "Mind and Socialism" *ISR* 1 (April 1901): 4; "Labriola on the Marxian Conception of History," *ISR* 4 (March 1904): 548–52; and "An Endless Task," *ISR* 7 (Nov. 1906): 285.

29. [Charles H. Kerr], "Why We Need Your Stock Subscription," *ISR* 3 (Nov. 1902): 317–18.

30. Eugene Dietzgen, "Joseph Dietzgen: A Sketch of His Life," in *Some of the Philosophical Essays of Joseph Dietzgen*, ed. Eugene Dietzgen and tr. Ernest Unterman (Chicago: Charles H. Kerr & Company, 1906). Financed by Eugene Dietzgen, Kerr also published Joseph Dietzgen's major philosophical enquiry, *The Positive Outcome of Philosophy*, in 1906. Unterman once again did the translating while Eugene and brother Joseph Junior edited the original German. That work contained an introduction by the noted Dutch astronomer and socialist theorist Anton Pannekoek, who would later make a number of valuable contributions to the *ISR* during World War I.

31. Dietzgen, "Joseph Dietzgen."

32. Ibid.; May Walden, various recollections, box 1, folder 2, and diary for 1944, box 10, May Walden Kerr Papers; Charles H. Kerr to Morris Hillquit, Oct. 4, 1905, box 1, folder 5, Morris Hillquit Papers.

33. Ernest Unterman to Marius Hansome, Feb. 28, 1938, reel 1, "Correspondence," Ernest Unterman Papers.

34. Ernest Unterman, "Editor's Note to the First American Edition," in Karl Marx, *Capital: A Critique of Political Economy* (Chicago: Charles H. Kerr & Company, 1906), 7–10; [Charles H. Kerr], "Publisher's Department," *ISR* 6 (June 1906): 705, 7 (Dec. 1906): 380, 7 (April 1907): 637.

35. [Simons], "Salutatory."

36. Ibid.

37. *Worker's Call*, May 26, 1901, 3.

38. [Charles H. Kerr], "Publisher's Department," *ISR* 3 (Feb. 1903): 507. Kerr explained to Wisconsin professor Richard T. Ely that "the *Review* is doing a necessary work attempted by no other periodical. It is not intended for the ignorant who

have no idea of what socialism is. It is intended for those who want to talk or write intelligently on socialism." Charles H. Kerr to Richard T. Ely, June 16, 1904, box 28, folder 5, Ely Papers, SHSW.

39. [Kerr], *ISR* 3 (Feb. 1903): 507.

40. For examples, see *ISR* 1 (1900–1901) or 2 (1901–2).

41. Kerr, *A Socialist Publishing House*, 15.

42. Algie Simons, "American Socialist Literature," *ISR* 2 (May 1902): 697.

43. For a detailed discussion of Algie Simons's contributions to the corpus of Debsian-era American socialism, see Kreuter and Kreuter, *An American Dissenter;* Huston, "A. M. Simons"; the discussion of Simons's writings in Paul M. Buhle, "Marxism in the United States, 1900–1940," Ph.D. diss., University of Wisconsin, 1975, ch. 1; and Paul M. Buhle, *Marxism in the United States: Remapping the History of the American Left* (London: Verso Press, 1987), 92–94. For Simons's connection with Upton Sinclair's *The Jungle*, see Huston, "A. M. Simons," 45–47.

44. Charles H. Kerr, comp., *Socialist Songs*, Pocket Library of Socialism, 11 (Chicago: Charles H. Kerr & Company, 1899); Charles H. Kerr, *Socialist Songs with Music* (Chicago: Charles H. Kerr & Company, 1901, rev. ed., 1902).

45. Charles H. Kerr, "The Ideas on which Socialism Rests: I. How We Explain People's Actions" *Chicago Socialist* June 24, 1905, 6.

46. Charles H. Kerr, *Morals and Socialism*, Pocket Library of Socialism 10 (Chicago: Charles H. Kerr & Company, 1899), 3–4, 10.

47. Kerr, *Morals and Socialism*, 12.

48. Ibid., 7, 15.

49. Ibid., 9, emphasis in the original.

50. Ibid., 18.

51. Charles H. Kerr, *The Folly of Being "Good,"* Pocket Library of Socialism 27 (Chicago: Charles H. Kerr & Company, 1901). This particular pamphlet passed through a revision and rerelease in 1905. It had a circulation of more than forty thousand.

52. Charles H. Kerr, "The Central Thing in Socialism," *What to Read on Socialism* (Chicago: Charles H. Kerr & Company, 1903), 1–3, emphasis in the original.

53. Charles Kerr, *What Socialists Think*, Pocket Library of Socialism 57 (Chicago: Charles H. Kerr & Company, 1907), 17–19, 21–22.

54. Kerr, *What Socialists Think*, 23.

55. Ibid., 24.

56. Ibid., 25.

57. Ibid., 27–28.

58. Ibid., 29. For another example of Kerr's early socialist thinking, see "Socialism and Business Men," *Chicago Socialist*, Feb. 13, 1904, 3. Kerr also contributed two series of articles, one on the principles of Marxism and a second on U.S. history and politics, to the *Chicago Socialist* during 1905: "The Ideas on which Socialism Rests," July 1, 8, 15, 22, 1905; "What Are We Here For," Aug. 5, 1905; and "Dualism and Monism," Aug. 12, 1905; he also wrote "Things as They Are,"

Aug. 19, 1905; "Chattel Slavery," Aug. 26, 1905; "Free Americans," Sept. 2, 1905; "Something Right Now" Sept. 6, 1905; "People Are Lazy," Sept. 23, 1905; and "Eternal Justice and the Class Struggle," Oct. 28, 1905.

59. May Walden Kerr, "Three Principles of Socialist Philosophy," *Worker's Call,* Oct. 26, 1901, 3.

60. May Walden Kerr, *Women and Socialism* (Chicago: Charles H. Kerr & Company, 1900), 20–21.

61. Kerr, *Women and Socialism,* 22–23.

62. May Walden, *Socialism and the Home* (Chicago: Charles H. Kerr & Company, 1901), 12.

63. Walden, *Socialism and the Home,* 30.

64. For a sense of May Walden Kerr's socialist outlook and perceptions as a party activist and columnist, see "In North Carolina," *Worker's Call,* July 13, 1901; "Woman's Place in the Socialist Party," *Chicago Socialist,* April 26, 1902, 3; "In the Shopping District," *Chicago Socialist,* Aug. 11, 1906, 2; "After Forty Years," *Chicago Socialist,* Sept. 1, 1906, 2; "Co-operative Housekeeping," *Daily Socialist* (Chicago), Oct. 30, 1907; "Organization Work for the Woman's Committee," *Daily Socialist,* Aug. 8, 1908; "True Homes under Socialism," *Socialist Woman* 1 (Jan. 1908): 5; "Woman's Slavery," *Socialist Women* 1 (Sept. 1907): 4; "The Twentieth Century Is Woman's," *Socialist Women* 1 (Feb. 1908): 4; "How to Organize a Study Club," *Socialist Women* 2 (June 1908): 11; and "Socialist Woman's Study Club," *Socialist Women* 2 (July 1908): 9.

Walden often took to the speaker's rostrum for the socialist cause. For a sense of that aspect of her political work, see the various newspaper clipping of her numerous speaking engagements in box 7, folder 13, May Walden Kerr Papers and *Worker's Call,* Nov. 24, 1900, 4. She worked for several months during 1909 on the Political Refugees Defense League, a group headed by John Murray to assist exiles fleeing the political turmoil in Mexico. Box 7, folder 12, May Walden Kerr Papers. During the spring and autumn of 1913, she embarked on two lengthy speaking tours for the Socialist Party that took her to numerous small towns throughout southern and central Illinois. For her itinerary and descriptions of her experiences as a soapboxer for the Socialist Party, see box 6, folder 2, May Walden Kerr Papers, also see box 2.

65. Walden, "Notes on C.H.K.'s Ancestry."

66. Aside from the suggestion of some infidelity on Kerr's part, there is no clear explanation for the couple's separation existent in the May Walden Kerr Papers. Writing years later, she stated that she loved her husband "dearly" and that their marriage was "a happy one up to a certain point and without ever any quarrel between us, we both cried when we said 'Goodbye'" (ibid.). The two had very little, if any, contact after 1904. They did correspond on occasion, but their letter writing mainly had to do with business involving their daughter Katharine.

When Katharine grew older, she often relayed news of visits with her father in correspondence with her mother, who resided in Florida. Those letters, spanning a number of years, give little sense of Kerr aside from the fact that he was always hard-pressed financially. Charles Kerr to May Walden Kerr, Jan. 28, Oct. 8, 1908; May Walden Kerr to Charles Kerr, Oct. 9, 1908; Charles Kerr to May Walden Kerr, Feb. 8, 1909; May Walden Kerr to Charles Kerr, Feb. 10, 1909; Katharine Kerr Moore to May Walden Kerr, Oct. 5, 1917, Nov. 11, Nov. 29, 1920, April 18, July 21, 1927, all in box 4, May Walden Kerr Papers. See also the exchange between Katharine Kerr Moore and May Walden at time of Charles Kerr's death in June of 1944, May Walden Kerr diary, box 10, May Walden Kerr Papers.

67. Biographical sketch and collection description, May Walden Kerr Papers; see also diaries, boxes 9 and 10, May Walden Kerr Papers.

68. *Worker's Call*, Aug. 25, 1900. Although maintaining the independence of the company, Kerr readily lent its subscription and mailing lists to the Socialist Party state organization. *Chicago Socialist*, March 8, Aug. 2, 1902.

69. Charles H. Kerr, "A Socialist Co-Operative," *Worker's Call*, June 29, 1901; Ernest Unterman, "The Co-Operative," *Worker's Call*, July 6, 1901; Ernest Unterman, "Socialist Co-Operative," Aug. 10, 1901; Charles H. Kerr, "The Co-Operative," *Worker's Call*, Sept. 7, Nov. 2, 1901; "Plan of the Proposed Socialist Temple" *Worker's Call*, Dec. 28, 1901; Charles H. Kerr, "The Socialist Co-Operative of Chicago," *ISR* 2 (Jan. 1902): 502–3; "Socialist Co-Operative of Chicago," *Chicago Socialist*, March 22, 1902; "Renewed Interest in the Socialist Co-Operative," *Chicago Socialist*, July 5, 1902.

70. Kerr published Walter Thomas Mills's *How to Work for Socialism* in 1900. Born in 1856 in rural upstate New York, Mills attended Oberlin College and subsequently moved to Kansas to work in the Quaker ministry. He joined the radical Kansas People's Party but left in disgust following the Bryanite fusion debacle of 1896. Shortly thereafter, he gravitated toward Julius Wayland's *Appeal to Reason* in Girard, Kansas. He created the International School of Social Economy, one of many socialist school experiments in which he became involved, at Girard in 1902. He also edited a short-lived monthly, the *Socialist Teacher*. His textbook, *The Struggle for Existence* (Chicago: 1904), a primer in social studies and history from a socialist perspective, passed through numerous editions and sold an estimated five hundred thousand copies. James R. Green, *Grass-Roots Socialism* (Baton Rouge: Louisiana State University Press, 1978), 41–42; DeLeon, *American Labor Who's Who*, 161; Oscar Ameringer, *If You Don't Weaken* (New York: Henry Holt, 1940), 263–67; Kipnis, *The American Socialist Movement*, 180.

George McA. Miller made occasional contributions to the Kerr Company's *New Time* during the late 1890s. It was Miller, according to May Walden Kerr, who first interested Kerr in the idea for a workingman's college in Glen Ellyn. Walden, "Notes on C.H.K.'s Ancestry."

71. A former liberal pastor in the Congregational church, George D. Herron became an early leading advocate of the Social Gospel. He became a professor of Applied Christianity at Burlington, Iowa's Iowa College (later Grinnell) in 1893. His relations with organized or denominational Christianity became increas-

ingly tenuous; toward the turn of the century his outspoken socialism necessitated his resignation from the college in 1898. He joined the Socialist Party in 1901,
and by that time he had come to deem the philosophy of Jesus as "inadequate to
the Social Revolution." An influential figure within radical religious circles, Herron's conversion to socialism received notoriety. He gave the nominating speech
for Eugene Debs at the Socialist Party of America's Chicago convention in
1904. For a discussion of Herron, see Henry F. May, *Protestant Churches and Industrial America* (New York: Harper, 1949), 249–60; Weisenberger, *Ordeal of Faith*,
123.

Parsons was a regular contributor to the *New Time* during the latter 1890s. A
lecturer at Boston University Law School, Parsons joined the faculty of Kansas State
Agricultural College following the Populist victory in that state in 1897. In 1899
he and his fellow radicals were dismissed by a returning Republican administration, and George McA. Miller offered him a position of dean of the lecture extension division at newly founded Ruskin. For a fuller treatment of Parsons, see Mann,
"Frank Parsons, the Professor as Radical," in *Yankee Reformers in the Urban Age*, ch.
6.

72. Ross Evans Paulson, *Radicalism and Reform* (Lexington: University Press
of Kentucky, 1968), 147, 161–62; Harman, *The Story of an Old Town—Glen Ellyn*,
86; Kaiser and Vandercook, *Glen Ellyn's Story*, 141–42; Weiser, *Village in a Glen*,
75; Charles H. Kerr, "The Real Facts about Ruskin University," *ISR* 4 (Sept. 1903):
102.

73. Kerr, "The Real Facts about Ruskin University."

74. *Ruskin Rays* 1 (Aug. 1903): 1–4 (Ruskin College periodical, courtesy of
Chicago Historical Society); "Ruskin University" [advertisement], *ISR* 3 (April
1903): 617.

75. "Clear Socialism in Clear English" [advertisement], *Chicago Socialist* July
26, 1902, emphasis in the original; [Charles H. Kerr], "Publisher's Department,"
ISR 3 (Aug. 1902): 126–28.

76. [Charles H. Kerr], "Publisher's Department," *ISR* 5 (July 1904): 62–64.

77. Ibid.

78. [Charles H. Kerr], "Publisher's Department," *ISR* 4 (Dec. 1903): 382–83.

79. Kerr, *What to Read on Socialism* (1902), 26–27; [Charles H. Kerr], "Publisher's Department," *ISR* 3 (Sept. 1902): 189–92; "Why We Need Your Stock
Subscription," *ISR* 3 (Nov. 1902): 317–18; [Charles H. Kerr], "Publisher's Department," *ISR* 4 (July 1903): 64; 8 (Feb. 1903): 509–10; 10 (April 1903): 636; 4 (Dec.
1903): 382; "More Capital for the Publishing House," *ISR* 4 (Feb. 1904): 509–12.

80. [Charles H. Kerr], "Publisher's Department," 3 (Feb. 1903): 507–8.

81. "The Future of the *ISR*," *ISR* 4 (May 1904): 719.

82. [Algie Simons], "Something about the *Review*," *ISR* 5 (June 1905): 750.

83. Kerr, *A Socialist Publishing House*, 3.

84. J. Howard Moore, *The Universal Kinship* (Chicago: Charles H. Kerr & Company, 1905); Edward A. Brenholtz, *The Recording Angel* (Chicago: Charles H. Kerr

& Company, 1905); Robert Rives LaMonte, *Socialism, Positive and Negative* (Chicago: Charles H. Kerr & Company, 1907); Oscar Lovell Triggs, *The Changing Order* (Chicago: Charles H. Kerr & Company, 1905); Charles H. Vail, *The Principles of Scientific Socialism* (Chicago: Charles H. Kerr & Company, 1900); William Thurston Brown, *The Axe at the Root* (Chicago: Charles H. Kerr & Company, 1900).

85. Writing in the early 1950s on the impact of Marxian economics on American thought, the economist Paul Sweezy referred to Boudin's book as the only one from the earlier period that "aside from historical interest, is worth reading today." Sweezy described the Boudin monograph as "a very able book." Boudin was "the first American Marxist to give proper weight to the theory of economic crisis." In Sweezy's judgment, "Boudin's book was one of the outstanding Marxist works produced anywhere in the early years of the present century." Paul Sweezy, "The Influence of Marxian Economics on American Thought and Practice," in *Socialism and American Life*, ed. Donald Drew Egbert and Stow Persons (Princeton: Princeton University Press, 1952), 1:462–63; Buhle, *Marxism in the United States*, 95.

86. For biographical background on Boudin and the significance of his work, see Theodore Draper, *The Roots of American Communism* (New York: Viking Press, 1963), 57–58; DeLeon, *American Labor's Who's Who*, 23; Bernard K. Johnpoll and Harvey Klehr, eds., *Biographical Dictionary of the American Left* (Westport: Greenwood Press, 1986), 39–41; Buhle, *Marxism in the United States*, 95; and Paul Buhle, "Louis B. Boudin," in *Encyclopedia of the American Left*, ed. Mari Jo Buhle, Paul Buhle, and Dan Georgakis (Urbana: University of Illinois Press, 1990), 102–3.

In regard to the actual publication of *Theoretical System*, Kerr voiced concern that the original title sounded too scholastic and therefore might not sell as well as it otherwise might, but Boudin persisted. The two carried on a lengthy negotiation over the publication. Boudin agreed to relinquish any royalties to the company in exchange for free copies of the imprint. He personally maintained the copyright, however. See Kerr to Boudin, Oct. 11, 18, Nov. 30, Dec. 5, 1906, Jan. 12, 14, March 4, May 20, 24, June 7, 1907, Louis Boudin Papers, Columbia University Library, New York (hereafter Boudin Papers). In regard to Boudin's reception in Europe, see Karl Kautsky to Boudin, July 4, 1910, Boudin Papers. The German translation of Boudin's work, *Das Teöretische Systeme von Karl Marx*, appeared in 1909.

87. *ISR* 4 (June 1904): 776–77, and 5 (Jan. 1905): 445–48.

88. [Charles H. Kerr], "Publisher's Department," *ISR* 5 (July 1904): 64.

89. *ISR* 5 (Jan. 1905): 445–46; 6 (July 1905): 64; 6 (Sept. 1905): 187–92; and 6 (Dec. 1905): 383–84.

90. [Algie Simons], "Something about the *Review*," *ISR* 7 (July 1906): 61–64; [Charles H. Kerr], "The Future of the *Review*," *ISR* 7 (Nov. 1906): 256.

91. *ISR* 7 (Feb. 1907): 506; 7 (May 1907): 699; and 7 (June 1907): 761.

92. [Charles H. Kerr], "Our Record for 1907," *ISR* 8 (Jan. 1908): 445–46.

93. [Charles H. Kerr], "Publisher's Department," *ISR* 8 (Jan. 1908): 448, 8 (Feb. 1908): 510.

Chapter 7: The Move Leftward, 1908–11

1. The standard sources on the development and rise of the socialist movement used for an overview of American socialism include Kipnis, *The American Socialist Movement;* James Weinstein, *The Decline of Socialism in America, 1912–1925* (New York: Vintage, 1969); David A. Shannon, *The Socialist Party of America: A History* (Chicago: University of Chicago Press, 1955); David Herreshoff, *The Origins of American Marxism* (Detroit: Wayne State University Press, 1967); Nathan Fine, *Labor and Farm Parties in the United States, 1828–1928* (New York: Rand School, 1931); Daniel Bell, *Marxian Socialism in the United States* (Princeton: Princeton University Press, 1967); and Quint, *The Forging of American Socialism.* A number of more recent works dealing specifically with the Debsian era socialist movement have made significant contributions to the historiography of that impulse. For example, see Buhle, *Women and American Socialism;* Meredith Tax, *The Rising of the Women* (New York: Monthly Review Press, 1980); and Green, *Grass-Roots Socialism.* For the general context, that is, the social and economic transformations that reshaped American society as the nineteenth century drew to a close, see Edward C. Kirkland, *Industry Comes of Age* (Chicago: University of Chicago Press, 1961); Robert Wiebe, *The Search for Order* (New York: Hill and Wang, 1967); Sidney Fine, *Laissez-Faire and the General-Welfare State* (Ann Arbor: University of Michigan Press, 1956); Ginger, *Altgeld's America;* Harold U. Faulkner, *The Quest for Social Justice* (New York: Macmillan, 1931); and Samuel P. Hays, *The Response to Industrialism, 1885–1914* (Chicago: University of Chicago Press, 1957). For a discussion of the importance and centrality of democratic and republican values in the thinking and world view of turn of the century socialists, see Nick Salvatore, *Eugene V. Debs, Citizen and Socialist* (Urbana: University of Illinois Press, 1982); for the continuities of that theme in the vision and analysis of American radicals, see Leon Fink, *Workingmen's Democracy: The Knights of Labor and American Politics* (Urbana: University of Illinois Press, 1983).

2. In his survey of the early years of the movement, Shannon argued that "never before or since in the United States has a political organization with any kind of socialist organization grown the way the Socialist Party did for the first ten or fifteen years of its existence." Morris Hillquit, a chronicler of and participant in the movement, estimated that the party had some ten thousand members the year it was founded. In 1904, at the time of Eugene Debs's second campaign for the presidency, the party had 20,763 members. By 1908 official membership tallies counted 41,751. Party membership almost tripled between 1908 and 1912 and increased to 117,984. In that latter year Debs polled some 897,000 votes. Shannon, *Socialist Party of America*, 4–5. The most extensive account of the early years of the Socialist Party is still Kipnis, *American Socialist Movement.*

3. Shannon's opening chapter, "The Early Socialist Party: A Regional Survey," conveys some sense of the diversity of the young movement. In *Socialist Party of America.*

4. For a glimpse into the nature of agrarian discontent that found its articulation in the socialist movement, see Garin Burbank, *When the Farmers Voted Red: The Gospel of Socialism in the Oklahoma Countryside, 1910–1924* (Westport: Greenwood Press, 1976). Green's *Grass-Roots Socialism* is the best work to date on the socialist movement in rural America.

5. For an understanding of the diverse nature and composition of the movement, see Shannon's second chapter, "Immigrants, Negroes, Intellectuals, Millionaires, and Ministers," in *Socialist Party of America.* The cultural, ethnic, racial, and class diversity within the party naturally led to numerous debates and disagreements, some of them fundamental, on party policy and the direction of the movement. See Kipnis, *The American Socialist Movement,* 107–36, for insight into the diversity of opinion within the party.

6. The Socialist Party had a decentralized structure from its inception. Power was not officially invested in any central national body or office. The National Committee, elected by the membership, worked as a coordinating body that assisted in the implementation of those policies the membership adopted in convention or through national referenda. State and local branches operated in an autonomous, independent fashion as well.

The decentralized nature of the party in part reflected its deep-seated commitment to truly democratic institutions and popular participation. It also reflected a national organization that had evolved as a coalition among formerly rival factions of the earlier socialist movement. Each major faction had a geographic base of support, as well as a leadership with different agendas, varying levels of political savvy and support, and preexistent organization. The Socialist Party's decentralization could thus be described as a practical move to keep any one faction or leader from acquiring too much power at the national level. See Kipnis, *The American Socialist Movement,* for a sense of the wrangling and maneuvers that elicited the coalition that became the Socialist Party.

7. According to one historian of the Second International, "Social democracy was a genuinely international force. It was believed that certain problems were common to the parties which were members of the Second International and that they could be met by common solutions. Thus the tactical behavior and the theoretical beliefs of one Socialist Party often had a profound influence on other parties; and, indeed, one of the main themes of the history of the Second International is the imposition by the strongest Socialist Party of Europe, the German Social Democratic Party, of doctrines and tactics on other parties." James Joll, *The Second International 1889–1914* (New York: Harper and Row, 1966), 1–2. For a much more detailed history of the Second International, see G. D. H. Cole, *History of Socialist Thought,* vol. 3: *The Second International, 1889–1914* (London: Macmillan, 1963).

8. *"L'affaire Millerand"* refers to the controversy that raged within the French movement and the Second International as a whole over the entry of Socialist deputy Alexandre Millerand, into the cabinet of Prime Minister Waldeck Rous-

seau. Millerand's willing participation in the bourgeois government destroyed any semblance of unity between the French movement's right and left wings. On the French events and their repercussions, see Cole, *History of Socialist Thought*, 3:345ff.

One of the earliest pamphlets that Kerr & Company published, a polemic against participation in bourgeois governments, was written by one of the father figures of the German movement, Wilhelm Liebknecht. Wilhelm Liebknecht, *No Compromise! No Political Trading!* (Chicago: Charles H. Kerr & Company, 1900). In the United States, with its different forms of parliamentary rule, the issue as spelled out by the party was one of opposition to fusion with any elements of the dominant parties. The Socialist Party considered independent socialist campaigns as "the most vital principle" of the movement. They viewed union or labor parties as traps and considered votes for a labor party as votes for capitalism. No socialist could accept an appointment from a nonsocialist administration except under accepted civil service procedures. Party members were not allowed to support or vote for candidates from any other party. Violation of this fundamental principle could lead to suspension or expulsion. Locals that flirted with fusion had their charters revoked. Socialist Party, *Proceedings of the National Convention, 1904* (Chicago: National Committee, the Socialist Party, 1904), 50; "National Committee Resolution No. 8, 1905," *Socialist Party Official Bulletin*, May, July 1905; Kipnis, *The American Socialist Movement*, 125–26.

9. One of the issues that divided Kerr and Simons was "the land question." Legitimately concerned with the plight of the small landholder and also desiring to attract farmers' votes, Simons over a period of time introduced a number of demands based largely on the Populist Party platform of 1892 to successive Socialist Party conventions between 1908 and 1912. Kreuter and Kreuter, *An American Dissenter*; Huston, "A. M. Simons."

10. On Simons's journey to the right, see Kreuter and Kreuter, *An American Dissenter*, and Huston, "A. M. Simons."

11. Several different works present insights into the ongoing battle, both within the AFL and the Socialist Party, over the role of the socialists in the trade union movement. Many contemporary socialists had become conscious of the conservative role that established labor leaders played within the skilled-craft unions. They helped develop the critique of the class collusion and collaboration of such "labor aristocrats" as Samuel Gompers, which aided in the formation of the "new unionism" that took shape after AFL's agreements with the Steel Trust and the rise of the National Civic Federation. See Philip S. Foner, *History of the Labor Movement in the United States*, vol. 3: *The Policies and Practices of the American Federation of Labor, 1900–1909* (New York: International Publishers, 1964), and vol. 4: *The Industrial Workers of the World, 1905–1917* (New York: International Publishers, 1965); James Weinstein, *The Corporate Ideal and the Liberal State* (Boston: Beacon Press, 1968); David Montgomery, "Machinists, the Civic Federation, and the Socialist Party," and "The 'New Unionism' and the Transformation of Workers' Consciousness in America, 1909–22," both in *Workers' Control in America: Stud-*

ies in the History of Work, Technology, and the Labor Struggle, ed. David Montgomery (New York: Cambridge University Press, 1979); *The I.W.W.: Its First Fifty Years* (Chicago: University of Chicago Press, 1955).

12. Algie M. Simons, "Chicago Conference for Industrial Unions," *ISR* 5 (Feb. 1905): 496–99.

13. Simons, "The Industrial Workers of the World," *ISR* 6 (Aug. 1905): 65. The standard readings on the political and social history of the IWW include Melvin Dubofsky, *We Shall Be All: A History of the I.W.W.* (New York: Quadrangle Books, 1969), esp. 531–40 for a bibliographical essay; Foner, *History of the Labor Movement in the United States,* vol. 4; Joyce L. Kornbluh, ed., *Rebel Voices: An I.W.W. Anthology* (Ann Arbor: University of Michigan Press, 1964); Joseph R. Conlin, *Bread and Roses Too: Studies of the Wobblies* (Westport: Greenwood Press, 1969); Paul F. Brissenden, *The I.W.W.: A Study of American Syndicalism* (New York: Columbia University Press, 1919); and Fred Thompson, *The I.W.W.: Its First Fifty Years* (Chicago: University of Chicago Press, 1955).

14. Kreuter and Kreuter, *An American Dissenter,* 95–96, 100–104, 110. Simons alluded to his appreciation of the Labour Party's success in his last *ISR* editorial. Algie M. Simons, "Looking Forward and Backward," *ISR* 8 (Jan. 1908): 433–35.

15. Charles H. Kerr, "Socialist Unity in the United States," *ISR* 8 (Dec. 1907): 325–29; "Unionism, Utopian and Scientific," *ISR* 8 (May 1908): 557.

16. A. M. Simons, "Editorial Note," *ISR* 8 (Jan. 1908): 435; Charles H. Kerr, "What the *Review* Stands For," *ISR* 8 (Feb. 1908): 493–94; "To the Readers of the *Review,*" *ISR* 8 (Feb. 1908): 493. The editorial board for the *ISR* at the time included Spargo, from New York; Unterman, then living in Idaho; and LaMonte, a key Kerr translator and author. Hayes edited a monthly department on "The World of Labor." For Max Hayes, see *Biographical Dictionary of the American Left,* ed. Johnpoll and Klehr, 188–89.

17. Walden, "Notes on C.H.K.'s Ancestry." In his biography of Simons completed in 1965, Huston suggests that the split between the Simonses and Kerr had a personal side to it and that May Wood Simons "had never felt comfortable with the relatively well-to-do Kerrs and had suspected them of being socialist dilletanti." See Robert Huston, "Algie Martin Simons and the American Socialist Movement," Ph.D. diss., University of Wisconsin-Madison, 1965, 171. The source for that observation was a series of interviews with the Simonses' daughter, Miriam Simons Leuck, in 1954 and 1955. Just the opposite was true. The Simonses, already set in their drift to the right, became better situated, whereas Kerr threw his lot in with the clearly more working-class elements in the movement and maintained a living standard that might be described as well-to-do only with some stretch of the imagination. Committed to the cause as he was and would continue to be after 1910, he certainly was no dilettante. He took every available penny that he ever accumulated and pumped it back into the company. He lived simply quite humbly. His daughter would note in correspondence to May Walden that he had to scrimp and save in order to take her to ball games and the theater and

that he always ordered the least expensive item on the menu if they happened to eat in a restaurant. A lengthy series of correspondence over the years between Walden and Kerr, mainly disputes over Katharine Kerr's support while she was growing up, and letters between May Walden and her daughter, Katharine, all refute any suggestion of Kerr being well-to-do. Charles H. Kerr to May Walden Kerr, Jan. 28, 1908, Charles H. Kerr to Walden, Oct. 8, 1908, Walden to Kerr, Oct. 9, 1908, Kerr to Walden, Feb. 8, 1909, Walden to Kerr, Feb. 10, 1909, Katharine Kerr Moore to Walden, Nov. 11, 1920, Moore to Walden, Nov. 29, 1920, all in box 2, May Walden Kerr Papers.

18. Charles H. Kerr, "The *Review* for 1908," *ISR* 8 (Dec. 1907): 384.

19. Walden, "Notes on C.H.K.'s Ancestry"; Kerr, "What the *Review* Stands For."

20. "News and Views," *ISR* 8 (Feb. 1908): 507–9.

21. [Charles H. Kerr], "Publisher's Department," *ISR* 9 (Jan. 1909): 559; "News and Views," *ISR* 11 (July 1910): 55; "The Growth of the *Review*," *ISR* 12 (July 1911): 1.

22. Charles H. Kerr, "To New Readers," *ISR* 9 (Jan. 1909): 559.

23. "Socialist Gains and Losses," *ISR* 9 (Jan. 1909): 533; Charles H. Kerr, "The Party Election," *ISR* 10 (Jan. 1910): 534–35.

24. Joseph E. Cohen, "Constructive Socialism," *ISR* 9 (Aug. 1908): 81–91. Cohen was born in Baltimore in December 1883, the son of a cigar maker. An autodidact typographer and amateur journalist, he became active in Philadelphia's Typographical Union in 1902 and played a leading role in the the strike for the eight-hour day by that city's printers in 1905 and 1906. He joined the Socialist Party in 1903 and was a delegate to the party's convention from 1905 on. Keenly interested in socialist pedagogy and workers' education, he organized the Philadelphia School of Social Science and the Philadelphia Labor College. He also served as the Philadelphia representative of Kerr & Company and *ISR*. Kerr published his *Socialism for Students* in 1910. Stemming from a request by Kerr for a study course in socialism, that collection of essays initially appeared as a serialization that ran in *ISR* from November 1908 to July 1909. It was subsequently released in hard and soft cover as an "introduction to the study of Socialism with references for further reading." Fairly popular in leftist circles, it passed through several editions (1910, 1912, and 1918). Solon DeLeon, "Joseph Cohen," *American Labor's Who's Who*, 44; "Brother Joe," George Caylor Papers, Tamiment Institute, New York University; Joseph Cohen, "Author's Preface," *Socialism for Students* (Chicago: Charles H. Kerr and Company, 1910).

25. Charles H. Kerr, "Educate, Organize!" [editorial], *ISR* 9 (Aug. 1908): 141.

26. Charles H. Kerr, "Socialist Unity in France" [editorial], *ISR* 9 (Dec. 1908): 464.

27. Thomas Sladden, "The Revolutionist," *ISR* 9 (Dec. 1908): 423–30.

28. Carl D. Thompson, "Who Constitutes the Proletariat?" *ISR* 8 (Feb. 1909): 603–11.

29. Louis Duchez, "The Proletarian Attitude," *ISR* 10 (April 1909): 788–

93. For biographical material on Duchez, a rising star in the industrial unionist, left wing of the party who died suddenly at the age of twenty-seven, see *ISR* 12 (Oct. 1911): 231–34.

30. Charles O. Kohler, "Serious Thoughts" [News and Views], 9 (June 1909), 1013.

31. Charles H. Kerr, "Socialism Becoming Respectable," [editorial], *ISR* 9 (June 1909): 995–96; "A Step Backwards: Shall We Take It?," *ISR* 9 (June 1909): 998–99.

32. Charles H. Kerr, "A Party-Owned Press" [editorial], *ISR* 10 (July 1909): 68–70. At the national Party Congress in 1910, John Work and Morris Hillquit, two leaders of the gradualist or "constructive" wing, spoke avidly in support of the centralization of socialist publishing. Work suggested that the independent papers should make their subscription lists available for organizational purposes. Hillquit noted that the existent movement literature conjured up "all the differences of opinion within our ranks." Citing a certain amount of inefficiency and waste in the system of propaganda distribution, he suggested that the party limit itself "to a few works covering the main aspects of our philosophy and movement." Members of the party's left certainly did not want Hillquit or any of his allies determining what was suitable. Morris Hillquit, "The Propaganda of Socialism," and John Work, "Report on Organization," both in *National Congress Proceedings, 1910* (Chicago: Socialist Party, 1910), 61, 67, 39.

33. Louis Duchez, "The Strikes in Pennsylvania," *ISR* 10 (Sept. 1909): 193–203; William E. Bohn, "Reformer and Revolutionist," *ISR* 10 (Sept. 1909): 204–11; Tom Mann, "The Way to Win: An Open Letter to Trade Unionists on Methods of Industrial Organization," *ISR* 10 (Sept. 1909): 220–26; Odon Por, "Work's Coming of Age: Revolutionary Unionism in Europe," *ISR* 10 (Sept. 1909): 249.

34. Charles H. Kerr, "Revolutionary Unionism," *ISR* 3 (Sept. 1909): 266–68.

35. Duchez, "The Strikes in Pennsylvania," 193–94; Louis Duchez, "Victory at McKees Rocks," *ISR* 10 (Oct. 1909): 289–300. For a detailed discussion of the McKees Rocks struggle, see Foner, *History of the Labor Movement in the United States,* 4:281–95; Dubofsky, *We Shall Be All,* 200, 202–8; and John H. Ingham, "A Strike in the Progressive Era," *Pennsylvania Magazine of History* 903 (July 1966): 353–77.

36. "An Inspiring Victory," *ISR* 10 (Oct. 1909): 359, emphasis in the original.

37. "An Inspiring Victory"; "The Steel Trust's Mistake," *ISR* 10 (Oct. 1909): 359.

38. Ibid.; "Equal to the Test," *ISR* 10 (Oct. 1909): 360; Charles H. Kerr to Louis Boudin, Feb. 19, 1910, Boudin Papers.

39. "What Is the Matter with the Socialist Party?" [editorial], *ISR* 10 (Nov. 1909): 449–51, emphasis in the original.

40. "Is the Charge True?" *ISR* 10 (Dec. 1909): 552, emphasis in the original.

41. "A Labor Party," *ISR* 10 (Jan. 1910): 594–96.

42. "A Letter from Debs," *ISR* 10 (Jan. 1910): 609; "Hillquit-Stokes Correspondence," *ISR* 10 (Jan. 1910): 656, 658–62, emphasis in the original. In addition, see

William E. Walling to E. V. Debs, Dec. 14, 1909, and Feb. 12, 1910, and Walling to Fred Warren, Feb. 26, 1910, William English Walling Papers, SHSW.

43. Kerr, "The Party Election," 644, emphasis in the original.

44. Charles H. Kerr, "Ten Eventful Years," *ISR* 11 (July 1911): 46.

45. Charles H. Kerr, "What the *Review* Has Done," *ISR* 11 (July 1910): 46.

46. Kerr, "What the *Review* Has Done," 46, emphasis in the original.

47. Ibid.

48. Chaplin, *Wobbly*; Franklin Rosemont, "Ralph Chaplin," in *Haymarket Scrapbook*, ed. Dave Roediger and Franklin Rosemont (Chicago: Charles H. Kerr & Company, 1986), 194. For a concise biographical sketch, see John R. Slater, Jr., "Ralph H. Chaplin," in *Encyclopedia of the American Left*, ed. Buhle, Buhle, and Georgakis, 127.

49. The cards were examples of the type of agitational pedagogical ephemera that Kerr & Company produced. Each card of the deck, issued in 1908, contained a rhyme by Marcy and an illustration by Chaplin. Each bit of doggerel wittily commented on the various types of characters that composed the class structure and power relations of the era. The only deck known is in a private collection. For a brief discussion of the deck, see Louis H. Orzack and Maressa H. Orzack, "Political Playing-Cards: American Examples," *Journal of the International Playing-Card Society* 11 (Nov. 1982): 33–49.

50. Jack Carney, *Mary Marcy* (Chicago: Charles H. Kerr & Company, 1922).

51. Karl Marx, *Capital*, vol. 3: *Value, Price and Profit* and *The Poverty of Philosophy*, trans. Harry Quelch (Chicago: Charles H. Kerr & Company, 1910). The Kerr edition (1909) of the exposition by Morris and Bax was an abridgment of a volume issued by Swann, Sonnenschein (London, 1893).

52. Kerr, "Our Record for 1907," 446; [Charles H. Kerr], "Publisher's Department," *ISR* 8 (June 1908): 718; [Charles H. Kerr], "Publisher's Department," *ISR* 9 (Dec. 1909): 479.

53. Samuel Levenson, *James Connolly* (London: Quartet Books, 1977), 154, 155, 171; Austen Morgan, *James Connolly: A Political Biography* (Manchester: Manchester University Press, 1988), ch. 4; Chaplin, *Wobbly*, 105. For a study of Connolly's years in the United States and their impact on his politics, see Carl Reeve and Ann Barton Reeve, *James Connolly and the United States: The Road to the 1916 Irish Rebellion* (Atlantic Highlands: Humanities Press, 1978).

54. James Connolly, "Ballots, Bullets, or ——— ," *ISR* 10 (Oct. 1909): 354–58, and "Industrialism and the Trades Unions," *ISR* 10 (Feb. 1910): 714–22.

55. Charles H. Kerr, "Publisher's Note," preface to William E. Trautmann, *Industrial Unionism* (Chicago: Charles H. Kerr and Company, 1908).

56. Austin M. Lewis, *The Militant Proletariat* (Chicago: Charles H. Kerr & Company, 1911); [Charles H. Kerr], "Publisher's Department," *ISR* 12 (Nov. 1911): 260; *ISR* 12 (Dec. 1911): 381.

57. Austin Lewis was born in England in 1865, the son of a schoolmaster at Lancastershire. He later attended the University of London, where he acquired both

bachelor's and law degrees. He became interested in the socialist cause and studied the writings of William Morris while a student in London. He immigrated to California in 1890, where he taught school in San Rafael for awhile. Admitted to the California bar in 1898, he campaigned for governor of California on the Socialist Party ticket in 1906 from his home in Oakland. An avid essayist and lecturer for socialism, Lewis published several works under the auspices of Kerr & Company. In addition to *The Militant Proletariat*, he also wrote *The Rise of the American Proletariat* (1907) and *Proletarian and Petite Bourgeois*. Well versed in Marxian theory, he also found time to do various translations, including Friedrich Engels's *Anti-Duhring*, published by Kerr as *Landmarks of Scientific Socialism* (1907). For biographical material on Lewis, see Lewis Francis Byington, *The History of San Francisco*, 3 vols. (Chicago: S. J. Clarke), 2:335–36; Agnes Foster Buchanan, "The Story of a Famous Fraternity of Writers and Artists," *Pacific Monthly* 17 (Jan. 1907): 73–74; and *San Francisco Chronicle*, Jan. 28, 1940.

58. Lewis, *The Militant Proletariat*; [Charles H. Kerr], "Publisher's Department," *ISR* 12 (Nov. 1911): 260; *ISR* 12 (Dec. 1911): 381.

59. Lewis, *Militant Proletariat*, 25.

60. Ibid., 28.

61. Ibid., 32.

62. Ibid., 32–34.

63. Ibid., 35–36.

64. Ibid., 36.

65. Ibid., ch. 2 and 108–14.

66. Ibid., 52.

67. Ibid., 70, 74.

68. Ibid., 179–81.

69. Ibid., 121–30.

Chapter 8: The In-House Battle, 1911–13

1. Duchez, "The Strikes in Pennsylvania," "Victory at McKees Rocks." For a detailed discussion of the McKees Rocks struggle, see Foner, *History of the Labor Movement in the United States*, 4:281–95; Dubofsky, *We Shall Be All*, 200, 202–8; and Ingham, "A Strike in the Progressive Era."

2. "News and Views," *ISR* 10 (Dec. 1909): 557–58; Elizabeth Gurley Flynn, "The Free Speech Fight at Spokane," *ISR* 10 (Dec. 1909): 483–89; Elizabeth Gurley Flynn, "The Shame of Spokane," *ISR* 10 (Jan. 1910): 610–19; Charles H. Kerr, "The Free Speech Fight" [editorial], *ISR* 10 (Jan. 1910): 642–43; Vincent St. John, "The Fight for Free Speech at San Diego," *ISR* 12 (April 1912): 649; Hartwell S. Shippey, "The Shame of San Diego," *ISR* 12 (May 1912): 718–23.

3. For example, see the account of the famous wildcat by forty thousand shirt-waist makers in New York that began in November 1909: Rose Strunsky, "The Strike of the Singers of the Shirt," *ISR* 10 (Jan. 1910): 620–27. See also the re-

ports of the Philadelphia street car strike of early 1910: Joseph E. Cohen, "When the Sleeper Wakes," *ISR* 10 (April 1910): 865–75, and 10 (May 1910): 976–82; or the strike wave among Chicago's forty-one thousand garment workers during the winter of 1910: R. Dvorak, "The Chicago Garment Workers," *ISR* 10 (Dec. 1910): 353–59; Eugene Debs, "Help! Help!! Help!!!" *ISR* 11 (Jan. 1911): 394.

4. For fuller accounts of Haywood's life, see Peter Carlson, *Roughneck: The Life and Times of Big Bill Haywood* (New York: W. W. Norton, 1983); Joseph R. Conlin, *Big Bill Haywood and the Radical Labor Movement* (Syracuse: Syracuse University Press, 1969); Melvyn Dubofsky, *"Big Bill" Haywood* (New York: St Martin's Press, 1987); and Bill Haywood, *William D. Haywood's Book* (New York: International, 1929).

5. For prime examples of the kind of witty, biting, and perceptive observations that made Haywood so popular with the left-wingers and such a thorn in the side of the party's right, see the collections of his aphorisms and sections of his speeches reproduced in *ISR*: "Pick and Shovel Pointers," *ISR* 11 (Feb. 1911): 458; "Shots for the Work-Shop," *ISR* 11 (April 1911): 588; "Pick and Shovel Pointers," *ISR* 12 (July 1911): 7; "A Detective," *ISR* 11 (Dec. 1911): 345; and "Blanket Stiff Philosophy," *ISR* 12 (Dec. 1911): 370.

6. Haywood used the opportunity of his trip to the International Congress to tour Europe, and he forwarded a number of articles on the state of the labor and socialist movement to *ISR*. See (all by William D. Haywood) "William D. Haywood in Europe," *ISR* 11 (Nov. 1910): 286–88; "William D. Haywood in London," *ISR* 11 (Dec. 1910): 352; "News from Europe," *ISR* 11 (Dec. 1910): 336–40; "Lockouts in Great Britain," *ISR* 11 (Jan. 1911): 415–16; and "The Fighting Welsh Miners," *ISR* 11 (Feb. 1911): 459–64.

7. For a detailed explanation of Kerr's plan for the *ISR* Lecture Bureau, see *ISR* 11 (Feb. 1911): 490–91.

8. Haywood briefly described his itinerary on that first *ISR* speaking jaunt. Beginning in Chicago, he spoke in Duluth, Minneapolis, St Paul, Butte, and several other mountain mining towns. He then proceeded to the Pacific Northwest, where he appeared in Spokane at the height of that city's free speech fight. He continued on to Portland and Seattle. Canceling a series of engagements in California, he turned north and worked his way across Canada from Vancouver to Cape Breton and down the East Coast to New York, where he challenged Morris Hillquit to public debate. William D. Haywood, *The Autobiography of Big Bill Haywood* (New York: International, 1977), 243–45 [originally *Bill Haywood's Book*, 1929]. For an additional partial listing of Haywood's itinerary, see "Haywood Dates," *ISR* 11 (June 1911): 761. For accounts of the tour, see "The Haywood Meetings," *ISR* 11 (March 1911): 557; "Haywood Drawing Record Breaking Crowds," *ISR* 11 (May 1911): 704–5; and "Haywood Hits Hard," *ISR* 12 (Oct. 1911): 242.

9. *Solidarity*, June 30, 1911, as cited in Foner, *History of the Labor Movement in the United States*, 4:394. Haywood apparently began his list of planned California stops but canceled the remainder, not so much because of the opposition raised

by the constructivists but because of a personal request made to him by Clarence Darrow, then in the midst of preparing the defense of the brothers McNamara in their sensational trial for the bombing of the Los Angeles Times Building. Darrow felt that appearances by Haywood in that already tense environment would have been to the detriment of public sentiment toward the case. Haywood abided by Darrow's request and went north to Canada instead. J. Edward Morgan, "Haywood in California," *ISR* 12 (Sept. 1911): 168–69; "Pages Torn From 'The Class Struggle' and Other Haywood Lectures," *ISR* 12 (Nov. 1911): 279–81; "Haywood in Ohio," *ISR* 12 (Jan. 1912): 436; "Haywood in Pennsylvania," *ISR* 12 (Jan. 1912): 436; "The Haywood Lectures," *ISR* 12 (Jan. 1912): 441; Haywood, *Autobiography*, 244–45; Kevin Tierney, *Darrow* (New York: Crowell, 1979), 243.

10. *"International Socialist Review* Lecture Bureau," *ISR* 11 (Feb. 1911): 490–91; "Bohn Organizing Locals," *ISR* 11 (May 1911): 698. For examples of Bohn's earlier contributions, see "Politics and the Proletariat," *ISR* 9 (Dec. 1908): 464–65; "The Failure to Attain Socialist Unity," *ISR* 8 (June 1908): 755; and "The Ballot," *ISR* 11 (Jan. 1911): 414–15. For biographical material on Bohn, see *Biographical Dictionary of the American Left*, ed. Johnpoll and Klehr, 38.

11. *ISR* 12 (Aug. 1911): 68.

12. "News and Views," *ISR* 12 (Sept. 1911): 186–87.

13. William D. Haywood and Frank Bohn, *Industrial Socialism* (Chicago: Charles H. Kerr & Company, 1911), 8.

14. Haywood and Bohn, *Industrial Socialism*, 10–22ff, 41.

15. Ibid., 43.

16. Ibid., 45, 48–52.

17. Ibid., 49–50.

18. Following his change of plea, James McNamara received a life sentence. His brother John received ten years. For a full account of the McNamara case and its affects, see Graham Adams, Jr., *Age of Industrial Violence* (New York: Columbia University Press, 1966), ch. 1; Tierney, *Darrow*, 236–75; Kipnis, *The American Socialist Movement*, 348–57; and Louis Adamic, *Dynamite: The Story of Class Violence in America* (1931, repr. New York: Chelsea House, 1967), 179–253.

19. In the immediate aftermath of the October 1910 bombing and the resultant accusations issued by anti-labor elements, an article in the *ISR* conjectured that a gas leak caused the explosion and that it was the logical outcome of Harrison Otis's disregard for workers' lives. After the April 1911 arrests of the McNamaras and their codefendant Ortie McManigal, *ISR* joined in the claim of frame-up, which received widespread support throughout the socialist and labor press. Haywood, then in the middle of his *ISR* lecture tour, went so far as to call for a general strike on the day that the McNamara trial began. See A Unionist, "The Los Angeles Conspiracy against Organized Labor," *ISR* 11 (Nov. 1910): 262–66; William D. Haywood, "Get Ready," *ISR* 11 (June 1911): 725–29; "Haywood Defends McNamara," *ISR* 11 (June 1911): 760–61.

20. Eugene V. Debs, "The McNamara Case and the Labor Movement," *ISR* 12

(Jan. 1912): 397–401; Frank Bohn, "The Passing of the McNamaras," *ISR* 12 (Jan. 1912): 401–4.

21. *Socialist Party Weekly Bulletin,* Nov. 23, Dec. 7, 1911, Jan. 1912; Kipnis, *The American Socialist Movement,* 395.

22. "A Letter from William D. Haywood," *ISR* 12 (Dec. 1911): 375.

23. Frank Bohn, "A Letter from Frank Bohn," *ISR* 12 (Dec. 1911): 375.

24. "Letter from Morris Hillquit," *New York Call,* Nov. 20, 1911, and "Letter from William D. Haywood," *New York Call,* Nov. 28, 1911, both cited in Kipnis, *The American Socialist Movement,* 382–83.

25. "Better Than Barricades," *ISR* 12 (Jan. 1912): 430–31; Kipnis, *The American Socialist Movement,* 382–83.

26. Charles H. Kerr, "Is Our Publishing House Co-Operative?" *ISR* 12 (Jan. 1912): 440–41; "The Haywood Lectures," *ISR* 12 (Jan. 1912): 441–42.

27. For a full stenographic report of the Cooper Union speech of Dec. 21, 1911, see William D. Haywood, "Socialism the Hope of the Working Class," *ISR* 12 (Feb. 1912): 461–71.

28. Eugene Debs, "Sound Socialist Tactics," *ISR* 12 (Feb. 1912): 481–86.

29. "Direct Action" [editorial], *ISR* 12 (Feb. 1912): 505–6.

30. Robert Rives LaMonte, "Socialist for Capitalist Law," *ISR* 12 (Feb. 1912): 500–504. LaMonte continued his discussion and clarification of the issues facing the party in subsequent *ISRs.* See Robert Rives LaMonte, "Tools and Tactics," *ISR* 12 (March 1912): 577, "You and Your Vote," *ISR* 13 (Aug. 1912): 116–22, and "The New Socialism," *ISR* 13 (Sept. 1912): 205–16. For a polemic on the question of the role of violence and its relationship to the socialist movement, a left-wing defense of Haywood and Bohn's *Industrial Socialism,* see Marcus Hitch, "Violence in Class Struggles," *ISR* 12 (Feb. 1912): 491–93.

31. In the middle of the strike, while Haywood appealed to party members to assist the hard-pressed Lawrence workers, the *New York Call* resumed its attacks on him. A party local from Yuma, Arizona, went so far as to introduce a referenda motion calling for his removal from the NEC. The motion needed a second, and the New York Central Commitee adopted it. A week after the Lawrence victory of March 13, the New York committee reconvened, however. Deciding that it had perhaps acted in haste, it withdrew the motion in support of Yuma, and the resolution died for lack of a second. Kipnis, *The American Socialist Movement,* 389–90.

32. Charles H. Kerr, "The Victory at Lawrence," and "The Socialist Party of America" [editorials], *ISR* 12 (April 1912): 679–80.

33. Frank Bohn, "Some Definitions," *ISR* 12 (May 1912): 747–49.

34. "Report of Clyde A. Berry and Stephen M. Reynolds to the Comrades of the Socialist Party of America, May 5, 1912," *Socialist Party Monthly Bulletin* (June 1912): 16–19; "Verdict—Not Guilty," *ISR* 12 (June 1912): 862–65.

35. For a detailed discussion of the convention proceedings, see Kipnis, *The American Socialist Movement,* ch. 18.

36. Ibid.

37. For the discussion of Legien's appearance at the Socialist Party convention, see Kipnis, *The American Socialist Movement*, 399–400. The major parties of Europe, especially the SPD, underwent a similar debate and censure of syndicalist elements. The SPD carried out a revision of its bylaws several months before the May 1912 gathering of the U.S. party. The Germans passed a resolution almost identical to that which the Americans would come to approve, which outlawed advocacy of violence, sabotage, and direct action.

38. Socialist Party, *Proceedings of the National Convention, 1912* (Chicago, 1912), 122, 134.

39. "An Appeal to Stupid Prejudice" [editorial], *ISR* 12 (June 1912): 874–75.

40. *Social-Democratic Herald* [Milwaukee], Nov. 24, 1912; Morris Hillquit, "In Self-Defense," *ISR* 13 (Aug. 1912): 163–66.

41. "The Case of Morris Hillquit" [editorial], *ISR* 13 (Aug. 1912): 170; "Minutes of the Executive Committee, Local New York, July 23, 1912," *New York Call*, July 25, 1912; letter from Charles Rice to the *Call*, Oct. 24, 1912.

42. For a full discussion of the role of Joe Ettor and Arturo Giovanitti in the Lawrence strike and their subsequent arrests and trial, see Dubofsky, *We Shall Be All*, ch. 10; Foner, *History of the Labor Movement in the United States*, 4:142.

43. "The Motion to Recall Haywood" [editorial], *ISR* 13 (Feb. 1913): 625.

44. "Annual Stockholders' Meeting," *ISR* 13 (Feb. 1913): 636.

45. M.E.M., "A Straw Man" [editorial], *ISR* 13 (March 1913): 691.

46. Ibid., 691.

47. Frank Bohn, "The State of the Party" [editorial], *ISR* 14 (Oct. 1913): 236–40.

48. Bohn, "The State of the Party," 236.

49. Ibid., 240.

Chapter 9: *The International Socialist Review, 1908–18*

1. Those years of dedication left an immense but underused, detailed record for social historians. Herbert Gutman, one of the first historians to point to the value of *ISR* as "a lasting historical source" of American social history, cautioned future scholars not to approach it solely as a source to the internal political squabbles of the socialist movement. In his estimation, it was "utterly foolish" to research *ISR* simply because it allowed a renewal of an "acquaintance" with the factional fights and debates of that past era. Rather than some "relic" of "an irrelevant past" or a "nostalgic reminder" of the "vitality of a submerged, neglected and quarrelsome radical tradition," Gutman called the *Review* "an exceedingly useful historical record for those historians concerned with understanding the successes and failures of American radicalism, the causes and consequences of American reform, the economic and social conditions of American society before 1917, and the patterns of protest and acquiescence characteristic of a developed but imbalanced capitalist society." Herbert G. Gutman, "The *International Socialist Review*," in *The*

American Radical Press 1880–1960, 2 vols., ed. Joseph R. Conlin (Westport: Greenwood Press, 1974), 1:82–86.

2. For examples of the range of discussions on socialism and the American farmer, see J. B. Webster, "A Farmer's Criticism of the Socialist Party," *ISR* 2 (May 1902): 769–73; Algie Simons, "The Socialist Party and the Farmer," *ISR* 2 (May 1902): 774–78; Karl Kautsky, "Socialist Agitation among Farmers in America," *ISR* 3 (Sept. 1902): 148–60; Algie Simons, "Socialism and the American Farmer," *ISR* 3 (Oct. 1902): 201–11; [Algie Simons], "The Farmer and the Wageworker in the Socialist Party," *ISR* 4 (Aug. 1903): 109–12; Isadore Ladoff, "The American Farmer," *ISR* 5 (Feb. 1904): 475–79; C. F. Dight, "Socialism and the Farmers," *ISR* 5 (April 1905): 604–9. For later discussions, see W. J. Bell, "Who Is the Farmer?" *ISR* 11 (Nov. 1910): 295; John Randolph, "Insurance against Crop Failure," *ISR* 12 (June 1912): 852–54; Bert Willard, "Farmer Jones on Party Problems," *ISR* 13 (Aug. 1912): 129–32; Bert Willard, "Farmer John and the Union Label," *ISR* 13 (Feb. 1913): 594–97.

3. For a sampling of such articles, see Algie Simons, "The Negro Problem," *ISR* 1 (Oct. 1900): 204–11; Charles H. Vail, "The Negro Problem," *ISR* 1 (Feb. 1901): 464–70; Clarence Darrow, "The Problem of the Negro," *ISR* 2 (Nov. 1901): 321–35; William Noyes, "Some Proposed Solutions to the Negro Problem," *ISR* 2 (Dec. 1901): 401–13; Eugene Debs, "The Negro in the Class Struggle," *ISR* 4 (Nov. 1903): 257–60; A. T. Cuzner, "The Negro or the Race Problem," *ISR* 4 (Nov. 1903): 261–64; Clarence Meilly, "Socialism and the Negro Problem," *ISR* 4 (Nov. 1903): 265–67; Eugene V. Debs, "The Negro and His Nemesis," *ISR* 4 (Jan. 1904): 391–97; Oscar Edgar, "A Study of Race Prejudice," *ISR* 4 (Feb. 1904): 462–65; Eraste Vidrine, "Negro Locals," *ISR* 5 (Jan. 1905): 389–92; E. F. Andrews, "Socialism and the Negro," *ISR* 5 (March 1905): 524–26. See also the series by Algie Simons: "Economic Aspects of Chattel Slavery in America," *ISR* 4 (July 1903): 25–33, 4 (Aug. 1903): 95–105, and 4 (Sept. 1903): 164–73.

The monthly continued its discussion of race and class and the "correct" position of socialists to black America in the period after the change in editorial direction at the beginning of 1908. For examples, see the lengthy series by I. M. Robbins, "The Economic Aspects of the Negro Problem," *ISR* 8 (Feb. 1908): 480–88, 8 (March 1908): 548–54, 8 (April 1908): 614–21, 8 (May 1908): 691–700, 8 (June 1908): 765–77, 9 (July 1908): 51–61, 9 (Sept. 1908): 161–71, 9 (Oct. 1908): 282–92, 9 (Jan. 1909): 499–510, 9 (March 1909): 690–702, 9 (June 1909): 985–94, 10 (July 1909): 50–59, 10 (Sept. 1909): 253–65, 10 (Dec. 1909): 527–41, 10 (May 1910): 1010–20, and 10 (June 1910): 1106–17; Ellen Wetherell, "In Ole Alabam'," *ISR* 11 (Dec. 1910): 341–44; Covington Hall, "Negroes against Whites," *ISR* 13 (Oct. 1912): 349–50; Anon., "The Southern Negro and One Big Union," *ISR* 13 (June 1913): 888–91; Upton Sinclair, "Spontaneous Combustion," *ISR* 15 (June 1915): 723; Palmer Hoke Wright, "The American Negro and the War," *ISR* 17 (Sept. 1916): 166–67. For a significant series of contributions by a noted black socialist of the period, see Hubert Harrison, "The Black Man's Burden," *ISR* 12 (April 1912):

660–63, 11 (May 1912): 762–64; Hubert Harrison, "Socialism and the Negro," *ISR* 13 (July 1912): 65–68.

4. Lalla Kufferath, "Women in Belgium," *ISR* 1 (Dec. 1900): 359–61; Edgard Milhaud, "Socialist Propaganda among Women in Germany," *ISR* 1 (May 1901): 713–18; Mila Tupper Maynard, "Woman Suffrage as Observed by a Socialist," *ISR* 5 (Jan. 1905): 385–88; Isadore Ladoff, "Sexual Slavery," *ISR* 5 (Feb. 1905): 449–59; Paul Lafargue, "The Woman Question," *ISR* 5 (March 1905): 547–59; May Wood Simons, "Living In," *ISR* 7 (July 1906): 1–5; John Jesse M. Molle, "The National Convention of the Woman's Movement," *ISR* 8 (May 1908): 688–90.

The discussion of the role of women in the socialist movement and the larger society continued in the *ISR*'s later period. For examples, see John Spargo, "Woman and the Socialist Movement," *ISR* 8 (Feb. 1908): 449–55; Lida Parce, "Woman and the Socialist Philosophy," *ISR* 10 (Aug. 1909): 125–28; Theresa Malkiel, "Where Do We Stand on the Woman Question?" *ISR* 10 (Aug. 1909): 159–62; Lida Parce, "The Relation of Socialism to the Woman Question," *ISR* 10 (Nov. 1909): 442–45; Maud Thompson, "The Value of Woman's Work," *ISR* 10 (Dec. 1909): 513–23; Georgia Kotsch, "The Mother's Future," *ISR* 10 (June 1910): 109–71; Rose Strunsky, "The Russian Woman and the Suffragette," *ISR* 11 (July 1910): 29–32; Caroline Nelson, "Neo-Malthusianism: The Control of Child-Bearing," *ISR* 14 (Oct. 1913): 228–30; Caroline Nelson, "The Control of Child-Bearing," *ISR* 14 (March 1914): 547–48; Modesto C. Rolland, "Mexican Feminist Congress," *ISR* 17 (Sept. 1916): 152–53.

5. *ISR*, from January through October 1901, featured a monthly column, "Socialism and Religion," by the well-known Christian Socialist George D. Herron. For examples of articles on the relationship of socialism and religion see "Paganism and Christianity," *ISR* 1 (June 1901): 753–64; J. Stitt Wilson, "Christianity and Paganism (a Reply)," *ISR* 2 (July 1901): 1–13; Peter E. Burrowes, "Paganism vs. Socialism," *ISR* 2 (Aug. 1901): 104–11; Robert Rives LaMonte, "Paganism and Christianity," *ISR* 2 (Dec. 1901): 435–37; W. T. Brown, "Open Letter from a Catholic to Pope Leo," *ISR* 2 (April 1902): 715–22; Owen R. Lovejoy, "Jesus and Social Freedom," *ISR* 3 (Sept. 1902): 165–71; Thomas J. Hagerty, "A Correction," *ISR* 3 (Oct. 1902): 229–30; A. M. Simons, "Bishop Spalding and Socialism," *ISR* 3 (Jan. 1903): 395–400; Austin Lewis, "The Church and the Proletarian," *ISR* 3 (Feb. 1903): 465–72; Lucien V. Rule, "Christ the Comrade," *ISR* 5 (Aug. 1904): 101; Peter E. Burrowes, "Religion of Science: Science of Religion," *ISR* 5 (March 1905): 534–43; Algie Simons, "The Jesuits' Attack of Socialism," *ISR* 5 (May 1905): 655–63; G. E. Etherton, "Why Revivals No Longer Revive," *ISR* 6 (May 1906): 686–88; Joseph E. Cohen, "Why the Workingman Does Not Go to Church," *ISR* 7 (July 1906): 28–32; Clarence Meilly, "Why the Workingman Is without a Church," *ISR* 7 (Feb. 1907): 459–61; Anton Pannekoek, "Socialism and Religion," *ISR* 7 (March 1907): 546–56; Thomas C. Hall, "The Element of Faith in Marxian Socialism," *ISR* 8 (Jan. 1908): 392–95.

An occasional article on religion, more specifically discussions of the relation-

ship and response of the movement to antisocialist activities on the part of organized religion, especially the Catholic church, appeared during the *ISR*'s second
phase. See Isadore Ladoff, "Historical Christianity and Christian Socialism," *ISR* 9
(Aug. 1908): 113–18; William Thurston Brown, "Christianity and Socialism," *ISR*
9 (Sept. 1908): 180–83; Thomas Hall, "Historical Christianity and Socialism," *ISR*
9 (May 1909): 881–85; Thomas Hall, "Marxian Socialism and the Roman Church,"
ISR 10 (June 1910): 1072–73; Timothy O'Neil, "Why Catholic Workers Should
Be Socialists," *ISR* (Oct. 1913): 216–17; Richard Perin, "The German Catholic
Unions," *ISR* 15 (July 1914): 397–99; Anon., "The Catholic Threat and the A.F.of
L.," *ISR* 14 (July 1914): 414–15; Anon., "The Catholic Church and the Unemployed," *ISR* 14 (April 1914): 608–9; Anon., "The Origin of Religion," *ISR* 16 (Oct.
1915): 225; J. Howard Moore, "The Source of Religion," *ISR* 16 (June 1916): 726–
27.

   6. Editorial [A. M. Simons], "The Chicago and St. Louis Strike," *ISR* 1 (July
1900): 58–63; Mary "Mother" Jones, "A Picture of American Freedom in West Virginia," *ISR* 2 (Sept. 1901): 177–79; [Algie Simons], "The Steel Strike," *ISR* 2 (Oct.
1901): 314–16; Mary "Mother" Jones, "The Coal Miners of the Old Dominion,"
ISR 2 (Feb. 1902): 575–78; [Algie Simons], "Socialism and the Trade Union Movement," *ISR* 3 (July 1902): 46–49; William Mailly, "The Anthracite Strike," *ISR* 3
(Aug. 1902): 79–85; Algie Simons, "The Western Federation of Miners," *ISR* 6 (May
1906): 641–48.

   7. For a sampling of such contributions during the *ISR*'s earlier period, see N. A.
Richardson, "Labor and Capital and China," *ISR* 2 (April 1902): 735–39; Sen
Katayama, "Socialism in Japan," *ISR* 4 (Oct. 1903): 202–3; Andrew M. Anderson,
"Political Unrest in Australia," *ISR* 5 (Nov. 1904): 265–68; Andrew M. Anderson,
"Australian Labor Convention," *ISR* 6 (Sept. 1905): 141–44; Tom Mann, "The
Political Position of the Labor and Socialist Party in Australia," *ISR* 6 (Sept. 1905):
137–40; Karl Kautsky, "Differences among the Russian Socialists," *ISR* 5 (June
1905): 705–17 (from *Die Neue Zeit*); Robert Rives LaMonte, "Socialist Unity in
France," *ISR* 5 (March 1905): 527–33; Odon Por, "The Italian Socialist Conven-
tion," *ISR* 7 (Dec. 1906): 342–46; Jean Longuet, "The Political Situation in France,"
ISR 7 (March 1907): 528–32; William M. Salter, "Socialism in France and Italy,"
ISR 7 (May 1907): 611–52; George Whitfield, "Present Conditions in Cuba and
the Outlook," *ISR* 9 (Aug. 1908): 137–39; Clarence Clowe, "The Situation in
China," *ISR* 9 (Aug. 1908): 119–25.

   8. Victor Serwy, "To the Labor Parties of All Countries," *ISR* 1 (May 1901): 795–
96; [Algie Simons], "Editorial," *ISR* 2 (May 1902): 811. For examples of bureau
communiqués, see "Events in Russia," *ISR* 3 (Aug. 1902): 86–88; H. M. Hyndmann,
"The International Situation and the International Socialist Bureau," *ISR* 3 (Sept.
1902): 129–32; Victor Serwy, "International Socialist Congress of Amsterdam," *ISR*
3 (Feb. 1903); International Socialist Bureau, "The Conference of the International
Committee," *ISR* 3 (Feb. 1903): 482–83; A. M. Simons, "International Socialist
Congress," *ISR* 3 (Nov. 1902): 300–301; Victor Servy, "The Kischniff Massacres,"

ISR (July 1903): 46; "The International Socialist Bureau," *ISR* 4 (March 1904); "Report of the Secretary of the International Socialist Bureau," *ISR* 7 (July 1906): 51–53; "Bulletin of the International Socialist Bureau," *ISR* 7 (Sept. 1906): 172–74; "To the Workers of the World: Manifesto of the International Socialist Bureau," *ISR* 8 (Aug. 1907): 88–91; "International Socialist Congress of Stuttgart," *ISR* 8 (Aug. 1907): 104–6.

9. The monthly carried coverage of every significant labor agitation carried out by the direct-actionists of the period. For a sampling, see Louis Duchez, "The Strikes in Pennsylvania," *ISR* 10 (Sept. 1909): 193–203; "The Shame of Spokane," *ISR* 10 (Jan. 1910): 610–19; Rose Strunsky, "The Strike of the Singers of the Shirt," *ISR* 10 (Jan. 1910): 620–27; Joseph E. Cohen, "'When the Sleeper Wakes': The Car Strike and the General Strike in Philadelphia," *ISR* 10 (May 1910): 976–82; Eber F. Heston, "The Street Car Strike at Columbus," *ISR* 11 (Sept. 1910): 133; Thomas F. Kennedy, "The Class War in the Coal Fields," *ISR* 11 (Sept. 1910): 141–48; Louis Duchez, "The Cossack's Club," *ISR* 11 (Oct. 1910): 193–94; Robert Dvorak, "The Chicago Garment Worker," *ISR* 11 (Dec. 1910): 353–59; Robert Dvorak, "The Fighting Garment Workers," *ISR* 11 (Jan. 1911): 385–93; Ed Moore, "The Strike at Baldwin's," *ISR* 12 (Aug. 1911): 90–95; Hartwell Shippey, "The Shame of San Diego," *ISR* 12 (May 1912): 718–23; Phillips Russell, "The Dynamite Job at Lawrence," *ISR* 13 (Oct. 1912): 308–11; Mary Marcy, "The New York Garment Workers," *ISR* 13 (Feb. 1913): 583–88; William D. Haywood, "On the Paterson Picket Line," *ISR* 13 (June 1913): 847–51; Mortimer Downing, "The Case of the Hop Pickers," *ISR* 14 (Oct. 1913): 210–13; Leslie H. Marcy, "Calumet," *ISR* 14 (Feb. 1914): 453–61; Clara Ruth Mozzor, "Ludlow," *ISR* 14 (June 1914): 722–24; Anon., "The Garment Worker's Strike," *ISR* 16 (Nov. 1915): 260–64; George Harrison, "The Mesaba Iron Range," *ISR* 17 (Dec. 1916): 329–32; Walker C. Smith, "The Voyage of the Verona," *ISR* 17 (Dec. 1916): 340–46.

10. Kerr, "What the *Review* Has Done," 46.

11. Bell, *Marxian Socialism in the United States*. In his discussion of the "failure" of Marxian socialism in America penned during the early dark ages of the cold war, Bell asserts that the main reason underlying the movement's inability to make substantive and lasting gains was the "unhappy problem" of "living *in* but not *of* the world." More polemic than history by the ideologue of the "end of ideology," Bell's interpretation held considerable sway with several generations of like-minded intellectuals who never looked closely at the movement themselves and therefore found it convenient to accept the assertions of a one-time leftist turned prodigal son. Flawed, imprecise, and selective to the point of distortion, Bell's essay was more a product of the political climate and era in which he wrote than an accurate assessment of socialists in America. Kerr and his close circle of intimates were very much of this world; they could not have run a publishing venture for as long as they did if they had their heads either in the clouds or in the sand.

12. Kerr, "What the *Review* Has Done"; Kerr, "Ten Eventful Years"; Charles H. Kerr, "What the *Review* Stands For," *ISR* 13 (Sept. 1912): 270–71.

13. The *ISR* had several memorable contemporaries that also had remarkable histories and political trajectories. Most notable among them was the weekly *Appeal to Reason* (published in Girard, Kansas, from 1895 to 1917), *The Comrade* (published in New York from 1900 to 1905), *The Masses* (published in New York from 1911 to 1917), and the *New Review* (also published in New York from 1913 to 1917). For a discussion of the strength and viability of the socialist movement press from 1912 to 1920, see Weinstein, *Decline of Socialism*, 84–93.

14. Kerr, "Ten Eventful Years."

15. Ibid., 46.

16. Ibid., 46.

17. For examples, see Mann, "The Way to Win," 220; J. A. Phillips, "Revolutionary Mining Machine," *ISR* 8 (Feb. 1910): 702–4; Robert J. Wheeler, "The Passing of the Bottle Blower," *ISR* 9 (Feb. 1911): 449–57; Thomas F. Kennedy, "Banishing Skill From the Foundry," *ISR* 9 (Feb. 1911): 469–73; Kennedy, "A Molderless Foundry," *ISR* 10 (April 1911): 610–12; Louis Duchez, "Scientific Business Management. What Is It? What Effect Will It Have on the Revolutionary Movement?" *ISR* 10 (April 1911): 628–31; Thomas F. Kennedy, "Revolution in the Coke Industry," *ISR* 11 (May 1911): 690–94; Robert J. Wheeler, "The Cement Monopoly," *ISR* 11 (June 1911): 734–41; Thomas F. Kennedy, "What Twelve Men Produce," *ISR* 12 (July 1911): 39; Lew W. Lang, "Pearl Buttons," *ISR* 12 (Dec. 1911): 342–45; Phillips Russell, "The Steel Trust's Private City—Gary," *ISR* 12 (Dec. 1911): 327–33; Edgar Llewellyn, "From Pick and Shovel to Breaker," *ISR* 12 (Jan. 1912): 407–11; J. H. Fraser, "Craft Unionism," *ISR* 12 (April 1912): 670–72; Peter Kinnear, "That Damn Steam Shovel," *ISR* 12 (May 1912): 769–71; Mary Marcy, "Things Doing in the Cement Industry," *ISR* 13 (July 1912): 58–60; L. A., "The Automobile Industry," *ISR* 13 (Sept. 1912): 255–58; Robert Johnstone Wheeler, "Modern Machinery and the Future of Industrial Education," *ISR* 13 (Sept. 1912): 265–68; Robert Johnstone Wheeler, "Automatic Machinery in the Glass Bottle Industry and Its Effect on the Employment of Skilled Craftsmen," *ISR* 12 (Nov. 1912): 408–12; "The Automatic Process—in the Cement Industry, Showing the Tendency Toward Automatic Machinery and the Minimum of Labor in the New Industries," *ISR* 12 (Nov. 1912): 533–39; Hugo Lenz, "The Passing of the Skilled Mechanic," *ISR* 13 (March 1913): 668–70; Winden A. Frankenthal, "New Labor Displacing Machines," *ISR* 14 (Nov. 1913): 289–91; Mary Marcy, "The Advancement of the Canning Industry," *ISR* 14 (Dec. 1913): 351–55; L. T. Rush, "The Passing of the Boiler-Maker," *ISR* 14 (April 1914): 592–93; James E. Griffith, "Modern Office Machinery," *ISR* 14 (April 1914): 622–24; Jack Morton, "Carrying Coal by Pipe Line," *ISR* 14 (May 1914): 691; Barbara Lidy Frankenthal, "The Advent of the Diesel Motor," *ISR* 15 (Sept. 1914): 163–66; Paul L. Wright, "The Revolution in Car Building," *ISR* 15 (Dec. 1914): 350–52; Mary Marcy, "Auto Car Making," *ISR* 15 (Jan. 1915): 406–12; Anon., "Good By, Section Gangs!" *ISR* 16 (Sept. 1915): 167–68; Fania Mindell, "Machine Millinery," *ISR* 16 (Sept. 1915): 173–74; Anon., "The Passing of the Telegraph Operator," *ISR* 16 (May 1916): 686; "Foot-Propelled Vehicles," *ISR* 17 (Oct. 1916): 218;

Anon., "Automatic Breadmaking," *ISR* 17 (Dec. 1916): 349–53; Austin Lewis, "Shop Control," *ISR* 17 (May 1917): 640–49; Scott Nearing, "The Man and the Machine," *ISR* 18 (July 1917): 43–48; Glenn Warren, "Coal Mining by Machine and the Changes It Has Brought," *ISR* 18 (Nov.-Dec. 1917): 288–91.

ISR not only chronicled changes occurring in the industrial sector but also examined the effects of mechanization and technical innovations in agriculture. For examples, see Ernest F. Lydison, "The Cotton Picking Machine," *ISR* 12 (July 1911): 29; Lynn W. Ellis, "How the Machine Is Making History on the Farm," *ISR* 14 (April 1914): 641–49; Grace Silver, "Capitalist Farming," *ISR* 13 (Oct. 1912): 358–62; Jean L. Haskins, "The Modern Flail," *ISR* 13 (March 1913): 677–79; Winden E. Frankweiler, "The New Harvester: Another 'Job-Killer,'" *ISR* 13 (May 1913): 810–12; Robert Johnstone Wheeler, "The Agriculture Industry," *ISR* 14 (July 1913): 34–39; *ISR* 14 (Aug. 1913): 94–98; D. Lopez, "The Land, the Machine and the Worker," *ISR* 15 (Nov. 1914): 306; Nils H. Hanson, "Threshing Wheat," *ISR* 16 (Dec. 1915): 344–47; J. A. MacDonald, "A New Chapter in the Industrial Revolution," *ISR* 16 (Dec. 1915): 347–49; Henry P. Richardson, "Scientific Organizing and the Farmer," *ISR* 16 (March 1915): 554–58.

For additional discussions of technological changes and managerial innovations and their effects on the work force, see Ellen Wetherell, "Uncle Sam's Wage Slaves at Work in the Washington Bureau of Printing and Engraving," *ISR* 13 (July 1912): 29–32; Rose Pastor Stokes, "The Slave Driver," *ISR* 13 (Aug. 1912): 133 (on the alarm clock); Robert M. Lackey, "How the Winchester Repeating Arms Company Rifles the Workers," *ISR* 13 (Nov. 1912): 396–99; W. S. Morrow, "Good-Bye, Morse," *ISR* 14 (Aug. 1913): 99–100; Winden Frankweiler, "The Latest in Shipbuilding," *ISR* 14 (Sept. 1913): 154–57; Ellen Wetherell, "Among the Cotton Mills," *ISR* 14 (Jan. 1914): 416–19; R. B. Tobias, "Spot-knocking," *ISR* 16 (Dec. 1915): 337–41; Harrison George, "Sulphur and Brimstone: A Hell of a Job!" *ISR* 16 (Dec. 1915): 351–52.

18. Robert Rives LaMonte, "The New Socialism," *ISR* 13 (Sept. 1912): 205–16, and "How to Kick," *ISR* 11 (Jan. 1911): 402–7.

19. For examples, see Mann, "The Way to Win," 220; Eugene Debs, "The Crime of Craft Unionism," *ISR* 11 (March 1911): 513–17; William D. Haywood, "The General Strike," *ISR* 11 (May 1911): 680–84; "Sabotage: A Successful Strike Weapon," *ISR* 13 (July 1912): 73–74.

20. Vincent St. John, "The Brotherhood of Capital and Labor: Its Effect on Labor," *ISR* 10 (Jan. 1910): 587–93; A. Ledots, "The National Civic Federation," *ISR* 10 (March 1910): 801–10. For earlier discussions of the National Civic Federation and the National Association of Manufacturers, see A. M. Simons, "Our Real Antagonist" [editorial], *ISR* 3 (June 1903): 745–47; Max Hayes, "The World of Labor," *ISR* 5 (March 1905): 565–68, and 7 (June 1907): 753–56.

21. For a sampling of the type of arguments put forward to counter the reform impetus, see "Suppose Everything Were Reformed!" *ISR* 11 (Oct. 1910): 241; Henry Slobodin, "Compulsory Compensation or State Insurance—Which?" *ISR* 11 (June

1911): 744–47; Phillips Russell, "Wage Minimummery," *ISR* 13 (Aug. 1912): 155–56 (a criticism of minimum wage laws); Frank Bohn, "The National Progressive Party," *ISR* 13 (Sept. 1912): 228–32; M.E.M. [Mary E. Marcy], "The White Flag Agreement Brigade" [editorial], *ISR* 13 (April 1913): 760–62 (a piece in opposition to binding agreements in contracts between capital and labor); Charles Edward Russell, "The Invisible Government," *ISR* 14 (Aug. 1913): 71–75 (a piece on the National Association of Manufacturers); Gustavus Myers, "Only One Goal," *ISR* 14 (Oct. 1913): 214–15 (an analysis of Canadian corporate liberalism); William E. Towne, "Straight Revolutionary Program the Only Solution," *ISR* 15 (Dec. 1914): 363–65; Carl Sandburg, "The Two Mr. Rockefellers—and Mr. Walsh," *ISR* 15 (July 1915): 18–25; Carl Sandburg, "That Walsh Report," *ISR* 15 (Oct. 1915): 198–201 (a series of discussions on the Commission of Industrial Relations). For an informative analysis from the monthly's earlier period, see Joseph E. Cohen, "Reform," *ISR* 7 (Dec. 1906): 347–53.

22. Kerr, "Ten Eventful Years."

23. "Our Opportunity" [editorial], *ISR* 13 (July 1912): 74.

24. Paulo Freire, *Pedagogy of the Oppressed* (New York: Seabury Press, 1970). For examples of the types of socialist pedagogy that Kerr and his associates promoted, see Joseph Cohen, "Socialism for Students," *ISR* 9 (Dec. 1908): 416–22; *ISR* 9 (Jan. 1909): 490–98; *ISR* 9 (Feb. 1909): 581–88; *ISR* 9 (March 1909): 674–82; *ISR* 9 (April 1909): 778–86; *ISR* 9 (May 1909): 870–80; *ISR* 9 (June 1909): 965–74; and *ISR* 10 (July 1909): 13–22 (Kerr later produced this particular serialization in pamphlet form under the same title, Joseph Cohen, *Socialism for Students* [Chicago: Charles H. Kerr & Company, 1910]). Also see Mary Marcy, "The Cause of Rising Prices," *ISR* 10 (March 1910): 769–74; "Beginner's Course in Socialism," *ISR* 12 (July 1911): 37–39; "Are You a Socialist?" *ISR* 12 (Aug. 1911): 106–7; "Can a Socialist Serve 'All the People'?" *ISR* 12 (Sept. 1911): 150–51; "Why the Socialist Party Is Different," *ISR* 13 (Aug. 1912): 157; "The Value of Immorality," *ISR* 15 (March 1915): 528–29; "What You Have to Sell?," *ISR* 16 (Sept. 1915): 141–43; "Economic Power," *ISR* 18 (Feb. 1918): 401–5; Guy McClung, "The Big Threes," *ISR* 13 (Sept. 1912): 222; "The Simplicity of Socialism," *ISR* 13 (Oct. 1912): 331; Leslie H. Marcy, "Why a Workingman Should Vote the Socialist Ticket," *ISR* 12 (Nov. 1911): 394–95; Gustavus Myers, "Capitalist Political Parties," *ISR* 13 (July 1912): 38–45; James Connolly, "Workshop Talks," *ISR* 17 (July 1917): 42; J. E. Sinclair, "Study Course in Scientific Socialism," *ISR* 14 (Nov. 1913): 294–95; *ISR* 14 (Dec. 1913): 358–62; *ISR* 14 (Jan. 1914): 424–28; *ISR* 14 (Feb. 1914): 487–92; *ISR* 14 (March 1914): 556–58; *ISR* 14 (April 1914): 611–13; *ISR* 14 (May 1914): 676–78; *ISR* 14 (June 1914): 748–51; *ISR* 15 (July 1914): 51–54; Austin Lewis, "What Do the Workers Work For?" *ISR* 18 (Feb. 1918): 410–13.

25. For examples from *ISR*'s earlier period, see Harlow Gale, "The Relation of Instructor and Student," *ISR* 1 (Feb. 1901): 486–92; May Wood Simons, "Education and Socialism," *ISR* 1 (April 1901): 600–607; George McA. Miller, "The Social Spirit of the N.E.A.," *ISR* 2 (Sept. 1901): 196–200; May Simons, "Democracy

and Education," *ISR* 3 (Aug. 1902): 89–96; and Editorial [A. M. Simons], "The Ignorance of Schools," *ISR* 4 (Sept. 1903): 174–78. For later examples, see Henry Leffmann, "Capitalistic Control of Education," *ISR* 9 (July 1908): 25–33; and Austin Lewis, "Socialism and Education," *ISR* 9 (Nov. 1908): 373–79.

26. See the ten-part serialization of J. Howard Moore's "Savage Survivals in Higher Peoples," which ran from March through December 1915, and Mary Marcy's lengthy series "Stories of the Cave People," which ran in two installments, from April to October 1909 and from October 1915 through June 1916. See Wilhelm Böelsche, "The Love Adventures of the Spider," *ISR* 15 (May 1915): 659–62; "The Love-Troubles of the Stickle Back," *ISR* 15 (June 1915): 744–46; "The Love Duel of the Snail," *ISR* 16 (Jan. 1916): 397–99; and "The Origin and Earliest Traces of Man," *ISR* 17 (Aug. 1916): 108–11. For other examples of articles drawing from the natural sciences, see August Schnitzler, "The Love Affairs of the Fiddler Crabs," *ISR* 16 (Nov. 1915): 289–91; Royal Dixon, "Electric Plants," *ISR* 16 (March 1916): 536–38; Frankenthal Weissenburg, "The Ways of the Ant," *ISR* 16 (April 1916): 606–8; Eliza Frances Andrews, "Socialism in the Plant World," *ISR* 17 (July 1916): 18–19; and Hennydena Nederd, "The House Fly as a Carrier of Disease," *ISR* 17 (July 1916): 26–28.

Concerned with scientific and technological advances, *ISR* often carried general informative pieces. See W. O. Wing, "Making Sugar in the Laboratory," *ISR* 10 (April 1910): 888–89; S. Walsh, "The Mono-Rail," *ISR* 10 (Feb. 1910): 738–40; William E. Dixon, "The Steam Engine," *ISR* 10 (Feb. 1910): 728–33; Jack Morton, "The Story of the Telephone," *ISR* 10 (May 1910): 1027–29; and J. O. Phillips, "Carrying Water 250 Miles," *ISR* 10 (May 1910): 982–84.

27. "The Library of Science for the Workers," a series begun in 1905, featured ten titles on evolution and natural history by 1917. The list of titles included, Wilhelm Böelsche's *The Evolution of Man* and *The Triumph of Life*; E. Teichmann, *Life and Death*; Dr. M. Wilhelm Meyer, *The End of the World* and *The Making of the World*; R. H France, *Germs of Mind in Plants*; Friedrich Nietzsche, *Human, All Too Human*; Ernest Unterman, *Science and Revolution*; Paul Lafargue, *Social and Philosophical Studies*; and Arthur M. Lewis, *Evolution, Social and Organic*. Kerr offered the "Library of Sociology," twenty of his previously published titles "on the subject of Sociology and closely related topics, . . . writen from the view of Marxian Socialism," to readers of the *Review* in 1916–17. "Library of Science for the Workers," *ISR* 17 (May 1917): 694. "Library of Sociology," *ISR* 17 (Aug. 1916): 127.

28. "Ridpath's *History of the World*," *ISR* 13 (Nov. 1912): 385; "Webster's *Universal Dictionary*," *ISR* 13 (Feb. 1913): 582; Buckle's *History of Civilization*," *ISR* 17 (Oct. 1916): 194, 196.

29. The early *ISR* contained a number of pieces on art and literature from a socialist perspective. See May Wood Simons, "Art and Socialism," *ISR* 2 (April 1902): 710–14; Austin Lewis, "The Revolt of the Artist," *ISR* 3 (June 1903): 720–24; Giovanni B. Civale, "Socialism and Art," *ISR* 8 (Jan. 1908); John Fry, "The Negation of Form," *ISR* 9 (July 1908): 20–25; and Francis Perkins, "Henrik Ibsen, the

Iconoclast," *ISR* 10 (July 1909): 40–49. Concern with the fine arts continued well into the later period. See Phillips Russell, "Constantin Meunier, Sculptor of Labor," *ISR* 14 (May 1914): 661–63; Arthur Ruskin, "The Potter and His Clay," *ISR* 16 (Sept. 1915): 158–60; Eleanor Wentworth, "Outcasts," *ISR* 16 (Jan. 1916): 418–19; and William Marion Reedy, "Robert Minor," *ISR* 17 (July 1916): 46–47.

For some of the best examples of biting wit and satire that appeared in the monthly consult the several pieces, mainly short, pithy aphorisms by William D. Haywood: "Pick and Shovel Pointers," *ISR* 11 (Feb. 1911): 458; "Shots for the Workshop," *ISR* 11 (April 1911): 588; "Pick and Shovel Pointers," *ISR* 12 (July 1911): 7; "A Detective," *ISR* 11 (Dec. 1911): 345; and "Blanket Stiff Philosophy," *ISR* 11 (Dec. 1911): 370.

For an engaging bit of fiction written by one of Kerr and Company's inner circle, see Mary Marcy's "Out of the Dump," a story that originally ran in monthly installments between June and November 1908. Several stories by Jack London also made their debut in the pages of the *ISR:* "The Dream of Debs," *ISR* 9 (Jan. 1909): 481–561, and 8 (Feb. 1909): 561–70; "The Apostate," *ISR* 9 (June 1909): 929–45; "Revolution," *ISR* 10 (Aug. 1909): 97–112; "The Army of the Revolution," *ISR* 14 (May 1914): 659–61; "South of the Slot," *ISR* 15 (July 1914): 7–17; and "The Enemy of All the World," *ISR* 15 (Sept. 1914): 167–75.

A compilation of the poetic contributions to the *ISR* over its span of eighteen years would fill a sizable volume in and of itself. Quite varied in tone, style, and literary merit, the poetry published in the monthly's pages conveyed the temper, emotion, and sentiment of the times and the artist militants who attempted to convey the sense of optimism and tragedy that shaped the subjective mood of the movement. See Frederick F. Rockwell, "Strike off Thy Chains!" *ISR* 9 (Sept. 1908): 197–98; Covington Hall, "In the Holy Name of Trade," *ISR* 9 (April 1909): 793; Mounce Byrd, "The Hand of Socialism," *ISR* 10 (July 1909): 49; Nicholas Klein, *ISR* 10 (Sept. 1909): 236; Jack Phelan, "The City Beautiful," *ISR* 10 (Feb. 1910): 713; Edwin Brenholz, "I Have Seen and I Have Vowed," *ISR* 10 (April 1910): 917–18; Arturo Giovannitti, "The Republic," *ISR* 13 (July 1912): 21, and "The Walker," *ISR* 13 (Sept. 1912): 201–4; Rose Pastor Stokes, "The Slave Driver," *ISR* 13 (Aug. 1912): 113; A Paint Creek Miner [Ralph Chaplin], "Mother" Jones," *ISR* 14 (April 1914): 604–5; Covington Hall, "Us, the Hoboes," *ISR* 14 (April 1914): 610; Ted Robinson, "The Ignorant Masses," *ISR* 14 (May 1914): 693; Upton Sinclair, "To Frank Tannenbaum in Prison," *ISR* 14 (June 1914): 756; C. S. [Carl Sandberg], "Boes," *ISR* 16 (Aug. 1915): 78, and "Child of the Romans," *ISR* 17 (Jan. 1916): 393; Wilfrid Gribble, "A Song of Revolt," *ISR* 16 (March 1916): 531; Carl Sandberg, "Ashes and Dreams," *ISR* 15 (May 1915): 671, and "Billy Sunday," *ISR* 16 (Sept. 1915): 152–53; Ralph Chaplin, "Joe Hill," *ISR* 16 (Dec. 1915): 325.

30. Robert Rives LaMonte, "Methods of Propaganda," *ISR* 8 (Feb. 1908): 456–65; William Restelle Shier, "How to Sell Literature," *ISR* 9 (March 1909): 703–5; J. G. Phelps-Stokes, "Campaign Methods," *ISR* 10 (March 1910): 835–38; Arthur M. Lewis, "Example Book Talks," *ISR* 11 (Aug. 1910): 11–112; Wilfrid Gribble,

"How to Spread Propaganda," *ISR* 9 (May 1909): 921; Sol Fieldman, "How to Agitate in the Open Air," *ISR* 12 (Aug. 1911): 109–10; "An Effective Co-Operative Press," *ISR* 12 (Sept. 1911): 173–74; "National Socialist Lyceum Bureau," *ISR* 12 (April 1912): 666–67; Guy McClung, "Some More Don'ts," *ISR* 13 (July 1912): 61; Arthur Brooks Baker, "Be a Party Builder," *ISR* 13 (Sept. 1912): 259–62; Grace Silver, "Public Speaking," *ISR* 13 (May 1913): 807–9; E. E. Kirk and Harry M. McKee, "Propaganda in Jails and Prisons," *ISR* 14 (Oct. 1913): 231–32; Frank Bohn, "The Local Headquarters as a Social Center," *ISR* 14 (Jan. 1914): 420–22; William D. Haywood, "Tactics of the Unemployed," *ISR* 15 (Nov. 1914): 266–68; Anon., "Make an Ally of Your Enemy," *ISR* 15 (Jan. 1915): 425–27; Jim Higgins (pseud.), "Talkers and Doers," *ISR* 16 (Nov. 1915): 300–301; Anon., "How to Fight on the Job," *ISR* 16 (April 1916): 619–21.

The Kerr Company maintained an ongoing concern for the spoken word. Instruction on the best methods and techniques of public speaking for the street, meeting hall, or auditorium appeared continually in *ISR:* Henry Gaines Hawn, "The Art of Public Speaking," *ISR* 13 (Feb. 1913): 601–2, and 13 (March 1913): 673–74; Frank Bohn, "Public Speaking: The Great Orations of American History," *ISR* 13 (Feb. 1913): 603–5; Jack Morton, "Debating," *ISR* 13 (Feb. 1913): 674–76; Grace Silver, "Public Speaking: Pratical Soap Boxing," *ISR* 13 (April 1913): 737–39, and "Public Speaking: Lecturing," *ISR* 13 (May 1913): 778–79; Jules Scarceriaux, "The Importance of a Library in Labor Organization," *ISR* 17 (July 1916): 43.

31. *ISR*'s circulation reached three thousand at the beginning of 1908. By the end of that year, it increased to ten thousand. By July 1910 circulation went up to twenty-six thousand; by June 1911 it climbed to forty thousand. [Charles H. Kerr], "Publisher's Department," 12 (July 1911): 1.

32. Organizers and militants used the *ISR* as a combination fund-raiser and organizing tool during protracted strikes or free speech fights. See "News and Views," *ISR* 10 (Dec. 1909): 557–58. For a sampling of the direct manor in which activists used the publication, see Elizabeth Gurley Flynn, "The Free Speech Fight at Spokane," *ISR* 10 (Dec. 1909): 483–89; "The Free Speech Fight," [editorial], *ISR* 10 (Jan. 1910): 642; Maurice E. Eldridge, "Preston and Smith," *ISR* 10 (April 1910): 894–98; Eugene Debs, "Help! Help!! Help!!!" *ISR* 11 (Jan. 1911): 394; Elizabeth Gurley Flynn, "Shall This Man Serve Ten Years in Sing Sing?" *ISR* 11 (May 1911): 685–88; William D. Haywood, "Get Ready," *ISR* 11 (June 1911): 725–27; "Ettor and Giovannitti Must Be Saved," *ISR* 13 (July 1912): 19; "Shall Ettor and Giovannitti Be Murdered?" *ISR* 13 (Sept. 1912): 245–46; Jack Morton, "The Trial of the Timber Workers," *ISR* 13 (Nov. 1912): 407; Vincent St. John, "The Fight for Free Speech at San Diego," *ISR* 12 (April 1912): 649; "To the Rescue," *ISR* 14 (June 1914): 757; "Save Joe Hill," *ISR* 16 (Aug. 1915): 126; William D. Haywood, "Sentenced to Be Shot: Act Quick!" *ISR* 16 (Aug. 1915): 110; "George Andreytchine," *ISR* 17 (Sept. 1916): 170; Robert Minor, "The San Francisco Frame-up," *ISR* 17 (Oct. 1916): 216–22; "Will Labor Stand for Another Haymarket?" *ISR* 17 (Dec. 1916): 360–63; "Keep Your Eyes on Everett," *ISR* 17 (April 1917): 608–9; Eugene

V. Debs, "Tom Mooney Sentenced to Death: An Appeal to the Organized Workers of America," *ISR* 17 (April 1917): 613–14.

33. For a sampling, see Clarence Clowe, "The Situation in China," *ISR* 9 (Aug. 1908): 119–25; George Whitfield, "Present Conditions in Cuba and the Outlook," *ISR* 9 (Aug. 1908): 137–39; "The Revolt in Spain," *ISR* 10 (Sept. 1909): 250–52; H. Scott Bennett, "Forces Making for Industrial Unionism in Australia," *ISR* 10 (Nov. 1909): 446–48; James Edwards, "The Same Old Spain," *ISR* 10 (Dec. 1909): 494–96; Dan Sproud, "The Situation in British Columbia," *ISR* 10 (Feb. 1910): 741–44; W. O. Wing, "Mining Graphite in India," *ISR* 10 (March 1910): 779–81; H. A. Talchekar, "Mill Operatives of India," *ISR* 11 (July 1910): 22–25; William E. Bohn, "Suppressing Socialism in Argentine," *ISR* 11 (Sept. 1910): 171–73; Omar Vayia, "Factories Abolish Caste in India," *ISR* 11 (Oct. 1910): 196–98; Jack Morton, "Capital in Guatemala," *ISR* 11 (Dec. 1910): 349–51; "Flashes from China," *ISR* 11 (March 1911): 518–19; Leah Gay, "Porto Rico," *ISR* 11 (March 1911): 545–48; Archibald Crawford, "The Class War in South Africa," *ISR* 12 (Aug. 1911): 76–83; Henry Flury, "Manila's Shame," *ISR* 12 (Aug. 1911): 108–9; Sun Yat Sen, "The Chinese Revolution and the Socialist Questions Involved," *ISR* 13 (Oct. 1912): 339–40; Lina Lane McBride, "A Voice from Porto Rico," *ISR* 16 (July 1915): 31–32, and "Women Workers of Porto Rico," *ISR* 17 (June, 1917): 717–19.

As part of the overall educational attempt to aid in the development of well-rounded, class-conscious worker-activists, Kerr and his associates quite often ran what might be described as left-wing travel pieces—articles from different parts of the world describing life in general and the living conditions of the popular classes. For a sampling, see Henry Flury, "The Bontoc Igorots," *ISR* 11 (Nov. 1910): 267–70; Lindley Vinton, "Tropical Agriculture," *ISR* 11 (June 1911): 754–58; Jack Morton, "The Story of Rubber in the Kongo Free State," *ISR* 11 (June 1911): 291–92; Mary Marcy, "Changing China," *ISR* 13 (Jan. 1913): 528–32; Estelle Baker, "The Molokai Leper Colony," *ISR* 14 (Jan. 1914): 411; George Hardy, "Black and White in the Congo," *ISR* 17 (Jan. 1917): 414–16; R. R. Hornbeck, "The Isle of Java," *ISR* 17 (Feb. 1917): 466–71; "Seeing Sarawak, in Borneo," *ISR* 17 (March 1917): 542–46; "A Ramble Through the Streets of a Chinese City," *ISR* 17 (May 1917): 679–81; S. G. Rich, "Notes on Natal," *ISR* 17 (June 1917): 723–26; Margaret Starr, "Filling the Sugar Bowl," *ISR* 18 (July 1917): 18–21; R. R. Hornbeck, "The Rubber Industry in Malaya," *ISR* 18 (Sept. 1917): 163–65; "Moving Pictures of the East," *ISR* 18 (Oct. 1917): 218–20. For a clear sense of this type of article submitted exclusively to *ISR* by a voyager with a critical eye, see the numerous articles sent from the Pacific by Marion Wright: "Glimpses of Formosa," *ISR* 14 (April 1914): 598–600; "Hemp Growing and Rope Making in the Philippines," *ISR* 14 (May 1914): 673–75; "The Poor Man's Smoke," *ISR* 15 (July 1914): 25–29; "Our Subjects in the Far South Seas," *ISR* 15 (Aug. 1914): 96–99; "The Cocoanut in the Philippines," *ISR* 15 (April 1915): 608–10; "The Japanese Farmer," *ISR* 15 (June 1915): 735–39; "The Story of Hawaiian Sugar," *ISR* 16 (July 1915): 27–31; "Taro: The Oriental Poor Man's Bread," *ISR* 16 (Aug. 1915): 88–91; "Philippine School Craft," *ISR*

16 (March 1916): 526–28; "Virgin Forests of the Philippines," *ISR* 17 (July 1916): 33–35; "The Hawaiian Pineapple," *ISR* 17 (Aug. 1916): 84–86; and "About Bananas," *ISR* 17 (Oct. 1916): 224–25.

34. Kerr insider and *ISR* illustrator Ralph Chaplin's memoir recounted several meetings with notable figures of the international left whom he met at the Kerr Company offices. They included Jim Larkin and James Connolly and a number of Mexican revolutionaries. Kerr developed a close friendship with the Japanese socialist Sen Katayama, who visited regularly on his several sojourns in the United States. Chaplin, *Wobbly*, passim.

ISR editorial board member William E. Bohn continued his monthly column of "International Notes" up to the period of U.S. entry into World War I. In summary form, that particular section of the magazine supplied one of the richest contemporary chronicles of developments of the socialist and labor movements globally. For examples of the types of articles concerning events in Europe that helped the left-wing iron out and substantiate its developing analyses, positions, and tactics, see J. O. Bentall, "The General Strike in Sweden," *ISR* 10 (Nov. 1909): 392–96; H. M. Hyndman, "Revolutionary Social-Democracy: The Curse of Compromise in Great Britain," *ISR* 10 (Feb. 1910): 681–85; Hendrik DeMan (trans. Charles H. Kerr), "The Working Class Movement in Belgium," *ISR* 10 (April 1910): 907–14; Giovanni B. Civale, "The Strike of the Seamen at Marseilles, France," *ISR* 11 (July 1910): 32–33; Robert J. Wheeler, "The Way to Win," *ISR* 11 (Oct. 1910): 226–27; William Bohn, "Carl Liebknecht," *ISR* 11 (Nov. 1910): 289–90; William D. Haywood, "News from Europe: The Great French Railway Strike and the Leaven of Socialism in England," *ISR* 11 (Dec. 1910): 336–40, and "Lockouts in Great Britain," *ISR* 11 (Jan. 1911): 415–16; Tom Mann, "The Class War in England," *ISR* 11 (May 1911): 706–9, and 11 (June 1911): 768–69; "The Masters of the Bread: The Great Strike in England," *ISR* 12 (Oct. 1911): 197–98; Ben Tillett, "On the Right Road," *ISR* 12 (Oct. 1911): 203–9; Tom Mann, "The Transport Workers' Strike in England," *ISR* 12 (Dec. 1911): 351–55; Samuel W. Ball, "Industrial Socialism in Italy," 13 (March 1913): 684–85; Anton Pannekoek, "The Election in Germany," *ISR* 13 (March 1913): 557–62; Tom Mann, "The Uprising of the British Miners," *ISR* 12 (May 1912): 711–16; "The Fight with Folded Arms," *ISR* 13 (June 1913): 864–68; "A Plea for Solidarity," *ISR* 14 (Jan. 1914): 392–94; Emile Pouget, "Syndicalism in France," *ISR* 15 (Aug. 1914): 100–105; Jim Larkin, "The Underman," *ISR* 15 (March 1915): 538–42.

35. Kerr purchased the book and pamphlet end of the Appeal to Reason Publishing Company early in 1909 when the *Appeal's* publisher, Julius Wayland, decided to forego the handling of books and pamphlets and concentrate his energies on his weekly. Kerr reprinted a few of the pamphlets from the newly acquired lists and removed the rest from circulation because most duplicated information contained in the standard books that the company published. As part of the deal negotiated with the Kansas publisher, Kerr agreed to pay for five years' worth of advertising space in the *Appeal*. Charles H. Kerr, "We Have Bought the Book Business of the *Appeal to Reason*," *ISR* 9 (Feb. 1909): 636.)

36. "Special to *Review* Readers," *ISR* 13 (March 1913): 691; "Combination Offer," *ISR* 16 (March 1916): 575.

37. "$10.00 Share and $15.00 Worth of Books Prepaid for $15.00," *ISR* 10 (April 1910): 956; "Share of Stock Free with $14.00 Book Order," *ISR* 12 (July 1911): 1, 4; "Forty Volume Socialist Library for $10.00," *ISR* 11 (Jan. 1911): 440.

38. "What Debs Says," *ISR* 12 (Oct. 1911): 256.

39. "We Will Pay Six Per Cent," *ISR* 10 (June 1910): 1144; "Four Per Cent and Safety," *ISR* 17 (March 1917): 627.

40. "A Socialist Library Free," *ISR* 13 (Nov. 1912): 448; "Full Set of Marx," *ISR* 15 (Sept. 1914): 189; "Free with Five Subscriptions, 20" x 16" Portrait of Marx," *ISR* 15 (May 1912): 750; "Stereopticon Par Excellence," *ISR* 13 (March 1913): 642; "Four Socialist Classics to Be Given Away," *ISR* 13 (April 1913): 710; "New Encyclopedia," *ISR* 14 (March 1914): 561; "Portraits of Revolutionary Comrades," *ISR* 16 (Nov. 1915): 320; "Buckle's *History of Civilization*," *ISR* 17 (Aug. 1916): rear cover.

41. *ISR* 12 (Dec. 1911): 383. The text of the advertisement, pitched to "Socialist Comrades and Locals," noted that the record player could be "so adjusted as to carry the sound to a large crowd" and suggested that it could enhance a wide range of left-wing gatherings: "Open and close your meetings with the 'Marseillaise' and other revolutionary songs and pieces. The more entertaining you make your meetings, the larger they will be."

42. "*Review* Will Send Fifty Comrades to Europe," *ISR* 14 (Oct. 1913); "Free Trip to San Francisco World's Fair," *ISR* 15 (April 1915): 668, 739.

43. "A Free Ford Five-Passenger Touring Car or Run About for You or Your Local," *ISR* 17 (July 1916): 2; "A Soap Box on Wheels: Fording It for Socialism," *ISR* 17 (Sept. 1916): 129.

44. "Write to Our Advertisers," and "The *Review* Enlarged Again," both in *ISR* 11 (April 1911): 652. Advertising revenue increased from $77.77 in 1909, to $1,774.28 in 1911, and to $2,811.42 in 1912. Total company expenditures for the latter year approached $75,000. *ISR* receipts increased from $10,913.54 in 1909 and $23,780.31 in 1911 to $25,887.10 the following year. "All Records Broken," *ISR* 10 (Dec. 1909): 569; "Annual Report," *ISR* 12 (Feb. 1912): 521; *ISR* 13 (Feb. 1913): 636.

45. For a sampling of the types of advertisements in *ISR*, see "Make $20.00 a Day," "Deafness Successfully Treated," "Let Me Cure You of Rheumatism Free," "Turkish Baths at Home Do Wonders," and "Don't Wear a Truss," all in *ISR* 13 (Feb. 1913): 640; "Law—University Instruction at Home," *ISR* 13 (March 1913): 643; "Let Us Make You Fat," *ISR* 13 (June 1913): 843; "Typewriter Sensation," "Tobacco Habit—How to Be Easily Rid of It," and "Electricity—Nature's Cure," *ISR* 17 (Aug. 1916): 114, 115, 121; "Write to Our Advertisers," *ISR* 11 (April 1911): 652; and "The *Review* Enlarged Again." *ISR* advertising revenue increased from $77.77 in 1909 to $1,774.28 in 1911 and $2,811.42 in 1912. Total company expendi-

tures for the latter year approached $75,000. *ISR* receipts increased from $10,913.54 in 1909, to $23,780.31 in 1911, and to $25,887.10 the following year. "All Records Broken," *ISR* 10 (Dec. 1909): 569; "Annual Report," *ISR* 12 (Feb. 1912): 521; *ISR* 13 (Feb. 1913): 636.

With the coming of World War I, revenue from advertisers declined. It dropped to $1,571.62 in 1914; by 1917 had it slowed to $811.50. Total receipts for the company plummeted throughout the war period, but operating expenses, mainly because of increases in the cost of paper, mounted steadily. "Annual Report," *ISR* 15 (Feb. 1915): 503; [Charles H. Kerr], "Publisher's Department," *ISR* 18 (Feb. 1918): 431.

46. Kerr had sold another two hundred shares by September 1913 and an additional hundred by March 1915. The capital garnered through the sale of shares went directly toward the production of new volumes and imprints. "Reason for Buying Stock," *ISR* 13 (Oct. 1912): 384, 14 (Sept. 1913): 129, 15 (March 1915): 575.

47. The arrangement with the American News Company allowed news dealers to return unsold issues to Kerr. That resulted in a heavy loss for the publisher because of additional freight, postage, and handling. Kerr halted the arrangement in December 1909. From then on he turned more and more to direct bulk distribution by movement "hustlers." [Charles H. Kerr], "Publisher's Department," *ISR* 10 (Dec. 1909): 567, and 10 (Jan. 1910): 668–69.

48. Kerr had initially used the subscription card system during the 1890s when he was publisher of *New Time*. The system was quite simple. An annual subscription to *ISR* came with three to five cards that offered a discount on the monthly. The subscriber made a small profit by selling the cards that covered the cost of the original subscription; if sold, they reimbursed the initial subscriber. [Charles H. Kerr], "Publisher's Department," *ISR* 12 (Dec. 1911): 381.

49. [Charles H. Kerr], "Publisher's Department," *ISR* 11 (July 1910): 60–61; *ISR* 12 (Feb. 1912): 521.

50. *ISR* 11 (Jan. 1911): 440. Circulation increased to fifty thousand early in the spring of 1912. *ISR* 12 (May 1912): 798–800.

51. "Hustler's April Combination," *ISR* 10 (April 1910): 954; "Socialist Hustlers Wanted," *ISR* 12 (Oct. 1911): 252. Individual hustlers ordered from one to seven or eight hundred copies monthly. The method worked so well that Kerr promoted the sales scheme on one occasion by suggesting that an *ISR* salesman could make a living wage. "News and Views," *ISR* 11 (July 1910): 55; [Charles H. Kerr], "Publisher's Department," 11 (Jan. 1911): 440.

52. [Charles H. Kerr], "Publisher's Department," *ISR* 11 (Feb. 1911): 506–7.

53. "Exchange of Stock for Literature," *ISR* 12 (July 1911): 4.

54. "Exchange of Stock for Literature," 1, 4.

55. "Socialist Partners Wanted," *ISR* 13 (Oct. 1912): 384.

56. "Annual Stockholder's Meeting," *ISR* 13 (Feb. 1913): 636–37; *ISR* 14 (Feb. 1914): 508–9.

Chapter 10: The War Years and After

1. The several standard works on the American left and the war period that informed this chapter include Weinstein, *Decline of Socialism in America*; H. C. Petersen and Gilbert C. Fite, *Opponents of War, 1917–1918* (Seattle: University of Washington Press, 1957); William Preston, Jr., *Aliens and Dissenters* (New York: Harper and Row, 1966); Draper, *The Roots of American Communism*; Robert K. Murray, *Red Scare* (New York: McGraw-Hill, 1955); Dubofsky, *We Shall Be All*; Robert Justin Goldstein, *Political Repression in Modern America* (Cambridge: Schenkman, 1978), chs. 4, 5; Philip S. Foner, *History of the Labor Movement in the United States*, vol. 7: *Labor and World War I, 1914–1818* (New York: International Publishers, 1987.)

2. The Socialist Party listed some 323 dailies, weeklies, and monthlies in 1913. Of those in existence at the time of U.S. entry into the war, few survived. Within five months after the declaration of war every leading socialist publication had been barred from the mails at least once. Other socialist papers, especially in smaller cities and towns, faced the wrath of "vigilance committees" that were often organized by local chambers of commerce. Those publications soon passed from existence. By mid-1918 the remaining socialist press consisted almost entirely of periodicals published in larger cities not dependent on the mail for distribution. Weinstein, *Decline of Socialism*, 84–93.

3. From its earliest days, *ISR* carried numerous poems, short stories, and essays that voiced ongoing opposition to militarism. See Ernest Crosby, "The Hero," *ISR* 2 (Oct. 1901): 280; Caroline Pemberton, "The Patriot," *ISR* 3 (Jan. 1903): 420–25; "Organized Labor and the Militia," *ISR* 3 (March 1903): 540–43 [reprinted from the *St. Louis Arbeiter Zeitung*]; Maurice E. Eldridge, "Universal Military Service," *ISR* 8 (April 1908): 608–13; George D. Herron, "War and Peace Under Capitalism," *ISR* 9 (Dec. 1908): 431–43; Louis Duchez, "The U.S. Regular Army," *ISR* 10 (Jan. 1910): 628–31; William D. Haywood, "In Prison with Hervé," *ISR* 11 (March 1911): 513–17; Cloudesley Johns, "Now Is the Time," *ISR* 11 (April 1911): 613.

4. Sen Katayama, "Attitude of Japanese Socialists toward the Present War," *ISR* 4 (March 1904): 513–14; Isadore Ladoff, "The Japano-Russian War: Its Actual Causes and Probable Effects," *ISR* 4 (June 1904): 740–42; Denjiro Kotoku, "Japanese Socialists and the War," *ISR* 4 (June 1904): 757–59; Ernest Unterman, "The Truth about the War," *ISR* 5 (April 1905): 618–22.

5. Gustave Hervé, "Insurrection Rather Than War," *ISR* 11 (Nov. 1910): 272–73. Kerr imported five hundred of the English version of Hervé's declaration *My Country, Right or Wrong!* and offered them as specially bound, limited-edition premiums to *ISR* subscribers. [Charles H. Kerr], "Publisher's Department," *ISR* 11 (Nov. 1910): 316.

The key debates within the International revolved around the question of socialist action in the face of a war threat. The left wing of the movement called for mass action—the political or general strike. The right, more concerned with its parliamentary role and the question of legalism, voiced its opposition to such tactics. Another related question focused on the issue of a just war—the legitimacy of defensive wars against the designs of a foreign aggression. With the outbreak of the world war, the various socialist parties ran aground on the shoals of defense of the motherland or fatherland as each belligerent defined the other as the aggressor. For an extensive discussion of the differing opinions on the question within the International, see Cole, *A History of Socialist Thought*, vol. 3, part 1.

6. G. L. Harding, "Socialism and the World-War," *ISR* 15 (Sept. 1914): 141–43; Editorial [Mary Marcy], "The Real Fatherland," *ISR* 15 (Sept. 1914): 177–78; Anton Pannekoek, "The Great European War and Socialism," *ISR* 15 (Oct. 1914): 198–204; William E. Bohn, "The War, the People, and the Future," *ISR* 15 (Oct. 1914): 241–44; Charles Ashleigh, "The Job War in Chicago," *ISR* 15 (Nov. 1914): 262–65; National Union of Brewery Workers, England, "War News from Abroad: The Workers and the War," *ISR* 15 (Nov. 1914): 274–75; Clarence Darrow, "The Cost of War," *ISR* 15 (Dec. 1914): 361–62; Editorial [Charles H. Kerr], "The War Through Socialist Lenses," *ISR* 15 (Jan. 1915): 433–34; Phillips Russell, "Yes, but How about the War at Home?" *ISR* 15 (March 1915): 526–27; William E. Bohn, "The Class Struggle and the War," *ISR* 15 (May 1915): 686–92; Frederic C. Howe, "The Flag Follows the Investor," *ISR* 17 (July 1916): 11–14.

7. Chaplin, *Wobbly*, 106–12.

8. John K. Murray, "Mexico's Peon-Slaves Preparing for Revolution," *ISR* 9 (March 1910): 641–59; "The Private Prison of Diaz," *ISR* 9 (April 1909): 737–52; Mañuel Sarabia, "How I Was Kidnapped," *ISR* 9 (May 1909): 853–62; John K. Murray, "The Mexican Political Prisoners," *ISR* 9 (May 1909): 863–68.

9. Cy O. Brown, "Capitalism International: The Case of DeLara," *ISR* 10 (Dec. 1909): 509–11; C. M. Brooks, "Mexico Replies to the Appeal to Reason," *ISR* 11 (Oct. 1910): 211–12.

10. John K. Turner, "The American Partners of Diaz," *ISR* 11 (Dec. 1910): 321–28. For a discussion of the story behind the publication of Turner's book, which Kerr & Company published in 1911, see Sinclair Snow's introduction to its re-release: *Barbarous Mexico* (Austin: University of Texas Press, 1969).

11. Turner, "The American Partners of Diaz"; Mary Marcy[?], "Mexico, Our Capitalist's Slave Colony" [editorial], *ISR* 11 (Dec. 1910): 364.

12. John Kenneth Turner, "The Revolution in Mexico," *ISR* 11 (Jan. 1911): 417–23; "Withdraw the Troops," *ISR* 11 (April 1911): 585–88; John Kenneth Turner, "Why Mexican Workers Rebel," *ISR* 11 (April 1911): 589–92; George D. Brewer, "Murder as Patriotism," *ISR* 11 (April 1911): 592–93; [Charles H. Kerr], "Barbarous Mexico and Capitalist America," *ISR* 11 (April 11): 637; Ed Moore, "When the Workers Fold Their Arms," *ISR* 11 (June 1911): 729–30; "Manifest Destiny" [editorial], *ISR* 11 (June 1911): 774.

13. Eugene V. Debs, "The Crisis in Mexico," *ISR* 12 (July 1911): 22–24; "The Situation in Mexico" [editorial], *ISR* 12 (July 1911): 47–49; William C. Owen, "What Mexico's Struggle Means," *ISR* 12 (May 1912): 739–43; Guy A. Aldred, "Behind the Scenes in Mexico," *ISR* 14 (Dec. 1913): 344–46.

14. Mary Marcy, "Whose War Is This?" *ISR* 14 (June 1914): 729–31, emphasis in the original. The same issue contained several pieces on the situation in Mexico: "More Murdered Children," 731, Mañuel Sarabia, "The Situation in Mexico," 732–35, and "A Rich Man's War" [an editorial], 750. Marcy had not developed the particular line on working-class action against war alone. The question of the particular action that workers should take in time of war had perplexed the Second International almost from its inception, and several contributors to the *ISR* had helped deepen that particular debate within the American movement over an extended period. See Robert Rives LaMonte, "War on War," *ISR* 11 (May 1911): 661–64; Anton Pannekoek, "War against War," *ISR* 13 (Feb. 1913): 589–93, and 13 (March 1913): 663–65; and Vincent St. John, "The Working Class and War," *ISR* 15 (Aug. 1914): 117–18.

15. Clarence Darrow, "Patriotism," *ISR* 11 (Sept. 1910): 159–60; Anon., "From an U.S. Marine," *ISR* 11 (May 1911): 665; Lindsay Lewis, "Our Glorious Navy?" *ISR* 11 (May 1911): 675–79; W. G. Henry, "Patriots and Parasites," *ISR* 12 (Sept. 1911): 166–68; William E. Bohn, "Nationalism and Internationalism," *ISR* 12 (Jan. 1912): 432–34; Marion Wright, "Fresh Bait: 'Ware Suckers," and "In the Navy: The Other Side of the Paper," *ISR* 13 (Oct. 1912): 344–47; Ex-Marines in the U.S. Navy, "Untold Tales in the Navy," *ISR* 13 (Nov. 1912): 400–407; Marion Wright, "Truths about the Navy," *ISR* 13 (Dec. 1912): 481–86; Ex-Sailors and Soldiers, "News about the Army and Navy," *ISR* 13 (Jan. 1913): 547–49; Anon., "The Army and the Navy," *ISR* 13 (Feb. 1913): 616–19; Anon., "The Recruiting Officer and His Reward," *ISR* 13 (March 1913): 679–80; Marion Wright, "School of the Butcher," *ISR* 14 (Oct. 1913): 197–99; Jack London, "The 'Good' Soldier," *ISR* 14 (Oct. 1913): 199; Wilhelm Lamszus, "The Human Slaughterhouse," *ISR* 14 (Nov. 1913): 278–80; Anon., "In the Army," *ISR* 14 (April 1914): 602–3; Tom McConnell, "Letters of a Soldier to His Dad," *ISR* 14 (May 1914): 670–72.

16. Articles dealing specifically with Mexico continued to appear up through 1917. They tied their a support of the revolutionary forces and an opposition to further U.S. intervention to a criticism of American "monied interests." Each article attempted to pierce the patriotic rhetoric and mythology shrouding the actual motivations of those forces pushing for further direct U.S. involvement in the civil war. See W. W. Pannell, "Mexican Workers in the Southwest," *ISR* 16 (Sept. 1915): 168–69; David Bruce, "Bleeding Mexico," *ISR* 16 (April 1916): 581–86; Dante Barton, "Mexico for the Mexicans," *ISR* 17 (Aug. 1916): 87–88; George P. West, "Face to Face," *ISR* 17 (Aug. 1916): 100–102; Modesto C. Rolland, "Petroleum in Mexico," *ISR* 17 (Sept. 1916): 149–52; Thomas Carter, "Going to School through Revolution," *ISR* 17 (Sept. 1916): 154–56; Robert H. Howe, "How We Robbed Mexico in 1848," *ISR* 17 (Nov. 1916): 277–80; Modesto Rolland, "Why Is Government Needed in Mexico?" *ISR* 18 (July 1917): 48–49; D. Bolspa, "Your Dream Come True," *ISR* 18 (Feb. 1918): 414–16. For a scathing, insightful critique of the Wilson administration's words and deeds at the time of the U.S. military incursion in 1916, see John K. Turner, "Marching through Mexico," *ISR* 16 (May 1916): 652–56.

17. G. L. Harding, "Socialism and the World-War," *ISR* 15 (Sept. 1914): 141–43; Mary Marcy [editorial], "The Real Fatherland," *ISR* 15 (Sept. 1914): 177–78; "War and the European Socialists," *ISR* 15 (Oct. 1914): 210–13.

18. Phillips Russell, "Europe in the Clutch of War," *ISR* 15 (Oct. 1914): 133–35.

19. Pannekoek, "The Great European War and Socialism." Pannekoek contributed several other analytical commentaries to the *ISR*. See "War against War"; "The War and Its Effects," *ISR* 15 (Dec. 1914): 325–31; "German Socialism in the War," *ISR* 15 (Feb. 1915): 455–59; and "The Third International," *ISR* 17 (Feb. 1917): 460–63. On the contributions of Anton Pannekoek to revolutionary left theory, see D. A. Smart, *Pannekoek and Gorter's Marxism* (London: Pluto Press, 1978); Serge Bricianer, *Pannekoek and the Workers' Councils* (St. Louis: Telos Press, 1978), passim. *ISR* also carried several essays by Pannekoek's comrade, Herman Gorter: "Imperialism, the World War, and the Social Democracy," *ISR* 15 (May 1915): 645–51; and "Mass Action the Answer," *ISR* 17 (Sept. 1916): 165–66. On Gorter, see Smart, *Pannekoek and Gorter's Marxism*.

20. Mary Marcy, "Socialist Unpreparedness in Germany," *ISR* 17 (Sept. 1916): 245–47.

21. For a sampling of the most significant articles on socialists and the war, see Anon., "War and the European Socialists," *ISR* 17 (Sept. 1916): 210–13; August Bebel, "August Bebel on the Franco-German War," *ISR* 17 (Sept. 1916): 247; Karl Kautsky, "Imperialism and the War," *ISR* 15 (Nov. 1914): 282–86; Sen Katayama, "The War and the Japanese," *ISR* 15 (Nov. 1914): 287; Harry Uswald, "Militarism and Socialism: An Analysis of the Factors That Led European Socialists to Support the War," *ISR* 15 (Nov. 1914): 289–300; Frank Bohn, "The Fallen Mighty," *ISR* 15 (Dec. 1914): 354–57; Roscoe A. Fillmore, "Keep the Issue Clear," *ISR* 15 (Jan. 1915): 398–403; William English Walling, "The Defense of the German Socialists," *ISR* 15 (Jan. 1915): 418–22; Austin Lewis, "The Russian Menace," *ISR* 15 (Feb. 1915): 460–63; and William English Walling, "Karl Kautsky—Nationalist," *ISR* 15 (Jan. 1915): 470–71.

22. For a sampling of the relevant reportage in Bohn's "Notes," see "This War What For?" *ISR* 15 (Sept. 1914): 178; "The War, the People, and the Future," *ISR* 15 (Oct. 1914): 241–44 and 15 (Nov. 1914): 309–12; "News from Europe," *ISR* 15 (Jan. 1915): 389–93; "Second Thoughts on the War," *ISR* 15 (Feb. 1915): 497–501; "New Thoughts on Socialist Theory," *ISR* 15 (March 1915): 562–70; "The Class Struggle and the War," *ISR* 15 (May 1915): 686–92; "'Socialists' and Socialists in Germany," *ISR* 15 (June 1915): 755–62; "German Socialists a Year Later," *ISR* 16 (Aug. 1915): 119–23; "A Socialist Split in Germany?" *ISR* 16 (Sept. 1915): 182; "Clara Zetkin Arrested," *ISR* 16 (Oct. 1915): 243; "The New Socialist Group in the Reichstag," *ISR* 16 (June 1916): 754; "Liebknecht in Danger," and "Progress of the German Minority," *ISR* 17 (July 1916): 48–53; "Berlin Socialists against War," *ISR* 17 (Aug. 1916): 112; "Anti-War Movement in Germany," *ISR* 17 (Sept. 1916): 179; "Karl Liebknecht's Defence," *ISR* 17 (Jan. 1917): 436–38; Frank Bohn, "The Reds of Germany Down but Not Dead," *ISR* 16 (July 1915): 79–82.

ISR carried a number of pieces, often compiled or translated by William Bohn, from key figures of Europe's antiwar left during that period. Bohn carefully chronicled the several tendencies that gradually had begun to coalesce around a call for a new International and the line forwarded by the Russians that called upon the left to intensify the war crisis and thereby convert it into an anticapitalist "civil war." See Rosa Luxembourg, "The Rebuilding of the International," *ISR* 16 (July 1915): 9–11; Franz Mehring, "From the Reds of Germany an Interesting Letter," *ISR* 16 (Nov. 1915): 273; "Manifesto of Editors and Publishers of the 'International,'" *ISR* 16 (Nov. 1915): 274–76; Alexandra Kollontay, "Do Internationalists Want a Split?" *ISR* 16 (Jan. 1916): 394–96; William Bohn, "International Notes: Russian Socialists and the Third International," *ISR* 16 (Jan. 1916): 436–41; S. J. Rutgers, "The Battle Cry of a New International," *ISR* 16 (May 1916): 647–49; William Bohn, "The Second Zimmerwald Conference," *ISR* 17 (July 1916): 53; Carl Wittman, "Socialism and Patriotism in Germany," *ISR* 17 (Sept. 1916): 163–65; Carl Wittman, "The German Minority and the War," *ISR* 17 (Nov. 1916): 303–4; S. J. Rutgers, trans., "From German Socialists: The Left Wing; New Methods of Parliamentary Action," *ISR* 17 (Dec. 1916): 363–65; Pannekoek, "The Third International"; Anon., "Manifesto of the Socialist Propaganda League of America," *ISR* 17 (Feb. 1917): 483–85; S. J. Rutgers, "The Future of International Socialism," *ISR* 17 (March 1917): 550–51.

23. "Better any Kind of Action Than Inert Theory!" *ISR* 15 (Feb. 1915): 495–96; "Where We Stand on War," *ISR* 15 (March 1915): 561; "Why You Should Be a Socialist," *ISR* 15 (May 1915): 700–702.

24. M.E.M. [Mary Marcy], "International Capital and the World Trust," *ISR* 16 (Oct. 1915): 241–42.

25. "When We Go to War," *ISR* 15 (June 1915): 753–54, emphasis in the original. For a further discussion on the efficacy of the general strike, see M.E.M. [Mary Marcy], "Direct Action," *ISR* 16 (Sept. 1915): 179–80.

26. For examples, see Edmund R. Brumbaugh, "A Billion-Dollar Bulwark," *ISR* 16 (Dec. 1915): 350; Eliza Frances Andrews, "An International Boycott?" *ISR* 16 (Dec. 1915): 431; Frank Bohn, "Preparedness," *ISR* 16 (Feb. 1916): 451–54; A Live Wire, "Looking 'Em Over," *ISR* 16 (Feb. 1916): 465–67; Guy Bogart, "From Foetus to Trench," *ISR* 16 (March 1916): 552–55; Anon. "When They Ask You," *ISR* 16 (May 1916): 650–51; Anon., "The Cat Is Out of the Bag," *ISR* 17 (Aug. 1916): 99–100; Eugene Debs, "The Class War and Its Outlook," *ISR* 17 (Sept. 1916): 135–36; Mary Marcy, "Killed without Warning by the American Capitalist Class," *ISR* 17 (March 1917): 519–22; Frank Bohn, "Whose War?" *ISR* 17 (March 1917): 529–32; Editorial [Mary Marcy?], "You and Your Country," *ISR* 17 (April 1917): 625–27.

27. "Ready to Kill," *ISR* 16 (June 1916): 710–11. For additional examples of antiwar poetry, see A Paint Creek Miner [Ralph Chaplin], "The Red Feast," *ISR* 15 (Oct. 1914): 196–97; Carl Sandburg, "Ashes and Dreams," *ISR* 15 (May 1915): 671; C.S. [Carl Sandburg], "A Million Young Workmen," *ISR* 16 (Nov. 1915): 268;

Bernard Gilbert, "He's Gone to War," *ISR* 16 (Dec. 1915): 358–59; Carl Sandburg, "Wars," *ISR* 17 (July 1916): 4; and Eleanor E. Carpenter, "The Way of War," *ISR* 17 (March 1917): 535.

28. Henry L. Slobodin, "Socialism and Preparedness," *ISR* 16 (Jan. 1916): 428–30. The participants in the American debate followed a similar course of exchanges, abruptly ended by the opening of hostilities, that had occurred in Europe. The debate grew, in part, out of the lack of clarity and often contradictory messages on the question of war within the corpus of Marxian theory. No clear, coherent body of doctrine existed. As the Russian historian E. H. Carr explains, several differing positions had long existed within the movement. The nineteenth-century tradition had always contained a strong strain of pacifism that condemned war, irrespective of its motives or objectives. Marx and Engels, however, conscious of the revolutionary potentialities of war, denounced all forms of pacifism. They often argued that socialists had to take sides in such conflicts on the basis of the progressive or reactionary nature of the belligerents. That war was the result of the economic contradictions of capitalism and would only disappear with the triumph of socialism became an accepted doctrine of the Second International, but that body could not draw any commonly held policies from that often stated belief. The International contained many shades of belief—from the mainly British pacifists, to the mainly French advocates of the general strike against war, to those (mainly German) who ironed out a position of worker's participation in "wars of national defense."

The Russian social democrats added a new element to the debate. At the 1907 Stuttgart Congress they succeeded in linking the question of social revolution and war in the International's pronouncement on the issue. Their motion, as adopted, called upon socialists "to use all their exertions . . . to prevent the outbreak of war." In the event that war occurred, however, they called upon the workers of each country "to act in order to bring it to a speedy termination." Significantly, they then called upon the movement "to strive with all . . . [its] forces to utilize the economic and political crisis caused by the war to . . . hasten the destruction of the class domination of the capitalist classes." *Internationaler Sozialisten-Kongress zu Stuttgart, 18 bis 24 August 1907* (1907) as cited in E. H. Carr, "Note E.: The Marxist Attitude toward War," in *The Bolshevik Revolution* (London: Penguin Books, 1966), 3:541–60.

29. For a discussion of the shifts and changes, the struggles over the political line of the International movement, leading up to the call for a Third International and a break with the "opportunism" of the "social chauvinists," see Merle Fainsod, *International Socialism and the World War* (New York: Octagon Books, 1935).

30. S. J. Rutgers, "Down with American Militarism," *ISR* 16 (July 1915): 33–35; "Far Eastern Imperialism," *ISR* 16 (Oct. 1915): 212–14, and 16 (Nov. 1915): 286–88; "Fighting for Peace," *ISR* 16 (Jan. 1916): 420–21; "Socialism and War," *ISR* 16 (Feb. 1916): 496–99; "The Left Wing—Imperialism" *ISR* 16 (June 1916): 728–31; "The Left Wing—Economic Causes of Imperialism," *ISR* 17 (July 1916): 29–

32; "The Passing of the Old Democracy," *ISR* 17 (Aug. 1916): 96–98; "The Left Wing Socialist Mass Action," *ISR* 17 (Oct. 1916): 233–37; "Mass Action and Mass Democracy," *ISR* 17 (Nov. 1916): 301–3; "The Left Wing: An Actual Beginning," *ISR* 17 (Dec. 1916): 365–66; "Mass Action in Russia," *ISR* 17 (Jan. 1917): 410–13; "The Future of International Socialism," *ISR* 17 (March 1917): 550–51; "Letter from Karl Liebknecht," *ISR* 17 (April 1917): 610–12. On Rutgers's role in the formative years of American communism, see Draper, *The Roots of American Communism*, passim.

Fully aware of Rutger's political acumen, *ISR*'s editors wrote a brief comment on the left-wing series at the beginning of its second installment. They called upon readers to study the Rutgers pieces, discuss them, and pass them on. "Note," *ISR* 16 (June 1916): 728–31. Some of the best examples of the developing left-wing position in the ongoing debate on the tactical and strategic direction of the movement in the context of the American drift toward war are Roscoe A. Fillmore, "How to Build up the Socialist Movement," *ISR* 16 (April 1916): 614–18; J. O. Bentall, "The Crisis in the Socialist Movement," *ISR* 16 (May 1916): 676–79; Austin Lewis, "Mass Action," *ISR* 17 (April 1917): 605–8.

31. M.E.M. [Mary Marcy], "Mass Action—Where We Stand," *ISR* 17 (Dec. 1916): 367–69.

32. M.E.M., "Mass Action," 369.

33. [Charles H. Kerr], "More Capital Needed," *ISR* 15 (Oct. 1914): 248.

34. Weinstein explains that many socialist leaders initially attempted to evade the issues raised by the failure of the European parties. As a result, the Socialist Party experienced a demoralization within its ranks and a general loss of public prestige. Party membership declined sharply during the first six months of 1915. *Decline of Socialism*, 120.

35. "Over 1500 New Readers," *ISR* 15 (Nov. 1914): 314–15; "From the *Review* Rebels," *ISR* 15 (Dec. 1914): 382; "We Must Raise a War Fund," *ISR* 15 (Dec. 1914): 383; "Annual Stockholder's Meeting," *ISR* 15 (Feb. 1915): 503, 505; [Charles H. Kerr], "Publisher's Department," *ISR* 15 (March 1915): 575, 15 (April 1915): 638, and 15 (May 1915): 641–42, 703; [Charles H. Kerr], "How to Get Socialist Books at Cost," *ISR* 16 (March 1916): 572–74; "Revolutionary Co-Operation," *ISR* 16 (Oct. 1916): 253–55; Charles H. Kerr, *What Socialism Is* (Chicago: Charles H. Kerr & Company, 1917), 28–29.

36. [Charles H. Kerr], "The Time to Strike Is Now," *ISR* 16 (June 1916): 660–61; "Annual Stockholder's Meeting of 1917," *ISR* 17 (Feb. 1917): 504–5; "Trying Times Ahead," *ISR* 17 (May 1917): 697.

37. [Socialist Party of America], *Proceedings: Emergency Convention of the Socialist Party of America, at St. Louis. April 7–14, 1917* (Chicago: Charles H. Kerr & Company, 1917); Leslie Marcy, "The Emergency National Convention," *ISR* 17 (May 1917): 665–69; "Resolutions on War and Militarism," *ISR* 17 (May 1917): 670–71; Weinstein, *Decline of Socialism*, 125–29.

38. Petersen and Fite, *Opponents of War*, 21–42, passim.

39. Anon., "Their Country," *ISR* 17 (April 1917): 589–97; Carl Sandburg, "Will Marshall Field III Enlist?" *ISR* 17 (May 1917): 660; Frank Bohn, "To the Old Guard," *ISR* 17 (May 1917): 685; "Conscientious Objectors in England," *ISR* 17 (June 1917): 719–20; S. J. Rutgers, "Our Action against Conscription," *ISR* 17 (June 1917): 721–22.

The July 1917 issue of *ISR* carried an excerpt from a book entitled *A German Deserter's War Experience*, which was published by B. W. Huebsch of New York and distributed by Kerr. A brief editor's note to the piece described the book as "a wonderful book which ought to be read by every workingman in America." "A German Deserter's War Experience," *ISR* 18 (July 1917): 15–17.

40. Various historians have made a great deal about the fact that a number of intellectuals in the movement favored the war following U.S. entry. The implicit message in such discussion suggests that the movement was left without a rudder or that those in the know somehow came to see the error in their ways and now understood the need to support the American "mission" (e.g., Shannon, *Socialist Party of America*, 83–84). The most influential leaders of the movement, center and right—Debs, Hilquit, and Berger—maintained their antiwar stance, however. Reasons for a socialist stance favoring the war varied greatly. Some movement intellectuals who shifted over to support of the Allies did so out of support for the Russian revolution. Germany's defeat would assure the survival of the infant social democracy. Weinstein, *Decline of Socialism*, 119–33 passim.

41. *Congressional Record*, 65 Cong., 1st sess., April 4, 1917, 209. For a discussion of the debate over the passage of the act, see Peterson and Fite, *Opponents of War*, 15–18.

42. Described as "the most omnipresent of the repressive organizations," the Justice Department-sponsored American Protective League developed a network of informants in more than six hundred cities. APL members, described as "the leading men in their communities," numbered well over 350,000 by the end of the war. Officially sanctioned vigilantes par excellence, they opened mail and carried out numerous illegal searches and seizures in an ongoing effort to enforce prowar conformity and expose disloyalty. APL operatives infiltrated radical or antiwar groups; they burglarized, wiretapped, and bugged the offices of such organizations and participated in the periodic raids carried out by "official" law enforcement agencies. Peterson and Fite, *Opponents of War*, 19; Goldstein, *Political Repression*, 110–12.

Chicago-based APL agents watched Charles H. Kerr & Company closely and filed periodic reports about it to the Military Intelligence Headquarters in Washington, D.C. A full APL sketch of the company, compiled October 8–10, 1918, listed not only the key members of the firm but also the company's long-time printer, John F. Higgins, and the various distributors from which Kerr purchased paper and other supplies. The APL agent in charge of the investigation had a friend write to the company for a list of publications. Kerr responded to the inquiry, and the list he sent out is now in a Military Intelligence file at the National Archives in Washington. U.S. Department of War, Military Intelligence Division, Record Group 165, National Archives, Washington, D.C. (hereafter MID, RG 165), box 3017, folder 6, item 334, "People's Council Secret Meetings" (typescript, dated Nov. 1, 1918), 4–5, and item 335, "Order List of Socialist Books—Charles H. Kerr & Company."

43. On the various roundups of radicals during the war and the effects of such attacks, see Dubofsky, *We Shall Be All*, 406–45, passim; Preston, *Aliens and Dissenters*, ch. 4; Peterson and Fite, *Opponents of War*, chs. 5, 15–21, passim.

44. The bombing, one of the great causes-célèbre of the era, occurred on July 22, 1916. Ten died, and forty were injured. Authorities arrested the labor activists Tom Mooney and Warren K. Billings and three of their associates. The prosecution satisfied a jury of their guilt, but subsequent disclosures revealed a trail of perjury. The three other defendants were released, but Mooney and Billings remained in jail until the late 1930s.

ISR carried continuous coverage and commentary on the plight of Mooney and Billings and their colleagues until it was suppressed in February 1918. See Robert Minor, "The San Francisco Frame-Up," *ISR* 17 (Oct. 1916): 216–17; Theodora Pollok, "Will Labor Stand for Another Haymarket?" *ISR* 17 (Dec. 1916): 360–63; Robert Minor, "The Suitcase Ghost," *ISR* 17 (Jan. 1917): 424–25; Eugene V. Debs, "Tom Mooney Sentenced to Death," *ISR* 17 (April 1917): 613–14; Robert Minor, "To the Shame of Labor," *ISR* 17 (May 1917): 675–77; "Mooney Plot Exposed!" *ISR* 17 (May 1917): 675; Robert Minor, "They Are Building the Gallows," *ISR* 18 (July 1917): 22–25; Mary Marcy, "A Month of Lawlessness," *ISR* 18 (Sept. 1917): 154–57; "Rena Mooney Acquitted," *ISR* 18 (Sept. 1917): 177–79; "The Frame-Up Collapse," *ISR* 18 (Feb. 1918): 420.

45. John MacDonald, "From Butte to Bisbee," *ISR* 17 (Aug. 1917): 69–71; J. Oates, "Globe-Miami District," *ISR* 17 (Aug. 1917): 72–74; Marcy, "A Month of Lawlessness"; Boardman Robinson, "Two Deportations—Take Your Choice" [cartoon], *ISR* 17 (Aug. 1917): 158–59; Leslie Marcy, "The Eleven Hundred Exiled Copper Miners," *ISR* 17 (Aug. 1917): 160–62; Anon., "From the Deported Bisbee Miners," *ISR* 17 (Oct. 1917): 204. For details on the strike in the Arizona copper region and the Bisbee events, see Dubofsky, *We Shall Be All*, 369–74, 385–91; and Foner, *History of the Labor Movement in the United States* 7, ch. 13.

46. Phillips Russell, "To Frank Little," *ISR* 17 (Sept. 1917): 133; Anon., "The Man That Was Hung," *ISR* 17 (Sept. 1917): 135–38. On the events in Butte during the period and the murder of Frank Little, see Dubofsky, *We Shall Be All*, 366–68, 391–93, 420–21; and Foner, *History of the Labor Movement in the United States*, 7:286–89.

47. Already constrained by war censorship and harassed by the fall 1917, *ISR* nevertheless attempted to provide news on the Socialist Party's electoral campaigns that November. Hampered by rising costs and a decline in revenue, Kerr put out a combined issue for November and December that contained little information on the election. The January 1918 number, however, carried an insert that clearly had

been placed in the issue after it passed the postal inspection. Written by Adolph Germer from the Socialist Party's national office, "Defeated?" provided a full summary of those elections based on a clear antiwar message. In addition, see "Dayton, Ohio Swept by Socialists," *ISR* 18 (Sept. 1917): 182; and "Watch the Election Returns" [editorial], *ISR* 18 (Nov.-Dec. 1917), 313.

48. "May Day in Cleveland," *ISR* 12 (June 1917): 757; "Word from the Rock Island Reds," *ISR* 12 (June 1917): 758; "Propaganda News," *ISR* 18 (July 1917): 8–12; "Riots in Boston," *ISR* 18 (July 1917): 75–76; "News and Views," *ISR* 18 (Sept. 1917): 187–89; "The I.W.W. and the Socialist Party," *ISR* 18 (Oct. 1917): 205; "Statement from the I.W.W.," *ISR* 18 (Oct. 1917): 206–9; William D. Haywood, "Inside," *ISR* 18 (Nov.-Dec. 1917): 268; "From the I.W.W. Indictments," *ISR* 18 (Nov.-Dec. 1917): 271–79; "Socialists Acquitted," *ISR* 18 (Nov.-Dec. 1917): 283; Harold Callender, "The Truth about the I.W.W.," *ISR* 18 (Jan. 1918): 332–42; "From Ohio," *ISR* 18 (Feb. 1918): 429–30.

49. The lead articles of each issue from April through July dealt with the situation in Russia: "The Russian Revolution," *ISR* 17 (April 1917): 619–20; Henry L. Slobodin, "The Russian Revolution," *ISR* 17 (May 1917): 645–47; "The Russian Revolution," *ISR* 17 (June 1917): 709–14; and "The Passing Show—'Root'ing in Russia," *ISR* 18 (July 1917): 5–6.

The last several issues of the monthly carried more material on Russia than on developments in the United States. That peculiar situation reflected not only the political predilections of *ISR*'s staff but also the hand of the censor, who found favorable news about an ally more acceptable than any critical reportage about the Wilson administration or the American war effort. The American mood toward the revolution changed after the Bolshevik seizure of power and Russia's withdrawal from the war.

The post office never gave Kerr a precise reason for the final suppression of *ISR* in February 1918. Perhaps it had something to do with the monthly's energetic positive reportage of the Bolshevik triumph and the linkages made between the Russian events and the domestic situation in the United States. The last two issues of the monthly contained lead stories on the October Revolution. For further reportage on Russian events, see Phillips Russell, "Thoughts about Russia," *ISR* 18 (July 1917): 21; Max Eastman, "Syndicalst-Socialist Russia," *ISR* 18 (Aug. 1917): 77–79; Mary Marcy, "German Socialists in Russia," *ISR* 18 (Oct. 1917): 216–17; "News from Russia," *ISR* 18 (Oct. 1917): 221–23; Charles Edward Russell, "New Russia in the Making," *ISR* 18 (Nov.-Dec. 1917): 261–67, 310–12; Anon., "The Russian Bolsheviki Victory," *ISR* 18 (Jan. 1918): 325–30; Leon Trotsky, "The Bolsheviki and World Peace," *ISR* 18 (Feb. 1918): 389–94; and "From the Bolsheviki," *ISR* 18 (Feb. 1918): 399–400.

50. Mary Marcy, "Our Gains in War," *ISR* 17 (May 1917): 650–52.

51. Mary Marcy, "The Cause of War," *ISR* 18 (July 1917): 28–29, emphasis in the original; Phillips Russell, "Thoughts about Russia," *ISR* 18 (July 1917): 21; "The Great Issue" [editorial], *ISR* 18 (Aug. 1917): 114.

52. Kerr procured permission from Trotsky's New York publisher, Boni and Liveright, to excerpt the work. An editor's note to the piece informed *ISR* readership that Trotsky had begun preparing a contribution for the monthly but developments in Russia had called him home.

53. [Charles H. Kerr], "July Ruled Unmailable," *ISR* 18 (Aug. 1917): 125–26; Charles H. Kerr, "*The Review* and the Censorship," *ISR* 18 (Sept. 1917): 181–82; "Announcement," *ISR* 18 (Nov.-Dec. 1917): 305; [Charles H. Kerr], "Publisher's Department," *ISR* 18 (Feb. 1918): 431.

54. See 1917 edition of Marc Fisher, *Evolution and Revolution*, with handwritten inscription on the front cover informing subscribers that it was a substitute for the July 1917 *ISR*. Pamphlet Collection, SHSW. Unable to mail the September *ISR*, Kerr sent subscribers copies of Paul Lafargue's *The Right to be Lazy* to each subscriber and had an explanatory note placed in each volume. Katharine Kerr Moore to May Walden Kerr, Oct. 5, 1917, box 4, folder 2, May Walden Kerr Papers.

55. "*The Review* and the Censorship"; "The New Censorship Law," *ISR* 18 (Nov.-Dec. 1917): 31. One Bureau of Investigation employee, upon reading that month's *ISR*, thought that it appeared "to be one of many avenues used for the dissemination of the seeds of discontent among wage workers, and spreading peace propaganda bearing the trade mark of made outside the U.S." and "particularly dangerous reading for the men who were to receive it in this community." For deliberations on the monthly within the Justice Department, see Federal Bureau of Investigation, Investigative Case Files, National Archives, RG 65, Military Intelligence Division, 1917–22 (hereafter RG 65), M1085, reel 380, item OG34769.

56. Lloyd Canby, "C. H. Kerr & Co., Investigation, July 26, 1918," MID, RG 165, box 3017, folder 6, item 10110–219:320; Kerr Company typescript mailing intercepted by the postal authorities, dated April 2, 1918, Records of the Post Office Department, Documents Seized under Enforcement of the Espionage and Sedition Acts, 1917–20 (hereafter RG 28), file 51343, entry 40.

57. Kerr advertised and excerpted Karl Liebknecht's 1907 tract, *On Militarism*, in the last several *ISRs*. The company distributed the pamphlet for the New York publisher B. W. Huebsch. Kerr either thought that the promotion and distribution of such a work might meet the postal censor's approval because it attacked Prussian militarism or had decided to insert the advertising and a portion of the work in order to test war regulations. Either way, he lost. Karl Liebknecht, "Militarism," *ISR* 18 (Jan. 1918): 345–49; "Three New Books You Want," *ISR* 18 (Jan 1918): 361.

Katayama was but one of many socialists from around the world who spent some time in the United States during the early decades of this century. Kerr had just begun to serialize Katayama's groundbreaking work on the history of the Japanese working class in *ISR* when the monthly ran afoul of the censor. The series stopped with the suppression of the monthly in February 1918.

The Japanese socialist contributed numerous pieces to the *ISR* over its eighteen-year span. For a sampling of his writings on a diverse range of topics, see "The Labor Movement and Socialism in Japan," *ISR* 2 (Sept. 1901): 188–91; "Socialism in Japan," *ISR* 4 (Oct. 1903): 202–3; "Capitalism in Japan," *ISR* 10 (May 1910): 1003–6; "Government Oppression in Japan," *ISR* 11 (Aug. 1910): 80–82; "How Japan Is Civilizing the Formosan Heathen," *ISR* 11 (Oct. 1910): 222–24; "The Japanese Miners," *ISR* 11 (Feb. 1911): 478–82; "Letter from Japan," *ISR* 12 (Aug. 1911): 102–2; "A Japanese Victory," *ISR* 12 (March, 1912): 581–82; "Old Japan and New," *ISR* 13 (March 1913): 656–62; "The Democratic Uprising in Japan," *ISR* 13 (April 1913): 740–43; "California and the Japanese," *ISR* 14 (July 1913): 31–32; "Japanese Wrestling and the Jiu-Jitsu," *ISR* 14 (Aug. 1913): 92–93; "Women in Japan," *ISR* 14 (Oct. 1913): 223–24; "Chinese Refugees in Japan," *ISR* 14 (Nov. 1913): 273–75; "What It Means to Be a Socialist in Japan," *ISR* 14 (Feb. 1914): 467–68; "Business and Patriotism in Japan," *ISR* 14 (April 1914): 600–601; and "The Japanese Geisha Girl," *ISR* 15 (Aug. 1914): 79–81. For a brief biographical sketch of Katayama, see S. J. Rutgers, "Introduction to History of Japanese Labor," *ISR* 18 (July 1917): 37–39. For an extended treatment, see Hyman Kublin, *Asian Revolutionary* (Princeton: Princeton University Press, 1964).

58. *The Labor Scrapbook* (March and May 1918). Although back issues are rare, copies of *The Labor Scrapbook* exist in the collection of material seized by the Post Office Department under the Espionage Act in Record Group 28 of the National Archives. For a photocopy of *The Labor Scrapbook* no. 2, see Federal Bureau of Investigation, Investigative Case Files, RG 65, reel 596, item OG191687.

59. In addition to *Women as Sex Vendors*, Marcy was also the author of *How the Farmer Can Get His* (1916), *Stories of the Cave People* (1917), and *Industrial Autocracy* (1919).

60. Both Mary and Leslie Marcy remained under regular government surveillance from 1918 to 1921. At one point in June 1918 Leslie Marcy was arrested while en route to a Socialist Party convention in Canton, Ohio. He was held incommunicado for two days, and his inventory of Kerr & Company publications was confiscated. For examples of reports on the Marcys, often passed from one federal agency to another, see (all in FBI Investigative Case Files, RG 65, roll 667, item OG253980): "Report of A. H. Loula on Leslie E. Marcy [*sic*] and Chas H. Kerr, June 16, 1919"; typescript facsimile of letter from Mary Marcy to Mrs. S. J. Rutgers, dated June 27, 1918, seized by the U.S. Postal Censorship, Seattle, Washington; and letter from the U.S. Embassy, London, dated March 17, 1919, signed by Edward Bell, to the Department of State, Washington, D.C., with enclosure, a facsimile of a letter from Mary Marcy and Esa [*sic*] Unterman to Ben Tillet, Labor M.P.

61. Passed as a set of amendments to the Espionage Act of 1917, the Sedition Act of 1918 broadened the realm of restricted speech and action for the war period. Significantly for Kerr & Company, it increased the censorship powers of Burleson's Post Office Department. On the Sedition Act, see Peterson and Fite, *Opponents of War*, ch. 19, and Preston, *Aliens and Dissenters*, 145. The full story of the level of repression faced by Charles H. Kerr & Company may never be fully known. Two differing accounts exist in the remaining popular memory, passed on

to present-day associates of the company from old-timers now gone themselves. One account asserts that a raiding party of federal authorities and/or Chicago police and APL volunteers descended on the office at some point in 1918 or 1919. According to the story recounted to Burt Rosen, former secretary of the Kerr Company, and by Al Wysocki, a company associate from the 1920s, the authorities destroyed company papers including a massive correspondence with the who's who of the prewar international socialist movement. Supposedly, the records that survived happened to be locked in a safe at the time of the raid. The "mob" supposedly burned a great deal of material in the street outside the office.

This particular recounting remains problematic and unverified. I have found no mention of such an episode in the Chicago press of the period, and one might assume that an event such as a raid on the company and the subsequent incineration of papers in the street would receive some notice. In his memoirs, written many years later when he had shifted ideologically, Ralph Chaplin asserted that the authorities intentionally spared the company at the time of the round-up of the IWW's leadership. But the police ransacked the Marcys' home in Bowmanville, Illinois, when Kerr lived there. They also seized materials at the Kerr-financed Radical Bookshop, a gathering place for radicals on Chicago's North Clark Street. To suggest that the various police agencies would bypass such a key center of revolutionist activity seems unlikely. The company certainly was under surveillance.

One fact remains. The massive correspondence file did disappear. What happened to it remains unanswerable and open to conjecture. Concerned with the safety of those individuals associated with the company, the Kerr inner circle may have taken precautions and destroyed some of the files for security reasons. Others on the left, hounded by the generalized repression of the era, disposed of letters and communications. The John M. Work Papers in the State Historical Society of Wisconsin contain numerous letters without the names of their authors. Work cut the names from the documents in order to conceal the identities of correspondents from the authorities. He also recounted, in his memoirs, that concern about security had become so great that he often flushed communications down the toilet lest they fall into the wrong hands. And Work was not a left-winger.

62. Lloyd Canby, "C. H. Kerr & Co., Aug. 6, 1918," MID, RG 165, box 3017, folder 6, item 10110–219:323. *The Crimson Fist* was not a Kerr & Company publication, but apparently one of innumerable small or ephemeral pamphlets, published independently, which the house helped to distribute.

63. Ibid., item 10110–219:219; "Subject: Chas. H. Kerr & Co., Aug. 9, 1918," MID, RG 165, item 10110–219:327.

64. For an informative personal account of the assault on the IWW, see Chaplin, *Wobbly*, part 4, passim. For a general narrative of the war roundups and the Red Scare arrests, see Dubofsky, *We Shall Be All*, chaps. 16–18, passim; Peterson and Fite, *Opponents of War;* Preston, *Aliens and Dissenters;* and Murray, *Red Scare.*

65. For some sense of the types of activities in which Mary and Leslie Marcy became involved in an attempt to win freedom for Haywood and other prisoners of the war repression, including Eugene Debs, see copy of an intercepted letter

from Charles H. Kerr & Company, Chicago (original signed by Mary Marcy) to Mrs. Sheehy Skeffington, c/o *The Irish Worker*, Dublin, Jan. 1, 1919, and "Amnesty League," typescript report of A. H. Loula, Sept. 12, 1919, both in MID, RG 165, box 3075, folder 1958. The Marcys subsequently became involved in public support activities in the case involving the arrest and trials of various members of the Communist Labor Party in 1920. See "Radical Meeting held at No. 8 Walton Place, Chicago, Jan. 4, 1920," typescript report, MID, RG 165, box 3075, folder 1958, item 10110–1584–19. This particular document conveys some marvelous insights into the level of surveillance that leftists faced during that period now commonly referred to as the Red Scare of 1919–20. The informant who filed the report had infiltrated the group of "Parlor Bolsheviks" (his description) and became treasurer and secretary of that informal body of socialists and civil libertarians that had come together in an attempt to raise funds and mount appeals for political detainees.

66. Katharine Kerr Moore to May Walden, August 12, 1919, and May Walden Kerr to Katharine Kerr Moore, Aug. 15, 1919, May Walden Kerr Papers. When Haywood left the country for the Soviet Union, he informed those who had contributed to his bail fund that they would be reimbursed. Russia's Bolshevik leadership promised to assist in the repayment. The money destined for the Chicago group never arrived, however, and the loss that the IWW and several of Haywood's long-time comrades incurred placed salt in the already open wound of political differences among the some members of the IWW, various Socialist Party people, and the pro-Soviet left-wingers who eventually moved into the ranks of the Communist Party, founded in September 1919.

The Bolsheviks had, however, attempted to make good on their promise. Journalist John Reed, on his way back to the United States after a stay in the Soviet Union, carried the money for Haywood's Chicago supporters. Reed, however, never got home. Finnish authorities, under the direction of British intelligence, intercepted and jailed the author of *Ten Days That Shook the World* and confiscated the fund. Chaplin recounts that Reed also carried a number of priceless gems that the Bolsheviks had seized from some czarist cache. The Chicago activists, of course, had no way of knowing what had happened with the payback. An unfortunate side effect of Reed's stint in a Finnish jail, the loss that the IWW, the Marcys, Kerr, and others experienced had numerous political and personal repercussions. For discussion of Haywood's flight and its effects, see Chaplin, *Wobbly*, 238, 302–3; Dubofsky, *"Big Bill" Haywood*, 459–61; and John Grady, general secretary-treasurer of the IWW to Mont Schuyler, Aug. 11 and 31, 1922 in the I.W.W. Collection, Wayne State University Archive, as cited in Bryan D. Palmer, "'Big Bill' Haywood's Defection to Russia and the I.W.W.: Two Letters," *Labor History* 17 (Spring 1976): 271–78.

67. For Mary Marcy's final years, see Carney, *Mary Marcy*; and Walden, "Notes on C.H.K.'s Ancestry." The precise reasons for an individual's suicide always remain a matter of speculation. Clearly, the political disruption and demise of the Debsian socialist movement played an important role in Marcy's case. A member of the Socialist Party since 1902, she spent a good part of her life in the move-

ment believing that the cooperative commonwealth was not only inevitable but also just around the corner and achievable and possible during her lifetime. The Russian Revolution briefly invigorated that assumption, but a number of factors—the failure of the revolution in Germany, the virulent attack on the American left, and the splintering and decline of the movement—all took their toll.

68. It is uncertain whether the *Shop Book* ever appeared. Reports of its projected release found their way into the reports of the federal authorities. J. G Tucker, "Radical Activities in Greater New York District, Special Report for Period Ending May 28, 1921," FBI Investigative Case Files, roll 938, item 202600–1628.

69. A number of major publishers had refused to handle *The Deportations Delirium of Nineteen-Twenty* before Louis Post took it to Kerr, who published the 338–page work with assistance from the American Civil Liberties Association. Dominic C. Candeloro, "Louis Freeland Post: Carpetbagger, Freetaxer, Progressive," Ph.D. diss., University of Illinois, Champaign-Urbana, 1970. The author of *Imperial Washington*, R. F. Pettigrew, was a former U.S. senator from South Dakota. Subsequently published in a number of reprinted issues, the first imprint of the life story of the "miner's angel," Mary "Mother" Jones, appeared in 1923.

70. Katharine Kerr Moore to May Walden Kerr, April 18, 1927, box 4, folder 3, May Walden Kerr Papers. The domestic American demand for socialist literature declined markedly in the 1920s, and Kerr looked to other markets overseas and found them in China, Japan, India, and Australia.

71. Kerr's connection to the Proletarian Party is not clear. He contributed several articles to their press, *The Proletarian*, during the early 1920s. A full treatment of the Proletarian Party awaits its historian. One of the early communist formations in the United States that vied for recognition from the Comintern, the party spanned the period from 1920 through the 1960s. Its members played an active role in the major labor union battles of the depression years in Detroit, Chicago, and elsewhere but remain invisible or ignored in both the consensus history of labor and the various sectarian communist histories. Various authors from across the ideological spectrum make fleeting mention of Keracher, Batt, and the Proletarian Party, see Draper, *The Roots of American Communism;* Weinstein, *Decline of Socialism;* James P. Cannon, *The First Ten Years of American Communism* (New York: Pathfinder Press, 1962); Bert Cochran, *Labor and Communism* (Princeton: Princeton University Press, 1972); and Roger Keeran, *The Communist Party and the Auto Workers* (Bloomington: Indiana University Press, 1980), 31.

72. Katharine Kerr Moore to May Walden Kerr, July 21, 1927, box 4, folder 3, May Walden Kerr Papers.

73. "Yearbook, 1944" [diary], box 10, May Walden Kerr Papers.

Conclusion

1. Oakley C. Johnson, "The Early Socialist Party of Michigan: An Assignment in Autobiography," *Centennial Review* 2 (1966): 147–62; "John Keracher," *Proletar-*

ian News, March 1958, 1. For Dennis Batt, see Records of the Federal Bureau of Investigation, Investigative Case Files of the Bureau of Investigation, 1908–22, RG 65, reel 936, item 202600–1362, "International Council of Trade and Labor Unions ('Red' Labor Union International) and Delegates to World Conference Moscow, Russia, May 1921"; and RG 65, reel 940, item 202600–1778–45x, dated July 20, 1921, "The Proletarian Party of America." For a fuller treatment of the Proletarian Party, see Allen Ruff, "A Path Not Taken: The Proletarian Party and the Early History of Communism in the United States," in *Culture, Gender, Race, and U.S. Labor History*, ed. Ron Kent et al. (Westport: Greenwood Press, 1993), 43–57.

2. Johnson, "The Early Socialist Party," 156.

3. John Keracher, "Ten Years of Communism in America," *The Proletarian* 12 (Sept. 1929): 2–3; Johnson, "The Early Socialist Party," 155; Foner, *History of the Labor Movement in the United States*, 8:237–55; Draper, *The Roots of American Communism*, 165–67; Weinstein, *Decline of Socialism*, 196–97. A similar call for a September 1 meeting had been issued on May 31 by the Left Wing Section of New York.

4. "Call for a National Convention for the Purpose of Organizing a Communist Party of America," box 14, item 607, RG 28; Johnson, "The Early Socialist Party," 155; Foner, *History of the Labor Movement in the United States*, 8:243–45.

5. "Communist Party Convention," *Proletarian* 2 (Oct. 1919): 1; Johnson, "The Early Socialist Party," 156–57.

6. Robert A. Rosenstone, *Romantic Revolutionary: A Biography of John Reed* (New York: Vintage, 1981), 341–43.

7. See the so-called Michigan Manifesto: "Manifesto and Program: Minority Report of the Committee on Manifesto and Program at the Communist Party Convention," *Proletarian* 2 (Oct. 1919): 13–16; Keracher, "Ten Years of American Communism."

8. Dennis Batt remained behind, however. On the basis of notes taken by a federal agent during his opening address to the convention, he was arrested September 3 by Illinois authorities and charged with violation of state sedition laws. Briefly held in the Cook County Jail and subsequently released under a hefty bond, he was trailed by federal agents and informers well into 1920. See, for example, "Report of Agent E. J. Wheeler, 11/1/19, 'Meeting of Communist Party of America, Erie, Penn'a, October 26, 1919,'" RG 65, reel 832, item OG379614.

9. *Proletarian* 2 (Oct. 1919): 13–16.

10. *The Communist*, Dec. 13, 1919, 6.

11. John Keracher, "Thirty-five Years of the Proletarian Party," *Proletarian News* 24 (July 1955), in box 36, Kerr Company Papers; "Report of Agent Roy C. McHenry, dated Feb. 4, 1920: 'Proletarian University of America, 174 Michigan Ave., Detroit, Communist Activities,'" RG 65, reel 386, item OG38115. For one account of the Palmer raid assault on the Proletarian Party, see Dennis Batt, "A Year Gone By," *Proletarian* 2 (Jan.-Feb. 1920): 1,4. For a general discussion of the Red Scare in Detroit, see Christopher H. Johnson, *Maurice Sugar: Law, Labor and the Left in*

Detroit, 1912–1950 (Detroit: Wayne State University Press, 1988), 92–94. Johnson, not necessarily sympathetic to the Reds in Detroit, states that "the Proletarians suffered most severely from the Palmer raids."

12. Al Wysocki, "John Keracher, His Life and Work," *Proletarian News* (March 1958): 3; "The Proletarian Party of America," typescript, dated July 20, 1921, reel 18, items 620–32, Military Intelligence Surveillance Collection, NA; Committee on un-American Activities, House of Representatives, 85th Cong., 2d sess., Aug. 1953, *Organized Communism in the United States* (Washington: GPO, 1953).

13. Keracher, "Thirty-five Years of the Proletarian Party"; Keracher, "Ten Years of Communism in America."

14. Wysocki, "John Keracher"; Committee on un-American Activities, *Organized Communism*; Franklin Rosemont, "Proletarian Party," in *Encyclopedia of the American Left*, ed. Buhle, Buhle, and Georgakas, 606–7.

15. "Rough Notes on Life and Funeral of Al Wysocki, Aug. 19, 1971 by Virgil Vogel," typescript in possession of Franklin Rosemont

16. Virgil Vogel, "The Story of America's Oldest Socialist Publisher," typescript mimeo, dated Nov. 17. 1978, Manuscripts Department, Chicago Historical Society; David Cochran, "Charles H. Kerr Publishing Company," in *Encyclopedia of the American Left*, ed. Buhle, Buhle and Georgakis, 400–401.

■ Bibliography

Primary Sources

Manuscript and Archival Collections

Alexander Kerr Papers, University of Oregon, Eugene.
Algie M. Simons Papers, State Historical Society of Wisconsin (hereafter SHSW).
Charles H. Kerr & Company Papers, Newberry Library, Chicago.
Ernest Unterman Papers, SHSW.
First Congregational Church Collection, SHSW.
First Unitarian Society of Madison Papers, SHSW.
George Caylor Papers, Tamiment Institute, New York University.
George E. Bowen Papers, Chicago Historical Society.
International Workers of the World Collection, Wayne State University Archives.
Jenkin Lloyd Jones Collection, Meadeville/Lombard Theological Seminary Library,
    Chicago.
John M. Work Papers, SHSW.
Louis Boudin Papers, Columbia University, New York.
May Walden Kerr Papers, Newberry Library, Chicago.
Morris Hillquit Papers, SHSW.
National Archives, Washington, D.C., Record Group 28: records of the Post Of-
    fice Department, Documents Seized under Enforcement of the Espionage and
    Sedition Acts, 1917–20.
———. Record Group 65: Department of Justice, Bureau of Investigation Papers,
    1908–22.
———. Record Group 165: Military Intelligence Division, 1917–22.
Richard T. Ely Papers, SHSW.
William English Walling Papers, SHSW.
William F. Allen Papers, SHSW.

Periodicals

Appeal to Reason (Girard, Kansas, 1895–1918)
Ayer's American Magazine and Newspaper Annual and Directory
Chicago Daily Socialist (1902–7)
Chicago Record-Herald (1901–17)
Chicago Socialist (1907–12)
Chicago Tribune (ca. 1897–1921)
Coming Nation (Chicago and Girard, Kansas)
Comrade (New York, 1901–5)
Geyer's Reference Directory of the Booksellers and Stationers of the United States and Canada (New York: M. S. Geyer, ca. 1890)
International Socialist Review (Chicago: Charles H. Kerr & Company, 1900–1918)
The Masses (New York, 1911–18)
New Occasions (Chicago: Charles H. Kerr & Company, 1893–96)
New Time (Chicago: Charles H. Kerr & Company, 1896–98)
Open Court (Chicago, ca. 1887–94)
Progressive Woman (Chicago, ca. 1911)
The Proletarian (Chicago, Proletarian Party, 1919–25)
Proletarian News (Chicago)
Publisher's Weekly (Chicago, ca. 1886–96)
Publishers' Weekly (1881–1928)
Radical Review (New York, 1917–19)
Revoultionary Age (Boston and New York, 1918–19)
Social Democratic Herald (Chicago and Milwaukee, 1898–ca. 1915)
Socialist Woman (Chicago, ca. 1907)
Unity (Chicago: James Colegrove Publishing Company; Charles H. Kerr & Company, 1878–ca.93)
Workers' Call (Chicago, 1899–1902)

Books and Articles
(in addition to the publications of Charles H. Kerr & Company)

Brewer, G. D. *The Fighting Editor; or, Warren and the Appeal.* Gerard, Kans.: Appeal to Reason Publishing, 1910.
Brooks, John Graham. *American Syndicalism: The IWW.* New York: Macmillan, 1913.
———. "Recent Socialist Literature." *Atlantic Monthly* 99 (1908): 278–83.
Bruce, H. A. "Books on Socialism." *Outlook* 87, no. 6 (1908): 386.
———. "More Books on Socialism." *Outlook* 87, no. 7 (1908): 537.
Casson, Herbert N. "Socialism: Its Growth and Its Leaders." *Munsey's Magazine* 33 (June 1905): 290–98.
Cross, Ira B. *The Essentials of Socialism.* New York: Macmillan, 1912.

Ely, Richard T., and T. K. Urdahl. "Socialist Propaganda." *Chatauquan* 30, no. 1 (1900): 381.

Flower, Benjamin O. *Progressive Men, Women and Movements of the Past Twenty Years.* Boston: Arena, 1914.

Freeman, William H., comp. *The Press Club of Chicago: A History.* Chicago: Press Club of Chicago, 1894.

Griffin, H. F. "The Rising Tide of Socialism." *Outlook*, February 24, 1912, 433–48.

Hardy, Moses. "Literary Chicago." *Munsey's Magazine* 12, no. 1 (1894): 77–88.

Hoxie, R. F. "The Rising Tide of Socialism." *Journal of Political Economy* 19 (October 1911): 609–31.

Hughan, Jesse Wallace. *American Socialism of the Present Day.* New York: Macmillan, 1912.

Hunter, Robert. *Socialists at Work.* New York: Macmillan, 1912.

Kaufmann, M. "Socialist Novels." *Lippincott's Magazine* 55, no. 2 (1895): 138.

"Latest Phase of the Socialistic Novel." *Literary Digest* 32, no. 18 (1906): 679.

Macy, John Albert. *Socialism in America.* New York: Doubleday, Page, 1916.

Mortimer, James Howard. *Confessions of a Book Agent.* Chicago: Co-Operative Publishing, ca. 1906.

Regan, James L. *The Story of Chicago in Connection with the Printing Business.* Chicago: Regan Printing, 1912.

Socialist Party of America. *Proceedings: National Convention of the Socialist Party.* Chicago, May 1–6, 1904. Chicago: Socialist Party, 1904.

———. *Proceedings: National Convention of the Socialist Party.* Chicago, May 15–21, 1910. Chicago: Socialist Party, 1910.

Trachtenberg, Alexander, ed. *The American Labor Year Book, 1919–1920.* New York: Rand School of Social Science, 1920.

Warner, Charles Dudley. "Studies of the Great West: Chicago." *Harper's New Monthly Magazine* 76 (May 1888): 871.

Secondary Sources

Abell, Aaron I. *The Urban Impact on American Protestantism.* Cambridge: Harvard University Press, 1943.

Adams, Frederick B. *Radical Literature in America: An Address.* Stamford: Overbrook Press, 1939.

Adams, Graham, Jr. *Age of Industrial Violence, 1910–1915.* New York: Columbia University Press, 1966.

Ahlstrom, Sydney E. *A Religious History of the American People.* 3 volumes. Garden City: Doubleday, 1975.

American Bookseller, June 16, 1884, 572, May 15, 1885, 288.

Avrich, Paul. *The Haymarket Tragedy.* Princeton: Princeton University Press, 1984.

Basen, Neil. "Kate Richards O'Hare: The 'First Lady' of American Socialism, 1901–1917." *Labor History* 21 (Spring 1980): 165–99.

Beautiful Glen Ellyn. Chicago: E. W. Zander, ca. 1905.

Bedford, Henry F. *Socialism and the Workers in Massachusetts, 1886–1912.* Amherst: University of Massachusetts Press, 1966.

Bekken, Jon. "The Working Class Press at the Turn of the Century." In *Ruthless Criticism: New Perspectives in U.S. Communications History.* Edited by William S. Solomon and Robert McChesney. Minneapolis: University of Minnesota Press, 1993.

Bell, Daniel. *Marxian Socialism in the United States.* Princeton: Princeton University Press, 1967.

Bloomfield, Maxwell H. *Alarms and Diversions: The American Mind through American Magazines, 1900–1914.* Paris: Mounton, 1967.

Bloor, Ella Reeve. *We Are Many.* New York: International Publishers, 1940.

Boller, Paul F., Jr. *American Thought in Transition: The Impact of Evolutionary Naturalism, 1865–1900.* Chicago: Rand McNally, 1969.

"Bookselling in Chicago." *Unity,* August 1, 1883, 230–31.

"The Books of 1888." *Publisher's Weekly,* February 9, 1889, 205, 208.

Bordin, Ruth. *Woman and Temperance: The Quest for Power and Liberty, 1873–1900.* Philadelphia: Temple University Press, 1981.

Bowden, Henry Warner. *Dictionary of American Religious Biography.* Westport: Greenwood Press, 1977.

Bragg, Raymond Bennett. *Henry Martin Simmons.* Minneapolis: n.p., 1944.

Brecher, Jeremy. *Strike!* San Francisco: Straight Arrow Press, 1972.

Bricianer, Serge. *Pannekoek and the Workers' Councils.* St. Louis: Telos Press, 1978.

Brommel, Bernard. *Eugene V. Debs: Spokesman for Labor and Socialism.* Chicago: Charles H. Kerr & Company, 1978.

Broun, Heywood, and Margaret Leech. *Anthony Comstock.* New York: A. C. Boni, 1927.

Brown, Emily Clark. *Book and Job Printing in Chicago: A Study of Organization of Employers and Their Relation with Labor.* Chicago: University of Chicago Press, 1931.

Brown, Jerry Wayne. *The Rise of Biblical Criticism in America, 1800–1870: The New England Scholars.* Middletown: Wesleyan University Press, 1969.

Brown, Marshall G., and Gordon Stein. *Freethought in the United States.* Westport: Greenwood Press, 1978.

Buder, Stanley. *Pullman: An Experiment in Industrial Order and Community Planning, 1880–1930.* London: Oxford University Press, 1967.

Buhle, Mari Jo. *Women and American Socialism, 1870–1920.* Urbana: Univeristy of Illinois Press, 1981.

Buhle, Mari Jo, Paul Buhle, and Dan Georgakis, eds. *Encyclopedia of the American Left.* Urbana: University of Illinois Press, 1992.

Buhle, Paul M. "Debsian Socialism and the 'New Immigrant' Worker." In *Insights and Parallels: Problems and Issues of American Social History.* Edited by William L. O'Neil. Minneapolis: Burgess Publishing, 1973.

———. "Marxism in the United States." Ph.D. dissertation, University of Wisconsin-Madison, 1975.

———. *Marxism in the United States from 1870 to the Present Day.* London: Verso Press, 1987.

Burbank, Garin. *When Farmers Voted Red: The Gospel of Socialism in the Oklahoma Countryside, 1910–1924.* Westport: Greenwood Press, 1976.

Canon, James P. *The First Ten Years of American Communism: Report of a Participant.* New York: Pathfinder Press, 1973.

Cantor, Milton. *The Divided Left: American Radicalism, 1900–1975.* New York: Hill and Wang, 1978.

Carlson, Peter. *Roughneck: The Life and Times of Big Bill Haywood.* New York: Norton, 1983.

Carr, Edward Hallett. *The Bolshevik Revolution, 1917–1923.* 3 volumes. London: Pelican, 1973–53.

Carson, Gerald H. "Get the Prospect Seated and Keep Talking." *American Heritage* 9 (August 1958): 38–41.

Carter, Paul A. *The Spiritual Crisis of the Gilded Age.* DeKalb: Northern Illinois University Press, 1972.

Caruthers, J. Wade. *Octavius Brooks Frothingham, Gentle Radical.* University: University of Alabama Press, 1977.

Cauthen, Kenneth. *The Impact of American Religious Liberalism.* New York: Harper and Row, 1962.

Chadwick, John White. *Old and New Unitarian Belief.* Boston: American Unitarian Association, 1894.

———. *Theodore Parker: Preacher and Reformer.* Boston: Houghton Mifflin, 1901.

Chaplin, Ralph. *The Centralia Conspiracy.* Chicago: Charles H. Kerr & Company, 1972.

———. *Wobbly: The Rough-and-Tumble Story of an American Radical.* Chicago: University of Chicago Press, 1948.

Cline, H. F. "Benjamin Orange Flower and *The Arena*, 1889–1909." *Journalism Quarterly* 17 (June 1940): 139–50.

———. "Flower and *The Arena*: Purpose and Content." *Journalism Quarterly* 18 (September 1940): 247–57.

Cochran, Bert. *Labor and Communism: The Conflict That Shaped American Unions.* Princeton: Princeton University Press, 1977.

Cole, G. D. H. *A History of Socialist Thought.* Volume 3, parts 1 and 2, *The Second International, 1889–1914.* New York: St. Martin's Press, 1956.

Commager, Henry Steele. *Theodore Parker: Yankee Crusader.* Boston: Beacon Press, 1947.

Compton, Frank C. "Subscription Books." *Bowker Lectures on Book Publishing.* New York: R. R. Bowker, 1957.

Conlin, Joseph R. *Big Bill Haywood and the Radical Union Movement.* Syracuse: Syracuse University Press, 1969.

——. *Bread and Roses Too: Studies of the Wobblies.* Westport: Greenwood Press, 1969.

——, ed. *The American Radical Press, 1880–1960.* 2 volumes. Westport: Greenwood Press, 1974

Cooke, George Willis. *Unitarianism in America: A History of Its Origins and Development.* Boston: American Unitarian Association, 1902.

Critchlow, Donald T. *Socialism in the Heartland: The Midwestern Experience, 1900–1925.* South Bend: Notre Dame University Press, 1986.

Curti, Merle. *The Growth of American Thought.* New York: Harper and Row, 1943.

DeLeon, Solon, ed. *American Labor's Who's Who.* New York: Hanford Press, 1925.

Destler, Chester McArthur. *American Radicalism 1865–1901.* New London: Connecticut College, 1946.

Dick, William M. *Labor and Socialism in America: The Gompers Era.* Port Washington: Kennikat Press, 1972.

Dickason, David H. "Benjamin Orange Flower, Patron of the Realists." *American Literature* 14 (May 1942): 148–56.

Dombrowski, James. *The Early Days of Christian Socialism in America.* New York: Columbia University Press, 1936.

Draper, Theodore. *American Communism and Soviet Russia.* New York: Random House, 1960.

——. *The Roots of American Communism.* New York: Viking Press, 1957.

Dubofsky, Melvin. *We Shall Be All: A History of the Industrial Workers of the World.* New York: Quadrangle, 1973.

Duffus, Robert L. *Books: Their Place in a Democracy.* Boston: Houghton Mifflin, 1930.

Durrie, Daniel Steele. *A History of Madison, the Capital of Wisconsin; Including the Four Lake Country to July, 1874.* Madison: Atwood and Culver, 1874.

Easton, Lloyd D. *Hegel's First American Followers: The Ohio Hegelians, John Strallo, Peter Kaufman, Moncure Conway, August Willich.* Columbus: Ohio University Press, 1966.

Egbert, Donald Drew, and Stow Persons, eds. *Socialism and American Life.* Princeton: Princeton University Press, 1952.

Ekirch, Arthur A., Jr. *The Idea of Progress in America, 1815–1860.* New York: Columbia University Press, 1944.

Eliot, Samuel Atkins, ed. *Heralds of a Liberal Faith.* 4 volumes. Volume 4, *The Pilots.* Boston: Beacon Press, 1910–52.

Fainsod, Merle. *International Socialism and the World War.* Oxford: Oxford University Press, 1935.

Fairfield, Roy P. "Benjamin O. Flower, Father of the Muckrakers." *American Literature* 22 (November 1950): 272–82.

Faulkner, Harold U. *The Decline of Laissez-Faire, 1897–1917.* 2d ed. New York: Rinehart, 1959.

Fine, Nathan. *Labor and Farm Parties in the United States, 1828–1928.* New York: Rand School, 1928.

Fink, Gary. ed. *Biographical Dictionary of American Labor Leaders.* Westport: Greenwood Press, 1974.

Fink, Leon. *Workingmen's Democracy: The Knights of Labor and American Politics.* Urbana: University of Illinois Press, 1983.

Fleming, Herbert E. *Magazines of a Market Metropolis.* Chicago, 1906.

Foner, Philip S. *The History of the Labor Movement in the United States.* Volume 4, *The Industrial Workers of the World, 1905–1917.* New York: International Publishers, 1965.

———. *The History of the Labor Movement in the United States.* Volume 5, *The AFL in the Progressive Era, 1910–1915.* New York: International Publishers, 1980.

———. *The History of the Labor Movement in the United States.* Volume 7, *Labor and World War I, 1914–1918.* New York: International Publishers, 1987.

———. *The History of the Labor Movement in the United States.* Volume 8, *Postwar Struggles, 1918–1920.* New York: International Publishers, 1988.

Ginger, Ray. *The Bending Cross: A Biography of Eugene Victor Debs.* New Brunswick: Rutgers University Press, 1949.

Glaser, William A. "Algie Martin Simons and Marxism in America." *Mississippi Valley Historical Review* 16 (Dec. 1954): 419–34.

Gohdes, Clarence L. F. *The Periodicals of American Transcendentalism.* Durham: Duke University Press, 1931.

Goldstein, Robert Justin. *Political Repression in Modern America, 1870 to the Present.* Cambridge: Schenkman Publishing, 1978.

Goldwater, Walter. *Radical Periodicals in America, 1890–1950.* New York: University Place Book Shop, 1977.

Golin, Steve. *The Fragile Bridge: The Paterson Silk Strike, 1913.* Philadelphia: Temple Univesity Press. 1988.

Graham, John. *"Yours for the Revolution": The Appeal to Reason, 1895–1922.* Lincoln: University of Nebraska Press, 1990.

Green, James R. *Grass-Roots Socialism: Radical Movements in the Southwest, 1895–1943.* Baton Rouge: Louisiana State University Press, 1978.

———. "The 'Salesmen-Soldiers' of the 'Appeal Army': A Profile of Rank-and-File Socialist Agitators." In *Socialism and the Cities.* Edited by Bruce Stave. Port Washington: Kennikat Press, 1975.

Gutman, Herbert G. "The International Socialist Review." In *The American Radical Press, 1890–1960.* Volume 1. Edited by Joseph R. Conlin. Westport: Greenwood Press, 1974.

———. "Protestantism and the American Labor Movement: The Christian Spirit in the Gilded Age." In *Work, Culture and Society in Industrializing America: Essays in American Working-Class and Social History.* Edited by Herbert G. Gutman. New York: Vintage Books, 1977.

Harmon, Ada Douglas. *The Story of an Old Town: Glen Ellyn.* Glen Ellyn: Anna Harmon Chapter, Daughters of the American Revolution, 1928.

Hays, Samuel P. *The Response to Industrialism, 1885–1914.* Chicago: University of Chicago, 1957.

Haywood, William D. *Bill Haywood's Book: The Autobiography of William D. Haywood*. New York: International Publishers, 1929.

Herbst, Jurgen. *The German Historical School in American Scholarship: A Study in the Transfers of Culture*. Ithaca: Cornell University Press, 1965.

Herreshoff, David. *The Origins of American Marxism*. New York: Pathfinder, 1973.

Hillquist, Morris. *History of Socialism in the United States*. New York: Dover, 1971.

Hofstadter, Richard. *Social Darwinism in American Thought*. Boston: Beacon Press, 1955.

Hopkins, Charles H. *The Rise of the Social Gospel in American Protestantism, 1865–1915*. New Haven: Yale University Press, 1940.

Howe, Daniel Walker. "'At Morning Blest and Golden-Browed': Unitarians, Transcendentalists and Reformers, 1835–1865." In *A Stream of Light: A Sesquicentennial History of American Unitarianism*. Edited by Conrad Wright. Boston: Unitarian Universalist Association, 1975.

————. *The Unitarian Conscience: Harvard Moral Philosophy, 1805–1861*. Cambridge: Harvard University Press, 1970.

Huston, Robert. "Algie Martin Simons and the American Socialist Movement." Ph.D. diss., University of Wisconsin-Madison, 1965.

Ingham, John N. "A Strike in the Progressive Era: McKees Rocks, 1909." *Pennsylvania Magazine of History and Biography* 90 (July 1966): 353–77.

Johnson, Christopher H. *Maurice Sugar: Law, Labor, and the Left in Detroit, 1913–1950*. Detroit: Wayne State University Press, 1988.

Joll, James. *The Second International, 1889–1914*. New York: Harper, 1966.

Kaiser, Blythe P., and Dorothy I. Vandercook. *Glen Ellyn's Story*. N.p., 1976.

Kaser, David. "The Booktrade and Publishing History." In *Research Opportunities in American Cultural History*. Edited by John Francis McDermott. Lexington: University Press of Kentucky, 1961.

Kelley, Robert. *The Transatlantic Persuasion: The Liberal-Democratic Mind in the Age of Gladstone*. New York: Knopf, 1969.

Kipnis, Ira. *The American Socialist Movement, 1897–1912*. New York: Monthly Review Press, 1952.

Kolakowski, Leszek. *Main Currents in Marxism: Its Origin, Growth and Dissolution*. Volume 2, *The Golden Age*. Cambridge: Oxford University Press, 1981.

Kornbluh, Joyce L. *Rebel Voices: An I.W.W. Anthology*. Ann Arbor: University of Michigan Press, 1972.

Kraditor, Aileen S. *The Radical Persuasion 1890–1917*. Baton Rouge: Louisiana State University Press, 1981.

Kreuter, Kent, and Gretchen Kreuter. *American Dissenter: The Life of Algie Martin Simons, 1870–1950*. Lexington: University Press of Kentucky, 1969.

Kublin, Hyman. *Asian Revolutionary: The Life of Sen Katayama*. Princeton: Princeton University Press, 1964.

Labriola, Antonio. *Socialism and Philosophy*. Introduction by Paul Piccone. St. Louis: Telos Press, 1980.

Laidler, Harry W. *History of Socialism*. New York: Thomas Y. Crowell, 1933.

Laslett, John H. M. *Labor and the Left: A Study of Socialist and Radical Influences in the American Labor Movement, 1881–1924*. New York: Basic Books, 1970.

Laslett, John, and Seymour Lipset, eds. *Failure of a Dream? Essays in the History of American Socialism*. Garden City: Doubleday, 1974.

Lehmann-Haupt, Helmut. *The Book in America: A History of the Making and Selling of Books in the United States*. New York: R. R. Bowker, 1952.

Leinenweber, Charles. "The American Socialist Party and 'New Immigrants.'" *Science and Society* 32 (Winter 1968): 1–25.

——. "Socialists in the Streets: The New York City Socialist Party in Working-class Neighborhoods, 1906–1918." *Science and Society* 41 (Summer 1977): 152–71.

Levenson, Samuel. *A Biography of James Connolly: Socialist, Patriot, and Martyr*. London: Quartet, 1977.

Lindsey, Almont. *The Pullman Strike: The Story of a Unique Experiment and of a Great Labor Upheaval*. Chicago: University of Chicago Press, 1942.

Lowenberg, Bert James. "The Controversy over Evolution in New England." *New England Quarterly* 8 (1935): 232–57.

——. "Darwinism Comes to America." *Mississippi Valley Historical Review* 27 (December 1941): 339–68.

——. "The Reaction of American Scientists to Darwinism." *American Historical Review* 28 (July 1933): 687–701.

Lyttle, Charles H. *Freedom Moves West: A History of the Western Unitarian Conference, 1852–1952*. Boston: Beacon Press, 1952.

Marty, Martin E. *The Infidel: Freethought and American Religion*. Cleveland: World Publishing, 1961.

May, Henry F. *Protestant Churches and Industrial America*. New York: Harper, 1949.

McCabe, Joseph, comp. *A Biographical Dictionary of Modern Rationalists*. London: Watts, 1920.

McCoy, Ralph Edw. *Freedom of the Press: An Annotated Bibliography*. Carbondale: Southern Illinois University Press, 1968.

McLoughlin, William G. *Revivals, Awakenings, and Reform: An Essay on Religion and Social Change in America, 1607–1977*. Chicago: University of Chicago Press, 1978.

Mead, Sidney. "American Protestantism since the Civil War: From Denominationalism to Americanism." *Journal of Religion* 36 (January 1956): 1–16.

——. "American Protestantism since the Civil War: From Americanism to Christianity." *Journal of Religion* 36 (April 1956): 67–89.

Mernitz, Susan Curtis. "The Religious Foundations of America's Oldest Socialist Press: A Centennial Note on the Charles H. Kerr Publishing Company." *Labour/Le Travail* 18 (Spring 1987): 133–37.

Meyerhardt, M. W. "The Movement for Ethical Culture at Home and Abroad." *American Journal of Relgious and Psychological Education* 2 (1908): 71–153.

Miller, Sally M. "Other Socialists: Native-Born and Immigrant Women in the Socialist Party of America, 1901–1917." *Labor History* 24 (Winter 1983): 84–102.
———. "Socialist Party Decline and World War I: Bibliography and Interpretation."
Science and Society 34 (Winter 1971): 398–411.
———, ed. *Flawed Liberation: Socialism and Feminism*. Westport: Greenwood Press,
1981.

Mock, James R. *Censorship, 1917*. Princeton: Princeton University Press, 1941.

Montgomery, David. *The Fall of the House of Labor: The Workplace, the State, and
American Labor Activism, 1865–1925*. Cambridge: Cambridge University Press.
1987.
———. "The 'New Unionism' and the Transformation of Workers' Consciousness
in America, 1909–1922." *Journal of Social History* 7 (Summer 1974): 509–29.

Moore, R. Laurence. *European Socialists and the American Promised Land*. New York:
Oxford University Press, 1970.

Morgan, Austen. *James Connolly: A Political Biography*. New York: St. Martin's Press,
1988.

Morris, Jack Cassius. "The Publishing Activities of S. C. Griggs and Company, 1848–
96; Jansen, McClurg and Company, 1872–86; and A. C. McClurg and Company, 1886–1900; with List of Publications." Master's thesis, University of Illinois,
1941.

Mott, Frank Luther. *American Journalism: A History of Newspapers in the United
States through 260 Years, 1690–1950*. New York: Macmillan, 1950.
———. *Golden Multitude: The Story of Best Sellers in the U.S.* New York: Macmill-
an, 1947.
———. *A History of American Magazines*. Volume 4, *1885–1905*. Cambridge:
Harvard University Press, 1957.

Murray, Robert K. *Red Scare: A Study in National Hysteria, 1919–1920*. New York:
McGraw-Hill, 1955.

Nelson, Bruce C. *Beyond the Martyrs: A Social History of Chicago's Anarchists 1870–
1900*. New Brunswick: Rutgers University Press, 1988.

Noble, David W. "The Religion of Progress in America, 1890–1914." *Social Research*
22 (Winter 1955): 417–40.

Norris, Jack. "Pioneer Marketing Associations of the American Book Trade, 1973–
1901." Ph.D. dissertation, University of Chicago, 1938.

"Obituary Notes: Joseph B. Keen." *Publisher's Weekly*, August 11, 1900, 356.

O'Harra, Downing P. "Book Publishing in the United States, 1860 to 1901, Including
Statistical Tables and Charts to 1927." Master's thesis, University of Illinois, 1928.

O'Neil, William L., ed. *Echoes of Revolt: The Masses, 1911–1917*. Chicago: University of Chicago Press, 1966.

Palmer, Bryan D. "'Big Bill' Haywood's Defection to Russia and the I.W.W.: Two
Letters." *Labor History* 17 (Spring 1976): 271–78.

Pease, William H. "Doctrine and Fellowship: William Channing Gannett and the
Unitarian Creedal Issue." *Church History* 25 (September 1956): 210–38.

Persons, Stow. *Free Religion: An American Faith.* New Haven: Yale University Press, 1947.

Peterson, H. C., and Gilbert C. Fite. *Opponents of War, 1917–1918.* Seattle: University of Washington Press, 1957.

Pierce, Bessie Louise. *A History of Chicago.* Volume 3, *The Rise of a Modern City 1871–1893.* New York: Knopf, 1957.

Preston, William, Jr. *Aliens and Dissenters: Federal Suppression of Radicals, 1903–1933.* Cambridge: Harvard University Press, 1963.

Putnam, George H. "A Survey of Book Publishing in the U.S. since 1860." *Publisher's Weekly,* August 14, 1915, 487.

Quint, Howard H. *The Forging of American Socialism: Origins of the Modern Movement.* Columbia: University of South Carolina, 1953.

———. "Julius A. Wayland, Pioneer Socialist Propagandist." *Mississippi Valley Historical Review* 35 (March 1949): 585–606.

Radest, Howard B. *Toward Common Ground: The Story of the Ethical Societies in the United States.* New York: Frederick Ungar Publishing, 1969.

Reeve, Carl. *The Life and Times of Daniel DeLeon.* New York: Humanities Press, 1972.

Reeve, Carl, and Ann Barton Reeve. *James Connolly and the United States: The Road to the 1916 Irish Rebellion.* Atlantic Highlands: Humanities Press, 1978.

Rideout, Walter B. *The Radical Novel in the United States, 1900–1954.* New York: Hill and Wang, 1966.

Roediger, Dave, and Franklin Rosemont, eds. *Haymarket Scrapbook.* Chicago: Charles H. Kerr & Company, 1986.

Rosenstone, Robert A. *Romantic Revolutionary: A Biography of John Reed.* New York: Vintage, 1981.

Rowbotham, Sheila. "In Search of Edward Carpenter." *Radical America* 14 (July-August 1980): 49–60.

Rowbotham, Sheila, and Jeffrey Weeks. *Socialism and the New Life: The Personal and Sexual Politics of Edward Carpenter and Havelock Ellis.* London: Pluto Press, 1977.

Ruff, Allen. "Charles H. Kerr and the Charles H. Kerr & Company, Publishers, 1886–1928." Ph.D. dissertation, University of Wisconsin-Madison.

———. "*International Socialist Review.*" In *Encyclopedia of the American Left.* Edited by Mari Jo Buhle, Paul Buhle, and Dan Georgakas. Urbana: University of Illinois Press, 1990.

———. "Mary Marcy." In *Encyclopedia of the American Left.* Edited by Mari Jo Buhle, Paul Buhle, and Dan Georgakas. Urbana: University of Illinois Press, 1990.

———. "A Path Not Taken: The Proletarian Party and the Early History of Communism in the United States." In *Culture, Gender, Race and U.S. Labor History.* Edited by Ron Kent, Sara Markham, David Roediger, and Herbert Shapiro. Westport: Greenwood Press, 1993.

———. "The Socialist Press and Repression in the World War I Era: The Case of

Charles H. Kerr & Company." *Journal of Newspaper and Periodical History* 5 (Spring 1989): 2–19.

———."Socialist Publishing in Illinois: Charles H. Kerr & Company of Chicago, 1886–1928." *Illinois Historical Journal* 79 (Spring 1986): 19–32.

Salvatore, Nick. *Citizen and Socialist: A Life of Eugene Victor Debs.* Urbana: University of Illinois Press, 1982.

Scharnau, Ralph William. "Thomas J. Morgan and the Chicago Socialist Movement, 1876–1901." Ph.D. diss., Northern Illinois University, 1970.

Scheiber, Harry N. *The Wilson Administration and Civil Liberties.* Ithaca: Cornell University Press, 1960.

Schick, Frank L. *The Paperbound Book in America: The History of Paperbacks and Their European Background.* New York: R. R. Bowker, 1958.

Schlesinger, Arthur M., Sr. "A Critical Period in American Protestantism, 1875–1900." *Massachusetts Historical Society Proceedings* 64 (June 1932): 523–47.

Schneider, Herbert W. "The Influence of Darwin and Spencer on American Philosophical Theology." *Journal of the History of Ideas* 6 (June 1945): 3–18.

Sears, Hal D. *The Sex Radicals: Free Love in High Victorian America.* Lawrence: Regents Press of Kansas, 1977.

Sereiko, George Eugene. "Chicago and Its Book Trade." Ph.D. dissertation, School of Library Science, Case Western Reserve University, 1973.

Shannon, David A. *The Socialist Party of America: A History.* Chicago: University of Chicago Press, 1955.

Sheehan, Donald Henry. *This Was Publishing: A Chronicle of the Book Trade in the Gilded Age.* Bloomington: Indiana University Press, 1952.

Shore, Elliott. "Selling Socialism: The 'Appeal to Reason' and the Radical Press in Turn-of-Century America." *Media, Culture and Society* 7 (1985): 147–68.

———. *Talkin' Socialism: J. A. Wayland and the Role of the Press in American Radicalism, 1890–1912.* Lawrence: University of Kansas Press, 1988.

———. "The Walkout at the 'Appeal' and the Dilemmas of American Socialism." *History Workshop* 22 (Autumn 1986): 41–55.

Shove, Raymond H. "Cheap Book Production in the U.S., 1870–1891." Master's thesis, University of Illinois, 1936.

Smart, D. A. *Pannekoek and Gorter's Marxism.* London: Pluto Press, 1978.

Smith, Timothy. *Revivalism and Social Reform.* New York: Abingdon Press, 1957.

Stern, Madeline B. "Keene and Cooke: Prairie Publishers." *Journal of the Illinois State Historical Society* 42 (December 1949): 442.

Stevenson, James A. "Daniel DeLeon and European Socialism, 1890–1914." *Science and Society* 44 (Summer 1980): 199–223.

Stow, Robert N., ed. "Conflict in the American Socialist Movement, 1897–1901: A Letter from Thomas J. Morgan to Henry Demarest Lloyd July 18, 1901." *Journal of the Illinois State Historical Society* 71 (May 1978): 133–42.

Taft, Philip. *The A.F.L. in the Time of Gompers.* New York: Harper and Brothers, 1957.

Tassin, Algernon. *The Magazine in America.* New York: Dodd, Mead, 1916.

Tax, Meredith. *The Rising of the Women: Feminist Solidarity and Class Conflict, 1880–1917.* New York: Monthly Review Press, 1980.

Tebbel, John. *The American Magazine: A Compact History.* New York: Hawthorn, 1969.

———. *A History of Book Publishing in the United States.* Volume 2, *The Expansion of an Industry, 1865–1919;* Volume 3, *The Rise of the Magazine Business, 1850–1905.* New York: R. R. Bowker, 1975.

Thistlethwaite, Frank. *The Anglo-American Connection in the Early Nineteenth Century.* Philadelphia: University of Pennsylvania Press, 1959.

Thomas, Richard Harlan. "Jenkin Lloyd Jones: Lincoln's Soldier of Civic Righteousness." Ph.D. dissertation, Rutgers University, 1967.

Tierney, Kevin. *Darrow: A Biography.* New York: Thomas Crowell, 1979.

Trachtenberg, Alexander, ed. *The American Socialists and the War.* New York: Rand School of Social Science, 1917. Reprint. New York: Garland Publishing, 1973.

Tripp, Anne Huber. *The I.W.W. and the Paterson Silk Strike of 1913.* Urbana: University of Illinois Press, 1987.

Tyack, David B. *George Tichnor and the Boston Brahmins.* Cambridge: Harvard University Press, 1968.

U.S. Bureau of the Census. *Census of Manufacturers, 1905: Printing and Publishing.* Washington, D.C.: Government Printing Office, 1907.

———. *Census of Manufacturers, 1914: Printing and Publishing.* Washington, D.C.: Government Printing Office, 1918.

U.S. House of Representatives, 85th Cong., 2d sess., Committee on Un-American Activities. *Organized Communism in the United States.* Washington, D.C.: Government Printing Office, 1958.

Warren, Sidney. *American Freethought, 1860–1914.* New York: Columbia University Press, 1943.

Webber, Christopher L. "William Dwight Porter Bliss (1856–1926): Priest and Socialist." *Historical Magazine of the Protestant Episcopal Church* 28 (March 1959): 9–39.

Weinstein, James. *The Decline of Socialism in America 1912–1925.* New York: Vintage, 1969.

Weisenburger, Francis P. *Ordeal of Faith: The Crisis of Churchgoing America, 1865–1900.* New York: Philosophical Library, 1959.

Weiser, Frederick S. *Village in a Glen: A History of Glen Ellyn, Illinois.* Glen Ellyn: Anna Harmon Chapter, Daughters of the American Revolution, 1957.

Wendte, C. W. *The Wider Fellowship: Memories, Friendships and Endeavors for Religious Unity, 1844–1927.* Boston: Beacon Press, 1927.

Wiebe, Robert. *The Search for Order, 1877–1920.* New York: Hill and Want, 1967.

Wilson, Harold S. *McClure's Magazine and the Muckrakers.* Princeton: Princeton University Press, 1970.

Wright, Conrad. *The Beginnings of Unitarianism in America.* Boston: Beacon Press, 1955.

————. *The Liberal Christians: Essays on American Unitarian History.* Boston: Beacon Press, 1970.

————, ed. *A Stream of Light: A Sesquicentennial History of American Unitarianism.* Boston: Unitarian Universalist Association, 1975.

————, comp. *Three Prophets of Religious Liberalism: Channing, Emerson, Parker.* Boston: Beacon Press, 1961.

Zurier, Rebecca. *Art for* The Masses: *A Radical Magazine and Its Graphics, 1911–1917.* Philadelphia: Temple University Press, 1988.

■ Index

Allen M. Ruff received his Ph.D. in United States history from the University of Wisconsin–Madison. An independent historian and activist, he resides in Madison, where he fishes in the morning, works in the afternoon, and studies at night.